INTIMATE SUBJECTS

Intimate Subjects

Touch and Tangibility in Britain's Cerebral Age

Simeon Koole

THE UNIVERSITY OF CHICAGO PRESS
CHICAGO & LONDON

PUBLICATION OF THIS BOOK HAS BEEN AIDED
BY A GRANT FROM THE BEVINGTON FUND.

The University of Chicago Press, Chicago 60637
The University of Chicago Press, Ltd., London
© 2024 by The University of Chicago

Published 2024
Printed in the United States of America

33 32 31 30 29 28 27 26 25 24   1 2 3 4 5

ISBN-13: 978-0-226-83432-0 (cloth)
ISBN-13: 978-0-226-83434-4 (paper)
ISBN-13: 978-0-226-83433-7 (e-book)
DOI: https://doi.org/10.7208/chicago/9780226834337.001.0001

Library of Congress Cataloging-in-Publication Data

Names: Koole, Simeon, 1990–, author.
Title: Intimate subjects : touch and tangibility in Britain's cerebral age /
    Simeon Koole.
Other titles: Touch and tangibility in Britain's cerebral age
Description: Chicago ; London : The University of Chicago Press, 2024. |
    Includes bibliographical references and index.
Identifiers: LCCN 2023057862 | ISBN 9780226834320 (cloth) |
    ISBN 9780226834344 (paperback) | ISBN 9780226834337 (ebook)
Subjects: LCSH: Touch—Great Britain—History—19th century. |
    Touch—Great Britain—History—20th century. | Neurology—Great
    Britain—History. | Psychology—Great Britain—History. | Great
    Britain—Social life and customs—19th century. | Great Britain—
    Social life and customs—20th century. | Great Britain—Civilization—
    19th century. | Great Britain—Civilization—20th century.
Classification: LCC BF275 .K664 2024 | DDC 152.1/82—dc23/eng/20240202
LC record available at https://lccn.loc.gov/2023057862

♾ This paper meets the requirements of ANSI/NISO Z39.48-1992
(Permanence of Paper).

To my parents

Contents

List of Figures *ix*

INTRODUCTION: ENTANGLED TALES 1
1 · LOVE IN THE TIME OF NEUROLOGY 27
2 · PEDAGOGIES OF TOUCH 67
3 · MIND THE GAP 103
4 · TEA SHOP TOUCH AND GLOBAL CAPITALISM 137
5 · REVELATIONS OF THE LONDON FOG 181
EPILOGUE: TENDER 221

Acknowledgments 235
Source Abbreviations 241
Notes 243
Select Bibliography 307
Index 331

Figures

1   Postcard of Liverpool Street Station, ca. 1900.   *3*

2   W. H. R. Rivers experimenting on Henry Head's hand, ca. 1905.   *41*

3   Christopher R. W. Nevinson, *Amongst the Nerves of the World*, 1930.   *45*

4   Henry Head's hand, May 17, 1903.   *48*

5   Letter from Ruth Mayhew to Henry Head, November 17, 1902.   *56*

6   Alfred Hirst, from *My Dark World*, 1898.   *69*

7   Massage training at St. Dunstan's Hostel for Blind Soldiers and Sailors, 1918.   *75*

8   Geography class at Royal Normal College for the Blind, ca. 1872–1912.   *87*

9   Cyril Power, *The Tube Train*, linocut, ca. 1934.   *105*

10   F. H. Stingemore, *Pass Down the Car Please*, poster, 1919.   *111*

11   Interior view of CSLR "padded cell" carriage, 1890 stock, ca. 1890–1900.   *113*

12   Interior view of 1923 "standard stock" car, no. 820, ca. 1920–1925.   *114*

13   Waterloo Underground Station, Bakerloo Line, January 17, 1936.   *115*

14   Escalator at Charing Cross (now Embankment) Station, ca. March 1914.   *124*

15   Aerated Bread Company tea shop, 32 King Street, City of London, 1912.   *144*

16   Tea pluckers on Lyons's Lujeri Estate, Nyasaland (now Malawi), ca. 1928–1938.   *162*

17   "Nippies" setting tables in a Lyons Corner House, 1939.   *164*

18   Basement plan for proposed rebuilding of Maison Lyons, January 1915.   *167*

19   Film set of *Underground*, Waterloo Underground Station, April 27, 1928.   *172*

20   Harold Davidson with Lady Waechter de Grimston, July 8, 1932.   *178*

21   Record of London's fog, *Daily Mirror*, December 11, 1924.   *182*

22   George W. F. Ellis, Piccadilly Circus at noon on a foggy day, 1924.   *192*

23   The Welcome Free Travelling Café, 1930.   *204*

24   Ground floor plan of Tower Bridge Police Court, 1907.   *211*

25   Blind children at Sunderland Museum and Art Gallery, June 1913.   *227*

Entangled Tales

Almost noon, Liverpool Street Station, London, around 1900. Arriving at the station during the midday bustle, it was as much as you could do to hang onto your luggage and allow yourself to be carried on one of the streams of people cascading down the station's eighteen platforms and breaking on the line of ticket barriers. The largest station in Britain after its expansion in 1894, the terminus of the Great Eastern Railway handled more than 172,000 passengers daily, most from the low gray suburbs of east and north London and the fens of East Anglia.[1] During peak times, as many as 20,000 passengers an hour passed through the station's perpetual twilight, beneath the great glass roof whose light only accentuated the pall of smoke and steam, and out into the glare beyond.[2] Bewildered visitors reaching for metaphors described the station in terms of a gigantic factory or a great flood, the twin descriptors of immensity and destruction.[3]

At the south exit you would find yourself on one of three ramps stretching down to a line of stout pillars and wrought iron gates giving access onto Liverpool Street.[4] No more than eight hundred feet in length, Liverpool Street served as the confluence of three railway stations including Broad Street Station, terminus of the North London Railway, and, across the road, Bishopsgate Station, a stop on the underground Metropolitan Railway connected with Liverpool Street Station by a pedestrian tunnel.[5] Here, thousands more converged in a maelstrom of humans, horses, and vehicles: the new "bedlam" on, appropriately enough, the site of the former infamous insane asylum. To pass along this street meant hustling through a thicket of newspaper hawkers, flower sellers, two-wheeled horse-drawn hansom cabs, their four-wheeled counterparts known as *growlers*, omnibuses and their trailing would-be fares, and the much-bemoaned obstructions of "gutter merchants" and costermongers' barrows heaped with fruits and vegetables.[6] Although the Great Eastern Railway employed porters to help beleaguered passengers with their luggage, the station and adjoining street were also popular among hawkers eager to carry, or carry off, what they could.[7] Once you had negotiated these threats to limbs and luggage, you reached, to the east, the thoroughfare of Bishopsgate Without, with its assortment of tall mismatched buildings making the street seem narrower than it was. Directly opposite, above a bookshop and Society of Friends meeting hall, was the Devonshire House Hotel, an unassuming smoke-grimed building where you might, for a while, escape the too-close press of the world.[8]

From the second-floor window of the hotel, it was possible to discern the first outlines of the crush from which you had emerged.[9] To the north, past the Great Eastern Hotel and Bishopsgate Institute, Bishopsgate Without gave way onto the wholesale drapers, music halls, and model housing of Shoreditch. To the south lay a sprinkling of banks, the first outposts of finance before you reached the Bank of England, Royal Exchange, and insurance offices beyond. Directly below, looking west toward the stations, pedestrians and street traffic massed and parted in a seething rhythm at the point where the City met the East End.[10] Here was an ideal location for that turn-of-the-century journalistic pastime, the ethnography of the street corner.[11] Hurrying to the stations from the west and south were typists, clerks, brokers, lawyers, and accountants of City offices and the waitresses and barmaids of its tea shops and taverns. Mingling with these people from the east, like two rivers converging, were purveyors of secondhand clothing from Houndsditch old clothes markets, warehousemen of the adjacent London and St. Katherine's Dock Company stores, and laborers from the innumerable factories and workshops stretching east into Whitechapel. Like all railway termini, Liverpool Street Station added to this throng by attracting those who profited from closeness. Among the workaday rush were cardsharps and pickpockets exploiting intimacy through sleight of hand and confidence tricksters "scraping acquaintance" with forged tender.[12] Standing at the entrance gates and on the concourse were flower sellers such as the twenty-one-year-old Alice Beswick, hard bitten by a constant traffic too eager to be somewhere else and often, the police alleged, hustling purchases by shoving flowers into the faces of passersby.[13] All surging, stopping, gathering, parting in an intricate choreography of intimacy and isolation.

The more you looked, the more you would discern the fleeting bodily encounters tying lives together. The street corner would become a study of how individuals avoided or courted bodily contact in order to protect

FIGURE 1 Liverpool Street Station at 11:50 a.m. April 16, 1902, or July 28, 1904; two days on which news broke of a Russian minister assassinated, advertised here by a newspaper vendor at the station entrance. Postcard. Author's collection.

themselves, fulfill desires, understand one another, or survive. On various days, you might have seen twenty-year-old waitress Alice Farrell making her way to one of the A.B.C. tea shops in the City, perhaps the one at 40 Old Broad Street, just south of Bishopsgate Station.[14] Obliged to wear her uniform on her journey to work, she stares down anyone hoping to try their luck with an "A.B.C. girl." If it were a Friday evening, you might have seen Henry Head, physician at the London Hospital a mile east in Whitechapel, battling through the commuter traffic to catch a train to Cambridge where he was conducting a curious experiment on his hand with psychologist William Rivers. The crowds were so thick at this time of day that train compartments were often filled to twice their capacity, with passengers jammed in like "herrings in a box."[15] Head holds his sensitive hand to his chest, but the pushing still jars. Discerning accidental nudges from surreptitious brushes in these crowds was Great Eastern Railway constable H. Cooper. You could find him around the lines of people buying tickets in the booking hall, near the cloakrooms, or at the curbside, considering how the bearing of a body, a particular posture or gesture, traced intention. And doing the same thing were those seeking intimacy from others in a city where crowded housing and large families made it impossible in their own homes. One of these might have been Alice Hutchings, a dressmaker, idling around the station entrance one Christmas Eve. There you could see her meet master mariner Josiah Tamylon, who persuaded her to join him at the Alhambra music hall and then for oysters afterward. We cannot know what words were exchanged that evening, but it ended with a night spent at Scott's Hotel in Euston.[16] Animating, intensifying, embodying these encounters was an experience so common as to be barely noticed: the sense of touch.

This book is a history of the brushes, grasps, and caresses, of the touches stolen and evaded, which, in late nineteenth- and early twentieth-century Britain, bound together lives. Following intimate encounters in spaces where touch became an open question, such as the subway car, the tea shop, the schoolroom, and the police court, it explores the constant but historical struggle to find ways of being together and apart. This is a history of the entanglement of knowledge and desire, the longing for and fear of contact, and of all the ways that individuals tried to make space for one another and for themselves. It is, therefore, also a history of how touch expressed and remade—and continues to shape—our ways of thinking about the world.

THE USES OF TOUCH

The seething crowds of Liverpool Street Station around 1900 suggest a familiar story. It is a story integral to accounts of the "modern" city, and one best told by the philosopher and sociologist Georg Simmel. "The deepest problems of modern life," Simmel wrote in 1903, "flow from the attempt of the individual to maintain the independence and individuality of his existence against the sovereign powers of society, against the weight of the historical heritage and the external culture and technique of life." The individual was caught in a constant struggle to maintain independence from their social and historical circumstances, and from the relentless incursions of everyday life. For Simmel, there was no better example of this than in the contemporary city. There, faced with a ceaseless barrage of stimuli, the city dweller found it increasingly difficult to distinguish between what they sensed, and between themselves and the sensible world. Threatened with the collapse of the boundary between their "inner life" and the world outside, the city dweller became "blasé" toward the endless succession of images and encounters. The result was a new mode of perception, in which they viewed the city as if from outside its restless change.[17] Whereas Simmel tied this perceptual shift to the acceleration of street life, it could also be seen, argued Walter Benjamin, in capitalism's conversion of the commodity, the department stores and arcades devoted to it, and the crowds drawn to them, into spectacles to be consumed.[18] In both cases, the city dweller ostensibly found themself caught between visual stimulation and distraction, synoptic knowledge and alienation.

An equally powerful story might then be told about how this sensory disorder was managed, and how its management became central to political and social order. The excess, unpredictability, and incessancy of stimuli overwhelming the nineteenth-century city dweller compelled municipal authorities to regulate the urban environment and how it was sensed. Through the ordering of new material systems—for water, transport, lighting, communication—and an emerging culture of inspection, local authorities sought to manage sensory stimuli and habituate city dwellers to new ways of sensing. What and how one sensed became central to the creation of a more rational, better integrated, and freer political and economic sphere, even if this was only ever an ideal.[19] Liverpool Street Station, handling in 1900 ostensibly the greatest volume of traffic through any railway station in the world, would be an example of this drive to regulate sensation through the managed movement of bodies.[20] In this story, the history of sensation is also one of capitalism and liberalism and their entangled relation.[21] We might extend this further, showing how emerging habits of sensing were also part of a longer history of self-management and social distinction.[22] How much one tolerated the odor, clamor, and scrimmage of other passengers in a place such as Liverpool Street marked the extent to which one had refined one's senses and, consequently, distinguished oneself from others. The regulation of the city became bound up with that of oneself; the city dweller's senses objectified and ordered, and honed as signs of distinction.

Yet even as these stories seem convincing, they also miss much of the picture. Indeed, overarching narratives of sensory change and its entangled relation to modernity, capitalism, and liberalism have obscured the very corporeality, contingency, and agency of the senses they aim to describe. Passengers hurrying across Liverpool Street Station around 1900 jostled and dodged one another in the fight for an omnibus or train. Once in a train compartment or tea shop or on the street, they continued the endless negotiations and adjustments of embodied existence that we most of the time forget: the bunching up on shared seats or circumspect distancing from others in line. Not only subjects of the attractions and imperatives of their "external" world, these individuals were also bodies whose sensing was inseparable from their physical involvement within it. What and how they sensed, and consequently how they thought, emerged from all these tacit, tactile interactions with the world in which they found themselves. In every minor gesture and restive hand, touch revealed their embeddedness in the world and the contingency of thought, feeling, and action on that spatial and temporal involvement.

What is the history of touch, and how can it offer a way of thinking differently about this condition of embodiment?[23] This book begins in the late nineteenth century, when across science, education, and everyday social relations touch emerged as a central object of concern. In the emerging disciplines of neurology and experimental psychology, scientists identified touch as key to unlocking the hidden, direct relationship between stimuli and sensations, and ultimately between body and mind. From the 1890s onward, British psychologists and neurologists experimented on touch to reveal the basis of perception in the workings and evolution of the nervous system: a history of the mind told through touch. Touch also became an object of pedagogical concern over the same decades, once the state required that children aged between five and thirteen receive an elementary education. After this requirement was extended to blind children until the age of sixteen in England and Wales in 1893, teachers, school inspectors, and blind commentators focused new practical attention on what could be known through touch and how such knowledge could be cultivated.

In urban public space, too, questions of the meaning and appropriateness of touch became increasingly important in the late nineteenth century. As Britain's cities expanded, and London in particular witnessed the spread of public transportation, proliferation of commercial leisure spaces, and challenges to the gendered segregation of public space, touch became the means through which understandings of consent, bodily conduct, and personal autonomy were contested and reconfigured. This was, in author D. H. Lawrence's words, the "*cerebral age*": an age in which the rise of the mind sciences, transformation of gender relations, and changing social constituency of public space at once produced new aversions to touch and made touch increasingly charged.[24] Disparaged and desired, touch was an increasingly important object of attention as well as a way of thinking more broadly about what it meant to be embodied.

Intimate Subjects traces this history of touch as one of practical, often ordinary encounters in spaces between which its protagonists moved. In this history, touch was not simply a mental process by which individuals responded to the world outside but emerged through active, situated involvement with the space occupied. On the "tube," as the subway is known in London, norms for how close passengers stood or what touches were overlooked developed in tandem with changes in tube car space, from the introduction of grab straps to the removal of guards. In hospitals and university studies, neurologists and physiologists studied the modes, thresholds, and location of touch by jabbing, stroking, and pricking one another and analyzing what they felt. How touch was conceptualized, and even how it felt, shaped and was shaped by what scientists did with their hands and how that changed over time. Meanwhile, in schools for blind children, students learned to refine their touch by running their fingers over the raised contours of relief maps or modeling what they had touched in clay. What these children felt, such exercises implied, was conditional on a skillful engagement with their environment, an engagement which in turn shaped how blind writers conceptualized touch.

The history of these encounters is also that of the changing meanings of touch. How and where individuals touched reshaped the very understandings of what touch was and meant. *Intimate Subjects* explores touch as physical contact and the feeling of being emotionally "touched." The understanding of how these were related—the science of head and heart—was shaped by how neurologists related their experiences of touch within and beyond their experiments. In the love letters of Henry Head and Ruth Mayhew, Head's analysis of touch as a discriminating sense met with fantasies of touch remembered and longed for. The book also examines touch as an "inner" sense that registered the position of one's limbs and body in space. Training this inner touch, teaching posture and bodily self-awareness through gymnastics or special desks, became a way of teaching blind children to attend to where they were and what they touched. This skill was equally important beyond the classroom. For those negotiating crowded public spaces such as elevators or escalators, learned embodied habits of posture and social distancing configured how one stood to avoid touch. More than only contact, touch involved a constant interaction between inside and outside, actual and potential, an interaction shaped by one's changing physical environment and social norms. How close was too close? How did one *know*?

This book is therefore also a history of when and where one could touch. Novels, plays, and films dramatized the opportunities for erotic chance encounters in spaces such as the tube but also the dangers of unwanted touch. In the film *Underground* (1928), which parodied how strangers negotiated a packed tube car, the depiction of new norms for managing bodily interactions reveals a hidden history of harassment, sexual violence, and nonconsensual touch in public. Behind eulogies to the intimacy possible between passengers sharing aprons on chilly open-top buses, or in "the more sequestered seats at the picture palace," there was always an unwritten, equally common story of fear and violation.²⁵ As well as touch that was tender, patient, or unrealized, this book also examines encounters where the very concept of "touch" was called into question by contact that was nothing more than assault.

These histories of touch offer new understandings of urban life, scientific and legal knowledge, disability, gender relations, and capitalism. From the embodied labor of tea shop waitresses and the thwarted desires of their customers emerges a longer history of precarious employment, failed trade unionism, and corporate competition. Out of the tussles of police constables and suspects and the mundane progress of paperwork through the police court unfolds a history of law, not as the application of rules but as the work of bodies enacting and contesting it. These histories are contained within those of touch. But the histories of touch also provide a new way of understanding how historical subjects understood and organized their world. For if one's sense of touch emerged through embodied, active involvement in the world, then so too did how one thought about that world. The history of touch is also a history of thinking with, through, and about the body. How passengers attempted or avoided touch on the tube was a history of how personal space and the very experience of bodily autonomy were produced or suspended in changing situations. The ways in which neurologists touched their subjects and explored desires through erotic poetry and the novels of Henry James were also a history of the location and constitution of scientific knowledge. Touch was a way of thinking about the world, of forming ideas and organizing knowledge, as well as of thinking about the body within it.

And the same is true for us: tracing the historical understandings, experiences, and practices of touch also provides a method for examining historical and theoretical questions about the nature of embodiment. *Intimate Subjects* explores three of these questions. First, a history of touch reveals how the senses have historically been educated to conform to, and in so doing constructed, the normative able-bodied subject. Examining how blind children were taught to refine their sense of touch to "fit" in a sighted world enables both a history and a deconstruction of the concept of bodily capability as an inherent, rather than contingent, experience. Second, a history of touch traces that of scientific and juridical knowledge to the changing embodied experiences through which it was produced. It recovers the touches enabling the ideas formulated in laboratories or courtrooms but at the same time erased by the constitution of science and law as autonomous domains of knowledge. Third, historicizing touch offers a way of reflecting on vulnerability—the capacity to affect and be affected by others—as a universal condition of embodiment but one realized and experienced in distinct ways depending on situated encounters. Through the histories of unwanted touching in spaces such as the tube car, we can discern not only a history of assault but one of the constitution of the subject for whom non-consensual touching was (or was not) experienced and categorized as such. The history of touch was also that of the autonomous liberal subject that was simultaneously produced through, and might be violated by, its embodied encounters. Taken together, examining how touch was enacted and experienced differently over time enables critical reflection on embodiment as the condition of our capability, knowledge, and vulnerability.

HISTORICIZING THE SENSES

The history of the senses has a long history. Half a century before Simmel's observations on the desensitizing effects of modern urban life, Karl Marx, too, reflected on the contingency of sensing in the industrial age. In *Economic and Philosophical Manuscripts* (1844), Marx saw the senses as conditioned by the relationship that individuals had to objects; how one sensed was shaped by one's relationship to what one sensed, a relationship transformed by the advance of industrial capitalism and regime of private property. "The forming of the five senses" was a result of humanity's changing relationship to what it produced and used, and therefore "a labour of the entire history of the world down to the present."[26] Despite the long view, Marx was acutely conscious of how his idea of the senses as historical developed during a period of profound sensory change. The very concept of historicity, and of the historicity of the senses, was itself a particular historical development of modernity.[27] Historicizing the senses became a way of explaining the apparently new existential condition of "modernity" through which Marx, Simmel, and others such as Walter Benjamin were living. Once one thought of vision, for example, as historical, it became easier to explain the new experience of space, time, and social relations brought about by innovations such as photography or the shopping arcade and that ostensibly marked the era as qualitatively different. Consequently, from their inception, understandings of the historicity of the senses were bound up with the sensory changes they sought to explain: explanation and experience were intimately tied.

This history of thinking about sensory experience as historical has shaped much subsequent writing about the senses, as well as about urban change in the nineteenth and twentieth centuries. Indeed, one might even say that the connection between the idea of the senses as historical and the history of social and subjective change during the nineteenth and twentieth centuries is both what has made sensory history so useful and what has restricted it. Consider Alain Corbin's *The Foul and the Fragrant: Odor and the French Social Imagination* (first published in French in 1982), the pioneering sensory history that continues to provide the conceptual coordinates for the field. Corbin's argument that between 1750 and 1880 French city dwellers became more sensitive to odor and consequently less tolerant of bad odors, and that this increased "vigilance" toward odor reproduced social distinctions, owed much to historian Lucien Febvre, but also to Georg Simmel's "Sociology of the Senses" (1907), published shortly after Simmel's essay on the mental life of the modern city.[28] Also discussing smell, Simmel attempted to explain the apparent "heightened sensibility" of his own era by theorizing a sensory change. Although the sense of smell in the "modern person" became less acute as "culture" advanced, Simmel argued, modern people became more sensitive to that which they sensed, explaining both the declining tolerance of bad odors and increasing efforts to regulate urban sensations.[29] Corbin's argument about smell was deeply embedded in discourses about disease and the body that predated Simmel's essay. Yet even while Corbin explained sensory change by relating it to medical and scientific understandings of the senses before the late nineteenth century, many of his framing concepts—overstimulation, sensory "vigilance," changing thresholds of tolerance, sensory discrimination as a means of social differentiation—echoed Simmel's comments on the decades immediately after.[30] The concepts of sensory change that Simmel and his contemporaries invoked to explain modernity have proved irresistible to historians of the nineteenth and twentieth centuries precisely because they emerged during the period addressed.

This tie between method and object of study has persisted in more recent sensory and urban histories, which continue to frame sensory change within terms posited by theorists of modernity, even while deconstructing these theories. The inrush of capital, the unprecedented size and density of population and reach and rapidity of transport; the proliferation of advertising, culture of exhibition, and inversion of inside and outside through the deployment of glass; the reordering of time and space through the spread of gas and electric illumination and technologies of urban flow such as the ticket machine and the escalator; the accentuation of rush through the enforced pause of spaces such as the waiting line and the waiting room: all of these made the city a disorienting place.[31] Consequently, the history of the senses in the nineteenth and twentieth centuries has often been told as a story of overstimulation and desensitization.[32] The person who, say, found themself on the pavement of London's Oxford Street in 1932 faced a barrage of sensations at once unprecedented and impossible to distinguish. Here, Virginia Woolf alleged, "news changes quicker than in any other part of London. The press of people passing seems to lick the ink off the placards and to consume more of them and to demand fresh supplies of later editions faster than elsewhere." And just as the press of people seemed to hasten the passing of news, so the mind itself seemed to become a newspaper onto which sensations were endlessly printed; "a glutinous slab that takes impressions and Oxford Street rolls off upon it a perpetual ribbon of changing sights, sounds and movement."[33]

For those animated by this turmoil of impressions, places such as Oxford Street became not only sites for consumption but also spaces to consume, as if one had shed one's outer "shell" and been reduced to a "central oyster of perceptiveness."[34] Yet for others the relentless flow of sensations reduced one to an observer inured against a sensory onslaught of other people and things that could no longer be processed. Newspapers, read while standing in line, on the tube, or over lunch, became essential barriers against, rather than metaphors for, the constant, unwanted stimulation. Seated in a train carriage, "five faces opposite," one learned of life from the eyes of others and hid one's knowledge of it by looking away. "One smokes; another reads; a third checks entries in a pocket book; a fourth stares at the map of the line framed opposite": all but perhaps one played the "game" of concealment. Embattled by the persistence of the world, the best solution was to fold the *Times* into "a perfect square, crisp, thick, impervious even to life."[35]

Intertwined with this story of sensory change is therefore another of spectacle and alienation. As commerce and leisure mingled, as dark streets were made legible by gas and electric and consumers entered into direct relation with commodities through displays under soaring arcades or in palatial department stores, as there emerged new sites of entertainment such as music halls and nightclubs dedicated to the observation of and by others, the city became a space in which vision and visibility were at once more significant and more scrutinized.[36] At the same time as the city became an increasingly visual phenomenon, new techniques and technologies emerged for observing, dissecting, and representing the experience of seeing.[37] Pausing on Oxford Street before the great glass expanse of a department store window, Woolf played with the possibilities. Gazing through the glass on a winter's evening, she wrote, the window-shopper might construct a "vast imaginary house," furnished with tables, sofas, and carpets of any kind and, when tired of the construction, dismantle the whole thing and start again.[38]

The department store enabled anyone to enter a fantasy of creation that was also a re-creation of themselves. Was the "true self," Woolf wondered, the person who stood before the illuminated display, or was it so multifarious "that it is only when we give rein to its wishes and let it take its way unimpeded that we are indeed ourselves?"[39] Yet while Woolf reveled in these visual fantasies, she also revealed the alienating effects of spectatorship. For although observers of the display window or the surging crowd might become anyone they wanted to be, they reduced themselves and others to a play of surfaces; to what Woolf characterized as the "glassiness" of modern London.[40] The observer who imagined themself able to, for a while, "put on [. . .] the bodies and minds of others" reduced selfhood to a performance in which appearance was everything and each remained an isolated member of what historian James Vernon calls a "society of strangers."[41]

Woolf's daydreaming points to a third story often told about the history of the senses: the intertwining of sensory and social distinction and its management through the urban environment. In this story, sensation is a historically specific attitude taken toward sensory stimuli that also expressed one's social or political relationship toward others. How one looked, listened, or touched, and how one represented the sensory characteristics and capabilities of others, also reproduced or contested social difference, whether in terms of class, race, gender, or political adherence.[42] One thread of this story follows the changing tolerance of, or sensitivity toward, sensory stimuli and how this served as a means of social distinction. New medical understandings about the porosity of the body and fragility of the self, new technologies for measuring sensory stimuli, a discourse of improvement, and cultures of inspection and expertise all combined to turn particular sensations into problems, which an emerging middle class tasked itself to solve. The street musicians who, in Woolf's words, "scrape for the harmonies that never come while the traffic goes thundering by," were no longer an inevitable, perhaps unnoticed, fact of city life but, for the delicate neurasthenic or harassed writer, an intolerable nuisance that at once defined one's gender or class distinction and legitimated unprecedented interventions in how the city was planned and administered.[43] The nineteenth- and twentieth-century European and American city therefore saw a host of ways by which what, where, and how one could sense were disciplined and managed, from sewage and transport systems to bylaws against noisy cars and new codes of looking in galleries.[44] The intensified regulation of sensations, and of the spaces of sensation, in everyday life was therefore a means of reproducing a particular social order and the values associated with it. More than this: ways of sensing, and of materially managing sensation, were ways of articulating broader debates about what "progress," "liberalism," or the ideal political community, for example, looked like.[45]

These stories are compelling because they resonate with those told about sensory change during the period about which they are written. Yet for the same reason, they have made it hard to imagine a history of the senses in which the senses were not overstimulated, alienated, or managed as a cause and consequence of urban, industrial, and social change. The entanglement of the method of sensory history with the history of the senses during modernity has proved both inescapable and insufficient for conceptualizing sensory change. One consequence of this entanglement is the implicit continuation of assumptions about the body and historical time rooted in the period explained. Although sensory histories have carefully attended to the spatial particularities of sensing, they have largely continued assumed distinctions between the mind, the body, and the world sensed. In these studies, the mind remains a device for representing what lies "outside": a cinema for projecting images of the world to be interpreted rather than continuous with a person's embodied presence within it.[46] Moreover, while sensory histories foreground change over time, they typically fail to consider both the temporality of sensing as an embodied, situated action and the nature of historical time over which change occurs. The implicit theory in much of this research is that sensory change occurs over a singular, linear temporality—one over which the senses become "more" or "less" sensitive, alienated, ordered, objectified, commodified—rather than being contingent on embodied actions and the multiple temporalities of the body and environment that afforded them. Alongside histories of "perceptual revolution," we need accounts of the intimate entanglement of bodies with particular spaces, of everyday efforts to make and find space and their intersection with multiple, distinct chronologies.[47]

BECOMING TACTILE

This book begins with the premise that before we sense, we are bodies already involved in the world. How touch is experienced, and how the world is conceptually organized based on that experience, emerges through ongoing embodied actions in particular spaces and over time. Traceable in Britain to Henry Head and Gordon Holmes's "Sensory Disturbances from Cerebral Lesions" (1911), this idea foregrounds the emergent nature of both the sensing subject and the world sensed and their inseparable relation through action. For Head and Holmes, investigating the sensory disturbances of nerve injury patients, the body produced models, or "schemata," of its posture and position through measuring each bodily movement against those which had gone before. What a person sensed of their embodied relation to the world emerged through the continual unfolding of their actions within it. That a blind person was equally able to conceive posture and position without producing mental "images" was evidence, Head and Holmes argued, that a person's sense of their body in space emerged through active involvement in the world—the probing of the blind person's stick—rather than a passive response to it.[48] Sensory experience, especially touch, was contingent on one's inherence within, and active engagement with, the world sensed.

Since Head and Holmes's reflections in 1911, this idea has been taken up by a range of disciplines, including cognitive science, psychology, and phenomenology. It was developed most fully by Maurice Merleau-Ponty's *Phenomenology of Perception* (1945), which drew upon but sought to elaborate the "immanent" potential of Head and Holmes's work. As first conceived, Merleau-Ponty contended, Head and Holmes's concept of the body schema did not go far enough because it understood the body's spatiality only in terms of its position in space, a position only grasped, moreover, through the intervening role of mental representations. Yet Head and Holmes's concept implied a more fundamental point that the body was not merely an object "in" the world but part of it—part of an unfolding *situation*—and, through this participation, conditioned what it was possible to perceive.[49] The body was in the world "as the heart is in the organism," and the world appeared to a person insofar as they inhabited it with a body.[50] What this reenvisioning of the body schema allowed was a more radical argument about the situated nature of perception. In this argument, perception was not merely a mental response to a world that was already made; it was a condition of the world and constituted through one's embodied involvement within it. Perception was less something one "had" than something one *did* within a world to which one already belonged. Through reconceiving the body as situated within a context of action, Merleau-Ponty also emphasized the temporality of sensing. Because perception depended on a person's active involvement in the world, it was not a process that occurred after the fact but in and through the duration of action. Like blood circulating within the body, sustaining it through constant motion, the body sustained the world, bringing it into being as an object of perception through unceasing action within it. Perception could be conceived only in terms of its constant unfolding over time.[51]

The implications of this argument for understanding the historicity of the senses are significant. By arguing for the situated, embodied, enacted nature of perception, Merleau-Ponty collapsed assumed distinctions between the mind, body, and world, suggesting instead their inseparable entanglement. This is an insight later developed by theorists of embodied cognition, who argue, to differing degrees, that perception occurs "in" the thing perceived, and the body engaging with it, as much as in the mind of the perceiver.[52] Nearly a century after Head and Holmes's theorization of the body schema, philosopher Alva Noë opened his book *Action in Perception* (2004) with the example of a blind person building their world through the tapping of a stick. In this example, which Noë saw as paradigmatic of all perception, what the blind person perceived occurred through their physical engagement with the world and extended beyond their cognitive or bodily boundaries—at the tip of the stick as much as in the brain or hand.[53] In this way, some theorists of embodied cognition forward a more radical conclusion about the location of perception. Whereas Head and Holmes distinguished between perceiver and the world perceived, Noë and others argue that perception emerges through the active engagement of mind, body, and environment, not as entities divided from one another but as parts of the same cognitive "system."[54]

Merleau-Ponty's attention to the situated nature of perception also called into question the determinacy of sensory experience. Instead, phenomenology suggested that what a person perceived was conditioned by what they did with their body, which changed spatially and historically. This is more than saying that a person's body "mediates" what they perceive. It is to say that the very horizons of perception are constituted by embodied action, which is itself conditioned by what a person's physical environment affords.[55] Psychologist James Gibson developed this idea in a theory of visual perception, arguing that what a person perceived of a room, for example, was constituted by their movement within it, which was made possible by the specific capabilities of that person's body and the layout of the room traversed.[56] Cognitive archaeologists extend this idea over the long term, showing how human perception has evolved in tandem with—through embodied engagement with—things. Returning again to Head and Holmes's article and the example of the blind person's stick, these theorists argue that perception and the things humans use each condition how the other comes into being, both over an individual's lifetime and over evolutionary time. This means it would be better to talk not of "minds" and "things" as discrete, preexisting entities but as continuous, and continually emergent, over history.[57] Together, these scholars encourage us to consider the senses not as independent from what is sensed but of both existing in a relationship of dependent, ongoing emergence. What history—and what ethics—comes into view when we think about touch as in a process of perpetual becoming with what is touched?[58]

Thinking about perception as a process emerging across mind, body, and world compels consideration of the time over which that emergence changes, as well as causal explanations attached to it. Philosopher Shaun Gallagher emphasizes that perception does not only change through action but also through changes in the bodies and social and physical environments affording it. A person's perception of a crowded subway car, for example, is conditioned as much by the bearing of their body, norms of social interaction, and the layout of seats as by their movement within it. Each change at different rates and over different durations of biographical, historical, and evolutionary time that intersect differently over history.[59] An account of perception as emerging from an entanglement of mind, body, and things therefore also asks for an understanding of history as an entanglement of temporalities, or what Reinhart Koselleck calls "sediments'" of time.[60] This book traces the emergence of touch through the coincidence of multiple chronologies running within and across chapters. Chapter 3, for example, shows how the experience of touch on the tube emerged through a constellation of habitual, economic, technological, and spatial changes, from the electrification of rail lines to changing patterns of rush, each with distinct temporalities. These changes intersected with other patterns of change and histories of touch above ground. The electrification of tube cars, for example, influenced seasonal incidences of London fog and the need to feel one's way around the city on winter days, the subject of chapter 5. This approach to historical time disrupts singular narratives of sensory change and their associated linear causal explanations.

This book is about touch, but discussion of the other senses, especially vision, sometimes creeps in. This is not incidental but inescapable: just as mind, body, and world can be conceived as impossibly entangled, so too can the senses. The senses are, in Michel Serres's words, "mingled," knotted and spliced together like threads in a tapestry, each implicated in and enlarging on the other in the moment of perception.[61] Touch informs and is informed by the other senses even when, as chapter 1 shows with blindness, it is ideologically defined against them. In a similar way, chapter 5 examines how the meaning and experience of touch were clarified by the obscuration of vision during London fogs. Such mingling makes analysis of sensory experience, which entails separation, partial at best. Rather, it is necessary to trace the

unfolding entanglement of body and world and of particular senses: to follow "patiently and with respectful diplomacy the delicate disposition of the
veils, zones, neighbouring spaces, the depth of the pile, the talweg of their
seams," and to "[display] them when possible."[62] The mingling of the senses
makes the history of touch one of emphasis rather than degree.

Phenomenological theories of perception and embodied mind suggest
the need for another kind of sensory history: a history of the body's entanglement with and emergence from the world sensed, or what might be called
an *immanent history* of touch. This would be a history that attends to the
emergence of touch, of the horizons of the tangible, through tactile practices,
and to the ideas about touch stemming from that history and by which it can
be written.[63] For while reading *Phenomenology of Perception* I always returned
to several questions. How did ways of conceptualizing touch, as situated or
otherwise, themselves emerge from everyday tactile encounters? How did
these encounters condition ways of thinking about the body—for example,
about personal space and how this should be maintained? How did tactile
encounters condition ways of producing knowledge within other areas of
life, especially those that erased the role of the body, such as science and law?
And how is the history of touch therefore a means of interrogating our own
categories of thought—for example, of vulnerability or disability—which
derive from historical embodied experience? I have tried to take seriously
Merleau-Ponty's precept that we make the world we perceive through how
we inhabit it by also showing the historical emergence of this idea, and other
ideas about the body, through everyday experiences of touch.

Intimate Subjects therefore makes a historical argument about the emergence of touch, and ideas about touch, through what individuals did with
their bodies in particular spaces—at tea shop tables, on tube platforms,
in courtrooms, and elsewhere. But this is also a methodological argument
about the history of touch as a means of critiquing ways of thinking about
embodiment in the present, as well as of interrogating its own theoretical
origins. For this reason, I pay as much attention to Head's experience battling
through the crowds of Whitechapel High Street or holding his fiancé Ruth
Mayhew's hand on a trip to the Tate Gallery as to his concept of the body
schema. For the same reason, the book examines the school life of blind
children after 1893, not as phenomenological tropes but as individuals whose
tactile explorations along school corridors or on relief maps conditioned
their perception of the world and ideas used to explain it.[64] Tracing these
everyday experiences of touch enables us to critique historical understandings of the body derived from them. Yet it also enables us to examine the

tactile origins of the concept of the body schema that has for a century been central to efforts to explain the emergence of perception. In other words, this is a history of touch as emerging from particular, embodied experiences of being-in-the-world, which is also a critique of this and other ways of thinking about the body resulting from those experiences.[65]

OVERVIEW OF THE BOOK

What ways of thinking about the body, and about the world inhabited, arise from a history of touch? That is, what ideas about the body historically emerged from touch, and how does this history contribute toward contemporary understandings of embodiment?

This book starts in the 1860s because that decade has conventionally been taken as the beginning of an epistemological shift in how the senses were understood, as well as marking the advent of novel urban spaces through which they were reconfigured. In 1860, physiologist Gustav Fechner argued that experiments on touch conducted by his mentor Ernst Weber provided a way of establishing a direct, measurable relation between stimulus and sensation, and therefore between body and mind. Fechner's claim stimulated the development of a whole program of research in experimental physiology and, from the 1870s, experimental psychology to differentiate and map the basic elements of touch and other senses and to quantify the normative relationship between stimuli and sensations. For Friedrich Kittler and Michel Foucault, such investigations were central to the production of a normative subject and means of assimilating, instrumentalizing, and regulating their life for the needs of capital, technology, or the state.[66] I have chosen the 1860s as a starting point to show how ways of understanding and experiencing touch were more diverse and contradictory than any archaeology of knowledge or genealogy of the subject can allow for, precisely because they emerged through situated, embodied actions in a multitudinous variety of spaces. This was a decade in which the appearance of new social spaces such as the first underground railway and first tea shops transformed tactile interactions in ways irreducible to the emergence of a singular sensory subject.[67]

The book ends in the 1960s for historical and theoretical reasons. By that point neurologists no longer believed that one could read back a direct relation between mind and body by analyzing what one felt when touched. Ideas about touch in relation to blindness lingered longer, but the 1960s represented a turning point when visually impaired activists shifted attention away from how touch could make up for blindness and toward how society could make space for those who sensed differently. Crucial attitudinal changes were also led by British feminists, who in the 1970s adopted the definition, developed by US women's groups and legal scholar Catharine MacKinnon, of unwanted advances as sexual harassment, which especially stemmed from gendered power inequality.[68] This argument continues to be the touchstone for debates about sexual violence today, even while some scholars locate its cause in a gnawing male fragility rather than self-assured control.[69] The 1960s also constitute an important conceptual close for this book. The publication in 1962 of the first English translation of Maurice Merleau-Ponty's *Phenomenology of Perception* marked the most influential formulation of the idea that perception is a situated, embodied event, conditioned by the body's involvement in the world perceived. This argument was founded on a critique of "mechanistic" physiological and psychological models of the body maintained, for example, by Fechner in the 1860s.[70] It was the culmination of a series of investigations into how the body gains a sense of itself—a "body schema"—which is traceable through the work of neuropsychiatrist Jean Lhermitte (1939), Gestalt psychology, neurologist Paul Schilder (1923), and back to Henry Head (1911 and 1893).[71] At the same time, *Phenomenology of Perception* continues to stimulate research in contemporary neuroscience, which investigates how perception is conditional on one's being-in-the-world.[72] Ending *Intimate Subjects* here returns contemporary theories of embodied mind to their origins in the attempts to understand touch in the late nineteenth and early twentieth centuries. In so doing, the book shows how the history of touch in this period was also that of the concept that enables us to historicize it.

Why focus on Britain, and to what extent is this a uniquely British story? If recent stereotypes are to be believed, a history of touch in Britain promises a short story. Popular belief held that British people hardly touch—until troubled (and made troubling) by the revelations of #MeToo.[73] Comparative psychological studies suggest that British people are more selective about where they are touched than are people from other countries, although the importance of touch for social bonding is universal.[74] Whatever their truth, precisely these tropes of aversion indicate the central, phantasmic importance of touch in Britain at a time when vision allegedly dominates.[75] Many of the changes examined here had parallels elsewhere. What is unique in this story is how ways of touching and understanding touch were shaped by Britain's status as a global empire and a comparatively urbanized and industrialized society. British colonies provided early experimental psychologists with a laboratory for formulating ideas about touch and its relation to evolutionary development and racial difference.[76] Commodity chains spanning the empire directly connected the bodily disciplining of colonial indentured laborers with that of workers in the imperial capital. The size of London, the most populous city in the world in 1900, made it a site for distinctive technologies and environmental pressures that also transformed touch. The world's first underground railway compelled travelers to learn new habits for dealing with proximity, which were replicated, in diverse ways, as this system was imitated by other cities.[77] Britain's role throughout the nineteenth century as Europe's preeminent producer of coal, and of carbon emissions, fueled London's famous fogs and the popular fascination among Britons and foreign travelers with their sensorially disorienting effects.[78] Britain's imperial reach and urban and industrial development generated these distinctive histories while ensuring that their impact was global.

The first two chapters are about knowledge of what touch was and how it worked. Chapter 1 is a history of scientific experimentation on touch and the resulting changing understanding of the relationship between mind and body. But it is also a love story that explores how early twentieth-century understandings of the nervous system were shaped not only by touch within experiments but also by memories and erotic fantasies of touch beyond them. Starting with science is not meant to imply that it was foundational but the inverse: scientific knowledge about the body was entangled with the changing sensory life of scientists beyond the experiment, even while its purported objectivity depended on the erasure of that sensory life. Chapter 2 traces changes in the way that touch was taught and conceptualized in schools for blind children, and how this shaped understandings of bodily difference and the sensory conditions for involvement in economic and political life. After the state mandated elementary education for all, teachers in specialist schools trained blind children to refine their sense of touch to "compensate" for their lack of sight. Refining touch became essential training for the tactile work of piano tuning, poultry farming, and typewriting for which it was assumed blind people were most suited. Elementary education taught blind children to adapt to a sighted world and so conform to an ideal liberal subject whose economic, political, and intellectual freedom was predicated, implicitly, on bodily ability.[79] I trace this story to the 1960s, when blind people challenged the language of compensation by reconceiving disability as a social effect distinct from impairment.

The central chapters concern questions of when and where one could touch in public. In late nineteenth-century London, an emerging landscape of department stores, restaurants, music halls, theaters, and offices offered new spaces for an increasingly fractured, and fractious, public. The growing presence of unaccompanied ladies who "shopped," "working girls," and female charity workers, and the new opportunities for their mixing with an emerging class of male clerks and civil servants, intensified anxieties about sexual harassment and forced reconsideration of personal boundaries in public.[80] One of the most fraught spaces for this conflict, given its containment, liminality, and increasingly heterogeneous composition, was public transport, and so in chapter 3 I turn to the London Underground to examine how changing experiences of touch reconfigured understandings of personal space. As the possibilities for and prohibitions against touch changed in tandem with infrastructural and economic change, understandings of what constituted personal boundaries, for whom, and when also shifted. This chapter makes a theoretical point about the contextual nature of vulnerability and a historical one about the production, rather than only defense or transgression, of personal autonomy. Chapter 4 continues this argument through examining another space made possible by the growth in commuter traffic: the tea shop. Touch between customers and waitresses was shaped not only by the new social and spatial opportunities of tea shops but also by waitress employment conditions. Waitressing work remained precarious, and with it the personal boundaries of those performing it. Tense labor relations shaped the emotional labor expected of waitresses and both the desire for and aversion to touch among those visiting and working in tea shops.

The final chapter is about how touch shaped the way it was known and regulated. Chapter 5 traces a history of law, and of law's fictional separation from the world, through that of the touches sustaining it. Through examining the bewildering sensescape of the London fog and its associations with crime, this chapter shows how legal narratives about illicit touch in London's police courts were shaped by touch within and beyond them. Fog connected touch inside and outside the court as both a material thing and a metaphor for legal process. As a thing that blinded streetgoers and made them newly conscious of their bodies, fog revealed how the plausibility of legal narratives about touch depended on the sensory possibilities of the street. As a metaphor, fog stood in for the breakdown of law, particularly of the bodies of magistrates enacting it. In these ways, fog showed how law was made through touch that it at the same time regulated and shaped. Chapter 5 therefore returns to a theme of chapter 1, and a core argument of the book, that touch conditions the concepts through which it can be understood and historicized. At the same time, it reprises some of the book's characters, from blind ex-servicemen to harried tube passengers, who return, coughing and spluttering, across its pages.

Together the chapters demonstrate that touch shaped not only the possibilities of perception but also understandings of the body and the world it inhabited. I make this argument by showing how touch in certain spaces shaped ideas about the body relating to three overlapping themes: bodily difference; ethical relations between bodies; and embodiment as the condition of knowledge. As such, each chapter or pair of chapters might be read as historical explorations into the ontology, ethics, and knowledge of (and through) bodies. Yet together they show how such understandings of the body were inseparable since they emerged from tactile encounters between individuals who crossed and recrossed the spaces thematized. While Henry Head revealed the workings of the nervous system through his eroticized experiences of touch, the subject of his fantasies, novelist Ruth Mayhew, fumbled through London fogs that rendered her briefly sightless; the priest defrocked for harassing tea shop waitresses loitered on the set of a film, featuring those same waitresses as extras, dramatizing tactile norms in a tube car: lives and paths entangled, and with them ideas about the body emerging from such tactile encounters. For how else to tell the history of touch except as one of "entangled tales"?[81]

THEMES

Examining the historical relationship between touch and ideas about the body also allows me to make methodological claims within interdisciplinary debates about embodiment. I focus on three of these debates shadowing the book's themes: on the constitution of disability; inequality of vulnerability; and the making of science and law. Chapter 2 traces the historical relationship between disability and the able-bodied liberal subject through the sensory education of blind children. In the first half of the twentieth century, teachers of blind children perpetuated a binary of disability and ability by representing blindness as a medical condition to "overcome" through the refinement of touch. Touch was the means by which bodily difference could be overcome as well as that by which blind children were cast as inescapably different. By the 1960s, blind adults, the products of this system, challenged the binary of disability and ability by redescribing disability as the result of an exclusionary social environment and therefore different from the physical reality of impairment. While this understanding of disability established the basis for what became the dominant theoretical model in disability studies, it also raised the field's central problem: how to collapse the distinction between disability and ability while recognizing the importance, and uniqueness, of bodily experience.[82]

Following the sensory education of blind children from the late nineteenth century thus allows several histories. In part, this is a "minor history" of the "co-constitution of disability and ability"; a history of the able-bodied, self-determining liberal subject as well as that of the blind child who was its constitutive outside.[83] In part, this is a history of disability studies itself; of the emerging conceptual distinction, developed by blind and other disabled people, between disability and impairment that challenged segregation from the sighted.[84] But it is also a response to the question of embodiment that this new understanding of disability posed. Disability studies scholars seeking to bring the body back into analysis have suggested that disability be conceived not as a consequence of impairment or environment but as a relationship between the two, a relationship experienced uniquely by every individual.[85] In Rosemarie Garland-Thompson's terms, disability materializes from a particular "misfit" between bodily capability and environmental possibility.[86] Conceiving of disability as arising from a person's situated and shifting interaction with their environment recognizes the potential universality of disability—all bodies misfit sometimes—as well as its irreducible experiential uniqueness. Tracing the sensory history of the classroom thus reveals how, through situated, embodied encounters, children's visual impairments materialized as difference. Yet it also reveals how that embodied experience became a resource for, and continues to stimulate, reflection on the universality and uniqueness of embodiment. Historicizing the pedagogies of touch is also pedagogical.[87]

The second theme—vulnerability—is addressed in chapters 3 and 4, which examine the changing ethics and experience of touch in public space. Increased opportunities for mixing between unaccompanied women and the swelling ranks of clerks and City "gents" generated anxiety over when, where, and what kinds of touch were possible. Commentators discussing women traveling alone variously represented them as, depending on their class, threatened or thrilled by freer conditions of interaction in new heterosocial spaces of travel and leisure. The interactions in these spaces tell a story of the shifting threat of, and need to regulate, unwanted touch. Yet they also reveal a history of the spatially, socially, and legally uneven constitution of the autonomous body able to be violated by touch and, by extension, able to grant consent.[88] New spatial and social conditions for touch, from tube escalators to tipping policies for waitresses, created new class- and gender-specific understandings of who had a right to personal space and under which circumstances. Touch generated new understandings of bodies that touched as well as, crucially, the differing vulnerabilities between them.

The history of touch in public space thus offers a double history of the experience and the concept of vulnerability. As feminist philosophers argue, vulnerability is both a universal condition of embodiment and realized through particular bodily encounters. While we all are vulnerable by virtue of the fact that we have bodies that can affect and be affected by others, the experience of vulnerability materializes through the particular ways our bodies encounter the world; through how a person is responded to and feels capable of responding.[89] Touch is the exemplary case of this experience of vulnerability because it both reveals our shared existence in the world, our mutual exposure to one another, and conditions, through every encounter, our particular experience of that shared existence.[90] The history of touch across tube car seats and tea shop tables is one of the variable, always incomplete actualizations of vulnerability for different individuals in different spaces, as well as of its indeterminate effects. These experiences of vulnerability were shaped by differences in class, race, gender, and other power inequalities, but they took form only through concrete embodied encounters: through touch.

Yet while experiences of vulnerability in new public spaces were unique to each encounter, collectively they shaped understandings of what it meant to be vulnerable that persist. Historian Judith Walkowitz influentially showed how in the late nineteenth century a heterogeneous public and an expanding press enabled women to articulate harassment as "a violation of their bodily integrity"; the central chapters of this book highlight how experiences of unwanted touch were just as important in shaping ideas of what bodily integrity was, and who might claim (and lose) it.[91] The experience and discussion of unwanted touch in public space both recognized and allowed those women involved to claim an autonomy that might be violated. Yet such discussion also paradoxically attenuated that autonomy as, for the same women, an ideal always already under threat because of their assumed vulnerability. In this way, tactile experiences in the nineteenth and early twentieth centuries prefigured the conceptual tension between vulnerability and autonomy as its desired, but always elusive, antidote that structures debates about sexual violence and its solution today.[92]

The third theme, the tactile conditions of knowledge, is central to the chapters bookending my argument. Chapters 1 and 5 examine touch as the ground for, and object of, knowledge in science and law: how tactile practices conditioned ideas about touch made through experiments or court cases, as well as the boundaries of science and law as domains of knowledge. Erotic recollections of kisses stolen in theater stalls; narratives of longing for touch in poetry and prose; the charged intimacies of collaborative experiment: in neurology quotidian touches within and outside experiments combined to shape understandings of where touch was and how it worked. In London's police courts, too, conflicting narratives of touch possible on the street, as well as embodied performances in court, conditioned how legal knowledge about touch was made and judged. These remembered, performed, and imagined touches were the sensory conditions of how touch was conceptualized in science and law.[93] At the same time, scientific and legal knowledge of touch reconfigured how it was experienced, practiced, and regulated within and beyond the experiment and court case. Whether exploring its private experience or public exposure, scientific and legal understandings of touch shaped how those involved felt when they were touched, or touched others, far beyond these contexts.

Together these chapters trace the sensory conditions of scientific and legal knowledge, as well as its lived effects. Yet in doing so they also show the shifting constitution and boundaries of early twentieth-century science and law as discrete domains of knowledge. What scientists and magistrates did with their hands during experiments or legal disputes not only brought touch into being as an object of knowledge: it also determined what it was possible to know, and therefore the parameters of science and law themselves.[94] Skin prickled and ached under the neurologist's instruments, hands parsed and reassembled a mass of files, and with these touches both the objects and objectivity of science and law—their distinction from what was observed—were constituted. In the terms of one legal historian, the constitution of touch in law determined what it was possible for law to touch—what world was tangible to it, and which it took as its field of intervention.[95] As neurologists and magistrates isolated touch through their tactile practices, they continually reconstituted science and law's isolation from the sensory world. In this way, the history of touch was also one of the changing conditions of science and law's intervention in the world.

...

Somewhat shaken, as you peered through the uncleaned windows of the Devonshire House Hotel, you may have pondered the congested street below. The everyday vicissitudes of touch pose questions both historical and lasting:

How do we find our place in the world when it so often feels beyond us? How do we reach one another even while touch exposes our many differences? How do we stay open to others while still protecting ourselves? This book explores historical responses to these questions, which also pose them for us anew.

CHAPTER ONE

Love in the Time of Neurology

On the night of January 16, 1903, lovelorn neurologist and physician Henry Head sat down at his desk in his Westmoreland Mansions flat, Marylebone, and began to write. Writing, however, did not come easily. Even as he poured out his thoughts to his beloved Ruth Mayhew, Head found her "vivid presence" so tangible that he could scarcely write. "Written words," he pleaded, "seem poor when offered to the palpitating happy living creature whose touch I feel on my arm, whose joy envelopes me as a cloud."[1] Three months later that arm would be all but insensible. On April 25, 1903, at Head's instruction, London Hospital surgeons Henry Dean and James Sherren severed the radial and external cutaneous nerves in Head's left forearm. Head's aim was to identify what feeling remained once these nerves were cut, and to measure the return of tactile sensitivity lost as they healed. Immediately after the operation, Head could feel on his hand neither heat nor cold, the prick of a pin nor the brush of cotton wool; nor could he feel Mayhew's caress.[2] By May 4, 1903, ten days after the operation, the affected skin on Head's hand had flushed crimson and become inelastic and scaly.[3] He could feel no touch.

In the five years that followed, Head and psychologist William Rivers followed a painstaking, often painful, procedure of recording the return of sensitivity to his damaged forearm and hand. The conclusions drawn from these observations, first published in November 1905 and elaborated in subsequent experiments and publications until 1920, set what was later eulogized as a dramatic new course for understandings of touch, and of the nervous system in general.[4] "No branch of medicine, except that of tropical medicine, has made such remarkable advance in a single generation as neurology," effervesced the London *Times*'s obituary of Head in 1940; Head, it continued, had led the vanguard of this advance.[5] Gordon Holmes, fellow-neurologist and Head's collaborator for five years, gave a more intimate appraisal: Head combined a "rigidly scientific and objective outlook" with "a vivid imagination which at times seemed to carry his ideas beyond the bounds of probability." Yet ultimately Head managed to tame his wayward thoughts, claimed Holmes, by subjecting his writings "to a rigid criticism which assured an accurate and reasoned presentation of the conclusions to which he had come."[6]

Holmes's judgment was unequivocal: Head had managed to curb his "imagination" in the service of "reason." But it also hinted at the impossibility of maintaining this distinction in practice. If Head's memory of Ruth Mayhew's touch inhibited his writing, then that memory also at once removed him from his work and became inseparably entangled with it.[7] On May 6, 1903, twelve days after the operation, Head recounted to Mayhew the long evenings of the previous week when, laboriously writing letters for patients, his thoughts flew to her. "Last Sunday walking hand in hand with you," he wrote, "the rushing fierceness of my life seemed to pass away [and] I was no longer a man devoted to the diseased and disordered aspects of life, a fighter who has to pluck the heart out of each moment lest knowledge should escape never to be recaptured, but just a little child walking quietly in the rain [. . .] with my hand in your dear warm hand."[8] Head's hold on Mayhew's hand temporarily transported him from the examination of his own, the need to capture, as Rivers pricked and prodded him, the essence of sensation as it played across his regenerating skin. A week later, the memory of this touch again spirited him away. Yet at the same time, Mayhew's touch haunted Head's work on his hand like a specter, transpiring in what he observed and wrote. Off to Cambridge Head would go that coming Saturday afternoon, ready for more tests on the "extraordinary condition" of his hand. And although Mayhew rarely accompanied Head on these trips, neither was she ever fully absent, either from his thoughts or their later "reasoned presentation."[9]

The experiment on Head's hand was part of a much longer, international history of attempts to quantify and map the types and capacities of touch. In the earliest of these experiments, conducted at the University of Leipzig in the 1820s, anatomist Ernst Weber measured the minimum distance required between two compass points touching the skin for these to be registered as distinct sensations. Weber identified this distance as the "threshold" at which a change in stimulus became one of sensation.[10] The implications of these investigations increased significantly in 1860, when Weber's student Gustav Fechner claimed that they provided a way of determining a fixed, mathematical relationship between stimuli and sensations and that a similar relationship could be established for every sense.[11] Measuring sensory acuity became seen as a way of determining the elusive relationship between body and mind.[12] Soon the uses of this approach for empirically analyzing mental objects was recognized by Wilhelm Wundt, also at Leipzig, who from 1879 used sensory physiology as the basis of his new method, and eventually field, of experimental psychology.[13] Throughout the nineteenth century, physiologists and psychologists used experiments on the senses to pinpoint a functional relationship between stimulus and sensation, and between body and mind. Head drew on these approaches, visiting Germany several times before his operation to study the latest advances in experimental physiology.[14]

The implications of these experiments were considerable. By quantifying the normative relationship between stimulus and sensation, experimental physiology made the senses sites for differentiating between, as well as developing and intervening in, individuals' capacities to discriminate. Sensory discrimination became a way of discriminating *between* individuals according to a norm, as well as of turning them into subjects that could be worked *upon*. The effort to differentiate individuals and cultures according to how they sensed was most marked in anthropology, in which Rivers also played a significant role. In anthropological fieldwork of the late nineteenth century, investigating subjects' sensory acuity became a way of establishing or questioning lines of cultural and racial difference.[15] When combined with evolutionary biology in race science, measurements of sensory acuity enabled the historicization of culture and race in terms of cognitive and "civilizational" development and sensory adaptation to the environment.[16] Although increasingly questioned in British anthropology by the 1910s, this understanding of race in terms of measurable differences in sensory acuity, themselves the result of historical differences in evolution and environmental adaptation, long provided a sensory legitimation of imperialism.[17]

Such thinking added a temporal dimension to sensory acuity, suggesting that the senses not only were subject to evolutionary change but could also develop over an individual's lifetime. Besides making touch a marker of individual and racial difference, experimental physiology therefore also underpinned assumptions that touch could be trained. For pedagogical theorist Maria Montessori, measurable differences in tactile acuity suggested the possibility that schoolchildren's sense of touch could develop if they were given appropriate tactile "didactic material."[18] As will be explored in chapter 2, this idea directly informed the education of blind children, which depended on the assumption that tactile acuity developed to compensate for the absence of sight. Through correlating variations in sensory acuity with those in the environment, pedagogical theorists reframed individuals as sensory subjects that could be cultivated and intervened in. This experimental production of sensory subjects occurred beyond education. In commercial entertainment, for example, the measurement of sensation informed and was informed by new spectacles intended to deceive.[19] Quantifying the relationship between stimulus and sensation rendered the senses assimilable to new technologies and practices directed toward them, and the individual a potential subject of capitalist intervention.[20]

The measurement of Head's touch participated in this wider experimental construction and differentiation of sensory subjects. Like other experimental physiologists and psychologists, Head and Rivers believed that they were uncovering the hidden structures and forgotten history of the capacity to sensorially and intellectually discriminate. Yet Head's baleful letter to Mayhew shortly after his operation hints at a contrasting history: one in which touch conditioned what Head observed and how this was conceptualized as a new theory of the nervous system. Touch was not only the object but also the method of the experiment, and Head its ambiguous subject-observer. Consequently, the investigation into Head's touch enables a history not only of changing understandings of the relationship between body and mind but also the changing role of scientists' bodies in establishing this new understanding.[21] What Head felt under Rivers's touch, and how he formulated this as a theory of nerve functioning, was shaped by how he was touched, physically and affectively, within and beyond the experiment.

This mutual shaping of touch and ideas about touch is most evident in the way that Head's experiment entangled with his developing relationship with Mayhew. Head's observations of touch during a sitting were often charged with or disrupted by memories and dreams of Mayhew's touch and interpreted in terms of the aesthetic literature they shared. The hundreds of letters Head and Mayhew exchanged between 1897 and 1904 and the "rag books" in which they shared criticisms of books and plays allow us to trace, often to the day, the ineluctably entangled relationship between Head's understanding of touch and his relationship with Mayhew. This examination points to a longer history of the domestic origins of scientific knowledge.[22] But it also reveals a particular conjuncture of love, literature, and neurology in the years before the Great War.[23] During these years, feeling observed and theorized through neurological experiment enacted, framed, and modulated that which was shared and discussed in the too-brief intimacies stolen, novels read, and letters hastily written between them.

We can glimpse this conjuncture even before Head and Rivers's experiment began. Writing seven months before Head's operation, Mayhew noted that she had recently realized a close connection between her senses of touch and taste. When cutting the leaves of her new volume of Walter Pater's *The Renaissance* (1873), Mayhew found that the contact of the steel paper knife with the thick, "woolly" paper "brought to my tongue the taste I knew as a child when we loved to put our disobedient lips to the iron railings of the Parks at home or liked to suck our pennies."[24] Head responded by recounting a "tactile dream" told him by a colleague in which the colleague had dreamed he was steering a ship and after waking still "felt the wheel in his hands."[25] Besides revealing Head and Mayhew's close attention to how touch blurred with other senses and leaped between past and present, sleeping and waking, the exchange also shows how they interpreted these observations through an embodied and intellectual engagement with authors of aesthetic literature such as Pater. Pater's attempt to seize, in his studies of art, "impressions unstable, flickering, inconsistent, which burn and are extinguished with our consciousness of them" became a model for both Head's self-experiment and his trade in sensations with Mayhew.[26]

This chapter therefore traces a history of understandings of the relationship between mind and body through that of the tactile practices that enacted them. It shows how ideas about touch were formulated through touch experienced, remembered, and longed for within and outside experiments, through letter writing, aesthetic literature, poetry composition, and autofiction.[27] Through so doing, it captures a moment in the tactile production of scientific concepts and how those concepts shaped tactile experience. But it also provides a wide-angle view of how scientists' embodied involvement in the world contingently constructed the object available to them and the very boundary between scientific knowledge and the phenomenal world.[28] The tactile production of scientific objects, or "intra-action" between observer and observed, contingently structured what of the world was tangible to scientists, including touch itself.[29]

THE PHYSIOLOGY OF TOUCH

Head and Rivers were not the first collaborators to make the scientist's body a laboratory for touch. If the questions they asked about touch were different, their methods drew on a well-established tradition of introspective self-experimentation stemming from early nineteenth-century Continental experimental physiology.[30] Seventy years before Head's self-experiment,

Ernst Weber, professor of anatomy at Leipzig University, and his brother Eduard, professor of physics at Halle University, performed a near-identical procedure. Through applying two points of a pair of compasses to different parts of Ernst's body, the Webers mapped how the threshold for perceiving two simultaneous touches varied across the skin.[31] In a separate inquiry, Ernst Weber also measured what minimum change in a stimulus was required to cause a change in perception: what he called the "law" of "just noticeable difference."[32] These experiments established for the first time an empirical relation between stimulus and sensation that could be mapped on the skin. Touch became a quantifiable entity, operating under fixed laws, to be hunted down, classified, and plotted onto the body.

Yet if touch was quantifiable, physiologists were less certain whether its elements—the sensation felt or its material "basis"—represented differences in kind or only in degree. In his *Handbuch der Physiologie des Menschen* (1834–1840) Johannes Müller, professor of anatomy and physiology at Berlin University, argued that a sensation did not provide knowledge of the external world, only of the effect the world had on nerves themselves: "We do not feel the knife which gives us pain, but the painful state of our nerves." Nerves were therefore not "passive conductors" of impressions of the world but the determinants *of* those impressions according to the specificity of the nerve itself.[33] Nerves had what Müller called specific "energies" that determined the sensation conveyed. But for Müller it proved impossible to determine *what* and even *where* these energies were.[34] Either nerves with specific energies maintained a sensation's specificity, or undifferentiated nerves conveyed qualitatively identical sensations that only acquired specificity in the brain.[35] Exactly what was specific in the law of specific nerve energies remained decidedly vague because of the mysteriously unlocatable, ineffable nature of nerve energy.

Müller's law was especially confusing when it came to touch. In the mid-nineteenth century, touch was not, like vision or smell, a distinctly defined sensation but a catchall term for a bundle of sensations also known as *common sensibility*. Common sensibility, an idea derived from Aristotle, acted as the clearinghouse in which the diverse claims made by all the senses were settled as a unified consciousness.[36] Müller defined common sensibility more narrowly: no longer was it a center for coordinating sensation but a category embracing the many forms of touch and "feeling." Itching, tickling, pleasure and pain, heat and cold, and sensations of touch "in the more limited sense" all featured.[37] Yet even within this narrower definition, the relation between these sensations and with other, "proper" sensations such as vision remained for scientists long after Müller an enigma.[38] In 1846 Ernst Weber made a further distinction, arguing that touch referred to sensations providing information about the external world and common sensibility to sensations registering changes in the body.[39] But still Weber left undefined the relation between elements included within touch, such as temperature and pressure, and between touch and other senses. Arguing that nerves showed no difference in their "mode of conduction" and therefore that all sensations acquired specificity in the brain, he at the same time claimed that "exactly what goes on in our nerves, brain, and mind" when a sensation occurs "will always remain a puzzle."[40] If Weber established touch as something to plot, Müller revealed the conceptual and linguistic difficulties of determining precisely what was being hunted and where it could be plotted. The conceptual and semantic vagaries of touch meant it was not only difficult to grasp but also to find.

Despite these difficulties, later researchers persevered in sharpening the specificity of touch. To a large extent this was made possible by physiologist Hermann von Helmholtz's suggestion, outlined in his *Handbook of Physiological Optics* (1856–1866), that not only senses had their own specific energies but also nerves subserving distinct sensations *within* categories of sense such as vision.[41] In 1882 and 1884, respectively, physiologists Magnus Blix and Alfred Goldscheider independently separated warmth and cold into distinct sensations with distinct receptors and nerves; these receptors could be mapped onto the body as constellations of warmth and cold "spots," in between which were interspersed spots sensitive to touch but not temperature.[42] Between 1894 and 1896, Max von Frey, professor of physiology at Leipzig, argued that pain was not merely the result of excessive stimulation but itself an independent sensation with its own specific receptors, or pain "spots," on the skin. Von Frey associated these pain spots with those of warmth, cold, and touch identified by Blix and Goldscheider; each spot, he argued, represented a distinct modality of touch with its own specific nerve and nerve ending.[43]

By 1900, neurologists had therefore arranged touch into a punctate formation. The skin, Liverpool professor of physiology Charles Sherrington explained, was like "a sheet of water wherein grow water-plants, some sunken and some floating." When an object disturbed the surface of the "water," this aquatic foliage, the end organs of the nerves, moved commensurately with the intensity, dimensions, and proximity of the stimulus.[44] To a large extent this was a case of scientists finding what they had themselves produced. Through using blunted compasses (esthesiometers), spring measures of pressure (baraesthesiometers) and pain (algometers), metal pencils of various temperature, and filaments of various give (von Frey hairs) scientists established touch as a sense measurable at precise points.[45] Moreover, as psychologist James Sully claimed in his 1872 review of German research on sensation, physiologists who investigated sensation by measuring the effects of external stimuli "simply assume the antithesis and connection of the external and internal—which indeed nobody questions."[46] The very method used to examine sensation assumed a commensurable relation between stimulus and sensation that was retrospectively validated by its results.

EPISTEMOLOGY OF THE TICKLE

Yet despite its growing acceptance, the model of touch Sherrington described left many questions unanswered. Still in 1900 neurologists had no clear explanation of the distinction between common sensibility and the other senses, touch included. Was this distinction qualitative or quantitative, and if the latter, was it anatomical, maintained by specific nerves and end organs, or functional?[47] At one level this problem was linguistic. Neurologists distinguishing between the perception of things and things themselves inevitably worried whether the words describing sensations—for example, "pain"—encapsulated independent reality or merely their experience of it.[48] At another level the problem was conceptual. Neurology predicated on a distinction between self and world struggled when, after Weber's distinction between common sensibility and touch, that distinction was transposed onto the body itself.

This puzzling relation between common sensibility and touch, and between "inner" and "outer" sensation, is particularly evident in debates about ticklishness. For Sherrington, tickling resulted when the sensation of "light touches" combined with a reflexive "feeling of shivering" from the muscles. Yet at the same time, tickling caused a very different response from touch, affecting breathing, heartbeat, and the muscles controlling emotional expression. This difference suggested that tickling combined sensations of touch and common sensibility—of the world and the body—even while appearing to follow a neurological path distinct from touch.[49] Psychologists such as James Sully, by contrast, identified the cause of tickling less in the relation between touch and common sensibility than in the "mental attitude" toward physical stimulation. But this interpretation replaced one conceptual quandary with another, Sully admitting that exactly why we sometimes feel ticklish and sometimes not remained difficult to tell.[50]

To explain the vexed relation between touch and common sensibility, physiologists and psychologists turned to a functional, rather than anatomical, model of the nervous system. In this model, exemplified by sociologist Herbert Spencer's *The Principles of Psychology* (2nd ed., 1870), the nervous system was not a pregiven network of sensory paths but had evolved and, moreover, itself showed an evolution of complexity and integration as one moved from the periphery to the center. Psychology therefore traced the successively more complex functioning of the nervous system over phylogenetic evolution and within the individual body.[51] Neurologist John Hughlings Jackson developed this idea through his work at the National Hospital for the Paralysed and Epileptic, Queen Square, London, in the 1870s. Jackson identified three functional levels of the nervous system, each representing a stage of phylogenetic evolution and degree of complexity and control. The highest level, the cortex, normally inhibited lower levels, but in exceptional circumstances such as disease or injury, this controlling mechanism broke down and the lower levels were allowed to function unhindered.[52] In this understanding of the nervous system, sensations registering changes in the body such as hunger and fatigue were derived from a lower phylogenetic and functional level of development. Normally kept in check, when sufficiently intense or when higher levels of nervous functioning broke down, they erupted into consciousness.[53]

Ticklishness from this angle was not just another variant of touch but a different kind of tactile sensation altogether. It was, psychologists G. S. Hall and A. Allin wrote in 1897, a remnant of the defense mechanism of "primitive organisms" that had since become redundant but could still be called into consciousness during particular mental states.[54] Psychologist Louis Robinson pushed this idea even further through a remarkable experiment at London Zoological Gardens in which the animals were subjected to a thorough tickling.[55] Animals "of a lower order" such as armadillos and crocodiles, while sensitive to touch of unarmored areas, apparently "showed no more pleasure at being tickled than does a sensitive mimosa or a snail." By contrast, animals higher up the evolutionary ladder proved more ticklish in vulnerable areas. Robinson found young chimpanzees ticklish in the same parts as humans, although he struggled against an uncooperative gorilla which sadly, being "morose and unwell," "could not be got in the mood."[56] For Robinson, these results suggested an evolutionary purpose for ticklishness. Ticklishness developed, he argued, among animals with sufficient intelligence to require additional tools for defeating their equally intelligent competitors in the fight to reproduce. By encouraging "mock battles" in an animal's youth, ticklishness equipped it with the strength and tactics for defeating opponents.

Humans had once required this ability, but it had since become redundant; ticklishness remained as a relic of this earlier age, "a revelation," Robinson claimed in a statement far exceeding Charles Darwin's own on the subject, "of man's past habits and history."[57]

But if ticklishness was an exceptional survivor of an earlier sensibility, how could scientists find broader evidence for this state? How could they examine something either erased or inhibited by newer, "higher" levels of nervous functioning? The solution came from the hypothesis, popularized by biologist Ernst Haeckel, that an individual human's development recapitulated that of the development of humans as a species: that "ontogeny recapitulates phylogeny."[58] To excavate the "primitive" state half-buried in the nervous system of "civilized" humans, one therefore had only to examine humans themselves at an earlier stage of phylogenetic evolution. What was needed was not zoological comparison of species but anthropological excavation of humans themselves.

Ironically, a zoologist spearheaded this first foray of experimental psychology into the field. In March 1898 Alfred Cort Haddon, professor of zoology at the Royal College of Science, Dublin, sailed with a team of physiologists and psychologists to a tiny island in the Torres Strait, the stretch of sea pinned between northern Australia and Papua New Guinea. William Rivers, head of the new experimental psychology laboratory opened at Cambridge the previous year, joined too. For Haddon, who had drawn on the law of recapitulation in his *An Introduction to the Study of Embryology* (1887), Murray Island (Mer) offered the ideal scenario for testing an evolutionary understanding of the nervous system.[59] First encountering missionary activity only in 1871, the 450 islanders promised to be the perfect "primitive" representatives of an earlier phylogenetic age.[60]

"Primitive" did not necessarily mean less sensitive, though. Rather, the expedition aimed to test travelers' rumors that "primitive peoples" possessed exceptional sensory acuity compared with the "growing sensory defects" of "civilised" humans—especially city dwellers.[61] According to Rivers, the islanders were good test subjects because their primitivism made them, in the terms of German physiology, *unwissentlich*: entirely "without knowledge" that might cloud their judgment when reporting a sensation.[62] This apparent lack of knowledge did not make Murray islanders entirely unproblematic subjects, however. William McDougall, physician of St. Thomas's Hospital, found it impossible to collect data on heat and cold spots because temporary markings were soon washed away by islanders' habit of "frequent seabathing."[63] But McDougall did manage to gather enough results in Weber's test of two-point discrimination for a comparison with English subjects. These representatives of "civilisation" were five men "of the educated class" and a group of male working-class residents of a convalescent home in Cheadle. From the data McDougall made a striking claim: Murray islanders had a threshold of two-point discrimination half that of Englishmen; or, "their power of tactile discrimination is about double that of Englishmen."[64]

The travelers' tales, it seemed, were true: the expedition's *Reports* concluded that Murray islanders were equally, if not more, sensitive to tactile stimuli than the "civilised."[65] But whereas McDougall understood this finding in racial terms, Rivers interpreted it as what historian Henrika Kuklick calls an "evolutionary adaptation" to the natural environment.[66] Rivers suggested that Murray islanders had developed a greater acuity in the particular sensations, such as discriminative touch, that were essential to survival in the tropics. Although this meant for the islanders a finer touch, it also meant weaker intellectual grasp: for although, Rivers argued, there was nothing to suggest that they lacked the intellectual potential of their English counterparts, the demands made on the islanders' energy by heightened survival senses left little room for the development of their "intellectual superstructure."[67] The comparatively acuter tactility of the islanders proved them to be throwbacks to an earlier phylogenetic age when the challenges of survival demanded the lion's share of their energy. Reviewing the *Reports* in 1904, W. H. Winch was thrilled by the conclusion's implication that sensory "development" was "not sporadic [...] but normal evolutionary process." Sensations, he enthused, could no longer be "considered as changeless identities, atoms of solid truth in a world of changing judgments."[68]

When, in early March 1903, Rivers lunched with Head in Cambridge after five months' research in the Nilgiri Hills in India, the understanding of touch had reached a critical juncture.[69] Since Weber's experiments in the 1820s, physiologists had assumed that what was experienced as a sensation—for example, what felt "hot"—correlated with its physiological and anatomical origins in the body: mental impressions established the terms for their own explanation in the body. From Müller's suggestion that there were specific energies for each sense developed the belief that the impulses subserving the various sensations *within* the senses also followed specific anatomical pathways.[70] But for a sense as amorphous as touch, it was difficult to determine how many distinct tactile sensations ("modalities") there were. Introspection struggled to resolve this question as it proved difficult to distinguish between a modality "itself" and the experience of a modality, as well as to formulate a language that maintained the distinction.

The evolutionary understanding of touch offered a potential solution. Implicitly questioning the interpretation that specific nerve energy meant specific nerves for every sensation, the evolutionary model imagined phylogenetic and functional levels between which impulses competed or cooperated, rather than existing in isolation. The nature of those impulses could be distinguished by simple comparison between subjects rather than complicated introspection. But excavators of "primitive" touch still prodded their subjects, hoping to reveal touch spots, and still assumed "specific" pathways for diverse tactile modalities without being precise about what made those pathways specific. What researchers did with their hands continued to produce a model of touch as a pattern of spots with specific pathways, even while the change in whom they touched questioned what that "specificity" meant.

Where Head and Rivers stood in this is difficult to tell. Already in 1901 Head and the surgeon James Sherren had studied the return of sensation in London Hospital patients suffering from damaged nerves. Situated on Whitechapel Road, the heart of Jewish migration in the capital, the London's patients were overwhelmingly poor (a condition of admission) and, as an expression of the whole East End, disproportionately Jewish.[71] Of approximately seventy thousand Jews in London in 1888, an estimated half of whom were "foreign-born," 90 percent lived in the East End; the vast majority settled in Whitechapel. Local animosity toward Jews significantly increased as persecution in Russia in 1881, 1882, and 1892 drove new waves of Jewish migrants to London.[72] Privately, Head did not conceal his distaste for Whitechapel's newcomers.[73] Publicly, his aversion to many of the London's patients shaped what he believed research on their sensations able to reveal.

Head argued that the enormous number of patients passing through the London annually—250,000 outpatients alone by 1910—made it possible to filter out "untrustworthy" experimental subjects.[74] But although most patients could answer "'Yes' and 'No' with certainty" to calculated prodding, Head argued that they could "tell little or nothing of the nature of their sensations."[75] Although never explicit, the way Head described the London's patients was comparable to Rivers's description of the limited introspective capabilities and "primitive" nervous systems of Murray islanders. With concerns over urban degeneracy and Jewish migration at their height, Head interpreted his research on the London Hospital's patients through the same prisms of Spencerian evolution and colonial difference as Rivers did—only this time the "colony" was Whitechapel, in the heart of the empire.[76] Both Head's and Rivers's early sensory experiments contributed to the reification and elision of racial, class, gender, and intellectual hierarchies by claiming that these were also hierarchies of sensory discrimination: the finer one's sensory discrimination, the greater one's social differentiation.[77] For Head, the ostensibly retrograde character of the London's patients limited what they might reveal about touch. Because nothing but the "simplest introspection" could be asked of patients, it was necessary to turn to "the personal experiences of a trained observer" to push the bounds of neurological knowledge.[78]

Two months after lunching with Rivers in Cambridge, sailing over a "steel-blue sea" while bound for a holiday in Morocco, Head sat in his cabin aboard the steamship *Orotava* testing the sensibility of his hand.[79] Coincidentally, the *Orotava* was one of the ships that had transported soldiers between Britain and South Africa during the Anglo-Boer War (1899–1902) the previous year.[80] Then, Head and Sherren had supplemented their experiments on London Hospital patients with studies of the recovery of sensibility in soldiers suffering from nerve injuries sustained during fighting in South Africa.[81] Now though, Head turned to experimenting on himself; he hoped, he told Mayhew, to complete his investigations before returning home.[82] For in only twenty-two days he would be lying in a hospital bed himself, his arm tightly bound to a splint, trying to piece together the curious new feelings coming from his red-raw skin.

A HUMAN EXPERIMENT IN NERVE DIVISION

The testing of Head's sense of touch began immediately. On the day after the operation, April 26, 1903, Sherren found the radial half of the back of Head's hand to be insensible to prick, heat, and cold, and unable to discriminate between two compass points. Head did, however, feel the blunt pressure produced by a finger or pencil. A sliver of the affected area was also abnormally sensitive to painful stimuli so that when pricked there, Head would cry out and jerk his hand away.[83] The splint was removed on May 23, and the affected area, which chemical antiseptics applied before the operation had caused to peel and appear like toad skin, was scrubbed free of scales.[84]

By this time Head and Rivers had established a weekly routine of testing in Rivers's rooms in St. John's College, Cambridge. As a physician in Harley Street and the London, and a lecturer at the London's medical school, Head had an unforgiving schedule that left little time for research.[85] For this reason, Head traveled to Cambridge on Friday evenings, worked with Rivers over the weekend, and returned to London on Monday mornings. After a morning's work, Head walked or cycled, or whiled away the afternoon on the River Cam. Between 5:00 and 7:00 p.m., Head carried out control experiments on unaffected skin and then marked warmth and cold spots on the damaged area, ready for the next morning.[86] All experiments were performed in Rivers's rooms in St. John's, a set on the top floor of the second court of the college, well away from even the minor distractions of Cambridge. Head would sit at a large table in the low-ceilinged workroom, his bare arm laid before him.[87] Rivers would sit to his left, variously pricking and prodding him with the familiar tests of touch: von Frey hairs for pressure; the needle-pointed "algesimeter" (a modification of the algometer) for pressure-induced pain; tubes of hot and cold water and cooled copper rods for warmth and cold spots; and "carpenter's compasses" for two-point discrimination.[88] Instead of the "slum" onto which his London laboratory looked, the set had windows overlooking the court and the fellows' bowling green of adjacent Trinity College.[89] There, Head wrote, it was possible to give himself over to experimentation.[90]

Rivers's rooms, filled with academic paraphernalia and isolated from the "petty worries of a busy life," reified the discrimination that Head endeavored to test.[91] A carefully staged photograph materialized this, reperforming the experimental performance that Head provided for Rivers (and himself) as he observed his sensations as well as the academic performance of Rivers's workroom, its books ranged behind the table in unassuming distinction.[92] In this setting, Head would close his eyes, rest his head on his right hand, and allow his thoughts to wander "like clouds on a windy day."[93] The aim was to achieve a state in which he was at once fully conscious of his sensations and yet fully detached from them as if observing something not of himself. Within this "flowing sea of thoughts," Head wrote, "there appears a flash of pain a wave of cold or the flicker of heat." The sensation "should appear with the suddenness of a porpoise, attract attention and again disappear leaving the untroubled sea to its onward flow."[94] Head's task was to seize that momentary impression and relate it to Rivers, who jotted it down.[95]

At times, Head's "negative attitude of attention" reached such perfection that he entered a trancelike state and, as during the experiments on October 26, 1907, drifted into sleep.[96] In this somnolent state Head apparently became so detached from his own sensations that he reported them with increasing accuracy up until the moment at which he lost consciousness. Head's ability to double as subject and observer, however, depended on "absolute freedom from all external appeal to responsible action."[97] The slightest inkling of the test employed or whether he had answered wrongly reminded him that he was a scientist as well as a subject and apparently "roused" him to such "an intense determination to do better" that he devolved into inferring, rather than merely reporting, his sensations.[98] Consequently, Rivers

FIGURE 2 "With my eyes closed I try to let my thoughts flow by like clouds on a windy day":
W. H. R. Rivers experimenting on Henry Head's hand in Rivers's workroom, St. John's College,
Cambridge, ca. 1905.
© Sir Henry Head; Wellcome Collection

was careful to avoid doing anything that might break Head's delicate self-
suspension. Every test was prepared beforehand to prevent apparently innocent sounds like the "clinking of ice against the glass" or "removal of the
kettle from the hob" from revealing the experiment.[99]

Head described this method of introspection as fundamentally different
from that of earlier researchers. "The day of the *a priori* psychologist is over
as far as sensation is concerned," he announced. "A man can no longer sit
in his study and spin out of himself the laws of psychology by a process of
self-examination."[100] Head's self-examination, he claimed, was different.
Head confined himself to simple tests that provided "measurable results"
and were therefore comparable with those of other researchers.[101] Introspection was to be a replicable method, not one which, intrinsically unique to its
practitioner, was carried solely by the authority of the researcher performing
it. More important, the results of Head's self-observations were recorded as
"a function of the test employed" rather than of the sensation being tested:
"light touch," for example, was expressed in terms of "results obtained with

'tactile' and 'pressure' hairs"; "painful pressure" in terms of results from the algometer. Rather than self-report using the normal "descriptive terms" for sensations, Head was to respond in terms that did not presuppose what was being tested.[102]

This noninterpretive report required Head to suspend himself as an observer at the same time as observing himself. Although Head's most accurate results apparently correlated with his greatest self-detachment, ultimately his introspective method rested on Head shuffling *between* the roles of subject and scientist.[103] The benefit of this approach, Head argued, was that sensations were not taken as a priori but rather as potentially more complicated in cause than effect. By reading toward a sensation rather than backward from it, Head's method allowed him to detect "a multitude of phys-iological transformations" between stimulus and sensation that "could not be discovered by [traditional] introspection."[104] No longer was a sensation the explanation of its origin but the thing to be explained.

For a long time, though, there was not much to explain. Weeks after the operation Head felt only pressure or pressure-induced pain.[105] Only after eight weeks, on June 20, 1903, did sensitivity to pricking begin to return, and still then Head was insensitive to "light touch." Sensitivity to extreme tem-peratures returned next, an area of the affected part on the forearm detecting cold on August 15 and heat on October 3, 1903, but intermediate temperatures had no effect.[106] At this stage of recovery, sensations were poorly localized and disproportionate to stimuli, any stimulus below 24°C (about 75°F) pro-ducing "an explosion of cold" regardless of its intensity.[107] Only many weeks later was Head able to discern subtle differences between sensations of the same kind, to localize them and differentiate their intensity and position on the skin. Sensitivity to cotton wool wisps and the two points of a pair of compasses returned 365 days after the operation, on April 24, 1904, and to moderate temperatures between June 5 and June 26, 1904.[108]

For Head, such distinct feelings at widely separated times suggested that the changes he reported represented the recovery of discrete functional levels within the nervous system. What is more, the ability of each of these levels to operate independently suggested they were anatomically, as well as functionally, separate.[109] Head's recovery, he argued, was stepped too distinctly to suggest that a sensation was directly connected to a stimulus and that nerve regeneration was a case of rewiring the connection. Instead, Head posited that the peripheral nervous system was divided into three lev-els, each of which recovered at its own speed. The first, "deep sensibility," served pressure and pressure-induced pain and was intact after the operation, indicating its separation from the shallow cutaneous nerves that had been severed. The second, which recovered from June 20, 1903, and which Head named "protopathic," detected temperature extremes and pricking pain; its sensations, which radiated widely and were poorly localized, often caused reflexive responses. Finally, the third level to recover, from April 24, 1904, and which Head named "epicritic," detected "light touch" and "finer grades of temperature"; this was the level at which accurate localization and discriminative responses became possible, including the discrimination of two points on the skin and minor differences in temperature.[110]

Yet if each stage of recovery represented distinct functional levels of the peripheral nervous system, and if each cutaneous level detected different qualities of the same stimuli, then the cutaneous levels had to interact for stimulus to progress to sensation. Head argued that as nerve impulses traveled from skin to brain, they combined with impulses of the same kind from another level. The incipient "sensation," at first divided between impulses, became simpler as those impulses integrated en route. Whereas impulses began as protopathic or epicritic, Head wrote, as soon as they reached their first synaptic junction in the spine, those impulses of the same modality were combined and sorted into pathways serving the four conventional modalities of touch: pain, heat, cold, and touch. It was just like the "central office of a newspaper," where "the various accounts of the same event, arriving by telephone, by tape, or by telegraph, are co-ordinated and distributed according to their subject matter."[111]

The analogy was not new: it appeared in various forms across the writings of nineteenth-century physiologists. Like his predecessor physiologist Hermann von Helmholtz, Head used the telegraph analogy to explain how the structure of the nervous system around a center enabled its discriminating functions.[112] While some impulses combined, others, Head argued, competed, inhibiting competitors from traveling farther. The clearest evidence for this argument was given by the sharp switch from protopathic to epicritic sensibility during Head's recovery. For Head, this switch indicated that epicritic sensibility was not merely a later stage of recovery but an independent system that normally inhibited protopathic sensibility.[113] Far from traveling unhindered from skin to brain, tactile impulses underwent "profound transformations" as they competed and combined to form sensations.[114]

Representations of the nervous system in telegraphic terms in turn influenced those of media in the early twentieth century. In C. R. W. Nevinson's painting *Amongst the Nerves of the World* (1930), the "newspaper office" of the central nervous system was transposed onto the "nerve centre" of Fleet Street, the heart of Britain's newspaper industry.[115] The painting's title punned on the newspaper *News of the World*, whose offices were located on Fleet Street and which became with other news publishers, in Nevinson's depiction, the center of a global neural network.[116] Here the web of telephone and telegraph lines conveyed the clash of information, itself replicating the sensory chaos of the street below, that Head located at the spinal synapse: the world of the nervous system now the nervous system of the world. In this way, media of the period became a way of theorizing neurological mediation in terms of selection and simplification, a theory that shaped how media, too, were understood.

The significance to this theory of Rivers's work in the Torres Straits and Jackson's theory of the evolution and dissolution of nervous functioning is unmistakable. Like Jackson, whose annotated volumes of the journal *Brain* Head acquired sometime after 1894 and himself annotated, Head conceived of the functional and anatomical segmentation of the nervous system in evolutionary terms.[117] Sensation, Head argued, was for the earliest organisms "originally a vague undifferentiated state." From this state sensory organs of increasing complexity evolved in distinction from one another. At the same time, distinct "sensory levels" within the nervous system gradually emerged, the interaction between these levels perfecting the integration of nerve impulses traveling to the brain.[118] Under normal circumstances the epicritic level acted as a "control" on the protopathic level, either inhibiting protopathic impulses or combining them with its own and so modulating their effect. Only during nerve damage, caused by disease or injury, or when protopathic impulses were especially intense—for example, during a burning hot stimulus—was this epicritic control lifted and protopathic impulses allowed to register as sensations.[119]

Head's conclusions, and not only his results, were evidently also a function of the test employed. If reading backward from a sensation assumed its a priori existence, then reading toward it presupposed a complex integration of impulses that it was the self-observer's task, at particular stages of recovery, to discriminate. Moreover, if this method presupposed a certain discriminating nous, then it also meant Head would discover, through careful self-observation, the progressive return of his own capacity to discriminate. From the moment his nerves were severed until Rivers's last prod, 167 days of testing later, on December 13, 1907, Head was always going to discover himself as a discriminating observer; what his self-observations crystallized was an understanding of this concept in evolutionary terms.

FIGURE 3 Christopher R. W. Nevinson, *Amongst the Nerves of the World*, 1930. 002762. © Museum of London

Head's practice of recording observations in a "day book" shaped and was shaped by this formulation. In the earliest stage of Head's recovery, the day book contained entries by Rivers, Sherren, and other London Hospital staff as well as by Head himself. The notes varied from scribbles of procedures to lengthy accounts of Head's hand and forearm. Gradually, though, Head became the dominant voice on his own condition, peppering the day book with such terms as "light touch" and "protopathic" that suggested it was not entirely true that he restricted himself to soberly reading toward sensations or refrained from interpreting them.[120] Head's use of these words, especially those he invented, made it seem as though he could measure the progress of his recovery precisely because the connection between the words and the sensations they designated was arbitrary. Because there was no way to establish a fixed connection between what he felt and the words denoting it, Head's use of the term "light touch" at one moment *seemed* correct as it could not be compared with its previous uses.[121] Consequently, the words used corroborated what Head already assumed to be true of his sensations. By transposing the temporality of Head's recovery into spatial form—converting days into pages—the day book also encouraged a conception of the nervous system as something that was spatially and temporally differentiated: stages of recovery became functional levels and moments in evolution. In this way, the record became a plan of the nervous system from skin to brain as well as a condensed history of human evolution itself (day zero: 9:30 a.m. April 25, 1903). Head's day book materialized his cognitive process of interpreting— and not just reporting—his sensations while also materially shaping the conceptual outcome of those interpretations.[122]

This mutual conditioning of method and conclusion was in turn reinforced by the ordering of Head's subsequent experiments. In papers published between 1906 and 1918, Head extended his investigations through studying sensory disorder caused by nerve damage in the spine and brain.[123] Head found that just as there were two functional levels in the nervous system's periphery, so there were two in its center. The thalamus, he argued, correlated functionally and phylogenetically with the protopathic level in the skin. It received impulses that caused pleasure or pain (such as extreme temperatures) and that reported on the body's condition. The cerebral cortex, by contrast, correlated with the epicritic level. It received impulses that allowed discrimination; the ability to localize stimuli, to differentiate between them, and to spatially position oneself. And just as the epicritic level modified or inhibited impulses from the protopathic, so the cortex did for the thalamus.[124] In the same way, then, that Head's introspection allowed him to read from the outside in, his experiments were ordered to progress from periphery to center, replicating the functional and phylogenetic divisions of the nervous system they discovered. The ordering of Head's experiments recapitulated the recapitulation they apparently revealed—something Head consolidated by slightly rearranging that order to form an "orderly sequence" from skin to brain when his papers were collected as *Studies in Neurology*.[125] Both the day book and Head's collected papers performed an archaeology of sensation that produced the strata they uncovered and the discriminating observer that was their prerequisite.

Head continued the archaeological theme by interleaving day book entries with photographs recording his changing condition. Sometimes Head used photographs to record a measurement of touch. Rivers would, for example, touch Head and Head would mark on a life-size photograph the point he felt touched.[126] Sometimes, though, Head used photographs to record a measurement of touch *and* to calibrate that measurement at the same time. At the end of each Sunday sitting, Rivers marked the points at which Head was sensitive to cold onto a checkerboard five square centimeters in size (about two square inches) that was inked onto Head's hand. When Head returned to London, photographer and radiographer at the London Hospital Ernest Wilson took life-size photographs of Head's hand and smaller-scale ones of his forearm. The next weekend Head marked out what he felt as cold spots on his hand and Rivers tested them; these were then compared with results from previous photographs, and if there were found to be any cold spots "missing," then Rivers tested Head again.[127] In this way, what Head saw and what he felt mutually supported each other, his sense of touch bound up with its visual representation on the skin and in photographs that at once cataloged and calibrated it.

This bind between seeing and feeling had troubling implications for Head's new method of introspection. For contrary to Head's efforts to read toward a sensation that was "simpler than its constituent elements," by calibrating his self-reports through their photographic representation Head assumed a direct, visualizable correspondence between what he felt and what caused that feeling in the skin.[128] Despite claiming the opposite, Head's self-reports continued a turn-of-the-century visual semiotics that assumed, like the clues in a Sherlock Holmes mystery or the physiognomic quirks of a criminal, that external, visible signs possessed a secret bond with an internal, invisible reality.[129] Photographic indexicality—the direct physical relation between a negative and its object—played a part in reinforcing this assumed connection between inside and outside. The referentiality of

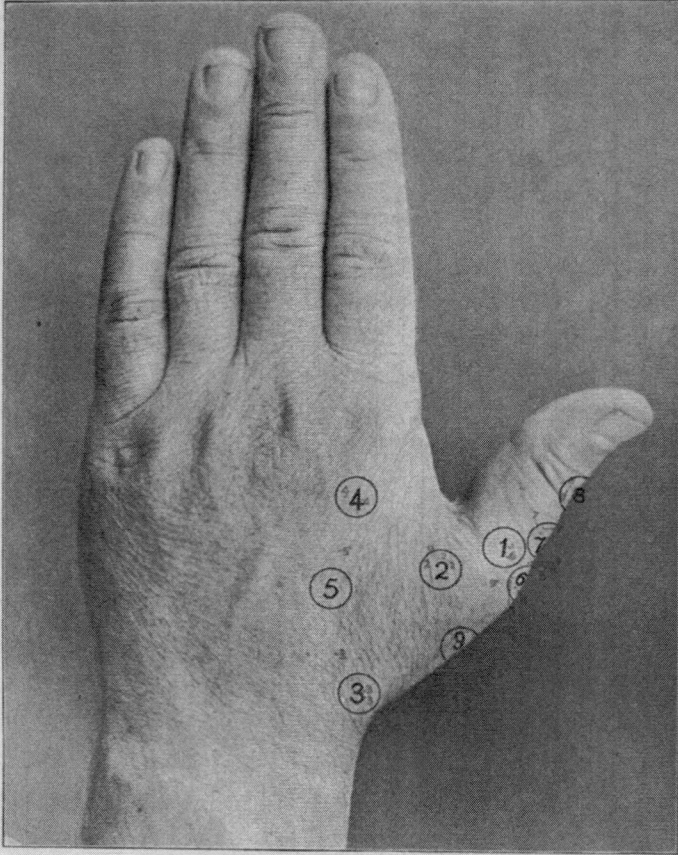

FIG. C3.

Reduced to two-thirds the natural size (May 17, 1903).
   Certain spots were marked on a life-sized photograph of H.'s hand. These are shown by black numbers within a circle of 1 cm. in diameter.
   H. was given a similar photograph and marked upon it in each case the spot he thought R. had touched.
   The photograph showing the spots stimulated and that showing H.'s localisation have been combined; the marks made by H. are printed in red. Thus, for instance, a red 3 shows the spot marked by H. as the locality of a stimulus applied by R. to the area marked with a black 3.
   The order of stimulation is given in the text.

FIGURE 4 Henry Head's hand, photographed by Ernest Wilson at the London Hospital on May 17, 1903, after Head's return from Cambridge. At this point in the experiment, Head could only feel pressure and localize touch. From Henry Head, *Studies in Neurology*, vol. 1 (London: Hodder & Stoughton, 1920), 251.

Head's photographs to their object, touch spots signifying tactile sensations, visualized and made durable sensations that were themselves invisible and would be forgotten by the next sitting, which gave to Head's reported sensations a kind of objectivity at first remove, if not that assumed were they to be "directly" photographed.[130]

Even more significant was the way the photographs visualized not only the invisible but that which Head had claimed was nonvisualizable and untenable: a direct referential connection between the site of a stimulus and the sensation that resulted. Photographing cold spots implied that impulses did not, in fact, only acquire specificity in the spine but, from their origin, directly corresponded with the sensations they caused: the old theory of specific nerve energies. Head counteracted this impression by arguing that cold spots detected only extreme cold and therefore represented only protopathic sensibility. But as his critic Francis Walshe, editor of *Brain*, later argued, this argument necessitated speculating a separate anatomical route for epicritic sensibility that was implied but nowhere located—or photographed.[131] Head's photographic record of his archaeology of sensation worked against it; paradoxically, it required the invention of an unrepresentable anatomy to support a theory of nerve functioning it was meant to make visible.

These inconsistencies did not stop Head's conclusions from becoming, for some observers, textbook knowledge.[132] But Walshe's article, published two years after Head's death, hinted at the way in which Head's imagination sometimes exceeded his results. Why, Walshe asked, would impulses be divided between protopathic and epicritic levels if, when they reached the spine, they were sorted into modality-specific pathways for heat, cold, pain, and touch that erased the distinction?[133] Even more perplexing was Head's explanation of what happened to impulses after they departed the spine. As well as positing specific pathways for the four touch modalities, Head also argued that tactile localization and two-point discrimination had their own routes to the brain. While it was possible to *think* of those qualities separately from one another and from their objects, it was absurd, Walshe argued, to treat them as things themselves, with their own physical existence and private nerves. Localization and discrimination were judgments *about* things touched and were inseparable from their objects and the touch they characterized. To argue otherwise was the same as speculating "pathways for truth or beauty"; equally "figments of the observer's mind."[134]

In short, Head got carried away. While arguing that tactile sensations were abstractions distilled from the complicated transformation of impulses, he also maintained a specific correspondence between sensations and stimuli that his introspective method aimed to refute. Readers journeying up Head's nervous system consequently found themselves teetering between nineteenth- and twentieth-century theories of touch, rather than propelled into the new era promised.

CORRESPONDING FEELINGS

Sometime in April 1903, just before Head's operation, Head and Mayhew engaged to marry.[135] The couple had met almost eight years earlier, in August 1895, and from 1897 onward had kept a weekly correspondence. Throughout this period, meeting unobserved proved to be a constant dilemma. While Head's work kept him in London and Cambridge, Mayhew, daughter of the chaplain of Wadham College, remained with her parents in Oxford, where she worked as an assistant mistress until becoming headmistress of Brighton High School for Girls in 1899. While they managed to meet at the Head family house in Buckingham or at a play or exhibition in London, for both of them these meetings were all too brief; Head's self-experiment, which required regular weekend trips to Cambridge, would become only another obstacle.[136]

Of the operation itself, Head only told Mayhew four days after, on April 29, 1903, but Mayhew was quick to reassure and encourage, writing of him "whom it is so wonderful and new [. . .] and strange to call mine in any sense."[137] Over the same months, Head and Mayhew read and corresponded on Henry James's *The Wings of the Dove* (1902), a novel that for each of them refracted and amplified the circumstances of their own relationship. The book told the story of Kate Croy and Merton Densher, deeply in love but wary of marriage because of Densher's modest earnings. Despite opposition from her family and her own limited finances, Croy nevertheless resolves to marry Densher using whatever means necessary. The rest of the novel unfolds the increasingly testing decisions the couple make in pursuit of marriage. After reading the "preface" repeatedly, Mayhew wrote to Head "that though I produce nothing, my way is that way."[138]

Whether Mayhew's statement referred more to the form or the content of the novel, James's actual preface, written several years later for the New York edition of his works, throws light on what she may have meant. James's intention had been to present two lovers "consumed by a sense of their intimate affinity" and so "impatient of barriers" to their marriage, and yet also each "with qualities of intelligence and character" to enable them to deepen that relationship and extend its possibility.[139] Just as Croy was sure of her match with Densher and, despite all obstacles, determined to marry, so Mayhew, after six years of courtship and still no end in sight, persevered with Head. With Head choosing to focus on unpaid research rather than his Harley Street practice, marriage was for him and Mayhew, as for Croy and Densher, "before them like a temple without an avenue."[140] In *The Wings of the Dove*, Densher consequently faced "the question of whether it were more ignoble to ask a woman to take her chance with you, or to accept it from one's conscience that her chance could be at the best but one of the degrees of privation."[141]

Head's comments on the novel are fewer than Mayhew's, but he clearly asked himself the same question. Returning late one evening to an empty apartment after a long day at the laboratory, Head wrote to Mayhew of his aching loneliness and the torment that it was caused by his own decision to continue work that did not pay and that itself caused such "toil & care."[142] Mayhew's response was assured. That Head's work was for him his "chosen mistress" she knew and accepted. The separation it caused was as unavoidable as Head's research was intrinsic to his life and was to be welcomed as unreservedly: "Forgive my writing this—it came to me who formulate so rarely as the slow hot tears pressed themselves out, and almost hid your writing from my wet eyes."[143] And so Mayhew and Head, apart for the while, wrote, even when writing was near impossible.

Over the course of this correspondence, Head's relationship with Mayhew entangled with the self-experiment simultaneously unfolding. Touch in and through their letters overflowed into touch practiced, felt, and thought about in Rivers's Cambridge study.[144] In part this was because Head wrote to Mayhew about his research in letters that materially stood in for the touch so often denied them: letters represented their authors, or sent a fragment of them, as traces of the hands that wrote them.[145] Head and Mayhew were, like many contemporaries, acutely aware of correspondence as a figurative and literal "touch" that both enabled and disrupted relationships.[146] The entanglement of touch in and through the correspondence and Head's self-experiment was also made possible by their intersecting temporalities. The present-centered quality of letters—how they encapsulate the moment of writing—as well as the way they develop in structure and form over a correspondence, intersected with the immediacy of Head's self-observations and the way his experiment, too, unfolded over the course of his recovery.[147] Consequently, letters became an extension of the real-time observation of feeling in Head's experiment, as well as the means by which changes in that feeling could be plotted, and progressively conceptualized, over time. Rather than being a "psychological activity" or a "performance" of selfhood, corresponding was how Head and Mayhew observed and interpreted the feeling they at the same time expressed.[148] Combined, the spatiality and temporality of letter writing enabled a correspondence of feeling between Head and Mayhew, but also between what they wrote and what Head felt in the experiment at the same time taking place.

Writing to each other every week enabled Head and Mayhew to share their lives while apart. But it also provided a material way to stay "in touch," the letters at once substituting the physical contact denied their correspondents and, by their existence, marking the absence of that contact.[149] For both, the letters were unique traces of the other and, as traces, tangible signs of their absence; for Head, Mayhew's letters were in particular markers of her distinction from other women and of the loss he felt in her absence.[150] One month into his self-experiment Head wrote to Mayhew of his recent trip to Cambridge, during which he stayed "in the ugly and cheerless rooms of a first year undergraduate":

> On the mantelpiece stood his sister, as she was presented, looking exactly like every other girl who ever made her bob to the queen, the Bishop of London and Wellson, the late head master of Harrow, in one frame, flanked on either side by Sophie Fulgarney [sic] (Vanbrugh) covered with a scrawled autograph—Among these offensive household gods stood your dear letter making the social, religious and artistic impulses of this youth seem increasingly crude & repulsive.[151]

Irene Vanbrugh played Sophy Fullgarney, a guileful yet good-hearted Bond Street manicurist engaged to a similarly dissembling "professional 'palmist,'" in Arthur Pinero's *The Gay Lord Quex* at the Globe Theatre in April 1899. The play followed Fullgarney's attempts to thwart Lord Quex, an apparently reformed roué, in his courtship of her young foster sister Muriel Eden using whatever means necessary.[152] Reviewers were both disturbed and electrified by the play's moral ambiguity. While questioning the licenser's laxity, they praised Vanbrugh's artful revelation of her character's contradictions. Fullgarney was "the ill-born, shrewdly-virtuous, meanly-enthusiastic, calculatingly-friendly type of girl sprung from the lowest rung of the lowest middle-class," explained the *Pall Mall Gazette*, and although the play was in bad "taste," Vanbrugh played her part faultlessly.[153]

Beyond the reviews, *Lord Quex* became the touch paper for a vigorous debate over morality in theater.[154] Three years later, in the autumn before Head stayed in the undergraduate's rooms, it resurfaced as the subject of a fierce exchange in the *Times* between Pinero and former president of the

Institute of Journalists Sir Edward Russell, who found its ostensible amorality more worrying than any suggested immorality.[155] For Head, though, *Lord Quex* had a more personal meaning. While the photographs of Fullgarney crowded out the other "household gods," they jarred with Mayhew's letter.[156] Celebrated photographically, Fullgarney's moral and social ambiguity was for Head a foil for Mayhew's qualities, sign of the undergraduate's vulgarity, and, by implication, testament to his own taste—in women as well as theater. Head's comment on Vanbrugh's "scrawled autograph," an addition to her photographs that, through its very denial, confirmed their reproducibility, only accentuated the contrast with Mayhew's letter as a sign of her distinction and a unique, tangible trace of her hand.[157]

Head and Mayhew's correspondence did not materially mediate their relationship only at the time it was sent. Through its sorting, storing, and rereading it enabled them to temporally as well as spatially bridge the distance between them, in turn reconfiguring that distance through the reencountered traces of their entire relationship. One October evening in 1902, Mayhew was riffling through old envelopes when she lost herself in Head's letters from four years earlier. She knew them well, Mayhew thought, but at the same time discovered in them "quite new and strange things," finding the Head she now valued—a man of "crystal sincerity" who weighed every word—in the Head she had then overlooked. The letters allowed her to "live again" her life with Head, "coloured and various and glowing"; and yet, like all repetition, they required her to live it differently, in turn also reshaping her relationship at the moment of writing.[158] Rereading the traces of her past relationship did not entail only reliving it; it also entailed rereading the self that remarked upon it, and the relationship of which it was *currently* a part.

The mundane details of how Mayhew collected, tied, and boxed their letters were as important to this process. Dreading that, should the worst happen, their correspondence fall into the hands of her legally "unscrupulous" mother, Mayhew left it to Head in her will and carefully sorted it into a state appropriate for a "precious heritage."[159] "It was extraordinarily interesting: I sat on a stool on the hearth rug and all around me they lay, long envelopes and little ones and here I read a bit and there I paused to think [. . .] and though I worked really hard I had not ended till after eleven, when there lay around me 20 packets various in length and thickness, all tied by their seasons, and fastened with green ribbon."[160] Mayhew stored all the packets in a large "Korean box." While enabling Mayhew to reconfigure her relationship through rereading its past biography, sorting the letters also allowed her to do so through an imagined *future*. Mayhew wrote that, while bundling

Head's letters, she often wondered what she could have said in her own and whether, in decades' time, they might put their collections together and read them as one. The thought chilled her: "I could bear it perhaps when I was very old—but I am not quite sure."[161] Yet by imagining them rereading their letters together, by temporarily closing the gap the letters mediated while Head and Mayhew lived apart unmarried, Mayhew was able to tell a story about their love that was otherwise not possible at the time of writing.[162] By imagining them remembering their relationship in the future, Mayhew embalmed the present into a love story even before it was complete, tying it together through anticipatory memory and judicious use of green ribbon.

While comparing their feelings with those of their earlier letters, Head and Mayhew also continually reformulated their relationship through corresponding on the letters of others. These published letters provided examples through which Head and Mayhew could configure their changing relationship, though they could destabilize as much as strengthen the part that Head and Mayhew's own correspondence played in maintaining "contact." When rereading Head's letters, Mayhew came across one commenting on the letters of Robert Browning and Elizabeth Barrett. Like Head and Mayhew's correspondence, these were written while the couple were courting and were first published in 1899, the same year as Head's letter. Mayhew found that rereading Head's letter "frightened me terribly." Head spoke, she wrote, "with such harshness of poor E.B.B.'s incoherency and their ridiculous attitude towards each other, at their age too when she was 40 and he was 34."[163] At the time Head wrote the letter, he was thirty-eight and Mayhew thirty-three. Both, like Browning and Barrett, corresponded on each other's poetry, and Mayhew, like Barrett, still lived with her parents.[164] Correspondence on the Browning-Barrett letters provided Head and Mayhew with a foil to their own relationship and its epistolary touching.

But as a tangible object with its own biography, Head's letter exceeded its original meaning every time it was thumbed and reread.[165] Reading Head's comments in 1899, Mayhew had felt "a pang"; "Now [in October 1902] it is something worse. Especially tonight because it has I fear been self-indulgent in me to write to you so often and so fully and you may all the time be blaming harshly my middle-aged folly."[166] If anything, Head felt the reverse was true. In August 1902, he had written approvingly on another love letter, this time between Gustave Flaubert and "Madam X," in which Flaubert claimed, Head glossed, that women "confid[ing] some personal experience to a man" most feared "anything more than polite interest" from him, lest his expression reveal she has actually told "the Truth."[167] Mayhew strenuously disagreed with this statement, claiming that Flaubert only meant that "every story will be flavoured by the personality of the narrator, however crystal clear her mind." "The aim of an educated woman, when she talks," Mayhew wrote, "is to record sincerely what she has observed, enjoyed or in any way made her own. She does not wish to be conceited nor egotistical, but she wishes her words to reflect truly her thoughts."[168] Head's writings on the love letters of others showed a different, at times cruel, assessment of sincerity between lovers from that of Mayhew. But just as important was the way that, as objects, they nudged his relationship with Mayhew into new patterns every time they passed through her hands.

As with all their correspondence, Head and Mayhew's letters on the correspondence of others were as significant for what they *did* as for what they said. Indeed, Head was particularly attentive to how telling a story threatened that which was told. "To keep a diary," he told Mayhew, "is foolish: for the very act of writing down that which has been felt changes its colour."[169] One way that Head and Mayhew tried to avoid this effect of writing, especially frustrating to the lover consequently unable to express love without attenuating it, was to keep a shared scrapbook (or "rag book") in which they compiled extracts and reviews of plays watched and novels read.[170] Through rag books, Head wrote, he and Mayhew were able to keep "a double diary without the crudity of attempt at mutual analysis." Rag books offered a medium through which Head and Mayhew could, although apart, enter into the same community of feeling, its oblique expression revealing that feeling better than "any [. . .] individual outpourings."[171] Yet because Head and Mayhew also directly discussed their responses to plays and books, the rag books became, as L. S. Jacyna suggests, a form of mutual self-constitution which continued that of their correspondence.[172] Such was the case especially because both Head and Mayhew favored works with a heavy emphasis on self-analysis, particularly analysis of sensory impressions.[173] By reproducing and discussing plays and literature, Head and Mayhew could keep in touch—emotionally and physically—in a way at once less and more intimate than the frequent declaration of love could achieve.[174]

Yet how, and for how long, this indirect touch supplemented the absence of the other depended on two very different temperaments. When, on the evening of November 10, 1902, Mayhew sat down with the volume of Pater that had sparked a vivid tactile memory of her childhood, she turned to the essay on eighteenth-century art historian Johann Winckelmann. The closing lines, she wrote to Head, gave her "such strong intellectual excitement, I might have been talking with some wonderful new friend or [. . .] with some enchanting old one." In these lines (actually those of Pater's conclusion rather than his essay on Winckelmann) Pater expanded on Victor Hugo's statement that "we are all under sentence of death but with an indefinite reprieve."[175] With this in mind, "our one chance," Mayhew enthusiastically cited Pater, "lies in expanding our interval of reprieve, in getting as many pulsations as possible in the given time."[176] For Pater, this "quickened sense of life" could be achieved through appreciation of art but also—the passage Mayhew cited for Head—from the "ecstasy and sorrow of love."[177] Four days later, inspired by Mayhew's letter, Head drew up his chair to the fire and read Pater's essay on Winckelmann. Delighting in Pater's "long sensuous senses [sentences]," Head told Mayhew, his pleasure was "inextricably mixed up with my feeling for you—it was through you that I came to understand that beauty in his writing which is not intellectual." Reading Pater's essay that evening was "as if you [Mayhew] had been with me & had gone."[178]

A few evenings later Mayhew conjured their meeting once again, this time reading her copy of Winckelmann alongside "parallel passages" in a

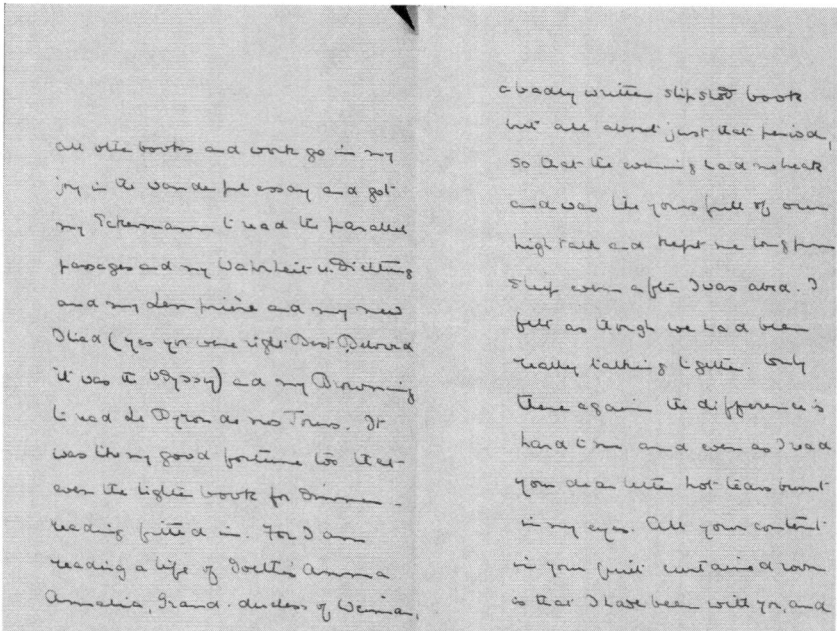

FIGURE 5 "Even as I read your dear letter hot tears burnt in my eyes": The letter as both material compensation for, and painful reminder of, another's absence. Ruth Mayhew to Henry Head, November 17, 1902. PP/HEA/D.4/12.
© Wellcome Collection

work by nineteenth-century poet Johann Eckermann.[179] Echoing Head, Mayhew also felt as though she and he "had been really talking together." But
although Mayhew agreed that shared reading brought the other into presence, she felt that this only accentuated an absence which Head, it stung her
to say, did not also feel. "All your content in your quiet contained room is that
I have been with you, and that *I am gone*—all my sorrow is that you are not
by me here" (emphasis in original)."[180] Through words not their own, Head
and Mayhew transported themselves into each other's presence.[181] Through
their letters, they reproduced this spectral tangibility of the other, calling
them as witnesses of the previous meeting. Yet for Mayhew even this double
encounter marked the absence of, rather than substituted for, the real presence of Head at her side.

Mayhew expressed this longing for touch through the figure of a wound.
In a particularly melancholic letter, she described the feeling of separation as
"like a wound that bleeds always," a wound only "healed" by "your hand in
my hand."[182] Writing three weeks into Head's self-experiment, Mayhew made
her emotional wound the counterpart and effect of Head's damaged hand.
Still tender from the operation, Head's hand kept him busy with research,
prolonging his absence and Mayhew's own tender state resulting from it.
Head's reply, written the day before the splint was removed from his arm,
was cautiously considered. "He bid me take love easy, as the leaves grow on
the tree," Head cited from W. B. Yeats.[183] While recognizing the pain that their
separation caused Mayhew, it was, Head wrote, precisely because Mayhew
already *knew* he was aware of this pain that she revealed it to him so openly.[184]
By exposing the wound caused by their separation, Head implied, Mayhew
only half forgot that she was not alone in her struggle.

Yet Mayhew not only attributed her "wound" to Head's absence but also
to the condition of his red-raw hand. A few days after Head's operation,
he and Mayhew spent a Sunday afternoon wandering the Tate Gallery. The
whole time, Mayhew recollected in a letter to Head, she could not stop herself from looking at the black and red marks dotting Head's hand. Although
only ink crosses recording Head's sensibility, they were "so like real wounds"
that Mayhew felt an upsurge of pride and helplessness. To Mayhew, Head
appeared "helpless, cut and wounded that others should have in this dark
world less pain," and while this sparked in her a strong longing to help him,
it equally pained her that their separation made this impossible.[185] For both
Head and Mayhew, the marks on Head's hand were signs. For Head, they
signified sensation "beneath"; for Mayhew, they signified, as the loved one's
body signifies to the lover scrutinizing it, the origin of her love for Head—

and the suffering it caused.[186] But while Mayhew understood her pain as caused by helplessness, it derived as much from the fact that Head's pain did not depend on her. Mayhew's wound was constituted by Head's precisely because his did not stand in relation to her, either caused by her absence or healed by her presence.[187]

More than this, Mayhew's pain at her separation from Head owed as much to the persistent suspicion that Head was not similarly affected. Attempting to account for this difference, both pointed to differences in the sensory power of their memory. For Mayhew, writing in October 1903, it was "curious" that Head only thought of her outside his ordinary hospital work, and then only as an image rather than a tangible presence. "To me," she wrote, "you are a voice speaking, hands holding, a presence enfolding, [. . .] and I cannot get at what I must be to you. Do you really never feel me in absence? Why the texture of your grey coat is the reallest [sic] thing to my fingers."[188] In an effort to explain an apparently equivocal experience of separation, Head reassured Mayhew that when they were apart he could still vividly "see" her. But he admitted that he could "never recall the touch of your hand, or the immense security of holding you in my arms." "Only once," he wrote, "have I recaptured this feeling as I lay half asleep some few days ago. For it would seem that as you never see but in sleep so to me touch can only return in non-waking consciousness."[189] This weak tactile memory shaped not only Head's relationship with Mayhew but also the results of his self-experiment occurring at the same time. "H.'s mental processes," his 1908 article reported, "are based upon visual images to a remarkable degree." While Head could easily recall "the memory-picture of an object," he was entirely unable to recall Rivers's touches once passed.[190] Yet, as we have seen, when Head drifted into sleep during testing, exactly four years after he had done the same thinking of Mayhew, his sense of touch progressively improved. Head's self-experiment elaborated his sensory experience of Mayhew in her absence, each condensing and transforming the other and the discourse of separation—physical and temporal—through which they were understood.

LOVE LETTERS, SELF-EXPERIMENTATION, AUTOFICTION

The intertwining of Head's self-experiment and correspondence with Mayhew did not result only from the feel of letters or figures of touch. It was also made possible by the peculiarly self-referential nature of love letters, which address not only a lover but one imagined by the writer, and therefore ulti-mately the writer themself.[191] While Head and Mayhew's letters spoke about touch, and vicariously mediated their touch of each other, they were also a way of speaking which touched *upon* the self that spoke. This made love letters, in which the writer explains and interprets how they feel to another imagined as much as real, analogous to the self-experiment in which Head attempted to both feel and observe himself feeling. Head and Mayhew's epis-tolary exchange could do nothing *but* amplify and be amplified by Head's self-experiment into sensation, both addressing and exploring another that was, inseparably, oneself. The mutual reinforcement of love letters and neu-rological self-experimentation was comparable to other entanglements of neurology with languages of selfhood before the Great War, particularly spiri-tualism and Pentecostal revivalism.[192] But distinguishing Head and Mayhew's correspondence and Head's self-experiment was how both, in different and intertwined ways, entailed Head and Mayhew occupying a space *between* explanation and interpretation, subject and observer.[193]

Head's checkered hand became the site where these thoughts and feel-ings from his relationship and research interacted. On July 21, 1903, eighty-seven days after the operation, Head reported that his arm was finally recov-ering.[194] The previous day his whole forearm and much of his hand had responded to pricking, though they remained insensitive to heat and cold.[195] Mayhew was delighted, willing the time when she might "sit on your left side as happily as on your right, without the chill feeling that the arm I am so proudly holding is only half-sensate."[196] For Mayhew, Head's arm and hand were representative not only of a physical but also an emotional inequality of feeling between them. In the same letter, she wrote how it was "such a ter-rible devastating thing to care so much," especially when her care met with Head's silent "reproof." Tortured by the fear that her care would "disgust" Head, Mayhew could equally not stop herself from telling him how all her worries as a headmistress paled into "supreme indifference [. . .] compared with the littlest finger of that Man's [Head's] most precious hand."[197] For Mayhew, Head's hand was a sign of their differing sensibility and a symbol of the care that she dared not, yet still did, speak.

For Head, too, the condition of his hand was inextricably linked to his relationship, his ability to sense and his feeling for Mayhew intertwining with and informing each other. Despite attempting a "negative attitude of attention" while working within the secluded rooms of St. John's, Head could not stop thoughts of Mayhew from erupting in his mind and scrambling what he felt under Rivers's touch. On November 27, 1903, Head told Mayhew that she "did not guess the curious way in which you were brought into my 'Dämmer zustand' as I sat with closed eyes on Sunday under the tests of Dr Rivers—'Vision qui dérange, Et trouble l'horizon de ma raison.'"[198] Elaborating his earlier claim that he was most perceptive during "non-waking consciousness," Head related a moment during testing when, in a state of "Dämmer zustand"—half sleep or semiconsciousness—visions of Mayhew suddenly seized him.[199] If semiconsciousness normally improved his tactile acuity, this time it entirely disrupted his ability to achieve an attentive inattention to his own sensations. Citing the love poetry of Paul Verlaine, concerned with the lover's passive reception of flickering sensations, Head implied that Mayhew's unexpected presence, a potentially erotic presence that could only be related in person, disordered the "horizon" of his "reason."[200] It was "as if," Head wrote, "we had been standing side by side watching the sea together—and my longing towards you made me neglectful of the stimuli that flashed into consciousness so preoccupied was I with the warmth of your presence."[201] In November 1903, Head for the first time began detecting sensations of heat at definite spots in his hand and forearm.[202] But as his mind wandered, these sensations were displaced by the altogether more tangible "warmth" of Mayhew's unexpected presence.

This bind between Head's sense of touch and his imagined touch of Mayhew also worked the other way. On March 8, 1904, the same day on which Head posted their banns of marriage, Head wrote to Mayhew of the "fiasco" of his last visit to Cambridge when, during particularly miserable weather, he developed a "steaming head cold." "The sensation of my hand went all to pieces: to the compass test I felt worse than a fortnight before & I was lamentably wrong over delicate shades of heat & cold." Head's sorry condition, he continued, not only disrupted his sensations but also his ability to articulate feelings for Mayhew; the "physical misery" seemed to "paralyse" him, preventing him from ordering his thoughts of her just as these thoughts had imposed themselves on his sensations the previous November.[203] For Head and Mayhew, the physical condition of Head's hand signified the condition of feeling existing between them. More than this, however, their letters hinted at an ineluctable tie between what Head felt for (and of) Mayhew, what he felt in his hand, and the ways in which his writing as a scientist and a lover conceptualized both, each folding into the other.[204]

The connection Head made between the sensibility of his hand and his feeling for Mayhew was not merely rhetorical. As Head wrote of his experiments in his love letters and sensed Mayhew's presence in his experiments, the feel of the carpenter's compass and of Mayhew's caress, and the language reporting them, became not only analogous but constitutive. On the evening of Saturday, May 23, 1903, twenty-nine days after the operation, Rivers removed the splint from Head's forearm. The following day, the pair mapped the borders of Head's almost total loss of sensitivity to touch, prick, heat and cold, the results of which Ernest Wilson photographed on Monday, May 25.[205] Apart from a curious triangular area banding his wrist, which appeared sensitive to wisps of cotton wool, Head could feel barely anything.[206] Yet what Head found most remarkable was the way this condition of feeling intruded on, animated, and expressed his feelings far beyond the experiment. Writing on the evening of Sunday, May 24, Head informed Mayhew of a curious discovery. Head had long been aware, he wrote, that his poetic composition followed a familiar pattern. A poem would begin forming in his head "last thing at night" and evolve during his dreams. By breakfast it would be gone, but then gradually return as he walked to the station to catch the Underground to Whitechapel. He had "always suspected that the lyrical stage in the early morning was physical" but now the proof came with his "dead arm": "For during the period on Saturday morning when I knew both by my internal feelings and by the fact that the lines were coming rapidly that my mood was lyrical the left arm glowed and tingled exactly as it did when you came into your room on the Wednesday after my operation."[207] At this key moment in his self-experiment, Head became acutely aware of how his tactile sensations, feelings for Mayhew, and lyrical mood mutually supported and signaled one another.

If this entanglement of feeling shaped how Head thought about his poetry, then it also shaped his understanding of the nervous system. The connection Head made between his condition a month after the operation and his poetic and emotional sensibility found its way into his publications through one particular concept: "feeling-tone." Before Head's self-experiment, neurologists unsure whether pain was a quality of sensation or a sensation itself spoke of "affective tone." All sensations, Sherrington argued in 1900, had affective tone, a quality of being "agreeable" or "disagreeable" that varied with the intensity, duration, and quality of stimuli. But while affective tone was shared by all sensations, it was particularly strong in sensations referring to the body: the four types of cutaneous sensation, particularly "pain spots," and, above all, the "inner" sense of common sensation.[208] Adapting this model, Head concluded from his self-experiment that "feeling-tone" varied between what he believed to be functional levels of touch: protopathic sensations were intensely affective, epicritic sensations less so. A pinpoint dragged over his tender hand, for example, caused an unpleasant feeling that was exceptionally intense and diffuse compared to one dragged over an undamaged area.[209] For Head, tactile sensations of different levels were therefore always already imprinted with affective qualities of varying degree, "lower" levels of touch imbued with greater affective content than "higher" ones.

In this way, Head gave anatomical form to musings tying his tingling arm, still at an early protopathic stage of recovery, to a rush of poetic and amorous feeling. Indeed, Head hinted at this thinking in his letter five years earlier. While his arm flared up when a new poem announced itself, seeing the completed version, Head wrote, left his arm "quiet" and was "obviously only intellectual."[210] If Head's lyricism was connected with the protopathic sensibility of his arm, then the appreciation of the final poem must have been connected with another, more "intellectual" sensibility, a sensibility Head later termed "epicritic" and directly associated with sensory and intellectual discrimination. Through connecting his sense of touch with his poetic composition and love for Mayhew, Head made his body a sign for his emotional and literary states and discovered in it a structure subtending them.

Sixteen years after making this observation to Mayhew, Head completed the connection. In 1919 Head published *Destroyers and other Verses*, a poetry anthology including the poem so intertwined with Head's "feeling-tone" that weekend in May 1903. Head dedicated the anthology "To Her without whose touch the strings would have been mute."[211] In the same way that Head found in his sense of touch a physical sign and structure for his poetic creativity and love of Mayhew, so in Mayhew's touch he found the source of that creativity and, over two decades, the neurological understanding of touch presented in his *Studies in Neurology* the following year.

The entangled self-referentiality of love letters and self-experiments continued also in Mayhew's writing long after Head's experiment ended. This time, however, fictionalizing her earlier relationship with Head offered a different perspective from which to observe and interpret feeling. In 1918 Mayhew published her first novel, *A History of Departed Things*.[212] The novel traced the life of Bettina, the daughter, like Mayhew, of an Oxford don, and of her unhappy marriage to a doctor named Francis. After Francis's death, Bettina falls for a consultant and scientist named Lucas Beck, a thinly veiled version of Head, whose maternal grandparents were surnamed Lucas and Beck.[213] Taking an epistolary form, the novel charted the development of Bettina and Lucas's relationship through, among other correspondence between its characters, part reproducing, part fictionalizing letters sent between Mayhew and Head. In this way, *A History of Departed Things* both retold Head and Mayhew's relationship and, to add the line following in William Wordsworth's *The Excursion*, from which Mayhew derived her title, provided "a mere fiction of what never was."[214] The novel was too fictional to be autobiographical but sufficiently autobiographical to complete the rereading of Head and Mayhew's correspondence that Mayhew had imagined in 1902.

Fictionalizing her past letters with Head enabled Mayhew, by 1918 Ruth Head, to explore feelings unexpressed at the time of writing, as well as to measure, as if scientifically, the change in feeling and her relationship with Head since then. If "the 'real' message of letters is not quite what is written," fictional letters enabled expression of what could not be expressed, because socially or emotionally inarticulable, and of how feeling changed since a letter's sending.[215] In this retelling Head did not come off well. Mayhew depicted Lucas as so preoccupied with work that Bettina eventually draws away and marries his former collaborator. But more important than changing the content of Head and Mayhew's relationship was the way fictionalization changed the interpretive work that letter writing did for each. Fictionalizing the correspondents of real love letters changed not only the real and imagined lovers to whom the letters were addressed but also the authors to whom they were "really" self-addressed.[216] The Mayhew who wrote to Head (and herself) became a different Mayhew who was self-addressed. The epistolary novel published fifteen years after the correspondence on which it was based allowed Mayhew to enact a different self-experiment in feeling; to explore the hidden recesses of the inexpressible and unthinkable, possible now because of a different relationship with Head and the passing of time. In so doing, Mayhew's novel enabled interpretation of that which was formerly beyond feeling, or at its uncertain margins, through a correspondence—emotional as well as literal—that had long since changed or ceased.

On April 28, 1904, Head and Mayhew married in St. Marylebone Church, a short walk from Head's Westmoreland Mansions apartment. A year and three days after Head's operation, Head's forearm and hand had shown the first signs of epicritic recovery four days previously.[217] Echoing this healing, on the day before the wedding Head wrote his "last little letter" to Mayhew, "clos[ing] a series of letters," and the metaphorical wound it had mediated, into which he had poured his "best thoughts."[218]

CONCLUSION

Despite decades of meticulous research, the understanding of touch presented in *Studies in Neurology* did not go unchallenged. From the publication of "A Human Experiment in Nerve Division" in 1908 through into the 1920s, neurologists, physiologists, and psychologists criticized Head for irresolvable inconsistencies, for illogical leaps, and for subordinating observation to an overactive imagination.[219] Yet even later research that seemed to move away from Head's methods and conclusions maintained, in a radical new form, some of the insights into touch he first outlined in 1905. Reading these later developments in the light of Head's findings reveals how touch was reconceived in spatial and temporal terms, in turn reconfiguring understandings of the relationship between body and mind. It also shows how technological change in observing and recording apparatus changed not only scientists' understanding of the relationship between body and mind but also their use of touch to explain this relationship.

In the same year as Head published "The Afferent Nervous System from a New Aspect" (1905), Cambridge physiologist Keith Lucas published a far less discussed paper on the effect of electrical stimulation on the muscle fiber of a frog. Lucas found that increasing the charge entering the muscle fiber caused the amplitude of muscular contraction to increase in sharp jumps. This suggested, Lucas concluded, that the contraction amplitude increased only when additional fibers were stimulated, and therefore that, once stimulated, individual fibers responded to the maximum extent: their response was "all-or-none."[220] In 1912 Lucas built on this work by adapting a device known as a *capillary electrometer*—a glass tube with a mercury meniscus that moved in response to the voltage passed through it. The amplitude and duration of the response was recorded on a photographic plate. By adapting the capillary electrometer to account for the small and fast impulses of nerve fibers, Lucas was for the first time able to photograph a recording of the impulse in flight.[221] Later research by neurologists Edgar Adrian and Yngve Zotterman, who used a triad valve amplifier to amplify the impulses measured, proved that Lucas's findings applied equally to individual nerve fibers: when an impulse was triggered, it traveled at full amplitude, regardless of additional stimulation. Impulses therefore did not vary qualitatively, only in number and frequency, and had an "all-or-none" relation to their stimuli.[222]

Lucas's, Adrian's, and Zotterman's investigations transformed the experimental configuration of scientists, instruments, and touch as an object of study, in turn causing renewed questioning of the relationship between body and mind. In the years following Head's self-experiment, electrophysiology enabled what Head attempted but could not achieve: the examination of sensations in terms of their constituent elements, rather than their psychological end result. By displacing the scientist's body as the ground for knowledge, prewar electrophysiology established that nerve impulses were qualitatively identical. The impulses subserving sensations could therefore not be explained in terms of "feeling-tone," only in terms of their frequency and route to the brain.[223] This meant that new efforts had to be made, across physiology and psychology, to explain how a sensory stimulus retained its specificity as a nerve impulse. Head's theory of a nervous system that was functionally divided yet maintained a fragile thread between mind and body through specific pathways could not last in its original form.

Yet while later research increasingly threw Head's theory into question, it also recaptured some of its crucial tenets in new ways. In particular, physiologists and psychologists continued Head's insights by recasting the nervous system in increasingly spatial and temporal terms. In 1929 physiologists Herbert Gasser and Joseph Erlanger established a direct relation between the conduction rate and diameter of nerve fibers. Gasser and Erlanger showed that thick, rapidly conducting fibers responded best to touch and thin, slowly conducting fibers to thermal stimuli.[224] This and later research suggested that stimulus specificity was maintained by the varying thickness of nerve fibers and speed at which impulses traveled, even though impulses themselves were nonspecific.[225] A more radical theory was put forward in the same year as Gasser and Erlanger's by psychologist John Nafe, who argued that stimulus specificity was maintained by the temporal and spatial pattern of impulses rather than by impulses or nerves themselves.[226] Variations in the frequency and distribution of impulses across nerves could, Nafe argued, account for an infinite variety of sensations without the need for corresponding anatomical variation.[227] Although these theories contradicted each other, they maintained Head's belief that touch was more complex in its formation than at its end result. No longer could the elements of touch be identified and mapped onto the skin, with the assumption that this correlated with what occurred beneath. Instead, touch was understood as a product of the spatial and temporal differentiation of the nervous system, whether those differences were between nerve fibers or how impulses traveled across them, or between phylogenetic evolution or the duration of individual nerve impulses.[228]

Most significantly, later research reveals the enduring importance of touch in conditioning its emergence as an object and consequently the very distinction between scientific knowledge and the phenomenal world. By the 1930s, the rejection of self-experimentation in physiology meant that what the researcher felt no longer preconditioned understandings of how feeling worked. But it remained true that how touch was defined as an object continued to depend on ever-changing *uses* of touch within and beyond the laboratory. Head's understanding of touch emerged in and through the instruments on Rivers's worktable, Pater's "sensuous" sentences, and the feel of Mayhew's hand on a rainy Sunday afternoon, an entanglement that Head consciously explored. Applying electricity to a frog's nerve involved a different but ontologically comparable "intra-action" between scientist, instrument, and object, which resulted in a different, though similar, understanding of the relationship between stimulus and sensation. Each entailed a distinct bounding of things in the world—of particular forms of touch, mind and body, observer and object—as well as of scientific knowledge *from* the phenomenal world.[229] Yet both revealed the emergence of touch, as object and experience, through scientists' ongoing embodied involvement in the world—and, consequently, the emergence of the world available for observation.

CHAPTER TWO

Pedagogies of Touch

A bright September morning, the air laced with the chill of autumn. Threading through the expanse of thigh-high barley, the wind rippling its spikes like the sea far below, it was easy to imagine oneself entirely apart from the world in this corner of the North York Moors.[1] This was the rolling farmland of Elizabeth Gaskell's heroine Sylvia, and it seemed unchanged a century later. Alfred Hirst had driven up from the fishing harbor of Whitby, where the River Esk met the North Sea, to try his luck on the first day of shooting season. The day started well, a familiar fluster signaling the first covey of partridges taking flight. But as Hirst raised his gun and closed his left eye, he saw through his right eye not the usual shapes accented against the sky but barely a brown blur. After an anxious but inconclusive trip to a local optician, Hirst discovered from a London ophthalmologist several days later that he had "amaurosis, or atrophy of the optic nerve." By Christmas Day 1874 the disease had spread to his left eye, and he found himself "practically blind."[2]

Despite this setback, however, Hirst launched himself into his business affairs with even more energy. On September 2, 1881, Hirst, a partner in a Huddersfield wool stapler's firm, boarded an Orient Line steamer to Melbourne, Australia, to purchase wool for the company direct from source.[3] Far from hindering his business, blindness, it seemed, made wool buying easier. "So thoroughly did I maintain, and even more improve my ability to judge the various classes of Colonial wool," Hirst wrote, that when in Melbourne he "bought no fewer than 10,000 bales, with results that gained for me some kudos in the Melbourne papers, and, what was of far more importance, the cordial praise of my partners." All of this Hirst accomplished independently, depending only on his secretary and his heightened sense of touch.[4]

Hirst published this story in the *Sunday Magazine* on April 19, 1897, and it was widely reported in the Australian press before the British and Foreign Blind Association (BFBA) reprinted it as a pamphlet a year later.[5] For the BFBA, Hirst's story provided an instructive message to readers that blind people could overcome any obstacle presented by blindness, even though the association undercut this assertion, in an appeal to stereotypes of the time, by entitling the pamphlet *My Dark World*. Prefacing the pamphlet was a photographic portrait of Hirst. It is difficult to know what to make of this photograph. On the one hand, it was an effort by Hirst, as the article was, to "recover" a body whose narrative had been taken from him by an ophthalmologist and by his own inability to see who he was.[6] On the other, it was doubly disempowering, Hirst unable even in his pose to return the gaze of photographer or viewer, his hands awkwardly half shoved into his pockets. Did Hirst feel able to influence a photograph that depended on his agreement to pose, even if it reproduced the sensory inequality that he aimed to contest?[7] What did the photograph do for the body that could never acknowledge it but that had apparently more than compensated for this impossibility?

These are thorny questions. But they highlight the intimate relationship between touch, vision, and independence in representations of blind people and blind people's relation *to* visual representations as these evolved from the late nineteenth century.[8] The portrait of Hirst suggests a distribution of power that, if never controlled by any participant, nonetheless remained unequal.[9] Yet by Hirst's account, this sensory and civil inequality was compensated by a sense of touch that allowed him to contest it in print and business. Through noting the admiration his successes in the Australian wool market earned him from business partners, Hirst showed how touch compensated for blindness and enabled his economic independence. This he demonstrated also through typing the article himself, which showed how touch could keep blind people participants in public debate. Emphasizing the potential for touch to substitute for vision claimed a place for blind people within economic and political life.[10] For this reason, Hirst noted how easily he learned Braille—being able to read and write it within three days—and his proficiency at typing, in which he argued all blind children should become "expert."[11] Indeed, Hirst introduced Braille to Australia during his visit in 1881, and he produced a pamphlet on *Types for the Blind* in 1894.[12]

Examining historical understandings of touch as a substitute, or "supplement," for vision in blindness therefore reveals changing assumptions

FIGURE 6 Alfred Hirst, wool merchant and bringer of Braille to Australia. From Alfred Hirst, *My Dark World* (London: British & Foreign Blind Association, 1898), facing 1. © The British Library Board

about sensation as the basis of independence.[13] Representations of the relationship between touch and vision articulated broader understandings of the relationship between disability and ability and, more fundamentally, about the body as the condition for involvement in economic and political life. Whereas Enlightenment philosophers considered the relationship between vision and blind people's touch in hypothetical terms, this question became practically important once embossed literature for blind readers was introduced to Britain in the 1820s. For sighted commentators, embossed literature demonstrated that a blind person's touch could substitute for vision if trained.[14] This understanding of touch as compensatory was institutionalized by the opening, starting in the 1790s, of the first specialist charity schools for blind children, which sought to refine their pupils' touch through haptic activities.[15] Embossed literature and schools teaching it reified the seemingly contradictory idea that blind people were defined by what they lacked, but might overcome this lack through cultivating touch.

Yet the connection between sensory substitution and independence became strongest once the education of blind children became the responsibility of the state. After Education Acts in 1890 and 1893 made the education of blind children until the age of sixteen mandatory, understanding how touch substituted for vision became vital for ensuring that those children later became economically and intellectually independent. Hirst's article, published four years later, therefore came at a crucial time, connecting the education of blind children's touch with his own independence as a successful merchant and commentator. In this way, the Education Acts made bodily independence—the condition of being "able-bodied"—essential to the economic, political, and intellectual independence defining the ideal liberal subject.[16] Teaching blind children to refine their sense of touch both contested and, ironically, produced the able-bodied liberal subject against which they were also defined.[17] As *My Dark World* made clear, the assumed relationship between touch and vision increasingly articulated that between the individual and the social body, and it was through this formulation that blind people staked a claim for, or were denied, equality.[18]

This connection between perception and political involvement is implicit in the way Hirst evoked other nonvisual senses too. Describing his journey to Australia in October 1881, Hirst noted how his sense of smell had become "much more sensitive since I lost that of sight," enabling him to detect even the waft of gum trees as he passed them during a stop in Cape Colony.[19] Yet by the 1960s an alternative discourse had emerged that understood blindness not as an impairment to overcome but as a disability constituted by societal attitudes *toward* impairment. In the following decades, this belief became the founding tenet of disability activism.[20] No longer was the emphasis on refining touch to a degree that blind and sighted people became "blind" to visual impairment. Instead, as became evident in several BBC programs broadcast in 1967 and 1968, the focus shifted to making blind and sighted people "see" how disability was constituted precisely through such attitudes. Over the first half of the twentieth century, the understanding of touch in blindness became central to the perceptibility of blind people as political subjects, and to their own efforts to recast what it meant to be disabled.

MASSAGE, THE GREAT WAR, AND TACTILE ACUITY

In its 1901 prospectus, the London Institute for Massage by the Blind justified its existence through calling attention to a common assumption: "It has been proved that the Blind can become expert in the practice of massage, and that when properly trained they attain a high standard of skill. In Japan, massage is commonly the work of the Blind."[21] Institute promotional literature and medical journals repeated the claim over the next decade, often assuming it self-evident enough to not require elaborating, besides passing reference to the long history of blind massage in Japan.[22] When explanation was given, periodicals and medical professionals commonly resorted to another apparent truism: that a blind person's sense of touch was "more finely developed than that of normal persons."[23] Praising the excellent work done by blind masseurs during the Great War, the superintendent of Alder Hey Military Orthopaedic Hospital claimed it "a well-known fact that when one of the senses is diminished in usefulness, by the law of compensation the remaining senses develop greater acuity. [. . .] It is remarkable how quickly the blinded masseur exhibits the value of his improved sense of touch, and I have personally seen many outstanding examples of this particular capacity."[24]

The assumption that blindness resulted in a compensatory increase in the acuity of touch was the London Institute's key tenet, and its minute books offer glimpses into attempts to justify the claim over its history. Founded at 64 Lancaster Gate, Bayswater, in 1900, the institute was the first dedicated solely to training blind students in massage, although the more established London School of Massage also opened its doors to blind students in the same year.[25] The course was a broad one covering massage, Nauheim and Swedish Remedial Exercises, and the electrical therapy popularized by American neurologist Silas Weir Mitchell. Students were given several months' training to enable them to secure a hospital post or set up their own practice, and the Institute solicited employment for those working on a freelance basis.[26] By 1910, the institute (which in 1908 became the National Institute for Massage by the Blind, or NIMB) had fifty-five masseuses and twenty-seven masseurs on its books, the lucky ones having gained appointments at St. Thomas's Hospital, the London Hospital, or a military academy.[27] So high was the demand for treatment at the Woolwich Military Academy that one masseur treated more than two hundred patients over eleven months and decided to resign his position at St. Thomas's.[28] Both an institutional record and a catalog of evidence for promotional material, the NIMB's minutes recorded instances where patients agreed that their blind practitioners were expert at massage. Writing to the institute in 1912, General Bainbridge found the "manipulation & touch" of his masseur "as near perfection as possibly could be."[29]

But if the NIMB assumed a blind person's acuter sense of touch and their proficiency at massage self-evident, this assumption did not go uncontested. Opposition to blind massage over the 1910s suggests that truth-claims about the potential for touch to compensate for blindness were themselves a product of institutional conflict within the emerging field of physiotherapy. As physiotherapy sought to distance itself from earlier scandals, disagreements over the gendered constituency of its professionals and patients translated into conflicts over the compensatory power of touch in blindness; over the degree to which a blind person could be considered "disabled."

The causes of these disagreements emerged before the existence of the NIMB. In July 1894, the *British Medical Journal* revealed that masseuses across London were using private massage practices as fronts for offering sexual services to clients. A week later, Home Secretary Herbert Asquith and Scotland Yard launched an investigation into the claims, their inconclusive reports further galling the *BMJ* into publishing another series of exposés in November. In response, four masseuses ventured to improve the professional standing of massage through the establishment of the Society of Trained Masseuses (later the Incorporated Society of Trained Masseuses, or ISTM) in December 1894.[30] At the preliminary meeting, held at the Midwives' Institute, a set of rules for good practice were listed in the temporary minute book, rules that all trainees of the society had to abide by if they were to become certificated. Massage was only to be given under "medical direction," advertised in "strictly professional papers," and refused to men unless specially prescribed by a doctor.[31]

The professional standing of massage gradually improved from the late 1890s onward, in part because of the society's careful regulation of members' professional conduct but also as a result of the instrumental role massage played in the treatment of amputees and those suffering from "shell shock" (known today as posttraumatic stress disorder, or PTSD) during the Great War.[32] No longer was massage primarily a treatment for female victims of neurasthenia (a condition similar to chronic fatigue syndrome), as it had been in the 1880s, but an integral part of rehabilitating the broken bodies of Britain's soldiers.[33] Society membership more than tripled to 3,641 in the war years alone (1914–1918).[34] Despite these advances, though, the press continued to publish allegations of improper conduct at private massage practices throughout the first three decades of the society's existence. A year after the society's founding, an undercover officer monitoring 4 Rupert Street, Soho, reported seeing masseuses dubiously "dressed in long tea gowns with the front open displaying lace underlinen and old gold stockings."[35] In April 1897, the Social Purity Department of the National British Women's Temperance Association again drew police attention to apparent improper conduct in London's massage trade, noting a *Figaro* article that described masseuses at one establishment wearing "uniform[s]" of a "chemise-like loose-fitting dress of the most diaphanous silk"; a sure sign, it seemed, that their primary role was not therapeutic massage.[36] Undercover police filed reports of a similar nature over the succeeding years, and suspicions were raised once again by a front cover *John Bull* exposé on April 24, 1920.[37]

Embattled into the 1920s, the ISTM was consequently reluctant to accept any claims for the special proficiency of blind people at massage, especially if this gave blind people a competitive edge. In part this reluctance was because the NIMB enabled the entry of men into a profession that the ISTM had attempted to restrict to women; although the society began training masseurs of the Royal Army Medical Corps in 1905, it did not welcome male members until 1918.[38] But the ISTM's reluctance was also likely attributable to the society's desire to maintain control over the system of massage certification, especially for masseuses, that was crucial to establishing the credibility of professional physiotherapy.[39] W. H. Illingworth, superintendent of Henshaw's Blind Asylum in Manchester, was aware of the threat that unregulated massage posed to physiotherapy in general, as well as perhaps that posed by a parallel system of certification to the ISTM in particular. His *History of the Education of the Blind* (1910), part history, part encyclopedia on all matters relating to the education of blind people, noted that there was "no better or lucrative form of employment" than massage to blind people "of good tact"—in both senses of the word. He warned, though, that "great care should be taken [...] that a certificate of efficiency in this art is never granted without a most searching examination as to qualifications and character."[40]

Anxiety over the propriety of some blind masseuses, or over the rigor of the NIMB's examination standards, came to a head in May 1912 when several blind masseuses staged a "Sale of Work" at an Albert Hall exhibition of women's work organized by the Society for Promoting Female Welfare. This demonstration went on despite the best efforts of the ISTM, which had called at the Society for Promoting Female Welfare's offices the week before, the NIMB minutes resentfully record, "to poison their minds against us." Although the ISTM failed to prevent the demonstration going ahead, it managed to intimidate one masseuse into declining attendance by using the same "falsehoods," provoking the NIMB to write to the ISTM to protest that "such slanders must not be propagated against us."[41] Precisely what these "falsehoods" were remains uncertain, as there is no record of the incident in the minutes of the ISTM; we do not know what accusations were leveled against the blind masseuses, but it is intriguing enough that they were kept off the books.[42] Perhaps wishing to avoid a repeated confrontation the following year, the Society for Promoting Female Welfare suggested to the NIMB, under the pretext of lack of space, that it only exhibit a stall this time rather than provide demonstrations.[43]

Relations between the two institutes remained sensitive throughout the 1910s. Yet attitudes toward blind massage, and the compensatory power of touch on which it was predicated, shifted significantly as a result of the rising public concern for those blinded during the Great War. At the center of this shift was St. Dunstan's Hostel for Blind Soldiers and Sailors, a large former private house with sprawling grounds in Regent's Park, London, where, in the words of its founder, National Institute for the Blind (NIB) president Arthur Pearson, ex-servicemen might "learn to be blind."[44] From an initial intake of sixteen upon its opening in March 1915, by December 1918 St. Dunstan's cared for seven hundred blinded ex-servicemen over five establishments.[45] For Pearson, former newspaper baron, and, on losing his sight to glaucoma by 1913, energetic philanthropist in causes for blind people, learning to be blind meant developing a new "mental outlook" and fostering the "latent and unsuspected powers" of other senses.[46] Careful attention was paid to the hostel's architecture and landscape to elicit these latent powers of touch. Linoleum paths ran through the house while outside boards denoted path intersections, steps, and walls, and handrails with knobs indicated turns.[47] In this way, residents might learn to navigate independently through trained attention to touch.

St. Dunstan's provided training in a range of vocational skills in which it was assumed that, because of their aural or tactile element, blind people could become proficient. Alongside carpentry, cobbling, basket weaving, telephony, and poultry farming, residents also learned typewriting and Braille.[48] According to Pearson, learning Braille had an intrinsic, as well as instrumental, value by providing the best training in substituting one "nerve-channel"—that of touch—for another.[49] Those who struggled to develop the requisite fineness of touch were advised to rub their fingertips with petroleum jelly before bed and sleep with a glove on to pique their sensitivity through deprivation.[50] St. Dunstan's residents also learned massage. Students first acquired knowledge of anatomy and physiology through models at the hostel and then gained practical experience at the NIB and at Middlesex and Hampstead Hospitals.[51] As more blind ex-servicemen learned massage and gained employment at military hospitals providing care for Britain's war wounded, the debate over whether touch compensated for blindness shifted grounds. Institutional conflict within the emerging profession of physiotherapy became less important than the political imperative of supporting blind ex-servicemen.[52] Consequently, it became harder to contest claims that touch compensated for blindness for those trained in massage. Indeed, the ISTM in 1915 began examining St. Dunstan's candidates—its first ever blind candidates—but only because, alleged principal of the NIB School of Massage and former student Percy Way, it was unable to refuse the rehabilitation of war casualties.[53]

Even with this change, though, the ISTM continued to resist claims about the self-evidence of blind people's tactile abilities. It remained skeptical about the ability of blind candidates to perform tasks as well as their sighted counterparts, notably in Swedish Remedial Exercises, a series of

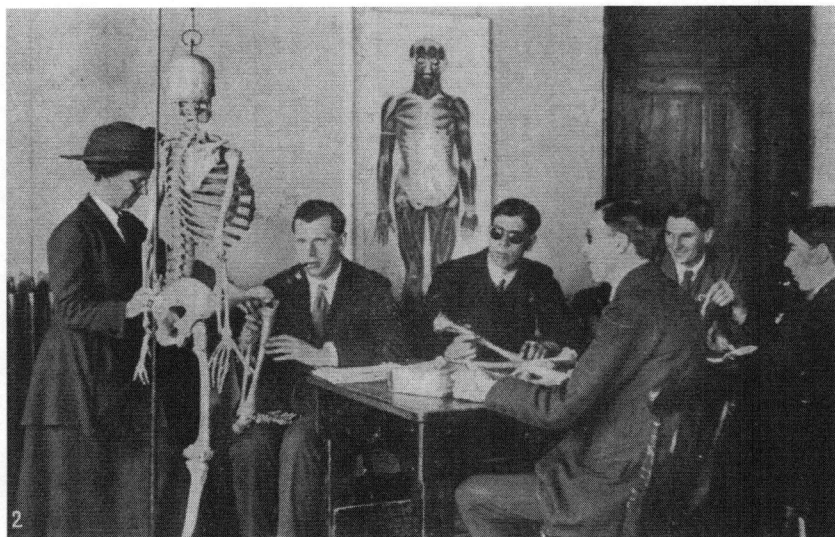

FIGURE 7 Blind ex-servicemen at St. Dunstan's Hostel for Blind Soldiers and Sailors learn anatomy during massage training. From "Blinded Soldiers at St Dunstan's," *St Dunstan's Review* 27, no. 3 (November 1918): facing 1.
© The British Library Board

stretching and flexing exercises designed to test a patient's movement. Two blind candidates acted as test cases for suitability in these exercises and despite passing the examination in 1917, "all Drs present considered that there must be limitations to the work that the blind undertake" and the suitability of Swedish exercises remained under question.[54] Shortly after obtaining his certificate, one of these candidates, Percy Way, gave a demonstration at King's College Hospital, but this elicited further criticism from the doctors present, which was forwarded to the Advisory Committee of the ISTM.[55] Only in 1919, when the ISTM needed NIB support in its bid for a royal charter, was it compelled by the NIB to adopt a more generous attitude toward blind candidates through forming an advisory standing committee composed partly of blind masseurs.[56] Even as it became increasingly impossible to contest the abilities of blind masseurs, institutional development within physiotherapy continued to shape the terms under which touch was believed to compensate for blindness.

Understandings of tactile substitution in blindness were a language through which the wider growing pains of physiotherapy were enacted. The ISTM's questioning of blind masseurs' tactile abilities reflected concerns both over the entrance of men into the profession and over its authority to certify candidates. Yet at the same time, it likely reflected anxiety over the effect a public discourse about tactile compensation for blindness had on the society's competitiveness. When the NIB opened a new physiotherapy clinic in 1934, the *Times* highlighted the unique proficiency of blind physiotherapists, claiming that "blindness has developed their sense of touch to an abnormal degree"; blind people massaged "not only as efficiently as the sighted but with a special skill born of their very affliction."[57] Claims such as these were common since the opening of the NIMB in 1900 and challenged the position the ISTM established for itself in the face of scandals surrounding massage. Consequently, the question of sensory substitution in blindness became entangled with the wider one of the place of newcomers within the expanding constituency of physiotherapy—as well as that of blind ex-servicemen within a reconstructed nation. The question of touch in blindness stood in for wider concerns about the integrity of physiotherapy—in both senses of the word—and of the national body it was tasked with healing.[58]

EDUCATING TOUCH

For all their promotion in the press, however, claims about the "natural" physical compensation of touch for blindness were not the only ones circulating. Alongside these claims existed a parallel and increasingly influential discourse about tactile substitution as a psychological compensation and, as a matter of mental application as much as physical functioning, therefore something that could be cultivated. In part this discourse derived from the growing emphasis in mainstream education on the health of schoolchildren, shaped by their meals, physical education, and built environment, as the basis for "national efficiency."[59] But it was also a product of a growing legal, medical, and institutional reification of blindness that made blind children supplementary to an ideal able-bodied liberal subject precisely through the way their touch was characterized as supplementary to vision.

The first schools for blind children opened long before the twentieth century; Liverpool (1791) Edinburgh (1793) and Southwark (1799) all provided specialist training for blind children before the NIMB was established. But only after the 1870 Education Act, which allowed school boards to include blind children in mainstream elementary schools, did blind children come within the purview of the state. In 1879 the London School Board opened a day school offering classes for blind children, but the trend by the 1890s was toward the expansion of voluntary specialist schools, which, with grants from the newly established Gardner's Trust for the Blind, were able to offer better provision for students seeking postschooling employment.[60] The vitality of specialist schools and the voluntary nature of board-funded provision resulted in an ambiguous situation wherein school boards remained uncertain over their responsibility to provide elementary education for blind children, an uncertainty identified by the 1889 report of the Royal Commission on the Blind, Deaf, and Dumb. The commission recommended that school be made compulsory for blind children between the ages of five and sixteen and that it be half funded by school boards, half by parents, with boards making up the deficit for parents unable to pay. The Elementary Education (Blind and Deaf Children) Act carried these recommendations into law in 1890 in Scotland and 1893 in England and Wales, and although the commission had advised mainstream schooling for at least part of the blind child's education, most boards preferred to fund existing specialist schools.[61]

These educational reforms had a twofold effect. As was also the case for "defective children" covered by a similar act in 1899, an emerging system of mandatory elementary education increased the need to determine the ways in which the diverse educational requirements of children could be categorized and provided for.[62] Thomas Armitage's *The Education and Employment of the Blind*, released a year after the 1870 Education Act and reissued in the same year as the investigations of the Royal Commission, especially sought to shape this conversation.[63] At the same time as incorporating blind children within the state education system, though, these reforms paradoxically sharpened their differentiation from sighted children through assuming their a priori difference. As Koven has noted for later legislation covering "defective" children, the 1893 Education Act always already assumed the difference and necessary segregation of blind children by defining them as those "too blind to read the ordinary school books used by children"; as those unable to benefit from the education given sighted children.[64] This paradoxical exclusion through inclusion within a state education system both underpinned and was informed by the understanding of tactile substitution in blindness that would develop on into the period between the two world wars.

Once they began receiving state grants in 1890, schools for the blind were required to provide the same minimum standard of education as all elementary schools, monitored by the Board of Education's inspectorate.[65] Although the beginning of state inspections of schools for the blind was intended to standardize the provision of elementary education, increasingly its effect was to demarcate the education of blind children as a distinct object of knowledge. In part this was a result of the terms of the 1890 and 1893 Education Acts, which inscribed the different education required by blind children within their provisions by granting special capitation grants for technical training in craft skills. Schools for the blind received three pounds and three shillings per year for each child meeting requirements in elementary subjects and an additional two pounds and two shillings per child showing "efficiency in manual work," likely the traditional handicrafts taught to blind children, such as basket weaving and chair caning.[66] In part, though, this differentiation of education for blind children emerged from within voluntary organizations themselves, which increasingly emphasized their specialist expertise in education. In July 1907, the British and Foreign Blind Association established the College of Teachers of the Blind to train and certify teachers in schools for the blind. Through lectures, a library, examinations, and its own journal, *Teacher of the Blind*, the college aimed at establishing the position of teachers in schools for the blind as, its foundation charter stated, "specialists in the work of education."[67] From the opening of the college, both the knowledge obtainable by blind children and the knowledge of teaching them were regarded as special domains requiring institutional segregation.

Most significant to this process of differentiation, though, was the requirement, under the 1907 Education (Administrative Provisions) Act, that every elementary schoolchild should be subject to periodic medical inspection.[68] As Zweiniger-Bargielowska notes, this requirement marked a change from the general regulation of the school environment to the individuation of each schoolchild, with their own health record, as the object of medical knowledge.[69] School Medical Service inspectors examined children three times over their elementary schooling and would often test for visual impairment during the first test, when children were aged five or six.[70] The Ministry of Health further sharpened the medical definition of blindness when in 1926 it informally adopted the Snellen test, the now familiar chart of different sized letters.[71] Although applied across the whole elementary system, medical inspections widened the distinction between blind and sighted children by turning blindness into a discrete condition to be diagnosed.[72]

The medicalization of blindness, and of supplementary touch within it, incorporated blind children within a wider discourse of preventative medicine gaining currency in the first decade of the twentieth century. Following the 1904 report of the Interdepartmental Committee on Physical Deterioration, charged with investigating the reasons for the alarmingly high rejection rates at military recruiting stations during the Anglo-Boer War (1899–1902), the Board of Education emphasized the importance of both a well-ventilated, hygienic school environment and a varied course of physical education in schools.[73] Alfred Eichholz, who inspected almost all schools for blind children from 1903 onward, testified before the committee.[74] As a primary advocate of the argument that physical "deterioration" resulted from environmental conditions rather than hereditary "degeneration," he stressed the benefits that improvements in sanitation, food, and clothing had on both the physical and psychological state of inhabitants of the poorest urban areas.[75] This contrasted with the strongly hereditarian view presented to the committee by James Cantlie, cofounder with Fletcher Little of the NIMB.[76] It is difficult to determine how much Cantlie's belief in the racial basis of physical "deterioration" underpinned the discourse of tactile compensation maintained by the NIMB; his *Physical Efficiency* (1906) made no direct reference to blindness.[77] For the committee, however, it was Eichholz's environmentalist argument that won out and governed both mainstream physical education and the understanding of touch in schools for the blind.

If, as the Interdepartmental Committee on Physical Deterioration concluded, physical deterioration was the product of a deleterious home and school environment, then schoolchildren could also be shaped into active, healthy subjects.[78] Prior to its report, physical education in schools, besides the competitive games played at public schools, consisted of military-style drill exercises standardized by the Board of Education, in consultation with the War Office, in its *Model Course in Physical Training* (1902). In the light of the findings of the Committee on Physical Deterioration, the Board of Education swiftly abandoned drill in favor of Swedish gymnastics in its 1905 *Syllabus of Physical Exercises* and subsequent 1909 *Syllabus*.[79] These syllabi outlined a holistic training that strengthened the "total unity" of the mind and body in the belief that efficient physiological functioning ensured a healthy nervous system and an attentive mind. Only through "the unity, balance, and equilibrium of the body as a whole," later reflected George Newman, chief medical officer at the Board of Education between 1907 and 1935, could body and mind achieve "growth."[80]

Schools for the blind readily included elements of this new thinking into their teaching. In 1921 Colville Street School, Nottingham, combined exercises and games from the Board of Education's *Syllabus* and *Handbook of Games* with four classes of Swedish gymnastics per week.[81] But, as was also the case for blind children's legislative and medical distinction, the adoption by schools for the blind of exercises recommended by the Board of Education reified blindness as a distinct "problem" even as it incorporated blind children within mainstream education. While teachers of blind children adopted Newman's understanding of the trained, mutual shaping of mind and body, they repurposed it to apply to the specific question of tactile substitution in blindness. Combined with current thinking in the psychology of blindness, physical education in schools for the blind became from the early 1920s onward a matter of shaping the mind through training the body, and tactile substitution increasingly became a matter of psychological rather than physical compensation.

This changing understanding of touch in schools for the blind is evident in the growing popularity of "eurhythmics," a dance-exercise devised by Émile Jaques-Dalcroze, former professor of harmony at the Geneva Conservatoire.[82] By 1920 E. Morley and E. Jones had released their version of the technique, adopted by the Queen Alexandra Kindergarten for the Blind in Birmingham and also translated into Braille.[83] The aim of eurhythmics was to foster a relationship between musical time and the listener's body; "to translate rhythms of music into rhythms of movement."[84] This translation enabled blind listeners to gain greater awareness of their posture and position within their surroundings. The difference from earlier drill training, recollected by Alfred Hollins, a former pupil at Wilberforce School for the Blind in Yorkshire in the 1870s, could not have been greater. After boot inspection the boys would order themselves in single file, place their right hands on the shoulder of the boy in front and, at the command, march smartly into breakfast.[85] Whereas drill standardized body habitus, the child's knowledge of space dependent on the body in front, eurhythmics experimented with it. While the correspondence between musical and bodily rhythms required "rules of grammar," this differed from drill as such rules were the condition for "free expression" rather than the limit to it.[86] Children were encouraged to formulate a bodily syntax that connected what they heard in a mutual but free relation to how they moved.

The unification of hearing with movement, though similar to Newman's emphasis on the "total unity" of mind and body, was uniquely important to blind children for several reasons. First, the quality of sound resonance was a way of determining the distance from and characteristics of objects, as well as perceptions of volume in enclosed spaces; aural correspondences with movement enabled a smoother negotiation of space.[87] The mind educated the body in "obedience" to the expression of an idea, and the body educated the mind in improvised decision-making.[88] Second, unlike the sighted, blind children lacked the visual means of learning good posture and unconsciously self-correcting postural "defects" and so benefited from training in managing the body. Their caution toward physical risk could also be overridden by a more confident interaction between mind and body.[89] Third, and most important in terms of touch, although eurhythmics focused on the body as a medium of expression, its encouragement of greater bodily awareness enlarged the body's capacity as a medium for sensation as well.[90] What eurhythmics enhanced was not touch as direct contact but consciousness of the physical conditions of possibility within which touch could occur: the potential to touch.

The interest in the mutual relation between blind children's mind and body, and the potential to train it, was not confined to eurhythmics. Between autumn 1931 and spring 1936, the College of Teachers of the Blind and NIB conducted a wide-ranging inquiry into the principles and methods of educating blind children. Chaired by Alfred Eichholz, and including representatives from the Board of Education and the Ministry of Health, the inquiry initially aimed at establishing an empirical basis for the psychological differentiation of blind and sighted children. Continuing an earlier, abortive investigation by F. M. Earle in 1927, the aim was to determine whether blindness, if at all, affected children's "native intelligence" or "acquirement of knowledge."[91] But after nine months' investigation, the inquiry failed to find any generalizable distinction, concluding that "no qualitative estimate of the mental life of a blind child was forthcoming."[92]

These findings both supported and subverted an assumed psychological difference that had already been institutionalized. On the one hand, they challenged an assumption that blindness necessarily deprived blind children of the same cognitive and emotional development as sighted children. On the other, they resonated with contemporary works on the psychology of blindness, such as Pierre Villey's *The World of the Blind* (English translation 1922) and John Ritchie's *Concerning the Blind* (1930), which argued that blind people differed from the sighted only in the means of acquiring knowledge, not in their intellectual or emotional potential. Touch was, these authors concluded, fully able to compensate for blindness, not through itself increasing in acuity but through psychological compensation enacted through an adjusted relation between mind and body.[93] In his contribution to the inquiry, Ritchie drew on the work of Charles Spearman, chair of psychology at University College London, to argue that the essence of intelligence, what Spearman termed the *g* factor, was unaffected by blindness; only the conditions within which intelligence could operate differed.[94] Following this thinking, the inquiry as a whole emphasized the importance of developing an active, reciprocal relation between blind children's bodies and minds.

The ability of touch to compensate for blindness, the inquiry stressed, depended on encouraging a child's early and active engagement with their environment.[95] Schools should be spacious, especially the infant school, where "corridors should be reasonably straight, with no jutting-out corners, and always kept free from casual obstacles."[96] They should also be "richly stocked with all that will appeal to the senses"; children required "the insistent call of external things," from boxes and canvas to "constructional toys," to incite them to mutually constituting mental and physical action.[97] Children aged between nine and fourteen should, for example, develop concepts of "form and proportion" through Plasticine modeling, an alternative to the tedious routinized movement of chair caning that had formerly been the mainstay of "handwork" in schools for the blind.[98]

This method of cultivating blind children's mind-body relation through play was embraced by the new NIB Sunshine Homes for blind preschool children. These residential nurseries, of which there were three by 1924, provided accommodation for up to ninety-six children from families that might struggle to care for them at home.[99] When the first of these Sunshine Homes opened at Chorleywood in 1918, NIB president Arthur Pearson capitalized on his press contacts to garner journalists' comments on the experiment, the resulting praise published as a book. In contrast with later guidance offered by the College of Teachers of the Blind, several visitors commented positively that few environmental changes were made to the home to cater for the needs of blind children.[100] This was likely a practical reason acquiring conceptual legitimation as Sunshine Homes tended to be converted private residences which resisted adaptation. It was nonetheless considered a strength as children were sensorially educated in a "normal" domestic environment more similar to life outside the home; one visitor noted how the children had learned to describe the "gay little figures" painted on their cots.[101] However, the keynote remained cultivating children's mind-body schema through concrete nonvisual experiences, often of specially adapted materials.[102]

This approach sat well with broader contemporary enthusiasm for the sensory autodidacticism promoted in Britain by educationalist Maria Montessori.[103] Children at Montessori schools, enthused the NIB journal, "become sense specialists." In these schools, "specially designed 'didactic material'" such as small, lightweight tables and chairs trained children's senses to appreciate "form, colour, dimension and weight."[104] This was not only a matter of training blind children's senses but a complex interplay between various forms of "sense." The teacher "acquires by practice the power of 'sensing' the inner working of the child's development and realising his state, and she can give him exactly the help he needs"; by "sensing" the way a child learned sensorially, teachers enmeshed their sensing, in both perceptual and physiological terms, with the child's.[105]

Besides emphasizing the importance of a sensorially appealing school environment, the joint inquiry also reviewed methods of teaching physical education. The review, conducted by orthopedic surgeon Dr. Anna Broman and teacher Miss V. Vulliamy, responded to the concerns of the College of Teachers of the Blind that examination candidates showed widespread ignorance of blind children's physical needs. Already in 1933 the college had charged Vulliamy with creating and reporting on a summer course on the subject for teachers of the blind.[106] While influenced by physical education of sighted children, like eurhythmics this course targeted the specific needs of blind children. Physical training, John Ritchie prefaced the report, should aim at removing the visual stigma of bad posture characteristic of blind children: "the well known droop at the shoulders, the drag and shuffle of the feet, the stolid springless slouch."[107] In line with the introduction of medical inspections, Vulliamy recommended that gymnastics instructors conduct annual orthopedic examinations to grade children from A to C.[108] She stressed that during training, instructors should avoid "stereotyping movement," as with drill, and instead encourage creative expression of the body.[109] The emphasis was on expanding the ease, energy, and scope of movement as a precondition of touch. In this manner, the mind worked in conjunction with the body as active touch fostered a more attentive mind and vice versa; the body schema integrated through a "habit of responsiveness."[110] The report illustrated the ideal-typical posture to be aimed for through photographs of statues at Dunfermline, diagrams of "good standing" produced by the early nineteenth-century formulator of Swedish massage Pehr Ling, and demonstrations by a schoolboy.[111]

Vulliamy continued her focus on poor posture in her contribution to the joint inquiry in 1936. Of 644 children she and Broman examined, 79 percent showed "postural and slight structural defects," and 10 percent had "marked postural defects" or "crippling deformities," including kyphosis (backward curvature of the spine resulting in a rounded upper back), knock-knee, and raised shoulders.[112] The culprit, it seemed, was the school desk. The report included an appendix illustrating the postural defects caused by particular desk types, also offering guidelines for their replacements and recommending that children should be regularly "fitted for their desks."[113] In her summer course report Vulliamy stressed the importance of developing good posture for the creation of "strong, lithe bodies" that were "efficient instruments of the will."[114] Good posture consolidated a physically active body in close connection with an attentive mind. This was especially important for blind children, both for developing their sense of touch and for guarding against bad habits to which they were ostensibly prone. As the joint inquiry report surmised in earlier chapters, the lack of incidental sensory stimulation and the inability to see "physical contingencies" reduced incentives for activity and could make blind children "cautious" and "sedentary."[115] The "relative scarcity of distracting stimuli" meant that "the emotional states of blind people tend perhaps to last longer than those of seeing people" and that the blind were "more prone to become introspective and moody and to yield to the attractions of a dream life, which in extreme cases may unfit them for grappling effectively with realities."[116] Encouraging good posture therefore helped develop both blind children's active, tactile engagement with their environment and their attention to the world beyond them.

The caution against a "dream life" creating a simulacrum of reality reveals an ethical basis to cultivating blind children's touch. In its discussion of blind children's "emotional world," the joint inquiry noted that "in many respects a blind person's conceptions of the external world must be only partial and may be erroneous, in consequence of which the exercise of his intelligence upon the relationships between the various parts of his knowledge or experience may lead him astray."[117] To be led "astray" here meant perceptually, but it had a subtext of moral straying. As the inquiry explained in the chapter on sex education, blind children relied principally on touch to understand sexual difference. Lacking "variety" in sensory stimulation, though, they could also fall into potentially harmful "self-exploration" and, by implication, masturbation.[118] The necessarily intimate means of gaining knowledge combined with the potential lack of alternative distraction repeated a similar link made between raised-print reading and masturbation in the late nineteenth century, as well as playing on broader contemporary fears concerning the dangers of escapist fantasy.[119] In the circumspect words of the inquiry, "where the mind is insufficiently occupied with agreeable matters, it will tend to seek relief in such outlets as present themselves. These are more restricted for the blind than for the seeing, and the danger that they may lead to undesirable forms of relief proportionately greater."[120] Encouraging blind children to develop an active tactile engagement with the world beyond themselves, the inquiry suggested, maintained a boundary between children's inner life and outer reality otherwise blurred by masturbation. As a principal means of improving posture and active touch, school desks therefore became central to mediating this relation between children's inner and outer worlds by directing their attention outward.

Prospectus photographs of school desks in subsequent decades show that the inquiry's recommendations remained the ideal rather than the reality for some schools.[121] But the recommendations significantly highlight an ethical dimension to cultivating blind children's active touch. Not only was cultivating touch essential to preventing harmful solipsism, it also ensured that blind children acquired the knowledge of the world necessary to form right judgments and constructive relations with others; to become responsible self-regulating subjects. Without blind children acquiring "direct contact with the world," the inquiry warned, "all subsequent formalizations of knowledge may be riddled with errors and misunderstandings, and all evaluations of what is good and worthy in life may be shattered by encounter with reality."[122] Likewise, training active touch was crucial for developing the communicative skills necessary for an integrated society: "The child must learn by experience how to control his bodily movements, and to acquire the innumerable forms of muscular skill that [. . .] enter most of his daily acts; he must learn the art of expressing his feelings and thoughts, and of interpreting those of others."[123] Only then could blind children become "mutually dependent members of an ordered society."[124] If cultivating active touch was important for blind children's moral and intellectual development, it was also, the inquiry implied, vital for acquiring the knowledge, values, and interpersonal skills necessary to become independent, responsible members of society.

"TACTUAL IMAGES" AND BLIND SELF-REPRESENTATION

By the 1930s, teachers had broadly accepted the importance of cultivating the reciprocal relation between blind children's bodies and minds. Yet for some, questions remained about the *way* information obtained from touch was converted into, and shaped by, thought. The joint inquiry by the College of Teachers of the Blind and the NIB boldly stated that the "thought processes" of blind and sighted people were the same; both employed "the same concepts," which, although potentially "fuller in meaning to the seeing because of the visual experiences with which they are associated," nevertheless "stand for the same things."[125] Yet the inquiry left unexplained whether there was a necessary connection between certain kinds of knowledge and the sensory means of acquiring it, or whether this connection disappeared once a concept was fully formed. The unexplored relation between sensation and thought consequently threw into question the presumed equivalence between the concepts blind children derived from touch and those sighted children derived from vision.

Teachers especially struggled to establish this equivalence when it came to teaching geography through maps. Geography had long been taught to blind children through raised maps, yet the laborious process of producing these, cutting and pasting an intricate topography, made them costly and relatively scarce throughout the nineteenth century.[126] While the Royal Normal College for the Blind in Upper Norwood provided individual embossed maps and a relief globe, at other schools teachers constructed basic maps with whatever was on hand.[127] Often made by sighted teachers, these maps tended to replicate the visual conventions of their flat originals, little attention being paid to how tactile reading might differ from seeing.[128] In the 1880s and 1890s, Thomas Armitage, founder of the Royal Normal College, and his secretary G. R. Boyle investigated the production of low-cost relief maps designed specifically for blind readers.[129] However, before the twentieth century, no systematic study was made of how touch substituted for vision and thus what visual concepts were available to blind readers of maps.

In 1930, Headmaster of Swiss Cottage School for the Blind John Ritchie returned to this vexed question of the relation between touch and thought

FIGURE 8 Children studying tactile maps, wheat, and a tactile globe in a geography class at the Royal Normal College for the Blind, Upper Norwood. From a photograph album prepared by and presented to Perkins Institution for the Blind, Watertown, Massachusetts, by Lady Francis Campbell, ca. 1872–1912. AG13/03/0012.
Courtesy of Perkins School for the Blind Archives, Watertown, MA

in his account of the psychology of the congenitally blind. Ritchie argued, as Villey also had, that through frequently handling objects blind people were able to create "an instantaneous mental image" that apparently divorced a concept from the sensory means of constructing it; the recollected "image" of a chair, for example, retained no traces of the touch that formulated it.[130] But while Ritchie claimed that blind people constructed mental "images," he regarded these as subtly different from those of the sighted. Grounding his argument in Lockean empiricism, Ritchie argued that, since every concept had its basis in sensation, there were some which, being entirely visually based, were inaccessible to the blind.[131] But most concepts, he claimed, derived from multiple sensations, meaning that the absence of vision did not prevent blind people forming their own "tactual images."[132]

The difference between tactual images and visual ones was a result of the degree to which the sensations forming each were mediated by thought. Touch, Ritchie argued, was "close to reality"; concepts derived from touch were "unambiguous" and required little intervening judgment. By contrast, sight was the subtlest of the senses and therefore visually based concepts required the most "mental correction."[133] Whereas "a blind man's images of objects are always tri-dimensional," Ritchie explained, "the ordinary man's are seen and remembered upon a plane background and must be over-ridden and corrected by his knowledge of the third dimension." This meant, Ritchie continued, that it was equally impossible for a blind person to develop mental images of plane surfaces—such as maps—without some mental correction. A picture of a fox, for example, could not be made perceptible to a blind person simply by embossing its outline, for this ignored how a sighted person's conception of the picture as a whole depended on their ability to conceive of objects on the plane, which blind people lacked.[134] Although Ritchie did not develop the point, this distinction between mental images presented problems when teaching blind children map work because their mental images, remaining stubbornly "tactual," could not replicate the two-dimensionality of maps. As the blind Pierre Villey noted, his mental images of relief maps were always "impregnated with tactile and muscular impressions," as the maps were covered with "too many intermingled lines, and too many different dots [. . .] for all this complex medley to be represented, as a whole, in my imagination."[135]

This thinking guided the recommendation by the joint inquiry on the education of the blind that teachers take a pragmatic attitude toward what could be accomplished with maps.[136] Nevertheless, between 1932 and 1937, Leonard Hardcastle, a partially sighted geography teacher at Leeds School for the Blind and a witness for the inquiry, crafted his own relief maps with the aim of determining just how much a two-dimensional representation might be converted into a "tactual image." At root was a semiotic dilemma: how to keep the same relation between a map and the world it represented when the touch of that map had a potentially different relation to the mind than its sight. How could the direct relation between the places marked on a map and those places in the world, a relation grasped instantaneously by a sighted person, be maintained in an object where that relation depended on the laborious successive movements of fingers across paper? Writing in May 1932, the NIB secretary-general proposed that Hardcastle develop relief maps of England similar to those already used at major train stations such as Paddington.[137] But Hardcastle replied that such maps, which converted all visible features into relief, were of little use for blind children because their detail was imperceptible to touch. Children easily overlooked coastline not bordered by cliffs while mistaking river valleys for train lines because their relief was so faint. Instead, Hardcastle argued, it was necessary to simplify and exaggerate relief representations—for example, marking coastline with a definite "step," removing "unimportant bends" in rivers, and indicating towns with round or square pegs according to population size.[138] The map Hardcastle suggested would approximate but bear only indirect relation to what it represented.

When Hardcastle sent his prototypes for evaluation at schools for the blind, it became clear that determining how much maps should differ from their referents—and, as a corollary, how much tactual images differed from visual ones—was a fraught exercise. While Swiss Cottage welcomed the prototype, Headmaster Ritchie wrote that it was likely blind people would gain "an equally vivid and more accurate impression" with a less exaggerated relief: "The impression which one might get from the Isle of Man, for instance, might be that anyone standing on it would be in grave danger of slipping off into the sea."[139] The report from Linden Lodge agreed that the elevation of relief was excessive, adding that "the perception gained from the map of the contour of the land can never be really translated into visual perception (the only adequate presentation of the real thing) so why trouble with so much detail."[140]

The belief that only vision adequately represented "the real thing" was telling. Linden Lodge's report assumed that only if maps maintained a direct relation with the world did they adequately represent "reality"—reality independent of the one observing it—and since touch was unable to perceive such detail, this reality remained inaccessible to the blind, and their tactual images were insurmountably poorer than visual ones. Even if blind children were trained, then, to substitute touch for vision, the resulting representation remained only a supplement to what sighted children could achieve. "After all," Hardcastle agreed, "a map is not a scale model"; a relief map did not, like a visual one, reproduce reality to scale, remaining directly proportional to it, but *stood in* for that reality in a relation that, like tactual images standing in for visual ones, retained their difference.[141] Just as relief maps maintained only a "functional" rather than "absolute" equivalence to reality, performing the same role but, unlike visual maps, unable to reproduce it, so was also the case for tactual images in relation to visual ones, which stood in for the same concepts but were unable to replicate them.[142]

Over the subsequent decade the NIB continued research into the psychology of blindness, but this research focused on developing intelligence tests for blind children rather than their ability to translate visual representations into tactile ones.[143] Between 1942 and 1956, teacher Myfanwy Williams worked for the National Foundation for Educational Research and the NIB adapting intelligence tests for use in schools for the blind.[144] But following the 1944 Education Act, a wider interest in the specific pedagogical needs of blind children returned. The act promised to desegregate blind from sighted children by allowing the education of disabled children in mainstream schools. But regulations from the minister of education in 1945 mandated that blind children remain in residential schools, further hardening the distinction by also categorizing them separately from partially sighted children. No longer was it possible for blind and partially sighted children to be educated together and hence the education of blind children became an even more specialist domain.[145] In 1951, the College of Teachers of the Blind created a research council for investigating "matters affecting the education and welfare of the blind," and in 1950 started to publish pamphlets under that theme, collated as a handbook for schoolteachers of the blind in 1956.[146] The handbook covered the now conventional themes of physical education and concrete learning, reiterating the rejection of the idea that blind people developed heightened sensory acuity and instead arguing for a theory of psychological compensation.[147] Yet, as had also been the case for the college's inquiry in the 1930s, the handbook did not explain *how* concepts derived normally from sight could be translated into ones derived from touch.

In the teaching of science at schools for the blind, this remained a knotty issue. Teachers had always struggled to teach blind pupils a broad science curriculum not just because of the expense of adapted apparatus and scarcity of Braille scientific and mathematical books but also because of the difficulty of transcribing "non-literal" scientific symbols into a form comprehensible to blind people.[148] Writing around 1960, William Bickley, a partially sighted professor of mathematics at Imperial College London, claimed that "science for the blind has resembled the mediaeval maps of the dark continent— empty, or decorated with fabulous or unreal objects."[149] The public schools had long taught theoretical and sometimes practical science, but they emphasized humanities teaching in line with the belief that blind children were better suited to nontechnical jobs.[150] Yet following the success of Adrian Magill, a partially sighted pupil from Worcester College for the Blind, at GCE Advanced Level Physics in the early 1940s, teachers of blind children increasingly focused their attention on developing new methods and apparatus for teaching science.[151] In 1959, the (now) Royal National Institute for the Blind (RNIB) invited Abraham Wexler, a teacher at the Royal Victoria Institute for the Blind, Melbourne, to visit Worcester College to reformulate existing methods of science teaching at schools for blind children.[152] The resulting manual, published in 1961, stressed that practical science teaching was not a matter of translating visual experience into tactile experience but of translating the *concepts* derived from the former into ones derived from the latter. Visual experiences remained inaccessible to the blind, but concepts derived from them did not.[153]

Soon after Wexler's visit, another major investigation into the uses of touch in science teaching at schools for the blind was launched. In 1965, Adrian Magill's brother Brendan wrote to a manufacturer of school scientific apparatus asking whether it would make adaptations for blind students.[154] The manufacturer forwarded the letter to the Nuffield Foundation, a charity that had already initiated a large-scale project aimed at reformulating the methods and materials used for science teaching in mainstream secondary schools.[155] In August 1965, the Foundation provided a three-year grant for research into the same area in schools for blind children, including investigations by Worcester College's craft instructor, W. Pickles, and physics teacher, W. VanClute.[156] The purpose of teaching blind children through practical science lessons was "to provide their minds with a schema by which objects of their world are comprehended in an ordered system of spatial relationships."[157] Surprisingly, the report recommended few adaptations of apparatus in subjects such as chemistry and biology as, Headmaster of Worcester College Richard Fletcher argued, blind children should learn, where possible, to use apparatus for the sighted both to enable them to work in a sighted environment and because commercial apparatus was cheaper.[158]

By contrast, the report emphasized the importance of training blind children to interpret what they felt within the same terms as the sighted, particularly for tactile versions of images. Discussing "the meaning of a line," Pickles argued that images were "completely artificial to the congenitally blind" and dismissed "nonsense about 'giving sight to the blind'"; visual experience would always remain inaccessible to them. Yet it was possible, he claimed, to teach the congenitally blind "sighted technique"; that is, to teach them the same "convention[s]" by which the sighted interpreted the relationship between representation and reality.[159] Crucially for Pickles, the act of translating visual representations into tactile ones came not at the level of experience, which was always incommensurate, but in the *way* blind children turned experience into concepts. If blind children learned to interpret embossed lines using the same "techniques" by which the sighted interpreted pictures, then they could develop the same concepts without requiring vision.

While Pickles experimented with lines of varying texture, he therefore also suggested methods by which blind children could learn to read images. Blind children struggled, he claimed, to gain the "overall" impression of an image that the sighted achieved with a "glance" because the blind built it through sequential touches. But they could be taught to gain this overall impression, either through resting the heel of their hand at the bottom of an image and allowing their fingers to spread outward, or by placing "all the fingers of both hands side by side flat on the diagram and giving them a rotatory rubbing action altogether."[160] These techniques allowed children both to build synoptic understandings of images and to develop a bank of images with which they could make comparisons in the future.[161] Yet while Pickles was tentatively optimistic that most blind children could learn "sighted" reading techniques, he stressed the limits to this. Texture might approximate color, for example, but no degree of interpretation of textured maps could replicate the mental images derived from a colored one. The irreducible difference between touch and sight meant that some concepts formed of visual representations remained beyond reach to blind children.[162]

For this reason, Pickles encouraged teaching blind children to produce their own tactile versions of visual representations in order to learn sighted techniques by doing.[163] As part of this study, in summer 1967 teacher Audrey Slater asked her students at Dorton House School to make several tactile drawings. Armed with ballpoint pens and sheets of clear polyester backed with rubber, her class of eight- and nine-year-olds created a range of drawings, including self-portraits. Some of these students Slater judged successful at producing work that was "realistic and had meaning." Others, however, seemed incapable of representing themselves in visual terms. Paul I., for example, "could trace round shapes, but did not succeed in creating any outlines with any obvious connection between them and what they were reputed to represent. His drawings without exception appeared to be random drawings wriggling across the page."[164] For Slater, such examples suggested that there were limits not only to the concepts available to blind children through touch but also to the conversion of these concepts into visual representations. In this way, the self-portraiture exercise turned the question of knowledge attainable by touch into one of self-conception and self-representation.[165]

As Slater and Pickles interpreted it, blind self-portraiture did not reveal simply alternative modes of perceiving but also the degree to which blind children could access a "reality" legislated in visual terms. In a comparison of two self-portraits, the report labeled the one best approximating a visual representation of a face as produced by an "intelligent child," the other by one "less intelligent." The "intelligent" child had captioned the portrait "THIS IS ME" in embossed Roman and Braille lettering, an additional mark that, like a signature, bound the representation to its author both through the caption's self-designating function and its existence as a tangible trace of the author.[166] Yet paradoxically, Slater and Pickles judged that trace "intelligent" precisely because it, like the self-portrait, was a *visual* representation standing in for its author's absence, so demonstrating the child's ability to convert their tactile sense of self into a representation linked to "reality." For Slater and Pickles, blind children's conception of reality was best judged in visual terms. Some blind children apparently approximated this conception whereas others did not, but in all cases the very terms of the inquiry—that a "realistic" self-conception depended on its visual representation—necessitated the difference between blind and sighted children the inquiry was ostensibly meant to test.

These working assumptions, as with those of earlier investigations into map reading, raised a deeper question underpinning that of tactile substitution. In the same way as medical examination reified blind schoolchildren's difference from the sighted, so too did investigations into teaching methods by which touch was trained to substitute for vision. By examining the degree to which touch "stood in" for vision, these investigations called attention to its apparently necessary difference *as* a substitute, or placeholder, to normative sensation. In the case of blind self-portraiture, this emphasis on the difference of touch called into question the very ability of blind children to form coherent selves, which were assumed to be grounded in visual terms—the old fear of a "dream life." At the same time, if examining the substitution of touch for vision revealed their necessary difference, then it questioned the ability of blind children to acquire the knowledge and reasoning required to become independent, self-reliant members of society. Just as touch apparently played a supplementary role in blindness, so these investigations inadvertently made blind children themselves supplements to an ideal, sighted subjectivity.

CONTESTING COMPENSATION

One year after Audrey Slater's students drew their self-portraits, in 1968, the RNIB celebrated its centenary. It was a year in which to take stock of what it meant to be blind in Britain, a theme the British Broadcasting Corporation (BBC) pursued through two programs released in the autumns of 1967 and 1968. On September 27 and 28, 1967, BBC1 broadcast a two-part television program called *BD8* that was produced by Philip Donnellan and given a sound montage by Charles Parker. On October 9, 1968 BBC Midlands Radio 4 followed with *The Blind Set*, a radio program produced by Parker, who had established a reputation by blending documentary, oral recordings, and folk song in what he called "radio ballad."[167] *The Blind Set* intercut folk songs with interview recordings made at schools, homes, and training centers for blind people across Britain between 1965 and 1967. Both programs aimed to counter what their producers perceived as a culture of pity toward blind people that assumed their unfortunate but inevitable dependence on the sighted. Instead, the programs stressed blind people's ability to "overcome" their impairment, particularly through new advances in mobility training enabled by the development of the now familiar white *long cane* in the United States. But whereas *BD8* received an overwhelmingly positive reception from both blind and sighted viewers, *The Blind Set* was, in Parker's assessment, "an unparalleled disaster," many blind listeners interpreting the program as a plea for pity that alienated them even more from mainstream society.[168] Through the hostility it received, *The Blind Set* inadvertently revealed a shift in the way that many of its blind listeners conceived of blindness, and touch in blindness, that contrasted with its own emphasis on tactile substitution.

In 1961, the British Pathé short *No Longer Alone* illustrated the training given to blind children at Condover Hall. Through ten graded exercises, children traveling in pairs advanced through a "privilege scheme" until deemed capable of traveling independently by bus to nearby Shrewsbury.[169] For *BD8* and *The Blind Set*, though, such training fell far short of what blind people were capable of by encouraging independence only insofar as their impairment allowed. *BD8* cited an example of such thinking in the case of Henry Taylor, teacher at the Scottish Blind School, who explained the purpose of the school's privilege scheme as producing "independent, mobile citizens within the limits of their handicap."[170] By contrast, *BD8* urged what the psychologist J. A. Leonard explained as a "standard" in which a blind person could "move about with the same degree of freedom [. . .] as a sighted person."[171]

This standard could be achieved, *BD8* argued, by making long cane training central to courses teaching blind students navigation techniques. Although long cane training was developed in the United States in 1946, *BD8* reported that the RNIB resisted its introduction for decades; it was taught in Britain beginning in 1966, when funding from the Nuffield Foundation enabled the establishment of the Midlands Mobility Centre and the RNIB introduced trials at its training center in Torquay.[172] *BD8* and *The Blind Set* presented long cane use as a matter of tactile substitution: of training the mind to direct movement according to tactile information derived from the cane tip. For Lee Farmer, the RNIB instructor, the cane was an "environmental sensor" continually providing information to its user. The blind person had to decide in a "split second" whether they needed to react immediately to that information, discard it, or store it as "money in the bank" for the future.[173] In the words of trainee Victor Horsley, "being able to use the long cane it's like having an extra long index finger, and it ferrets out for us the things, the information that we really need to know." Early in this interview Donnellan asked Horsley what independence meant to him. The reply, reproduced at the beginning of *The Blind Set*, was that "independence, of course being very much allied with mobility, is one of the most important things in life."[174] Taking up this message, BD8 and *The Blind Set* foregrounded long cane training, and the tactile substitution on which it depended, as the path to blind people's independence.

While countering the assumption, held even by sighted sympathizers, that blind people were inevitably dependent, this claim also challenged what Donnellan and Parker saw as blind people's own pessimism about their abilities.[175] Donnellan wrote, "The blind have been conditioned [. . .] to accept a state of non-information and prejudice, which has been alarmingly fostered by all sorts of reputable organisations."[176] Parker especially singled out the RNIB, whose resistance to long cane training had, he believed, conditioned blind people to accept lower levels of mobility. In this way, the RNIB perpetuated the dependence of those it was meant to help, reproducing what Parker understood as the class inequality at the heart of blind welfare. Underpinning blind people's self-conceived disability, Parker asserted, was "the reality of CLASS WAR and property [and] the utter refusal of the bourgeois to concede human parity to his class inferior."[177] Parker formulated this belief in part through an article by Anne Lapping reporting on the condition of blind people in Britain, published in the left-leaning journal *New Society* in March 1968. Lapping asked whether the strength of welfare organizations for blind people in Britain had paradoxically slowed the advance of welfare initiatives by allowing the state to evade its responsibilities toward disabled people.[178] She particularly drew attention to the apparent subordination of blind people, especially working-class blind people, to a predominantly sighted and middle-class RNIB. In a section Parker heavily underlined, Lapping reported the split occasioned in 1961 when the RNIB claimed the right to negotiate on behalf of kiosk workers represented by the National League for the Blind, a trade union whose members mainly worked in sheltered workshops.[179] For Parker, the assumption of blind people's inevitable sensory inequality from the sighted reproduced and was reproduced by an equally pernicious class inequality.

The Blind Set therefore faced a difficult task: while exposing what Parker believed to be many blind people's false consciousness regarding their abilities, it also needed to demonstrate what might be achieved once they thought of themselves in new terms. Constrained by the BBC's rules on political commentary, Parker believed the best way of achieving this critique was through careful attention to the form of radio documentary. Through intercutting contrasting material, for example, Parker highlighted the legitimacy of one viewpoint over another without the need for direct comment. In one section, an actor read an extract from Thomas Carroll's *Blindness* (1961) describing blindness as the "death" of one life and "birth" of another. This was succeeded by a clip of Tom Drake, manager of the RNIB center at Torquay, concurring with Carroll that blindness was a kind of "dying" in which the blind person was "born" as someone "functioning, competent, but different." Parker then critiqued this belief in blind people's inevitable difference through juxtaposition with a clip from Lee Farmer: "People haven't asked 'what can we do?'; the desire to get by, to make a token adjustment to a problem seems to be the predominant way of handling the situation here."[180] Parker also conveyed his message by weaving commissioned folk songs between interview extracts, a technique known as "radio ballad." Fortuitously for Parker, one blind interviewee compared overcoming blindness with the "life/death struggle" of humans over their environment, a struggle she believed English folk myths particularly drew inspiration from: "St. George killed the dragon but you—in essence this is the same thing as you've got to do." She speculated that "I think if you are searching for why the anxiety to blindness you have to go to folk-lore and primitive beliefs."[181] Parker followed this claim with a song recounting a hero "battling with a dragon" and, apt for blindness, the "king of darkness." Interspersed between verses were snatches of blind people describing moments when they overcame barriers presented by blindness, so conquering their own "dragons."[182]

"It will make your hair stand on end!" Parker wrote a week before the broadcast.[183] He was right, but not in the way he expected. Far from showing blind people's sensory equality with the sighted, to many listeners *The Blind Set* seemed to accentuate their difference even more. In the weeks following the broadcast, Parker received a torrent of critical letters, especially from blind listeners. Listeners variously described the music as "drooling," "dreary," "a sop to the contemporary folk-fad," and as "doggerel ditties" that distracted from program content and "presented the blind as half-witted."[184]

In addition, the audience report based on responses from a survey of 317 listeners noted that "nothing was said of the many who had triumphed over their disability with courage and good humour, nor had sufficient attention been paid to the fact that most sighted people did their best to treat them with 'courtesy, kindness, and respect.'"[185] Listeners especially rejected the impression given by the program that blind people were pitiable dependents. An exasperated H. Dudley, herself blind, wrote, "I don't quite know who you at the B.B.C. think you are, but will *our* point of view *never* sink in," suggesting that the BBC produce a program depicting blind people as "the same as everyone else."[186] An injured Parker replied, "You say that you fight every day against the public? ["who think we are either stupid or wonderful," Dudley had written] I feel that perhaps you should first fight against you[r] own organisations who perpetuate the charity image."[187] A mollified Dudley agreed that the RNIB was responsible for cultivating a culture of dependency but that *The Blind Set* did little to combat it: "Did you know that there are people looning round the streets of everywhere who actually think the blind don't and can't work!!!!"[188] D. Lineham wrote that her blind daughters knew some of the program contributors but "could not understand [. . .] why such knowledgeable people consented to have their voices drowned by raucous cries of 'PITY THE BLIND.'"[189] Some correspondents rejected the program's apparent condescension through the act of writing itself, Joy Gilbey pointing out that she was "a blind shorthand typist" who had typed her letter "on my office machine."[190]

For Parker, though, the most unsettling letters came not from critical listeners but from those who conscientiously interpreted the program as a plea for help. S. Wilson's letter, Parker wrote, was "the most disturbing I have ever received, and I am very nearly at a loss at how best to reply [. . .] in the face of such an extraordinary failure on my part to communicate. [. . .] What is most horrifying about your letter is its reasonableness and genuine and informed concern about the condition of the blind."[191] Wilson's letter, heavily underlined by Parker, read, "I listened to your programme 'Blind Set,' but *I am not really sure what you were trying to do*. Was it an appeal for funds on behalf of the R.N.I.B.—*in one part reference was made to sending donations to them*."[192] One listener did in fact donate two shillings and sixpence in sympathy for the blind, hoping that Parker received "lots & lots of Half Crowns & other big moneys" on their behalf.[193] If angry letters written to Parker revealed his failure to communicate, they at least showed blind listeners' rejection of the condescending attitude he was attempting to expose. By contrast, sympathetic letters, whether from blind or sighted listeners, devastatingly evidenced the persistent assumption that blind people were, indeed, necessarily deserving of pity.

The widespread misconstrual of *The Blind Set*, Parker believed, resulted from the failure of the radio ballad form. For Parker, radio ballad was not simply a way of overcoming the BBC prohibition on political commentary but also the only way in which the experiences related by blind interviewees might be related without being subsumed within a controlling narrative. After the magnitude of hostility toward the program became apparent, the Controller of Radio 4 (CR4) and Head of Programming Midlands (HPM) sent Parker sharply critical memos; enraged, Parker scribbled a vigorous rebuttal, which was never sent, explaining the importance of radio ballad and why it had failed. For CR4, complex intercutting of speech and music rendered the program unintelligible. Parker argued instead that intercutting placed blind people's experience, directly related, "in a context deliberately provocative (as for instance immediately following a description, or direct quote, from a TV commercial on make-up)" therefore juxtaposing "social matters" with the reality of a blind person's "deprivations."[194] Countering CR4's exasperation that the technique made "the thread of the programme [. . .] impossible to follow," Parker contended that radio ballad was "dialectical," deliberately "leav[ing] space in the 'thread of the programme'" for the listener "to enter and join up—so himself participating."[195] The point was to offer multiple possible interpretations that were only realized through their reception by each listener. At the same time, intercutting presented blind people's experience in a way that did not reduce it to "evidence" in an inquiry that always already turned those people into objects. The word rankled Parker:

> The real give away is "evidential": what an adjective, with all its legalistic/journalistic overtones, for such devastatingly human and social sources. Really that one work [word] *damns* C.R4 as having no concern for or understanding *of* the nature of Actuality, and its overwhelming potency as the oral expression of experience and so charged that at its high point, the experience seems to burst out of the loudspeaker as [at] first-hand, re-forged on the anvil of the speaker[']s passion to communicate every time that piece of tape is played.[196]

Adding force to the "Actuality" was the role folk music played not, in Parker's interpretation of CR4's criticism, as "BACKGROUND" aimed at "souping it up emotionally," but as an "unequivocal *statement*" that activated the spoken material interweaving it.[197] For Parker, "the *Common speech* ('actuality') and the *true Popular Song* ('folk song') are galvanically related," each animating the other and so conveying the immediacy of an experience otherwise attenuated by narrative.[198] Only in this way was it possible to convey his subjects' experiences without turning them into objects of pity.

More than this, Parker believed that radio ballad was particularly appropriate for blind listeners, whose assumed heightened hearing enabled them to discern his message beneath complex editing. The dispute with CR4, wrote Parker, revolved around the meaning of *impact*. CR4's understanding of the word was only of "impact as a machine gun hail of leaden information pellets, consistently clanging on the armoured hide of the [. . .] 'ordinary listener,' (a hide ever thickening by exposure to just such 'impact'!)." He, by contrast, aimed for "impact as that sense of excitement which irresistibly draws a listener to personal involvement."[199] For Parker, blind people were uniquely suited to this kind of impact because their acuter hearing made them especially sensitive to hidden messages.[200] The failure of *The Blind Set*, however, suggested that the reverse was true:

> One of the most terrible revelations for me, was the extent of the cultural deprivation of the blind. I had fallen [. . .] into the trap of assuming that the blind would be much more perceptive and sensitive where sound was concerned. In fact, [. . .] the absence of correctives available through the eyes meant that fed on the standard sound fare of broadcasting and middle-class utterance, they are, in fact, much more deprived than the sighted. This I believe is why the allusive method I was forced to use in "The Blind Set" [. . .] were [sic] just taken straight and interpreted by the blind as wounding and offensive.[201]

Blind listeners' misconstrual of Parker's message proved to him that they lacked not only the usual critical "correctives" of vision but also any compensatory ones from hearing. Blind listeners were not, after all, more perceptive but in fact exemplars of the unreflexive "ordinary listener."[202] In his very effort to counter the assumed difference of blind people by highlighting their tactile powers, Parker ultimately recentered that difference in his "discovery" that their hearing did not make them particularly attentive to his message. If blind people were now like "ordinary" listeners, this did not make them equal to those listeners, only woefully unable to grasp a message that might lead to their full independence.

Parker had conceived of radio ballad as a way of directly re-presenting blind people's experiences without reducing those experiences to "evidence" in a story over which they had no control. It was meant especially to impact blind listeners, whose acuter hearing would enable them to discern a message intended specifically for them, and in so doing raise them to a higher consciousness about their ability to become, through touch, wholly independent. In this way, blind people might challenge the assumption that blindness always already meant disability, an assumption that reified their difference as members of a subordinate "class," and so claim equality with the sighted. For Parker, *The Blind Set*'s failure therefore represented not only the failure of hearing to compensate for blindness but also the depth of blind people's "blindness" to their own subordination. The failure of hearing to substitute vision also entailed the failure of blind listeners to become perceptible to *themselves* as subordinated subjects: impairment, Parker concluded, did apparently necessitate disability. While Parker did not relate this conclusion to his earlier claims regarding touch, the potential for touch to enact the political—and perceptual—transformation he believed necessary seemed increasingly uncertain.

Yet another story is possible. While Parker believed the hostility *The Blind Set* provoked pointed to an intransigent sensory and political inequality between blind and sighted, it instead, the program's listeners might have contended, meant the opposite. Parker's case for the independence attainable by his blind listeners depended on the potential for touch and hearing to compensate blindness: social equality was contingent on sensory substitution. But the angry letters sent to the BBC suggest that by 1968 the question of tactile substitution was no longer the right one to ask. Instead, paralleling contemporary civil rights movements, blind listeners' rejection of what they construed as a call for pity challenged the very terms under which disability was understood. While missing Parker's point, their letters converged with his intention to reframe blindness from an impairment that necessarily meant disability to a state that was *constituted by* the attitudes of blind and sighted people themselves.[203] For both Parker and his listeners, disability arose not from impairment but from the social and environmental exclusion of those who were impaired. Once one thought of disability as a contingent condition distinct from impairment, it was then possible to challenge the assumed inherent difference between disability and ability that the language of sensory substitution had for so long reproduced. In this way, *The Blind Set*'s listeners anticipated an understanding of disability that would become, after the publication of the edited volume *Stigma: The Experience of Disability* (1966), foundational to the nascent field of British disability studies.[204] Through rejecting the centrality of impairment, and implicitly the language of sensory substitution, these listeners contested the very basis on which they, and disability itself, were construed as different.

CONCLUSION

On June 27, 1901, a fund-raising meeting was held in the Egyptian Hall at Mansion House on behalf of the Royal Normal College for the Blind, Upper Norwood.[205] In an attempt to rouse support, the Reverend H. J. R. Marston called for subscriptions to the college "on grounds of public economy, no less than on grounds of Christian charity." Referring to the college principal's claim that 89 percent of his students became "self-supporting," Marston argued that it was economic good sense to educate blind children rather than allow them to "remain a dead loss to society." For only £2,600 a year, eighty-nine blind children could be made economically independent for their adult lifetimes; by contrast, merely supporting the thirty thousand blind people in Britain at the same level of ten shillings per person per week would cost approximately £780,000 a year. For this reason, Marston contended, funding the college would make blind people "an asset" rather than "a bad debt" and was not only "sound Christianity" but also "sound political economy."[206]

An extract from this speech was reprinted in *The Law of Compensation: Blind but Self-Reliant* (1904), a pamphlet outlining the activities and successes of students at the Royal Normal College and repeating the call for public subscriptions. The pamphlet argued that the college, which specialized in musical training, amply demonstrated the "law of compensation." Although this "law" was apparently too self-evident to require explanation, the pamphlet pointed to the successful careers of former students as organists, pianists, professors of music, and pianoforte tuners as proof enough that a blind person's hearing "compensated" for blindness.[207] Understood in the light of Marston's speech, then, *compensation* assumed a double meaning. Not only did teaching blind children musical vocations enable their hearing to compensate for blindness, it also compensated society for its initial investment by preventing those children from becoming a future burden on welfare organizations and the poor law.

The Law of Compensation made explicit a link between sensory substitution and blind people's economic and political independence that defined the education of blind children well into the twentieth century. The reason for encouraging tactile substitution changed between the beginning of the century and the 1930s, from economic thrift to national rehabilitation and efficiency. Changing attitudes toward provision for disabled people after the Great War and new education legislation transformed the concept of tactile substitution from one of natural compensation to one of trained attentiveness. Yet until at least the 1930s, the assumed ontological difference between touch and vision in blindness reproduced a political difference between blind and sighted, disability and ability, in wider society. Specialist schools taught blind children to "compensate" for blindness through refining their sense of touch, so producing an ideal, able-bodied liberal subject that the language of compensation implied was almost, but not quite, within reach.

With the furor over *The Blind Set* in 1968, a new story emerged. Charles Parker's expressed intention for the program and the hostile reception it received revealed a desire to contest the binary of disability and ability by shifting attention away from impairment and toward society's treatment of visually impaired people. In this understanding, social and political equality depended not on sensory equality, and hence tactile substitution, but on societal attitudes toward sensory difference. Over the first half of the twentieth century, the history of touch in blindness traced an equally fraught political one of the shifting construction and deconstruction of the able-bodied liberal subject and the disabled Other against which it was defined. The understanding of disability that emerged from this history presented new theoretical problems, reifying a distinction between the "natural" fact of impairment and "social" attitudes toward it that defined debates for decades to come.[208] Yet nonetheless, the furious reception of *The Blind Set* by blind former students of special schools revealed how particular experiences of touch could become a resource for rethinking the nature and distinction of disability itself.[209]

CHAPTER THREE

Mind the Gap

Teresa Lubienska was not without enemies. As a countess who had been in the Polish Resistance, interned in the Ravensbrück concentration camp, and since migrating to Britain in 1946 chaired the association providing relief to Polish former political prisoners, she had ample reason and means to settle old grievances and, the police inferred, make new ones.[1] Nonetheless, it was still shocking news that on the night of Friday, May 24, 1957, the seventy-three-year-old woman had been stabbed on a platform at the Gloucester Road Station of the London Underground (known familiarly as "the tube") in West London. Ticket collector Emanuel Akinyemi stood alone in Lift No. 3 with the gates closed, listening for passengers who would ride the elevator up from the platform to street level. When the cry "Bandits!" reached him, he glanced down the passageway, catching sight of Lubienska staggering by the stairs. Akinyemi brought her up to the booking hall, containing the ticket office at street level, from which she was rushed to St. Mary Abbot's Hospital.[2] Doctor Vivian Devan pronounced Lubienska dead at 11:00 p.m.[3]

A Polish priest who attended a party with Lubienska that evening reported that he had accompanied her on the tube home as far as Earl's Court, and that she had only one station to go after he alighted.[4] But the murder was never solved. More revealing than her puzzling death are the 575 statements collated by the police inquiry, a snapshot of the eighteen thousand interviews allegedly conducted between late May and late August 1957 and most from tube passengers volunteering information about their journeys that they thought pertinent to the case.[5] As textured accounts of 1950s tube travel, these statements provide openings into thinking more broadly about the relation between touch, personal space, and time in an intimate space exemplary of, and peculiar to, modernity. Often recounting when normative passenger relations were transgressed, these statements reveal ordinary conditions of travel through extraordinary occurrences: an archive of the incidental. Through exposing how passengers expected to relate to one another in a 1950s tube car, the statements show how personal space was actually historically specific to the changing spatial and social conditions of the tube. In so doing, they show how the meaning and experience of unwanted touch, and of the ability to articulate and protest it, changed over time. The statements allow, in short, a backward glance into the hidden, shifting constitution of personal space through touch on the tube.

Since at least the early twentieth century, the tube has exemplified the apparent loss of personal space and, for some people, increased vulnerability attendant on "modern" city life. Population increase, the rise of commuting, and the diversification of labor in central London brought into more frequent and intimate contact an increasingly heterogeneous crowd of shop assistants, shoppers, clerks, laborers, brokers, and typists of both sexes and all classes. As these individuals encountered one another in new, less regulated, spaces of commercial leisure, commentary proliferated about the heightened dangers of unwanted touch and the possibilities for erotic chance encounters.[6] One of these spaces, the train compartment, drew special attention in the late nineteenth century; the sexual assault of twenty-two-year-old Kate Dickinson on a train between London and Woking in 1875 resulted in extensive comment on train compartments as sites of sexual danger and possibility.[7] Even in less traumatic cases, passengers commented on the uncomfortable proximity of strangers in train compartments, a proximity one either ignored by reading or looking out the window or used for sly observation.[8] By the 1920s, however, tube cars had displaced train compartments as the paradigm of new embodied relations between city dwellers. Once the tube became, after extensive expansion in the first decade of the 1900s, the most popular means of public transport in London, how one negotiated the uniquely awkward experience of clutching a strap amid jostling strangers while hurtling through darkness became a subject of intense scrutiny.

Consider Cyril Power's 1934 linocut *The Tube Train*. A decade earlier Power argued that the "satanic strength" of modern industry called for an equivalent artistic "sternness of treatment."[9] His image bore this out, the oversized bodies of passengers conforming to the car's curvature, angular limbs mirroring the angularity of newspapers that preserved each passenger's isolation in the midst of their proximity. Touch was prevented at all costs. For some historians, the apparently alienating experience of tube travel

identified by Power and his contemporaries stands in for a broader reconfig-
uration of social relations encapsulating "modernity."[10] As the size, density,
and mobility of Britain's population increased over the late nineteenth and
early twentieth centuries, frequent, fleeting, often close encounters with
strangers, especially in new public spaces such as the tube, became increasingly common. Although these changes in some cases reanimated personal
relationships, tube cars emblematized the alienation, loss of personal space,
and risk such encounters entailed as an increasingly diverse mix of passengers were thrown together and forced to develop new strategies of indifference.[11] Yet while representations such as *The Tube Train* are compelling, their
resonance with present-day tropes of the tube as alienating obscures the
contradictory and contingent realities of touch on the tube.[12] Power's linocut
expressed more his ambivalence toward modern technology than the com-
promises and small victories of the beleaguered commuter. The statements

FIGURE 9 Cyril Power, *The Tube Train*, ca. 1934, linocut. RED64214.
© Redfern Gallery, London/Bridgeman Images

collected after Lubienska's murder reveal instead a more complex reality, one in which personal space was not "lost" but contingently produced in interaction with seemingly minor changes in tube travel including electrification, de-compartmentalization, and straphanging.

Far from preexisting, personal space crystallized only in and through bodily transactions that informed and were informed by physical transformations of the tube. How these bodily transactions were experienced and interpreted was in turn shaped by differences of race, class, gender, and national identity. When Arthur Tribe, a witness in Lubienska's case, informed a "young foreign looking man" rushing down the stairs of South Kensington Station that "we keep to the right in England," he expressed a tacit etiquette of space that only emerged with the introduction of escalators in the Underground in 1911.[13] But the statements call for more than a history of tube architecture and technology or even a history "of" personal space, as if the concept predated the practice.[14] They instead show that, like an embodied speech act, personal space was realized only in the particularity of every passenger action, its conceptual existence contingent on each interaction between changing tube space and the bodies occupying it. Tribe did not merely "articulate" an existing etiquette of space but brought it into being anew, investing it with his own, national connotations. Personal space was *improvised*, concept and bodily practice mutually shaping one another, rather than either preexisting or being passively "determined" by physical changes in the tube.

If personal space was improvised, then it was also increasingly improvisational. The opening up of tube cars since the early 1900s—for example, through introducing central doors in cars—meant that by the 1950s, passengers faced a physically indeterminate space within which they had to improvise relations with one another. June Kitchin recounted how, one night in May 1957, three standing "youths" spent the journey "trying to kick each other in the pants and standing on each other[']s toes" until they were told to stop.[15] As rising passenger numbers and innovations such as grab straps made it more necessary and possible to stand, passengers had to improvise between tacitly agreeing on and explicitly enforcing personal space. Underpinning this improvisation were two major transformations: the transferal of private tube lines to public ownership and rising passenger anxiety over the need to rush. I argue that the switch from competition to coordination between lines and the paradox that efficiency improvements only encouraged more rushing together drove the restructuring of the tube and the improvisational personal space that resulted. It was these changes that, ultimately, meant passengers came to "mind the gap" between each other as much as that between train and platform.

Tracing this change rethinks key explanatory frameworks through which nineteenth- and twentieth-century Britain is often understood: histories of subjectivity, governmentality, and modernity. A contained space where the routinization of touch and movement appear paramount, at first glance the tube seems the perfect example of liberal governmentality: a site where, to adapt Patrick Joyce's phrasing, passengers were ruled to rule themselves. It might appear a site where, through sustained intervention in the material environment, the state paradoxically evacuated itself from direct intervention in the lives of its subjects, creating a space in which those subjects were ostensibly free to act. This would be a space where the careful planning of entrances and exits, lines of movement and points of stasis would, through habituating tube passengers to particular ways of moving, thinking, and interacting, enable them to self-regulate as "liberal" subjects and, ultimately, ostensibly monitor the state that at the same time guaranteed their freedom.[16] We can find echoes of this idea in J. B. Priestley's account, published in 1932, of how rush hours on the tube turned passengers into "parcels" to be ordered and made self-ordering: "Labels are pushed into their hands; trains are promptly loaded with them to full capacity; doors are opened and shut to admit them; they are hustled out, shot up in lifts, and only then, when the sweet cold rush of real air comes to meet them, are they allowed to turn back into ordinary men and women."[17]

But the evidence of everyday encounters on the tube suggests a different story. Even for a critic such as Priestley, for whom the tube presented a strange "nightmare of machinery," it would have been a mistake "to deduce the inner from the outer facts of life, to imagine that the mere mechanics give the key to everything."[18] Focusing on specific, incidental tube encounters avoids reducing passenger interaction to an expression of material change itself manifesting the pervasiveness of the liberal state. Instead, it foregrounds a more interactive, variable, and localized relation "between" bodies and their environment than that allowed by the paradigm of governmentality as often applied. Although recent work on liberal subjectivity counters these problems by highlighting how the use and failure of technology shape its power effects—pipes burst, concepts of privacy and secrecy conflict with attempts to make the city visible and legible—this work nonetheless remains within a paradigm in which action is overdetermined by "the rules of the liberal game."[19] This chapter instead shows how touch on the tube was not shaped only within these rules but rather involved what Michel Foucault conceived as "practices of the self" standing *independent* of and in relation to techniques of government.[20] In brief, personal space as it emerged on the tube by the 1950s followed its own improvised and improvisational logic.

This argument has two important implications. First, if personal space was not pregiven but contingently made, then historicizing it reveals the shifting, uneven constitution of the autonomous body that might be violated.[21] The history of encounters on the tube is one of the changing threat of unwanted touch, but also of the spatially and socially specific constitution of individuals *as* bodies with personal boundaries and therefore as both vulnerable to, and able to consent to, touch. Whether tube passengers understood themselves as vulnerable to unwanted touch was mediated by differences of class, race, gender, and every other way lives are made unequal. No touch escaped differentials of power conditioning its possibility and experience. Yet experiences of vulnerability and autonomy cohered only through particular bodily encounters, themselves conditioned by spatial and social changes and the economics of mass transit driving these changes. Tracing these encounters therefore also historicizes the experiential and conceptual constitution of particular bodies as vulnerable, and the subsequent centering of consent within debates about sexual ethics.

Second, examining the constitution of personal space reorients accounts taking modernist representations of tube travel at their word. If personal space was only ever contingent, then it could never mark the point at which Britain "became modern."[22] It could never mark the point at which Britons "finally" became indifferent strangers but instead calls into question the concept of modernity as a singular, successive condition of being itself.[23] It is not just that we have never been modern.[24] The contingency and variability of personal space instead questions the very possibility of a singular way of being, of sensing, that might be called modern. The statements gathered after Lubienska's death suggest a different, more incidental history of touch on the tube than the theories of modernity with which sensory history has historically been entangled.

MAKING PERSONAL SPACE

The problem of minding the gap emerged at a point of crisis for the tube. Over the Great War (1914–1918) tube traffic increased by two-thirds and came to constitute half of London's total public transport journeys.[25] Partly this was an effect of wartime conditions as over a third of buses were commandeered for frontline service, resulting in a shift of passengers from overground to underground.[26] But it reflected a longer-term trend caused by the mushrooming of London's population by over 4.2 million between 1861 and 1911 and the development of the West End as a leisure district and Whitehall as a nexus for commuting bureaucrats.[27] Traffic increase reached a critical point during the war as labor and materials shortages made the repair or addition of new rolling stock impossible. On the District Line alone, only 504 of 544 railcars owned were serviceable because there were no means to repair the remaining 40.[28] This, combined with rising passenger numbers, resulted in worsening overcrowding, with a 36 percent increase in the average number of passengers carried per Metropolitan Railway car over the course of the war.[29] An epidemic of pickpocketing followed as London's "light-fingered fraternity" exploited the crush of passengers, particularly on the route between Trafalgar Square and Waterloo often taken by soldiers on leave.[30] By 1919, the particular economic exigencies of the tube forced a new economy of bodies within it.

The problem was not just insufficient tube cars but also uncooperative passengers. At the 1919 London Traffic Enquiry, one company manager stated that the maximum service of forty trains per hour required stops of no more than twenty-five seconds, an increase to an average of fifty-five seconds thereby reducing the number of trains by ten per hour, and carrying capacity by a quarter.[31] Delays caused by congestion and dawdling passengers meant that in practice the timetable rarely converged with reality.[32] Various measures were attempted to align passengers with the tube's accelerated rhythm. At exceptionally busy stations such as Oxford Circus, barriers were erected on platforms to delay the crush until passengers had alighted, at which point a sliding bar was opened and boarding allowed. But this strategy proved to be self-defeating as, given a free exit, alighting passengers were "perhaps a little more leisurely in their movements," thereby extending the layover the measure was supposed to reduce. Knightsbridge Station experimented with "organized queuing"; while effective at quiet stations, the scheme proved unworkable at congested stations servicing multiple destinations.[33] The difficulty was finding solutions with sufficient flexibility to accommodate variations in traffic between stations and at various times of day.

The layout of endgate rolling stock was especially troublesome. With the exception of Metropolitan and District stock, which had doors to every railcar compartment, the noncompartmentalized cars of every other line were only accessible from gated platforms at their ends before central doors were experimentally introduced in 1915.[34] Passengers were slow in moving between train and platform because the procedure happened at only two points of a car, or for the City and South London line at only one point, and was regulated by gatemen assigned to each car. Limited accessibility increased average layover as it took longer to board and alight and meant that full car capacity was often not reached because passengers alighting at the next station refused to inconvenience their exit by moving to the center of the car. Longer stopping times meant fewer trains, less carrying capacity, and, combined with unequal distribution of passengers in cars, longer waiting times for would-be passengers. Although a perennial problem, immediately after the Great War these structural complaints converged with the explosion and ostensible naivete of passenger traffic and the rolling stock shortage to demand radical changes to the tube. Underlying those changes was a transformation in the tube's source of capital.

Tube lines were expensive. In the mid-1920s, a line cost £850,000 per mile to construct and equip. It could be operated at a cost of two-thirds of its traffic receipts at the scale of fares for 1926, meaning it had to carry fifteen million passengers a year if every passenger traveled an average of three miles.[35] That was a lot of traffic for a line to generate by itself without buses depositing additional passengers at stations.[36] Because demand responded negatively to even small fare increases, raising fares to boost revenue was not a serious option. In 1913 the upper fare limit for the average commuter journey was estimated at four pence, any increase above this severely deterring passengers. The viability of tube lines primarily depended on traffic quantity. Given postwar overcrowding, this might not seem problematic, but at the same time as being expensive to operate, tube lines were also unprofitable even when paying their way. In 1913, the Combine—that is, all tube railways excluding the Metropolitan—produced only enough profit for a meager 2 percent dividend.[37] Low profits made private investment unattractive as well as making it expensive to borrow capital. The tube therefore depended on heavy traffic to cover costs, but even then it remained a low-profit enterprise.

This presented a paradoxical situation in 1919. Though overcrowding was severe, it was because of the rolling stock shortage rather than because lines were running at maximum capacity. Because the tube's economic viability depended on traffic volume, it had further to increase its traffic, yet it could only do so with the addition of rolling stock to alleviate existing congestion and expand long-term capacity. At £3.65 million, the changes required could not be met by even optimistic projections of the amount the Combine could raise through profits or borrowing. The estimated shortfall was £2.75 million.[38] Prospects worsened when the economy slumped in 1920, reducing

UNDERGROUND

PASS DOWN THE CAR PLEASE

By not Passing Down the Gangways only **60** Passengers per Car are Carried.

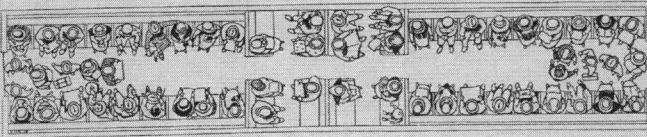

By Passing Down the Gangways **80** Passengers per Car can be Carried.

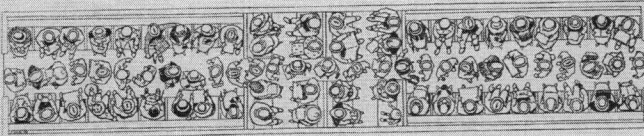

20 MORE PEOPLE ON EACH CAR OF A **4**-CAR TRAIN MEANS **80** MORE PEOPLE PER TRAIN THE ACCOMMODATION OF **1** CAR

PASS DOWN AND ADD CARS TO THE TRAIN.

FIGURE 10 F. H. Stingemore, *Pass Down the Car Please*, 1919, poster. 1983/4/808.
© TfL from the London Transport Museum collection

annual passenger journeys per capita from 410 to 380 the following year.[39] The tube simply could not fund itself.

Relief arrived with the 1921 Trade Facilities Act, which enabled tube companies to borrow at below-market interest rates guaranteed by the Treasury and so raise the capital necessary to expand service capacity. Though a palliative measure, its significance was far greater as the first public financial intervention, common to all companies, in the tube's history. The act increased the size and unity of the tube's capital base, accentuating a trend toward financial integration between tube companies and with buses. It presaged a move from private to independent administrative control, from competition to coordination across all London transport, underlain by a shift from private to public ownership of capital. Most of these changes were only fully realized a decade later, but what is significant here is how the changing economy of the tube already intersected with a changing economy of touch on the network.

Work soon began refitting the City and South London Railway (CSLR). When it opened in 1890, the line carried three-car trains pulled by the first underground electric locomotives. Excluding end platforms, each car was a stunted twenty-six feet long, accommodating 36 passengers seated on facing longitudinal seats; no provision was made for standing passengers. High-backed upholstery and slit windows soon earned the cars the wry nickname of "padded cells." Their cattle-truck exterior, sparse lighting, and absent seat or class divisions did nothing to dispel the impression. Under the renovation program, the line's tunnels were widened to comply with the standard diameter of 11 feet, 8.25 inches, and its platforms were lengthened to accommodate more and longer railcars. The new "standard" stock, introduced first on the CSLR in 1923 and subsequently rolled out on other lines, increased seating capacity to up to 48 passengers per car. This change potentially increased overall seating capacity from 160, or at a push 180, passengers per five-car CSLR train (1890 stock) to what in 1920 had been considered the ideal of 336 seated passengers per seven-car train (1923 stock).[40] This change also transformed the conditions of passenger relations on the CSLR. More spacious railcars meant more flexible space for passengers to choose when they sat next to others and who those others were. A mixture of transverse and longitudinal seating divided by armrests reduced the possibility for passengers cramming in next to each other, eyeballing those opposite, though this remained possible for facing longitudinal seats.

Although such changes were important, they continued developments in tube car space that had started when four new lines opened between 1900

FIGURE 11 Interior view of the City & South London Railway "padded cell" carriage, 1890 stock, ca. 1890–1900. 1998/75396.
© TfL from the London Transport Museum collection

FIGURE 12 Interior view of 1923 "standard stock" railcar, no. 820, ca. 1920–1925. 1998/81322. © TfL from the London Transport Museum collection

and 1907. More significant was the inclusion of automated central doors on new rolling stock. Central doors were automated on forty new railcars in 1919 but only became a widespread occurrence when introduced on the CSLR in 1923. Between 1923 and 1927, 736 cars with automated central doors were ordered to entirely replace the manually operated gate stock on all Combine lines.[41] Seemingly a minor change, automated central doors fundamentally reordered touch on the tube for decades to come. By changing how passengers moved between train and platform, they eased movement within cars and shifted the way passenger conduct was regulated.

Albert Francis's journey one evening in May 1957 is an example. A man sat opposite Francis eating a bar of chocolate, and another sat to his right. Two women sat to his left. The man to his right asked the man eating chocolate, whom he did not seem to know, for a piece, which he was given. A minute later he asked for more chocolate but was told it was "all gone." He then spat on the other man, drew a knife, and leaned over him just as the train pulled into Gloucester Road Station. The threatened man alighted, but the knife-wielding man remained.[42] This kind of occurrence owed much to the removal of gatemen effected by 1920s tube stock. In contrast to trains requiring up to six gatemen to operate the car gates, by 1927 automated doors required only one guard and removed the need for gatemen.[43] At the same time, "minding the gap" entered London Underground discourse as new central doors created gaps at curved platforms. No longer a regulating presence of conduct on trains, tube staff came to manage the gap between train and platform while passengers were left to manage the gap between each other. While at Gloucester Road, Francis leaned out of the car to report the incident to a porter, who only replied "O.K. And mind the doors," and took no further action. The new tube stock opened up a gap between train and platform but also a charged gap between passengers freed from direct regulation and the constraint on movement imposed by endgates.

When the train pulled away, the man with the knife sat next to the two women, who then got up and sought reassuring seats next to Francis.[44] Left to themselves, passengers developed mutual understandings of personal space through which it was at once reified *and* transformed in every iteration.[45] Being a "stranger" on the tube, as Cyril Power's linocut depicted it, necessitated a cooperation that *deferred* the inviolate boundaries it was meant to fix. If tube travel exemplified modernity, then this was a modernity in which spatial relations between passengers became increasingly contingent, uncertain, and necessarily negotiated. Through the introduction of

FIGURE 13 Mind the Gap: the curve on the Bakerloo Line platform, Waterloo Underground Station, and warnings to beware, January 17, 1936. 1998/88454.
© TfL from the London Transport Museum collection

automated doors in the 1920s, the tube developed a spatial undecidability requiring tacit agreement between passengers rather than the fixed anomie depicted by Power.

The novelty of this tacit knowledge of the tactile was shown by its advent in 1920s film. Opening in a crowded tube car, the melodramatic romance *Underground* (1928) depicted the ways passengers could, literally, put a foot out of place.[46] After a panning shot of a packed station taken from the front of an arriving train, the action cuts to the awkward negotiations within. At the entrance of a young woman, a soldier and sailor jointly defer their seats, only to have them filled by other passengers. One of these seat grabbers, an arrogant electrician named Bert, slyly reads the newspaper over the shoulder of his neighbor, who glowers back. At the next stop insult is redressed with injury as the departing sailor gleefully treads on Bert's foot, while Bert's exasperated neighbor flings the newspaper onto his lap. Unperturbed, Bert tries to catch the eye of his new neighbor, an attractive shopgirl named Nell, by grinning in her powder box mirror and pressing his foot against hers. An exasperated Nell impishly seizes Bert's cap and throws it across the car, inviting a standing woman to take his place. By introducing its protagonists through their tube car misdemeanors, *Underground* reveals how tacit norms of personal space were gaining currency by the 1920s yet also remained new enough to require satirical, visual explication.[47]

Whereas *Underground* satirized such transgressions, Alfred Hitchcock's *Rich and Strange* (1931) made the demands of the tube car stand in for the inescapable but unbearable conventions of urban life.[48] The film reused *Underground*'s opening footage of a crowded platform before cutting to its own vignette of tube car relations, which consequently stood out in relief.[49] In this retelling, awkward encounters in the tube car reenacted the constraints of a life not fully lived. As the train jolts forward, Fred, a world-weary clerk, lurches into a seated elderly woman, grabbing at a feather in her hat, which the woman snatches and jams back in. Another jolt and Fred's newspaper prods the face of a neighboring straphanger, who angrily shoves it away. Shot from the passenger's point of view, *Rich and Strange*, like *Underground*, showed the emerging tacit norms of the tube car. Yet rather than representing these as one of the unavoidable, uniquely interesting, conditions of urban life, the film had them exemplify what made that life unlivable—and act as the impetus to escape the city for a new one elsewhere. Chastened, Fred looks down at his newspaper to see an article entitled "Are You Satisfied with Your Present Circumstances?"

The contrast between *Underground* and *Rich and Strange* was also one of the gendered experience of new tactile norms. While *Underground* high-lighted the wiles of the attractive shopgirl, compelled to innovate new ways to be left alone, *Rich and Strange* followed the careworn male clerk unable to escape others' lives. These differing experiences were especially explored by *Underground*, whose plot followed the entwined amorous relations, and contrasting gender performances, of its four protagonists above and below ground. After Nell alights from the train, she is followed to the escalators by Bert. Noticing Nell's discomfort, a winsome railway porter named Bill trips Bert at the foot of the escalators, "rescuing" Nell from his advances. From the confined intimacy of the tube car, the story moves to the contrasting social and spatial dynamics of the department store where Nell works. There Bert tries his luck with Nell again, this time in a less confined space where she is, however, obliged to remain. While Bert's conduct was checked by other passengers in the tube car and an official on the station, in the department store the disapproving presence of a floorwalker halts his unwanted advances.

These encounters between Nell and Bert are contrasted with those she has with Bill. Whereas Bert capitalizes on the forced intimacy of the tube car, where passengers knew to tacitly manage personal space, Bill courts Nell on the deck of an open-top bus, a common trope for romantic trysts. Forward-facing, two-person "garden seats" and the ability to look out made the open-top bus a space of eroticized ambiguity, where female travelers might experience harassment or find a space for chosen intimacy.[50] After being forcibly kissed by Bert in a quiet side street, Nell escapes to Embankment, where she meets Bill for a planned day trip to a spacious London park. The couple share a seat, and chocolates, on the bus deck, watching London unfold filmically in imitation of the couples watching the film of which they are a part.[51] This cinematic, first-person perspective of London by bus drew upon earlier photographic and filmic versions and encouraged viewers to identify with Nell and Bill while differentiating their experience from the preceding side street assault.[52] Through such contrasting encounters above and below ground and between Nell and her two admirers, *Underground* emphasized the spatial particularity of sexual threat—different in open-plan tube cars compared with backstreets, open-top buses, and parks—as well as the ways in which it was managed.

Yet *Underground* also warned of how the sexual threat of the tube cut both ways. Desperate to win him back, Bert's lover Kate, a seamstress struggling by on piecework at their shared lodgings, agrees to frame Bill by faking an assault. Feigning illness at the foot of a tube station's escalators, Kate is led by Bill to the emergency stairs, where she suddenly ruffles his hair, pulls out his tie, and cries for help. Kate's plot is foiled when Nell makes her reveal all in a confrontation at her lodgings. Just as Bert's arrogance is contrasted with Bill's humility, Kate's hopeless attachment to, and dependence on, Bert is contrasted with Nell's independence, a contrast underpinned by their roles of the visible, desirable shopgirl selling clothes and the hidden, undesirable seamstress repairing them.[53] Through its spatial and social contrasts, *Underground* not only examined but enforced emerging norms of personal space on the tube, using these to tell stories about appropriate and inappropriate gender roles. The film's genre as a melodramatic romance meant it emphasized Nell's independence and Bill's reticence over Bert and Kate's sexual threat. Yet the film also showed how vulnerability materialized differently above and below ground, and how, in the spatial indeterminacy of the late 1920s tube car, it depended particularly on tacit agreements between passengers.

ECONOMIES OF COAL AND BODIES

Underground concludes with a vertiginous fight between Bert and Bill on the rooftops of Lots Road power station. As the tube's principal power source in 1928, Lots Road is the ultimate stage for enacting the sexual jealousy that drives the plot and which originates in a tube car. The film's return to its primal scene highlights a crucial factor governing tactile relations on the tube: its power source. Two decades before automated doors, the possible forms of passenger interaction were already being reshaped by the restructuring of railcar space attendant on the transition from steam to electric power.

In part, worsening travel conditions necessitated this transition. In 1897 a Board of Trade inquiry estimated that the 19 trains run each way per hour on the Metropolitan Railway emitted approximately 825 gallons of water as steam. With 528 passenger trains and 14 goods trains running on this line per day, and with few ventilation shafts, the atmosphere in the tunnels was becoming insufferable. In response, the inquiry approved additional shafts on the condition that the Metropolitan electrified its trains within three years of an act sanctioning the additional shafts.[54] Competition from other railways provided an even more important inducement for electrification. Charging a flat fare of twopence and offering smoke-free tunnels, the new electric Central London Railway, opened in 1900, poached a healthy portion of Metropolitan traffic, which fell from ninety-six million in 1899 to eighty-eight million in 1901.[55] Made possible by the creation of the giant Underground Electric Railways Company of London (UERL), more electric lines quickly followed. The Bakerloo, Charing Cross, and Piccadilly lines all opened between March 1906 and June 1907. Anticipating the inevitable, the Metropolitan began a partial electric service in January 1905 while the District, now absorbed into UERL, followed suit.[56]

UERL opened a coal power station at Lots Road in 1902 while the Metropolitan operated its own at Neasden from 1904. The tube's power source was relocated from locomotives to colossal Thames-side power stations, in turn shifting the possible ordering of bodies within tube cars themselves. In an analogy made on a poster at the time, "The turbines sleep / Like tops, and out / Of their sleep / Comes the strength / To move London."[57] That movement occurred not just across the space that tubes traversed but also *within* the restructured space of their cars as electrification ushered in the decompartmentalization of rolling stock and subsequent mixing of classes and genders.

Prior to the CSLR opening in 1890, all tube stock was one of three classes and divided into compartments. In the 1860s the Metropolitan's first-class cars were divided into six compartments, with total seating for up to sixty, and its second- and third-class cars into eight compartments.[58] While it still reserved separate cars for women and for smokers, the CSLR was the first line to provide classless, noncompartmentalized cars, but in practice a car half-partitioned into two sets of sixteen seats was not much different from a compartment on the Metropolitan, even if all classes now sat together. The major change to tube stock arrived with the electric *motor cars* (motorized railroad cars) of the Central Line and the UERL lines and Metropolitan Line competing with it. At 13 feet longer and 1 foot, 8 inches wider than CSLR cars and with seating for an additional sixteen passengers plus straphangers, the classless, noncompartmentalized Central cars provided far more potential for social and spatial mixing.[59] The same was true of the three new UERL lines that ran electric motor cars with seating capacity of around forty-two passengers and trailers with seating capacity of around fifty-two passengers in trains up to six cars long. All cars were classless, noncompartmentalized, and entered by endgates.

Electric trains with longer and more cars were made possible by the development in 1897 of multiple-unit *control cars*, or motor cars jointly controllable from a single point on a train. Long trains could now be powered without the necessity for heavy electric locomotives. Single UERL multiple-unit cars far exceeded whole CSLR trains in terms of power (480 horsepower compared with 100) while still carrying more than forty seated passengers.[60] Greater power meant quicker acceleration, which, combined with an electric system of automatic signaling and the introduction in 1930 of electropneumatic braking, enabled shorter intervals between trains and a more frequent service.[61] Trains could also travel faster. Whereas the average underground steam train traveled ten to eleven miles per hour in the 1860s, electrification increased this average speed to fourteen miles per hour by 1900 and eighteen to nineteen miles per hour by 1929.[62]

It was not only distance that increasing speeds eliminated but the spatial differentiation of class. Shorter journey times reduced the necessity for class and gender divisions by cutting the duration of potentially awkward social interaction. Where class divisions remained, as with some Circle Line trains in 1906, the more luxurious accommodation of new classless rolling stock made them redundant as passengers waited for the latter rather than shelling out for second class on the former.[63] Electrification was the final blow to a spatial layout that had only infrequently worked as intended. One first-class passenger in 1883 recalled his horror when, "on arriving at the South Kensington platform, a seething, distracted, and vociferous crowd" poured into the station from the Fisheries Exhibition. A "forlorn hope" of people "tumbled and hustled" into every compartment, regardless of class, until each car became "a miniature 'Black Hole of Calcutta.'"[64] While overcrowding in first-class cars here resulted from the tube's limited additional capacity in the face of traffic fluctuations, by 1919 the rise in average passenger density made straphanging in first-class cars more norm than exception. Even if this did not entail class mixing, one member of Parliament at the London Traffic Enquiry still regarded it as a breach of contract to not provide seats for all first-class passengers and suggested that segregated cars be abolished.[65] In practice, changes in passenger traffic had already overtaken the suggestion. In 1913, nearly all lines were classless, and first-class traffic accounted for only 4 percent of all traffic, excluding workmen's and season tickets.[66] For nearly all lines, electrification made class segregation no longer socially necessary or, increasingly, practically possible.

The discontinuation of class segregation and women-only compartments converged with the increasing presence of white-collar female passengers to dissolve the former ordering of tactile relations on the tube.[67] After the removal of gatemen, women in vulnerable situations in noncompartmentalized cars were more compelled to manage their surrounding space, especially relying on the tacit cooperation of other passengers. When Mabel Petley caught the tube from Wimbledon one evening in May 1957, she chose an empty car. But a young man soon joined her and stood at the doors nearest her seat, clutching a knife and staring. After an older man entered and sat at the end of the car Petley joined him, pretending she needed a light for her cigarette. Besides the obvious wish to distance herself from the knife, this was also a case of readjusting a postural economy by substituting oppositional with adjacent proximity, so interrupting eye contact, and disparate height with the equal height of two seated passengers. The gesture also enacted a response to the subcultural challenge posed by some 1950s adolescents, the forty-nine-year-old secretary reclaiming a bodily forfeited social status by moving from the standing man "of Teddy boy appearance" to her seated peer, though in so doing calling that status further into question.[68]

This economy of bodies was particular to higher numbers of independent female travelers and anxiety surrounding teddy boy culture in the 1950s. But it also owed to earlier changes in the speed and shape of tube cars caused by the relocation of coal as a power source from within tube tunnels to outside them. The bodily techniques of personal space on the tube were informed by and responded to transformations in the technology of the electric engine.

THE HISTORY OF IMPATIENCE

At 5:26 p.m. on February 13, 1928, Mr. J. Broom was in a hurry. As a compartment stock train drew away from Baker Street Station, Broom dashed down the platform steps and, disregarding shouts from dispatch staff, leaped toward a compartment. Somehow his foot slipped, though, causing him to fall between the car and the platform and be wrenched onto the permanent way. He did not survive the incident.[69] Though Broom no doubt had reason to rush, the next train would not have been a long wait. When the Circle Line opened in 1884, the average interval between peak-time trains was ten minutes; by 1897, it had been cut to three. Electric trains were even more regular, with peak-time trains arriving every two minutes when the Piccadilly and Charing Cross Lines opened in 1906 and 1907.[70]

Yet rather than resulting in nonchalant acceptance that a missed train meant briefly waiting for another, efficiency improvements failed to alleviate passenger frustration. Interwar Metropolitan Railway accident books show that Broom was not the only one to suffer injury when rushing for a train despite the decreasing reason to do so.[71] It was almost as if passengers hurried *because* tube travel was more efficient.[72] One of the causes of this paradox was the increased regularity of electric tube trains: as intervals between trains dropped, their perceived duration increasingly diverged upward from their actual duration, generating continued frustration at the perceived inefficiency of the journey overall. That is, because we tend to overestimate short time periods and underestimate long ones, a reduction in the duration of a short interval—that of waiting for a train—paradoxically led to increasing *over*estimation of that interval.[73] In short, as tube passengers had to wait less time for trains, they became more keenly aware of the time they *did* have to wait. Accidents caused by hurry were, in this sense, prefigured by the technological development of the tube.[74]

Although not exclusive to electric tube travel, this sense of time assumed a particular coherence on the tube in a way it did not on buses until after the mid-1920s.[75] Whereas tube trains stopped at every station in short, uniform intervals, before the 1920s motorbuses had neither a timetabled service nor fixed stops. They instead collected and deposited passengers as and when required. Fixed stops were experimentally introduced in 1920, with an average of four compulsory stops per mile and an additional two optional ones, but it was only after the 1924 London Traffic Act that buses were required to provide a regular service on set approved routes.[76] Waiting for the bus was therefore different from waiting for the tube. The length of the wait and duration of the journey depended on the quantity of bus traffic and number of stops a bus made before and after collecting a passenger. Even though the time between trains might be shorter than that between buses, it was precisely its predictable brevity that generated impatience.

This impatience might seem even less reasonable given that in 1920 the average tube train speed was eighteen miles per hour compared with ten miles per hour, including three to four stops per mile, for buses.[77] But in their early years motor buses appeared more convenient than tube trains, as they surely were for short distances. Buses compared favorably against the tube because they were accessible at street level and because tickets could be purchased on board; bus routes and the quantity of buses could also respond to geographical and temporal variations in demand.[78] While these features already applied to horse-drawn omnibuses, they combined with the increased acceleration of motor buses to place them beyond tramways in terms of speed (averaging nine miles per hour) and in competition with the tube in terms of convenience.[79] "On the comparatively short journeys with which we deal," worried the tube's superintendent of the line in 1918, "any time spent in waiting [...] bears a large proportion to the total time occupied on the journey, and, if unduly lengthy, will be sufficient to deter passengers from using the Railways." Inefficiencies could reduce the speed of a tube journey to only four miles per hour, and the actual time spent traveling to less than a third of the total journey time, making it much quicker to travel short distances by bus.[80]

The disparate experiences of waiting for tube trains and buses meant that rising passenger impatience with the former did not represent a general experience of time that might be called "modern." The perception of time differed between modes of transport, times of day, and purpose of travel, precluding any simple periodization of perceptual shifts.[81] Tube trains arrived overfilled, buses not at all; idleness mingled with impatience. Yet while time consciousness was variable, the superintendent's concerns highlighted how impatience was particularly problematic for the short duration—and, one could add, short intervals—of tube journeys, despite the rising speed and regularity of trains.

One solution to the problem of impatience was to streamline how passengers moved between platform and booking hall.[82] Electrification made more powerful elevators possible, but early models attracted negative comments from passengers who resented cramming together.[83] The alternative, developed soon after, was the escalator. The first made its remarkable debut in 1906 at Holloway Road Station as a rotating double helix that conveyed passengers through a vertical shaft. It was declared irredeemably unsafe after a day of service. The next to enter operation, a linear design, opened at Earl's Court Station in October 1911.

Escalators rationalized movement between booking hall and platform by changing the relationship between the distribution of passengers and the speed at which they moved. What escalators lost in speed compared to elevators they gained through evenly spacing passengers and dividing them from those in a hurry. At a rate of 100 feet per minute, the first escalator was, albeit optimistically, projected to carry 10,800 passengers each direction per hour.[84] By contrast, the three high-speed elevators at Hampstead Station, which operated at 360 feet per minute, or a thirty-second service over 180 feet, were conservatively estimated to carry only 2,400 passengers in only one direction per hour.[85] Through the regular arrangement of space occupied across time, escalators conveyed a greater number of passengers per hour. Though elevators traveled faster, their discontinuous service condensed space into a smaller number of discrete blocks occupied across time; passengers crossed the distance quicker, but only through collecting at elevator entrances and jostling in when it arrived, which increased overcrowding, frustrated passengers, and caused further delays. In an incident at Lancaster Gate Station, one passenger left behind by an ascending elevator rang the call bell continuously until it reached the top landing and returned. When he arrived at the booking hall, he expressed annoyance at the elevator attendant by jamming his walking stick between the elevator doors to prevent them from closing.[86] In contrast with elevators, escalators achieved a continuous sequentialization of space and time between booking hall and platform, reordering tactile relations between passengers through regular spacing and reducing impatience by leaving room for sprinters. If, that is, passengers stood on the right.

The etiquette of standing on the right of escalators coincided with, and in part resulted from, the apparent convenience of motor bus travel. Curbside access to faster buses necessitated rationalizing access to tube trains, part of which involved enabling passengers to overtake. Barriers and signs prompted the new conduct. On the first escalators the handrail cut diagonally rightward across the point where the steps evened out, allowing those standing on the right to step off without being suddenly impeded by those walking on the left. The handrail also prevented women's long dresses from getting caught in the teeth of the step slats. Early signs seem to have directed passengers to step off with the left foot first, but at some point this changed to the right foot.[87] The latter instruction was sufficiently well established by 1928 to be satirized by *Underground*, which showed a puzzled soldier struggling not to step off left foot first, the convention used in the military.[88]

FIGURE 14 Stand on the right: upper landing of the escalator connecting the District and Bakerloo/Northern Line platforms at Charing Cross (now Embankment) Station, ca. March 1914. 1998/73649.
© TfL from the London Transport Museum collection

Although these instructions standardized the space between passengers, they did not, however, prevent unwanted touch and in some instances encouraged it. One afternoon in May 1957, Susan Haynes arrived at the Lyons Corner House on Coventry Street for her shift. Before she began work, she discovered a vertical cut running nearly five inches down the back of her skirt, slightly to the left. A little earlier, when stepping onto the Piccadilly Circus Station escalator, she had noticed a young man standing at the bottom walk smartly behind her onto the lower step and, thinking this suspicious, clung onto her handbag. It only later transpired that it was not her handbag she had to watch, the position of the slit being consistent with the area exposed as she stood on the right of the escalator.[89] Since escalators equalized the distance between passengers and separated the fast from the slow, the hustle of elevators gradually gave way to the apparent safety of open, regularized space—and the risk that assurance created.

By 1919, the severe bus shortage in London meant less competition with the tube and so less cause for impatience with its comparative inconvenience. The growing coordination between tube services and London General Omnibus Company (LGOC) buses since 1912 also meant passengers increasingly saw each as supplementing rather than substituting for the other. But new grounds for impatience soon emerged that contributed to further rolling stock restructuring. One of these was the increasing difference between running for the tube and running for the bus. After automated central doors were introduced to new rolling stock in 1919, hurrying was no longer dictated by gatemen closing railcar platforms but by air-compressed doors. Boarding buses, by contrast, was regulated by conductors, automated doors not appearing on public central London services until 1965.[90] Automated doors induced further hurry by presenting a "beatable" target. Initially, the edges were sensitized with contact breakers, allowing passengers to cut the circuit of closing doors and force their way into cars, but this feature was soon removed, apparently because by encouraging hurry the system was causing the delays it was intended to resolve.[91]

The ferocious resurgence of competition between buses also caused impatience with the tube. Between late 1919 and mid-1924, total bus stock rocketed from 2,761, with a seating capacity of 93,000, to 4,790, with a seating capacity of 220,000, increases of 73 percent and 137 percent, respectively. Over the same period, annual bus traffic increased from 727 million to 1.34 billion, an 84 percent increase that nearly negated the capacity gains.[92] Within this growth in bus numbers the new player, the first of which began running in August 1922, was the independent, or "pirate," bus.[93] Although only a fraction of the total increase, independents offered alternative bus travel separate from the LGOC and in some cases altogether more frenetic.[94] Rather than carving out new routes, some independents tried to capture existing traffic by racing competitors or even changing direction if there was a larger line of passengers waiting on the other side of the road. Convenience and accessibility, not fares, were the competitive stakes; a contrast to the tube, it seemed, with its labyrinthine tunnels and synchronized denial of automated doors working on a timetabled service.[95] For Lord Ashfield, UERL general manager, the solution to passenger impatience was to provide express lines running parallel to regular stopping services. But their prohibitive cost meant that the only viable alternative was not to increase speed but to increase train capacity to reduce waiting in stations during rush hour.[96]

"RUSH HOUR" AND THE RISE
OF THE STRAPHANGER

Although the tube had always experienced daily rush periods, the coalescence of "rush hour" from 1919 shaped the particular form taken by tube car restructuring and contrasted it with the simultaneous restructuring of buses.[97] Between 1919 and 1920, trade union efforts won an eight-hour workday for seven million workers nationwide.[98] This reduced the preferred window of time for commuting and raised pressure on the tail end of "workmen's" tube trains, as Ashfield categorized trains predominantly taken by working-class men that offered reduced fares for early-morning travel. Although workmen's traffic constituted only 16 percent of total traffic in 1913, it was responsible for the dominant morning peak.[99] The standardization of the eight-hour day meant that the peak in workmen's traffic increasingly converged with the smaller peak in later traffic, compressing a greater number of people into a smaller time, worsened by the overall postwar increase in traffic.[100] Unlike the tube, buses in 1913 did not have workmen's fares. They consequently did not have comparable traffic peaks as the tube deprived them of a large share of traffic before 8:00 a.m. By contrast, Lord Ashfield pointed out that motor bus traffic "consists of traffic casually picked up all day long, so long as there is traffic in the streets. The motor buses are always reasonably full throughout the day."[101] When the consolidation of the eight-hour day pushed workmen's traffic into "ordinary" traffic, the tube therefore suffered a greater intensification of peak traffic than buses did, which likely fed into existing impatience particular to the intervals between tube trains. Rush hour overcrowding reduced the probability of catching the first train, making the interval between the one missed and the one anticipated seem increasingly critical.

As with the tube, the postwar increase in traffic necessitated restructuring bus space to increase capacity, but the greater daily fluctuation on the tube, and the particular impatience it caused, meant this occurred differently on each. Since 1906, a standard double-decked motorbus had carried only thirty-four seats, sixteen of which were longitudinal seats running along the lower deck. Because police regulations strictly limited bus dimensions, any increase in capacity had to be achieved through changing their layout rather than their size. In 1919, the development of wheel arches made it possible to lower the floor of the bottom deck, reducing the distance between it and the road and so, when combined with a reduction in the height of the bus, lowering the bus's center of gravity. This and improved suspension allowed buses to carry the weight of additional passengers. LGOC consequently replaced its longitudinal seats with transverse seats in sets of two facing the front of the bus, increasing lower deck capacity to twenty-two; it also increased upper deck seating, bringing total capacity to forty-six.

This restructuring set the pattern for enduring differences between bus and tube travel as bus passengers no longer sat in rows facing each other but on segregated seats facing forward. A mixture of longitudinal and transverse seating, roughly a two-to-one ratio, persisted on the tube. The removal of longitudinal seating on buses also reduced standing space; the new K-type bus accommodated at most ten standing passengers.[102] Partly this number reflected the police prohibition on standing, relaxed during the Great War, when five standing passengers were allowed, but reimposed shortly after.[103] Writing in 1920, Frank Pick, assistant managing director of UERL, hoped this restriction would soon be lifted.[104] However, it arguably fitted the growing functional differentiation of buses from tube trains resulting from the consolidation of rush hour: buses were not to absorb the daily peaks in traffic but to service the constant flow of casual, mainly short-distance traffic.

Tunnel dimensions, not police regulations, limited tube car size but similarly meant that capacity could only be increased by changing car layout. Unlike buses, though, there were no restrictions on standing. Besides, it was easier for more passengers to cram in if they were standing, making increasing standing space the best way to meet the greater quantity and fluctuation of tube traffic. Ashfield calculated that an arterial road with a maximum of 150 forty-six-seater buses running each direction per hour could carry 7,000 passengers. A tube line already managed 13,500 seated passengers per hour, but with the addition of only half of its estimated standing capacity, this ridership increased to 20,000.[105] While buses maximized capacity by increasing seating, the growing functional difference of the tube, occasioned by rush hour, meant that capacity increases were expressed as much through standing space as seating. Although the Central Line introduced the first grab straps for standing passengers in 1900, straphanging became more of a phenomenon in the interwar period because the increasingly distinct roles that buses and tube trains played were also increasingly materially expressed: seats on buses; standing space in tube cars. So emblematic of ordinary life was straphanging by the 1920s, especially on the tube, that Arnold Palmer used it to title his work on the lives of Londoners defined by their "ordinariness" and whom one might encounter, swaying "like marine vegetation," in the same tube car.[106]

If impatience with the tube depended on its contrast with buses, how were the tube's structural solutions to this impatience and the personal space that resulted also different? The experience of twenty-two-year-old Ann Pilcher is an example. Pilcher commuted daily from a boardinghouse on Gloucester Road to her work as a secretary at St. Thomas's Hospital, Westminster, in spring 1957, and recounted the following episodes:

> About February of this year I first became aware of a man who later attracted my attention a number of times. [. . .] We were both standing. At first we were apart but later, as people moved about, he came close to me. He leered and half smiled at me but I took no notice. He didn't speak to me on that occasion or touch me but about three days later he was again on the same train as me and he then said, "Good morning to me" [sic]. I didn't speak.
>
> He made no further effort to engage me in conversation but continued to stare and smile at me. I saw this man three or four times more in the mornings but he made no further approach to me.[107]

The option and, as here, increasing necessity to stand on the tube during rush hour configured passengers in a different way from buses. Not only could the man in this incident move to join Pilcher, he could also press closer than if they were seated, making it harder to avoid eye contact. The freer movement of standing passengers required them tacitly to formulate a concept of personal space in a way that bus seating did not.

In part, the fact that all tube seats faced each other whereas all bus seats faced forward supported this tacit formation of personal space on tube trains, but in a way different from straphanging. Late one evening in June 1957, twenty-year-old Patricia Miatt, also a secretary, was traveling home from the West End. She sat "on the inside seat of the type that face each other" and found herself opposite a young man "with very dark blue 'staring' eyes." The man struck up conversation about the book Miatt was reading, but she gave terse, noncommittal responses. She continued reading but was nervously aware of the man watching her in the window reflection.[108] Oppositional seating made avoiding eye contact just as hard as standing did and so similarly compelled passengers to tacitly agree on personal space. But though Miatt's experience was similarly awkward to Pilcher's, the latter's was less determinate, less predictable, because the space she occupied was less demarcated. Regardless of its orientation, seating delimited physical and social boundaries for touch in ways absent from standing space, which is perhaps why Miatt, albeit reluctantly, responded to conversation whereas Pilcher did not.

Pilcher's and Miatt's experiences reflected the spatial differences between straphanging and sitting. Yet experiences of personal space were also shaped by power inequalities conditioning one's relationships with others—in these examples, being young, lower-middle-class women traveling alone. Differences of gender, age, class, and race conditioned both the likelihood of discomforting close encounters and the experience of discomfort itself. Miatt's youth and gender emboldened a male passenger about her age to speak to her as well as accounting for her bodily unease at his reflected gaze. Crucially, though, Miatt's experience of autonomy and vulnerability was specific to the particularity of this interaction. Power inequalities shaped others' response to Miatt's body, in turn conditioning her bodily response to others—her experience *as* a body-in-the-world—but this experience cohered only through the concrete circumstances of each encounter.[109] Window reflections, traveling after 10:00 p.m., and the absence of other passengers all conditioned Miatt's sense of being a body at once autonomous and vulnerable to another. That both Pilcher and Miatt reported their experiences, in the context of widespread underreporting, suggests how marked their sense of personal space and, implicitly, the question of consent was on these occasions.

For standing male passengers, too, the indeterminate space between themselves and others also compelled an improvised response, although a different configuration of power mediated this in other ways. Vigilance could displace violation as the embodied response. Passenger vigilance revealed the assumption of common rules for personal space but admitted the indeterminacy of those rules and the need to enforce them. At almost the same time that Lubienska was murdered, Frederick Ayres caught a Piccadilly Line train from Knightsbridge Station. The train was crowded, and Ayres stood in the doorway. Just before the train departed, a "very agitated" man leaped in next to Ayres: he appeared to be "a nasty character in spite of the fact that he was very well dressed." Because of this, Ayres thought to himself, "I will keep an eye on you in case you start something." The man "kept looking round at everybody in the train as though he was looking for somebody or somebody was looking for him," and so Ayres "was determined at all costs to be ready for him."[110] Aware of a set, collective understanding of personal space, Ayres was equally aware that open tube car space was unpredictable and might require an improvised response. Rather than defending an already existing concept of personal space, Ayres brought that concept into being *through* a practice that was just as contingent; one that emerged as it became easier to move around tube cars and that reified and risked itself every time it was enacted.

Open space heightened the dialectic between tacit norms of personal space and explicit improvisations, such as reprimanding passengers, when these collapsed. It is not just that norms and improvisations were conditions for each other but that the particular *indeterminacy* of open cars demanded determination of personal space yet became, through that attempt, inde-terminable. Passengers therefore had to improvise. "With elbows wedged into your ribs, and strange hot breaths pouring down your neck," wrote the author Thomas Burke in 1919, "you need all the serenity you have stored against such contingencies; and the attitude of the other people about you can mitigate your distress or enhance it."[111] If the tube represented "moder-nity," this was a condition of an ongoing making and remaking of subjective boundaries in conditions of intrinsic *in*-determinability, not the final estab-lishment and defense of those boundaries.

QUEER SPACES

While Mary Eastwood rode the tube one Friday evening in 1957, she noticed a man "wearing a vivid yellow sweater with coloured stripes running diag-onally across it." She confessed, "He was the type of person I hoped would not get off the train at the same time as myself."[112] Her concerns hint at the difference between tube cars and platforms as social spaces. As sites of inter-change, platforms expressed a liminality different from cars. Passengers' presence on platforms was conditioned only by the interval between trains, whereas their presence in cars was of unpredictable duration, although potentially equally transitory. While it compelled improvisation, the inti-macy of cars was as much a benefit as a threat to vulnerable passengers compared to the expanse of stations. Without the constant presence of other passengers, stations offered more possibilities and risks to the socially marginal to suspend the very conditions under which their marginality materialized: to "queer."

I do not mean *queer* as an identity defined by same-sex desire, or by its opposition to the norm. I mean instead a temporally and spatially specific position *outside*, or in relation to, a sexual or social identity, and the way in which this position occurred through particular bodily encounters. Queer entailed a relation to the conditions of possibility under which distinctions of social or sexual difference were determined.[113] As Pilcher's and Miatt's unsettling experiences indicate, social and sexual differences shape and cohere through how bodies inhabit space with one another. How one is corporeally responded to and feels capable of responding in a given space both reflects and materializes perceived differences of race, gender, and sexuality.[114] The recognition of oneself *as* a Black elevator attendant or a woman traveling alone: these are lived experiences that cohere through how much one feels at home in particular spaces. Queerness can name that experience of being at odds with what one's social and physical environment affords. It is the experience of being "out of place" in an unaccommodating environment; a corporeal unease that reifies one's social and sexual difference from those for whom the space provides.[115]

And yet, when read in relation to the liminality of tube stations, queerness might instead mean a *disruption* of this process. In this context, queerness occurs when bodily encounters, and the categories of difference they cohere, are underdetermined by the spaces in which they take place. This is not an experience of being "out of place" but *in between* the spaces in which bodily experience expresses and materializes difference. Such an experience was particularly true of tube stations, whose streamlining—for example, through escalators or the cavernous "ambulatory" booking hall opened at Piccadilly Circus in 1928—accentuated their function as in-between spaces to traverse as quickly as possible.[116] The liminality of tube stations offered possibilities for encounters in between the times and spaces in which identity distinctions of normality and difference cohered. That is, the "transitive" aspect of queer—its relationship *to* or *across* identity categories—intersected with the transitory quality of station space.[117]

This social and sexual liminality applied to men seeking sex with men. As popular meeting places, central London's tube stations offered opportunities to be at once inconspicuous and visible to those who knew how to look. Few people in the stations remained long enough to notice the loiterer, and those who did might assume innumerable reasons for their presence.[118] After a month grubbing up potatoes in Jersey, twenty-seven-year-old Michael Griffin was newly returned to London and in between jobs in spring 1957. Around the time Lubienska left the party in Ealing Common, Griffin arrived at Piccadilly Circus Station, where he hoped to come across a man named Mark O'Malley. Griffin had met O'Malley before at the tube station, which the latter often frequented after his Friday and Saturday evening rounds of Piccadilly's pubs. On this occasion, Griffin returned to the station three times in forty-five minutes before he met O'Malley around 10:30 p.m. and was, after saying he had nowhere to sleep, invited to stay the night at O'Malley's house in Putney.[119]

Accounts differed, however, when Mark O'Mahony—not O'Malley—was interviewed the same day at a different police station. O'Mahony said he had known Griffin for six months rather than the nine the latter claimed and to have met him at Piccadilly Circus Station at 1:00 p.m. that day, rather than 10:30 p.m. But he confirmed that Griffin had stayed the night on May 24 and that they had several times met before at Piccadilly Circus Station, though "not by arrangement."[120] Griffin's and O'Mahony's imprecisions indicated the contours of their relationship and the importance of the tube station for maintaining its indeterminacy. The mistaken names, nighttime meetings, and shared night at O'Mahony's house—despite, Griffin's statement revealed, already having somewhere to stay—all suggested a fleeting sexual relationship. Yet its origins and continuation in Piccadilly Circus Station, where the constant flow of evening traffic meant Griffin's repeat visits went unnoticed and where both could meet unarranged, prevented its determination, by themselves or others, as anything more than friendly. Station space afforded ephemeral encounters outside the spaces and patterns of sociability in which same-sex relations cohered as "homosexual." This ephemerality was especially significant in the concluding months of the Wolfenden Committee, which in September 1957 recommended the decriminalization of sex between consenting men in private on the basis of evidence that discursively cohered the "homosexual" through the exclusion of other, "unrespectable," public sexual practices.[121] Griffin would stay at O'Mahony's again, on May 31, the same day he began work as a kitchen hand at the Spanish restaurant Martinez. Martinez was on Swallow Street, five minutes' walk from O'Mahony's office at Bryce Hanmer & Co. accountancy and less than five from Piccadilly Circus Station.[122]

The queerness of tube stations, however, applied not only to men seeking sex with men but to all encounters in which spatial and social liminality

intersected: encounters in which the "in-betweenness" of escalators or platforms briefly, unevenly, fragilely enabled bodily responses different from
those which reminded passengers "who" they were. Such was the case for
the racial as well as sexual dimensions of chance pickups. Take Frederick
Williams, a West African student, whose encounter with a flirtatious white
woman in Gloucester Road station on the night of the murder offered queer-
ing possibilities and limitations. Williams was leaving a platform when a
young white woman with a non-English accent approached him, asked for
a light, and began playing with his jacket lapels. She chatted up Williams
and then jotted down her number and said she would like to hear from him
again.[123] Williams, like other West African migrants, would have been used to
a different response, one in which the bodily attitude of white others reified
him as Black and compelled him to see himself, as if at one remove, in these
terms. In this logic, which philosopher Franz Fanon argued in 1952 structured
potentially every encounter experienced by Black people in the metropole,
the irreconcilable difference between how one felt and how one's body was
externally perceived resulted in a "corporeal malediction."[124] Race was an
experience of being out of place.

In Gloucester Road Station, however, the platform's liminality briefly
afforded Williams a social liminality temporally and spatially in between
the conditions under which his Blackness cohered as difference. On a nearly
deserted platform at past 10:00 p.m., it was possible for Williams to imagine
himself in a different interaction from those which circularly assumed and
reified racial difference—although this possibility was interrupted when the
mortally wounded Lubienska staggered through a passage from the adjoining platform.[125] The liminality of platforms, at once spaces of anonymous
rush and eerie quietness, temporarily disturbed the way in which bodily
encounters reified categories of social and sexual identity. In other words,
they queered.

Yet there were limitations to how station space disturbed identity
categories as well as to our knowledge of this. The liminality of platforms
varied temporally and between stations: crowds gathered; others lingered
unexpectedly. The social and sexual liminality afforded by platforms is here
only known through police records, which, to varying degrees, retrospectively erased it. Three times Williams sought the woman at various Lyons tea
shops, where she had said she worked, but to no avail. He tried her number
from multiple exchanges. Yet he also claimed to have resisted her initial
advances, trying only to escape.[126] Partly retrospective justification of contact
with a woman he now suspected of murder, the contradiction also shows

how Williams's experience was transfigured through the conditions of its retelling. Williams's account was structured more by his encounter with the detective inspector recording it in a room at Kensington Police Station than by that which it described. Any experience of being in between spaces where race materialized was obscured by its retelling in a space that unequivocally structured and was structured by racial difference. This reinscription of social or sexual difference was even more obvious in the case of Michael Griffin, on whose statement a police officer had scribbled, in both recognition and erasure of ambiguity, that Griffin was a "homo-sexual."[127]

The inconsistencies in Williams's account reveal what divided midcentury tube cars and platforms as social spaces. Whereas passengers traversed the fixed space of platforms, they were fixed within the moving space of cars. The open-plan space of 1950s tube cars demanded the fixing of personal space but also, because of its indeterminacy, precluded it and necessitated improvisation. But because tube cars were *confined* and more consistently occupied, rather than traversed, passenger cooperation made it possible, if not certain, for improvisation to redetermine personal space. This temporary determination of personal space was also one of differences between bodies spaced from one another. Class, gender, racial, and other distinctions materialized in and through how passengers sat or stood in relation to one another, and how they experienced this corporeally. By contrast, the traversed space of tube stations—equally indeterminate—had fewer tacit rules of tactility and fewer consistently present passengers with which to improvise them. Here, tactile relations between passengers might remain underdetermined, and with them the social or sexual categories they shaped and were shaped by—although by how much is difficult to say. This was a space disturbed by constant movement and constitutive of social relations that disturbed.

What unites the queerness of tube stations and personal space in tube cars is the contingency of these as explanatory categories themselves. "Queer" relations or "having" personal space depended on particular bodily interactions, themselves shaping and shaped by the material transformation of the tube: they depended on the particular *use* of tube space at particular times in its development. Examining this interaction therefore destabilizes narratives treating categories of queerness and personal space as historical or analytic givens.[128] The queerness of Frederick Williams's encounter with an unknown woman was at once particular to the space of Gloucester Road station in 1957 *and* called into question the stability of "queer" as a transhistorical analytic category. If tube stations disturbed social relations, they also disturb our own categories for explaining the passenger interactions occurring within them, and on the tube as a whole.

CONCLUSION

We do have one piece of evidence for Lubienska's practice of personal space on the tube: the statement of her companion, the priest Kazimerz Krzyzanowski. When they entered Ealing Common Station, Krzyzanowski recalled, they "walked twelve paces from the staircase on the East Bound side and entered a smoking carriage at that point. We sat on a seat which ran across the train, on the offside [. . .]. The Countess sat by the window and I was at her side." There were other passengers in the tube car, but Krzyzanowski disregarded them as he was immersed in conversation with Lubienska. He did, however, recall that they were quiet. Upon arriving at Earl's Court, he alighted from the same side on which he had been sitting, and "had to walk about twelve yards towards the front of the train to a lift."[129] Through this recollection Krzyzanowski reenacted a whole commerce between his mind, his postural disposition, and his relation to other bodies. He reenacted a finely calibrated relation between the arrangement of his limbs and the arrangement between himself and others that it effected. This was a transaction contingent on the particular instance in which it was enacted but, more important, on the *confined indeterminacy* of the 1950s tube car. Seemingly pregiven, this practice of personal space emerged as cause and effect of a series of transformations in the experience of tube travel, from automatic doors to the intensification of hurry.

Tracing the historical contingency of personal space calls into question accounts of modernity as a dialectic of intimacy and anomie for individuated bodies already "possessing" it. Personal space was not owned but practiced, not constant but specific, in turn reshaping the delineation of the body itself in its relation to other bodies. This is not to say that the emergence of personal space on the tube enacted a new relation "between" inner and outer self and between self and other, as if these were stable binaries. Instead, it *produced* these binaries and, because it was practiced in an indeterminate space, produced them *differently* on every occasion.[130] This story compels a reassessment of governmentality narratives that assume the stabilization of these binaries by the 1920s.[131] If the tube produced neither stably individuated subjects nor a stable relation between inner and outer that encouraged those subjects to self-regulate, then it was not a space through which citizens were governed to govern themselves. It did not manage, or even produce, the relation between a passenger's thought and embodied experience required to create the self-governing liberal subject. It could not, in short, reduce the biological life of its passengers to a political effect; the "politicization of bare life" that philosopher Giorgio Agamben argues underlies modern liberal democracies as much as dictatorships.[132] In narrating this ostensible history, historians of governmentality unwittingly reproduce it, denying the possibility for past or future forms of existence outside those circumscribed by the liberal state. Historicizing the conceptual and practical coevolution of personal space and how it mediated the relation between subjectivity and the state points us away from this spiral, toward histories containing the possibility for their own, different futures.

CHAPTER FOUR

Tea Shop Touch and Global Capitalism

At midday in early August 1929, Thelma Rogers went out for lunch. It was still a little early to eat, and so upon entering the first-floor dining room of 233 Oxford Street, an Aerated Bread Company (A.B.C.) tea shop, she found herself alone in a sea of tables. Locating an inconspicuous seat near the entrance, she began reading the menu. Shortly afterward, a scruffy clergyman entered and, disregarding the other forty-nine empty tables, settled upon hers. Apparently oblivious to any faux pas, he could not resist offering an opinion on Rogers's order—stewed oxtail: "Oh, I should not have that; you do not know what they put in it. I should have a cut off the joint." After quarter of an hour, the clergyman found a new target for his uninvited solicitude. He called the waitress Phyllis Holt away from a newly arrived customer she was serving and asked whether she would meet him at Oxford Circus tube station after she finished her shift. Holt refused; this was not the first time he had invited her out. Soon after she started working at No. 233, the clergyman had offered her two theater tickets and asked, when she mentioned going with another waitress, whether he might accompany her instead. On that earlier occasion, Holt laughed and did not reply; the second time, the clergyman put only one ticket under his plate when he left.[1]

The attention given to A.B.C. waitresses by Reverend Harold Davidson, later known commonly in the press as Rector of Stiffkey, was nothing new. On September 22, 1888, A.B.C. waitress Alice Farrell charged twenty-five-year-old George Hawkes with forcibly kissing her in a train carriage the previous evening. Farrell admitted knowing Hawkes as a regular at the tea shop where she worked but denied having encouraged his attention by serving him before other customers. The case was swiftly dispatched, with Hawkes sentenced to a five-pound fine or ten days' hard labor.[2] Davidson's treatment of waitresses was in some ways similar to such cases. But whereas Farrell's case occupied only a few paragraphs in the next day's papers, in spring 1932 Davidson's played out over a highly publicized, twenty-four-day consistory court trial in the Great Hall of Church House, Westminster. The bishop of Norwich, to whose diocese Davidson belonged, charged him with five counts of "immoral conduct" under the 1892 Clergy Discipline Act; even before the trial Davidson became a press sensation.[3] The final verdict came on July 8, 1932, when Chancellor of Norwich Frederick Keppel North found Davidson guilty of all charges: subsequently he was deprived of his living, was deposed from holy orders, and spent the remaining five years of his life protesting his innocence through ever-more-scandalous methods on Blackpool Beach.[4]

What might explain the difference in attention devoted to Davidson? Davidson's case was in some respects more serious. He was a married rector, and although four of his alleged offenses were similar to that committed by Hawkes, such as kissing and caressing seventeen-year-old Barbara Harris in Wah Yeng Chinese restaurant, Bloomsbury, he was also accused of attempted sex with the prostitute Rose Ellis. But more significant was the ambiguous entanglement of desire and empathy apparently motivating Davidson. At the same lunch that Davidson sought an evening with waitress Holt, Thelma Rogers recalled, he also "ran after" the tea shop's assistant manager "caught hold of her arm and started to speak to her."[5] According to Davidson, assistant manager Williams had "rather a 'down' on some of the girls"; there were a few that "she did not seem to understand, and I was giving her a little advice as to how to handle them."[6] That the prosecution did not call Williams to dispute this claim was telling. For lead prosecutor Roland Oliver, it was this confusion of intention that presented "the great issue" of the case: "Was his association with these young women [. . .] an association in which he was seeking to rescue them from a life of sin [. . .], or was it an association for his own self-indulgence?"[7] Why, Oliver asked, would rescue work be necessary for "perfectly respectable women in perfectly respectable employment"?[8]

This chapter takes Oliver's question as a starting point for exploring the broader relation between capital, labor, and desire as it was tactilely enacted in the London tea shop. The association between rescue work and desire, and contemporary anxiety over their entanglement, has been well elaborated for late nineteenth-century London, especially around the discourse of "slumming."[9] As Roland Oliver's rhetoric implied, by the 1930s it was possible to suggest that rescue work, at least by lone middle-class men, had been consigned to less compromised domains as charity institutionalized, the Metropolitan Police tasked women police with protecting women and children, and precariously employed laborers unionized.[10] Historians have argued that tea shops were important for women customers as refuges where they could dine with male company or alone without being harassed.[11] By the 1930s, palatial Lyons "Corner Houses" offered spaces of democratic heterosociability where customers of both genders and all classes could mix with, apparently, less sexual threat.[12] But Davidson's case, and Thelma Rogers's evidence, hints at a different story. It suggests an accentuated relation between the increasingly alienated labor of tea shop waitresses and an ambiguous, empathetic desire on the part of tea shop customers: an entwined history of labor and desire expressing global shifts in capital and commodity flows in a new era of mass consumption. Charting this entwined history emphasizes the historically and spatially specific causes, harms, and meanings of unwanted touch and, given its current persistence, the possibility for a different future.

Tea shops were one example of the new era of mass consumption. First appearing in the 1860s, they rapidly became ubiquitous in central London, particularly as the West End developed into a hub for shopping, night-time entertainment, and, in adjacent districts, office work. As the London Underground spread outward and suburban commuting became an increasing possibility, tea shops accommodated a fluctuating daytime and night-time population looking to refuel somewhere accessible, not unpleasant, and cheap.[13] The proliferation of tea shops was also sustained by a growing national habit of tea drinking, which cut across all classes and cohered further in the first quarter of the twentieth century.[14] By 1931, per capita adult consumption of tea in the United Kingdom had reached 11.24 pounds, an increase of 51 percent since 1901.[15] While much of this tea was consumed at home, it was partially accounted for by the emerging "iniquitous habit" of office workers going out for a coffee—but above all tea—at eleven o'clock in the morning and four in the afternoon.[16]

The increasing consumption of tea was made possible by an explosion in production, and a shift, beginning in the 1860s, away from Chinese producers and toward plantations in colonial Assam (in India) and Ceylon (present-day Sri Lanka). Between 1859 and 1900, Indian tea production increased from almost nothing to 220 million pounds, while Chinese tea exports to England fell from 70 million pounds to only 15 million pounds. Indian tea plantations increased production through mechanized processing and indentured labor, the majority of which consisted of women and children.[17] Consequently, the economic fortunes of tea shops—and the conditions of waitresses working in them—were shaped not only by the rising consumption of tea but also by changing capital flows and labor conditions of plantations in India.

Although tea shops depended on much more than tea sales, their profits were nevertheless affected by shifts in Indian tea production, which shaped the wages, working conditions, and bodily labor of tea shop waitresses. The labor of indentured, predominantly women and child, tea pickers and tea shop waitresses was intimately connected, and, combined with other economic factors, shaped the forms taken by touch and desire in early twentieth-century tea shops.[18] Touch in tea shops therefore reflected, and serves as a prism for examining, global shifts in consumer tastes, capital flows, and gendered labor conditions: for providing, in Koven's words, an "intimate history of capitalism."[19] Touch becomes, in short, both a topic and an optic for examining the connected histories of labor and capital in Britain and colonial India.

At the same time, the history of touch in tea shops is also one of the changing capitalist conditions of desire and vulnerability. Feminist historians of labor and consumption have long traced how the development of new work opportunities, commercial leisure spaces, and means of public transport in the late nineteenth century provided women of all classes with more access to the public sphere while increasing the real and perceived sexual risks associated with it. In the 1880s, Walkowitz argues, the rising public presence of women shoppers, workers, and philanthropists, among others, disrupted imagined "spatial boundaries" between the East and West End and public and private that formerly maintained class and gender distinctions.[20] These women claimed for themselves the role of urban spectators, formerly dominated by men, and became part of the urban spectacle.[21] While some commentators sought to manage this relationship, and the disruption it caused, with narratives of "sexual danger," others emphasized the freedom and safety of (predominantly middle-class) women in public.[22]

Narratives about the sexual dangers and possibilities experienced by women in public especially focused on women service workers. As Rappaport, Sanders, and others show, novels, newspapers, and musical comedies represented commercial leisure spaces as sites where class and gender inequality, the ambiguous spatial demarcation of work, and precarious employment compelled women workers to flirt with male customers and employers, as well as combat unwanted touch.[23] Of particular concern were department store assistants, or "shopgirls," and barmaids. While musical comedies portrayed flirtation as all part of the shopgirl's performance and the first step in a successful marriage plot, romantic novels highlighted their vulnerability to harassment—even while still presenting marriage as the only "escape."[24] Representations of barmaids and their customers depicted them as amorously teasing one another while containing the performance through the physical separation of the bar; a managed intimacy through which "touch took on a new expressive charge."[25] Together, these discourses represented women service workers in the late nineteenth century as potential consumers and objects to be consumed, and as managing a difficult bodily performance of desirability and distance from the customers they served.

As ostensibly better-paid and, at the chain Lyons, banned from accepting tips, tea shop waitresses of the 1920s fitted less clearly within this narrative of economic and sexual risk. Walkowitz has examined how, starting in the mid-1920s, Lyons expected its waitresses to embody a model of demure English femininity while managing relations between the diverse social groups visiting its tea shops, from Jewish couples to queer men. The self-disciplining of waitresses' bodies was intended to ensure that of Lyons's customers in a socially heterogeneous space.[26] Walkowitz places the competing "social performances" of Lyons waitresses and customers within a wider cultural change in early twentieth-century London to which women were central: a consumerist cosmopolitanism which encouraged "expressive bodily practices" for some and new regimes of "strict bodily management" for others.[27] This was not London of the 1880s, with its sharply contrasting narratives of sexual danger and self-determination, but one in which cosmopolitan spaces such as tea shops, dance halls, and nightclubs enabled social and sexual transgression—albeit managed by the "glamorized service worker."[28]

This chapter builds on these histories but directs attention away from spectacle and social performance and toward bodily interactions themselves: to what relations between actual, situated bodies *did* to condition what individuals desired, and how they experienced the touch of others—touch that was unwanted, violent, and, because shockingly normalized, often unrecoverable by historians.[29] In part this is an attempt, following Bourke, Beecher, and Wright, to more fully historicize the perpetrators of sexual violence.[30] Existing histories of women service workers highlight how harassment was enabled and encouraged by conditions of class and gender inequality and notions of masculinity—by power. Focusing on bodily relations between waitresses and customers examines how desire itself—the desire to touch inappropriately—was also historical: it was produced through embodied, situated interactions with others.[31] This does not relieve perpetrators of their responsibility but emphasizes, once again, the persistence and pervasiveness, rather than exceptionality, of sexual violence.[32] While Davidson's defenders claimed he was an "eccentric" with "nervous hands," he and similar others were neither unusual nor unresponsible but both agents and effects of the spatial and temporal ordering of bodies and their interrelations under capitalism.[33] For this reason, this chapter especially traces the changing layout and rhythms of tea shops from the 1860s to the 1930s and the specific interactions, and subjectivities, these produced.

At the same time, focusing on embodied interactions in tea shops builds on recent attempts to particularize the experience and concepts of vulnerability and consent. Because historically, as now, the majority of cases of harassment went unreported, historians of women's expanding public role during this period have focused on competing narratives of sexual threat and possibility—from the "feminist melodrama of sexual danger" to the "glamorized tale of the sexually available working girl."[34] This reveals new narratives of autonomy among some, principally middle-class, women (and men). But it makes it hard to see beyond historical discourses that homogenized and fixed women's experience, divided it into a binary of passive victimhood and sexual agency, and could be paternalistic or overstate autonomy, often in the self-interest of "male pests."[35] Feminist phenomenology provides an alternative approach by focusing on the biographical, spatial, and historical specificity of vulnerability itself.[36] Central to this approach is the argument that subjectivity is always embodied, and derived from embodied relations with others. How an individual experiences and conceives of their body is conditioned by concrete, embodied interactions with others, themselves shaped by class, gender, race, and other differences.[37] Autonomy is not a given but rather a unique effect of relations with others, and so too are the experience of vulnerability and perceived possibility to consent.[38] This is what made the vulnerability of tea shop waitresses, specific to each encounter, also different from that of shopgirls or barmaids. Whereas the latter were mostly confined behind the counter or bar, the former moved between tables, making it easier to escape unwanted attention and harder to avoid touch when close. "Terror is always local," writes Joanna Bourke of sexual violence, and histories must pay attention to these spatial and individual differences.[39]

Tracing the long history of embodied interactions in tea shops enables a history of harassment but also that of the spatially specific, socially differentiated experience of being a violable body and of being able, therefore, to articulate this experience. The trial of Harold Davidson—nearly two thousand pages of court testimony including accounts of tea shop encounters that were at once violent, quotidian, and underreported—offers a rare chance to historicize this experience and its conception by working women such as Phyllis Holt.

PRECARIOUS LIFE

In November 1894 Davidson was walking along Thames Embankment one particularly foggy night. As he passed Charing Cross tube station, he noticed a girl attempting to throw herself off the parapet into the river below. The girl, he related forty years later, was sixteen years old. She had run away from her home in a village near Cambridge ten days previously, chanced her luck in London, and, having failed to find work, decided to jump. Davidson clambered after her and, once she was consoled, sent her back to her mother with a letter; it was from this moment, he alleged, that he began taking an interest in helping vulnerable young women in dire straits.[40]

The girl, if Davidson's story was true, was unlucky but not uncommon. She was one of many drawn to London in the 1890s seeking work in the expanding service and white-collar sectors.[41] One of the places to which she might have applied for work was the A.B.C., which opened its first tea shop in 1864 and by 1893 operated seventy across London. Capitalizing on custom provided by the growing army of West End shoppers and clerks, the A.B.C. offered cheap fare in an unfussy atmosphere. Prior to the A.B.C., women caught in central London at lunchtime had little option but to provide for themselves or venture into the dark backroom of a "pastrycook's shop" or the overwhelmingly male preserve of London's coffee shops.[42] Whiteley's and Debenham and Freebody's department stores featured rooms "where women could lunch," but with their focus on "hot joints and poultry," these options were beyond the means of lower middle-class workers; the high prices and social graces of posh tearooms such as the Ladies' Tea Association were similarly prohibitive.[43] Tea shops, by contrast, offered both a new employment prospect and a welcome lunchtime escape for women workers—as well as refuge from London's stifling fogs of the 1890s. "How crisp and fresh were the plates of tongue," wrote novelist Shaw Desmond, "when the incandescents went up in the winter evenings with the yellow fog clammy on the panes!"[44] Focusing on customer turnover rather than comfort, tea shops were "a godsend for the impecunious," even if some customers found the whole experience rather harrying.[45] For *Hearth and Home* columnist Talbot Coke, the "rush and push of an ordinary tea-shop with its American cloth-covered tables, sawdusted floor, 'ready made' tea, and overworked, 'snappy' attendants" was a world away from the ideal tearoom.[46]

If tea shop waitresses were snappy, they had reason to be. In the 1890s, A.B.C. waitresses earned between eight and ten shillings for a fifty- to sixty-hour week. The diligent became counter assistants or managers; most did

FIGURE 15 Aerated Bread Company (A.B.C.) tea shop, 32 King Street, City of London, 1912. King Street lies in the center of the City, directly south of Guildhall. Although this tea shop advertises a "ladies room" in gilt lettering on the window, the photograph suggests this remained a tenuous enclave in the male-dominated City; six men and boys loiter outside while a seventh observes from a window above. SC/PHL/01/013/79/5060.
© London Metropolitan Archives, City of London

not.[47] In the same decade, a road ganger in Hackney, by contrast, earned twenty-eight shillings a week working considerably shorter hours.[48] The A.B.C. justified low wages by pointing out that they were only intended to "supplement" the support waitresses received from their families. It required its waitresses to live with relatives, a condition enforced by the company's own "lady visitors."[49] Backed by the certificated approval of a clergyman, this condition was ostensibly to guarantee a waitress's respectability— particularly important during anxiety over the "new girl" of the 1890s.[50] As Assistant Commissioner Eliza Orme reasoned for the 1893 Royal Commission on Labour, there was "great risk" for women serving a mixed clientele during the day and living alone in common lodging houses at night.[51] Yet over the 1890s, this justification seemed increasingly hollow as the A.B.C.'s profits grew while wages remained below subsistence level. The combined effects of expanding white-collar work and agricultural depression meant that by 1895, A.B.C. shareholders could vote themselves an enormous 28 percent dividend; wages remained static.[52]

This disparity between wages and dividends ignited small but persistent dissent among A.B.C. shareholders. At every annual shareholders' meeting between 1891 and 1893, shareholder Sidney Thomson called for an increase in waitresses' wages reflecting the A.B.C.'s growing profits, but each time he was silenced.[53] At a particularly raucous meeting in November 1892, Thomson pointedly drew attention to "those members of the Christian Church" seated before him who determinedly resisted waitress wage increases. "Don't talk such rubbish," rejoined an excited Reverend A. Pitt. "I live among the poor and know their wants, and I do all I can to relieve them, and would assist these young women if I thought they were badly paid, but I don't."[54] These comments earned Pitt strong censure in the liberal press; a stark contrast to the tabloid treatment of Harold Davidson forty years later, whose claim that he had been assisting underpaid waitresses was regarded with skepticism. By November 1891 the *Woman's Herald* and the *Star* had taken up the waitresses' cause. Three years after championing the 1888 strike of match girls at Bryant & May's match factory in Bow, the *Star* opened its columns to readers voicing their dismay at the treatment of A.B.C. waitresses and calling for a boycott of all A.B.C. tea shops until wages increased.[55] A flurry of letters provided updates of individual boycotts, suggestions for tea shop cooperatives, and even more scandalous details of waitresses' working conditions.[56]

The A.B.C. response failed to address the underlying problem, as the *Pall Mall Gazette* understood it, that it expected from its waitresses "a maximum of respectability" with "a minimum of remuneration."[57] When shareholder Dr. Furnivall suggested at the 1895 shareholders' meeting that the A.B.C. provide its waitresses with one free daily meal, deputy chairman B. W. Richardson replied that they were already able to buy hot meals for "a small charge."[58] This comment referred to a cooperative system of buying meals introduced shortly after the papers began expressing concern over waitresses' wages.

Under this scheme, managers bought ingredients from a common fund contributed to by participants. Tea shop cooks made a hot meal that waitresses ate together between 11:00 a.m. and noon. Much vaunted by Eliza Orme, the scheme likely caused resentment among waitresses wanting higher wages rather than added expenses. Each meal cost on average 3½ pence; at 1 shilling and 9 pence per six-day week, that was a significant deduction from a total weekly wage of 8 to 10 shillings.[59] Although the scheme seems to have been voluntary, the common mealtime may have placed uncomfortable pressure on waitresses for whom wages did not merely "supplement" existing income.

The A.B.C. was not the only tea shop chain that became a contested site for women's labor relations in the 1890s. Its younger competitor Lyons faced equivalent difficulties, this time forced into view by waitresses themselves. Lyons opened its first tea shop at 213 Piccadilly in September 1894, and by the end of 1895, there were a further twelve. With a hint of retrospective mythification, Nell Bacon, one of the first waitresses at No. 213, recalled that early Lyons waitresses worked seventy-four hours a week "and thought nothing of it."[60] It seems more likely that these long hours were encouraged by Lyons's payment method rather than any thoughtless self-sacrifice on the part of waitresses. Rather than receiving a basic wage, waitresses received 5 percent commission per sale, any additional income derived from tips. Although this resulted in higher weekly earnings than A.B.C. waitresses, Lyons waitresses—who, significantly, were not required to live with relatives—suffered more deductions for expenses. Of an average weekly income of fourteen shillings, an estimated eleven shillings and one pence went to rent, bus fares, fines for breakages, the washing of caps and aprons, and a weekly deduction to pay for uniforms. Lyons waitresses, unless supported by relatives, therefore had a razor-thin margin of around two shillings and eleven pence per week to buy food and maintain "respectability."[61]

When in late October 1895 rumors spread that new waitresses would be paid only 2.5 percent commission, Lyons's waitresses were unsurprisingly horrified. On October 23, waitresses of the Strand and Piccadilly tea shops walked out, gathering in St. Andrew's Restaurant at 81 Bride Street to draft their demands. Tom Mann, renowned leader of the 1889 London dockers' strike, also attended.[62] Mann's presence gave the waitresses' strike added political significance. Since the strikes of the dockers and the Bryant & May "match girls" the year before, a wave of "New Unionism" had swept the country.[63] Excluded from the unions of higher-skilled fellow laborers, unskilled laborers increasingly organized their own unions to press their demands and coordinate strikes. By May 1891, New Unionism had gained enough momentum to precipitate the appointment of a Royal Commission on Labour, of which Tom Mann was a member.[64] Just a year before the Lyons waitresses' strike, Mann signed the minority report condemning the commission's "scanty reforms," implicitly referencing Eliza Orme's evidence by calling attention to the long hours and low wages of many women workers and their limited union representation.[65] He was, therefore, well placed to advise the waitresses on their next move, his presence adding weight to the comparisons made between the conditions of dockers and waitresses during the first press campaign against the A.B.C. in 1891.[66]

For their part, the waitresses were reluctant to ally their cause with broader union activity and rejected calls to join with the Women's Trade Union League.[67] Instead they followed Mann's advice to ask Lyons director Isidore Salmon to receive a deputation outlining their complaint.[68] Salmon, however, demanded that each waitress apply for individual hearings. On October 24, the waitresses therefore met again at St. Andrew's Restaurant where, under the presidency of New Zealand–famed trade unionist William Belcher, they condemned their "tyrannical treatment" and called for a public boycott of Lyons tea shops.[69] Whether because of the public response or not, the waitresses brought enough pressure to bear on Lyons for the company to replace the commission system with a fixed weekly wage starting on November 11, 1895. Yet at only 10 shillings, this wage did not place them at any advantage over their A.B.C. counterparts, and in fact worsened their economic situation once deductions had been made.[70] Even after direct action, tea shop waitresses struggled to resolve the contradictions between what was expected of them and what they were paid to fulfill those expectations.

Tea shop waitresses could not become standard-bearers of New Unionism largely because of variations in indirect payment and tipping across companies. While some companies paid minimal wages but supplemented this remuneration with cheap board, others paid higher wages but deducted more for laundry and uniform costs. The A.B.C. theoretically did not allow tips whereas Lyons did until November 1895, thereafter encouraging customers to contribute to the tea shop's Provident Fund box rather than to individual waitresses.[71] As Charles Booth and Jesse Argyle argued, this variation in payment made it impossible to establish any standard wage as a ground for union formation. Moreover, while there were already catering unions—two for cooks and carvers, one for waiters—these principally offered emergency relief and matched members with vacancies rather than campaigning on trade union lines.[72] So although waitresses continued to meet at St. Andrew's Restaurant to air their grievances until at least February

1896, no collective campaign materialized.[73] With little means of redress, tea shop waitresses, especially those living independently, remained caught in a kind of respectable deprivation, the dangers of which sympathetic commentators delicately pointed out. "Under such circumstances," Booth and Argyle wrote, "and thrown so much into contact with persons of the opposite sex, it is not difficult to perceive what must be the result in some instances." Although experienced witnesses claimed that "questionable morality" was more a problem of women in hotels and restaurants, "this," Booth and Argyle claimed inscrutably, "we are not disposed to assert."[74]

Davidson was only nineteen when he allegedly rescued the unfortunate runaway on Thames Embankment. He had just left school and was two months into the start of his brief professional career as an actor before he began attending Oxford part-time in 1898. The furor over A.B.C. waitresses' wages would repeat itself for the fourth year running that month; the strike of Lyons waitresses would occur in nine months' time. Davidson may have been only at the fringes of these developments, but his interest in young women's work was already involving him in the labor conditions shaping, and exposed by, the tea shop customer's desiring touch.

EMOTIONAL LABOR AND ITS UNCERTAIN LIMITS

On May 21, 1932, the eleventh day of the consistory court trial, Harold Davidson took the witness stand for the second time. Examined by Ryder Richardson, his defense counsel, Davidson was not reticent about his contact with waitresses. He claimed to know between four hundred and five hundred Lyons waitresses alone, for many of whom he had provided references.[75] But his relations with the company itself, he alleged, had long been strained. In 1910, a Lyons commissionaire (a uniformed ex-serviceman employed by the company to regulate access to and behavior in its tea shops) assaulted Davidson at Coventry Street Corner House. Davidson successfully sued Lyons for the assault, receiving two hundred pounds' compensation plus costs; Lyons requested that Davidson in the future take his business elsewhere, a request he willfully ignored over the next twenty years. According to Davidson, he was assaulted because he had shown too much interest in waitresses' pay. Since then, he told Richardson acerbically, Lyons had "always had their knife into me."[76]

When questioned about the matter, Lyons chief inquiry officer Frederick Stevens confirmed that the assault had occurred and that Davidson had been paid damages, though whether Davidson's explanation was correct he refused to say.[77] But what is more important than the incident itself is the productive plausibility of Davidson's account.[78] The commissionaire's assault and the question of waitress pay, placed in 1910, reveal something both about waitress labor relations during four years of national labor unrest and about new forms of disorderly and regulatory touch produced by, and giving bodily form *to*, those relations before the Great War.

Davidson's apparent interest in waitresses' pay is made clearer in light of his involvement with newsboys the same year. In December 1910, the newspaper printers of the London Society of Compositors launched a strike to campaign for an eight-hour workday. The strike rode the crest of what became known as "the great unrest," a wave of militant trade union action across Britain lasting until the outbreak of the Great War in July 1914. Newsboys, however, were nonunionized. Calling out the news alone on the streets at night, with no union representation, newsboys were visible and vulnerable, and by the time of the printers' strike, they were a new target of philanthropic concern. In October 1910 the Newsboys' Club, funded by voluntary contributions and open to all, opened at 67a Farringdon Street; Davidson was honorary treasurer. As Davidson later described it, the club's purpose was to provide a social center and "cheap restaurant" for newsboys, "to discourage the boys from vicious habits and associates," and "to help them obtain skilled employment."[79] The club provided a gymnasium, washing facilities, a bicycle store, and technical classes in such crafts as carpentry and boot making. Honorary officers led activities and acted as mentor-friends for each boy.[80] Despite its moralizing, newsboys themselves seem to have welcomed the club. By 1912 more than twelve hundred boys had signed up, placing severe pressure on the club's finances and resulting in repeated pleas for funds and personal assistance.[81]

Tea shop waitresses in the 1910s faced a comparable predicament to that of newsboys. Pay remained low, weekly hours were limited only by the sixty-five-hour maximum imposed by the 1913 Shops Act—if their employer chose to adopt it over the 1912 act, which imposed no maximum—and, most significant, they were similarly nonunionized.[82] In part this lack of unionization was because of the variation in payment methods that had hindered concerted action in the 1890s. But it was also because of the gendered nature and wider problems of the catering industry immediately before the Great War. In contrast with tea shop waitresses, men who were waiters in London hotels and restaurants had long been part of clubs and friendly societies. Some of these organizations were international, such as the Geneva Association of Hotel and Restaurant Employees, but many were exclusive to London and divided along nationality lines—for example, the Italian and Swiss Societies of Hotel and Restaurant Employees. These organizations advertised vacancies and provided old-age pensions and relief to the sick, but they did not involve themselves in matters of pay or hours.[83] The first exception to this model was the Amalgamated Waiters' Society, established in 1896, which campaigned for a minimum wage of thirty shillings a week and a twelve-hour workday.[84] Yet even with these modest aims, the society struggled to retain members and disbanded in 1904.[85] Better provided for than tea shop waitresses, waiters nevertheless struggled to organize around the conditions of their labor.

Attempts by waiters to unionize were hampered by the deep national divisions cutting across the catering industry prior to the Great War. While French, German, and Italian waiters dominated the trade in large hotels and restaurants, British waiters were confined mainly to City chophouses and West End clubs, making common cause difficult to find.[86] Following the collapse of the Amalgamated Waiters' Society, several friendly societies formed a "cartel" and successfully secured from employers a fixed weekly wage of five shillings for the youngest boys.[87] But deepening distrust between British and non-British waiters in the immediate prewar years weakened the cartel's effectiveness. In autumn 1909, the Loyal British Waiters' Society was established with the aim of securing preference for British waiters and improving the training of British boys as waiters so that they might displace their foreign competitors.[88] Regular press articles on "waiters and patriotism" kept the issue alive, and by 1912, the society numbered five hundred members.[89] Although the International Caterers' Employees' Union, formed in 1909, briefly succeeded in uniting waiters regardless of nationality and organized several "stay-in" strikes and demonstrations, it fell apart with the onset of war when German and Austrian waiters were interned, French and Italian waiters returned to their own countries, and English waiters were conscripted.[90]

Waiters therefore offered tea shop waitresses few options for unionization, or models for their own union activity. While deeply divided among themselves, waiters also found little common ground with waitresses, who occupied what Fabian Barbara Drake termed their own "special sphere."[91] Waiters on average received far higher wages than waitresses, even a *commis de rang* (waiter's assistant) receiving twenty to twenty-five shillings a week, and had their own systems of deductions and tip distribution, making coordinated action over pay difficult.[92] In other unorganized trades these issues did not preclude unionization, the charwomen of London County

Council elementary schools, for example, successfully organizing to join the National Federation of Women Workers and press for a minimum wage.[93] Women from the jam and pickle, bottle-washing, and cocoa-making trades, too, joined the strikes erupting throughout 1910.[94] But with deepening mistrust between waiters and no potential equivalence in earnings across restaurants and tea shops, there were few common issues over which waiters and waitresses could unite. Waitresses, like newsboys in their relations with printers, consequently remained outside even the limited protests launched by waiters in the prewar years.

By the time of Davidson's assault in 1910, tea shop waitresses' labor conditions and representation were therefore little better than in the 1890s.[95] Yet as the trade diversified to meet rising demand, the dangers Charles Booth and Jesse Argyle had associated with those conditions increased. For Barbara Drake, who investigated the condition of tea shop waitresses for the Women's Industrial Council in 1913, the A.B.C.'s requirement that waitresses live with relatives provided little protection. Often a parent died or moved away, leaving the waitress to find cheap lodgings; for those earning twelve shillings a week or less and paying two shillings on weekly travel fares, plus accommodation, the temptation was strong to accept gifts from customers "over and above the regulation tip." Even without this hardship, Drake alleged, around 25 percent of tea shop waitresses allowed customers to "treat" them with taxi rides, restaurant dinners, or theater trips. For some couples, especially where the men were of equivalent class status, Drake found the treating "innocent enough," with marriage often resulting. "It is the older man, the married man, the so-called 'gentleman' of another class," she reported, "who is said to be responsible for the dark places of a waitress's career." Here was one possible incarnation of Davidson—the version the commissionaire assaulted—but also the shadow of another, the customer who varyingly exploited or alleviated waitresses' vulnerable predicament. While there was obvious danger in "treating," Drake avowed that the tea shop waitress, who was required to be "a girl of 'savoir-faire,' and quick parts," was "able as a rule to take care of herself."[96]

Yet sometimes the gray area of tea shop treating shaded into more explicitly illicit territory. While the A.B.C. ostensibly guaranteed waitress respectability through its no tipping policy, in the 1910s other, less salubrious, tea shops carved out a niche by doing the opposite: encouraging intimate relations between waitresses and customers by creating the financial necessity and environmental opportunity for waitresses to boost tips by kissing and cuddling customers. The trend became visible with the prosecution of Marian Hawes, manager of the Ashanti Tea Rooms in Hercules Passage, just off Threadneedle Street, in December 1914, and continued into the 1920s. Most of the tea shops involved were located in the City. The City's situation at the interstice of central London and the East End made it a site of mingled economies, classes, and, in the case of basement tea shops, precarious interpersonal boundaries. High business rubbed shoulders with grinding service work, while in tea shops below ground, this took a more literal form.

The turn to erotic touching between waitresses and customers represented both the enduring economic vulnerability of tea shop waitresses and a change in their labor as competition between tea shops increased. With no control over their working conditions, and no effective organization to change this situation, waitresses' labor was already commodified: an abstract quantity to be bought or sold to which individual workers could have no attachment. But as tea shops fought for business in a crowded market, in some places that labor became what Hochschild terms an "emotional labour"—especially one that was metaphorically and physically tactile.[97] Because of rising competition in the 1910s, waitresses' labor in some tea shops became a matter of easing boundaries between themselves and customers; of allowing themselves to be physically and affectively "touched" and "touching" customers in return. In this way, waitresses became potentially alienated both from their own labor and from the varying levels of "touch" increasingly constituting it.[98] However, if tea shop waiting became an emotional labor, then waitresses at the same time became adept at managing their own emotions within this work. Tactile habits and the desire to touch among waitresses and customers derived from changing labor conditions but also negotiated, reworked, or rejected those conditions in unpredictable ways in each interaction.[99]

The Ashanti Tea Rooms first came to public attention on December 23, 1914, when Marian Hawes was summoned before the Lord Mayor at Mansion House court for failing to stamp the insurance cards of two waitresses. But the insurance commissioners' visits to the tearooms made it clear that insurance fraud was not the only dubious activity in which the Ashanti was engaged. Commissioner Henson reported that on one visit he saw a woman smoking a cigarette while perched on a man's knee.[100] Henson's allegation was confirmed the same day when Hawes was also hauled before City Common Sergeant F. A. Bosanquet to answer charges of misrepresentation. Doris and Monica Conran Smith, purchasers of a four-fifths share of the Bonanza Tea Rooms from Marian Hawes, alleged that at the time of sale Hawes had misrepresented the Bonanza's revenue and outgoings, consequently exaggerating its profitability. But the real nub of the issue, and probable reason for the false account, seemed to be the way the waitresses behaved. The Conran Smiths alleged that the waitresses were not given food but had to have it bought for them by customers, many of whom were "rather forward young men."[101] The subtext behind the allegation, which the Conran Smiths were reluctant to reveal, was that Bonanza waitresses supported themselves through less-than-respectable relations with customers. This suspicion gained added credibility when Hawes admitted that Ashanti waitresses received only six shillings a week plus one shilling commission for every pound of sales, though she denied that anything indecent ever occurred.[102]

A few months later, May Perryman, proprietor of Carlton Tea Rooms at 1 Copthall Chambers, just north of the Bank of England, was summoned before Guildhall Justice Room for permitting disorderly conduct between waitresses and customers. Plainclothes policemen had visited the Carlton at lunchtime on five occasions and each time seen conduct of "a scandalous and disgraceful character," according to Assistant City Solicitor T. G. Vickery.[103] During their first visit on June 30, 1915, Detective Constable Challis and Police Constable Walton ordered two cups of coffee. Waitresses "Fifi" and "Dorothy," both allegedly dressed in "rather short skirts" and "low necked blouses," brought over the order, along with—apparently without asking—two sodas, milk, and two sandwiches for themselves, which they consumed alongside the policemen. Challis and Walton unquestioningly paid for everything. Describing the visit later in court, Challis explained with a sketch map how couches were arranged around the tearoom; on each couch occupied by a customer also sat a waitress. One of these waitresses, "Rose," balanced on the arm of a couch, her feet resting on the seat, her dress raised above her knees. The customer seated at her feet placed his hand beneath her dress. When the customer stood up to leave, Rose put her hand on his genitals, outside his trousers; he paid, Rose kissed him, and then she handed the money to Perryman.[104]

Similar scenes repeated on every occasion Challis and Walton visited. Waitresses sometimes kissed and cuddled, sometimes unfastened a customer's fly and placed their hands inside his trousers, but they apparently never passed beyond passive touch; this was disorderly conduct, not public indecency or prostitution. On the fifth visit, July 5, Challis and Walton were seated drinking their coffees when Rose allegedly pulled her dress up to her thighs and flashed her drawers to waitress "Millie," who, goaded by a customer, flashed hers in return. In answer to a compliment from May Perryman, who was unfazed by the whole affair, Rose said that she was trying to sell a few pairs to Millie and was showing her the size.[105] During the trial, Millie denied the accusation and alleged instead that Walton had "behaved like a cad," trying to kiss her and inviting her to a "tennis party" at his mother's house in Twickenham. Unconvinced, Alderman Sir George Truscott, who felt it particularly distasteful that men should be wasting their time in such activities while others were fighting for their country, found Perryman guilty on all counts.[106] He ordered a fine of five pounds, two shillings, and twopence costs or one month's imprisonment per offense.[107]

Perryman's prosecution was just the beginning. In November 1915, T. G. Vickery successfully prosecuted Eveline Fawcett, proprietor of the Café Bean, Bow Lane, and Kathleen Newton, proprietor of the Club Tea Rooms, Bishopsgate, for permitting six and four counts of disorderly conduct, respectively.[108] In each case the details were similar. Provocatively dressed waitresses brought customers their order along with refreshment for themselves and then allowed a limited amount of fondling—though how much this was stereotyped and routinized by police evidence is difficult to tell. Plainclothes officers noted the meager portions (sandwiches 3 inches by 2½ inches) and high prices; tea and coffee fourpence, sandwiches sixpence, plus the waitresses' refreshment and an undefined "service" charge.[109] Through this arrangement proprietors maximized revenue, minimized wages, and escaped paying for waitresses' meals, while waitresses supplemented their low wages through commissions or tips, if these were subsequently shared. Waitress Millie, for example, claimed that she received wages of ten shillings a week, plus tips of up to ten shillings.[110] Contrary to the A.B.C.'s dictum, low wages, and a liberal attitude on the part of some waitresses, had far more influence on tea shop disorderly conduct than a waitress's living situation; some of those accused, like Millie, lived with parents, while all three waitresses prosecuted when the Ashanti again came under scrutiny in September 1922 were married.[111] Even when partially supported, a basic, "supplementary" wage was insufficient to prevent waitresses from seeking other ways to increase their incomes.

Aware of this fact, City tea shop proprietors facilitated disorderly behavior through careful spatial planning. Several tea shops that were prosecuted—such as the Royal Exchange Tea Rooms below the Exchange, the Mocha Café at 20 Ironmonger Lane, and the Ashanti—were discreetly situated in basement rooms, away from innocent passing custom. Small already, the Mocha measuring only thirty feet by ten feet, they were often further divided by multiple partitions.[112] As the customer descended the stairs into the Ashanti, they came across a "deep recess" on the left-hand side partitioned by a wall and hangings; further down, another room opened up on the right-hand side, with "four recesses partitioned by six-foot folding screens."[113] The Mocha was divided into five sections, each section "lighted with electric light heavily shaded so as to give the least possible light"; the same was ostensibly true of lighting in the Ashanti.[114] According to one correspondent, a visitor to the Ashanti was "accommodated in a cosy corner dimly lighted by shaded lamps which create a warm, voluptuous atmosphere." In this intimate setting, waitresses could sit with, or on the knees of, customers, "accept[ing] caresses and endearments" in partial privacy.[115]

In the days surrounding Armistice Day, November 11, 1918, the need for these material boundaries was temporarily suspended as tacit norms regulating public intimacy eased. On one undercover visit to the Royal Exchange Tea Rooms on November 12, Detective Johnson saw two waitresses, a sailor, and another man cuddling one another. Returning again on November 21, Johnson ostensibly heard proprietor Millicent Gibson tease another customer: "Kiss me: I haven't had a peace kiss yet."[116] The end of hostilities offered a rare license for erotic touch between strangers in public.[117] But this language of temporary license revealed the normal importance of producing privacy in basement tea shops, especially since those involved in previous prosecutions attracted criticism for engaging in "disgraceful frivolity" while others fought for their country.[118] The ordering of public space into private niches was necessary to shield waitresses and customers from prying eyes and, less successfully, laws on disorderly conduct defining "public" in terms of what could be seen by others.

Despite T. G. Vickery's energetic campaign, disorderly conduct in tea shops continued throughout and beyond the Great War.[119] Beginning with the prosecution of May Perryman in July 1915, Vickery launched a further eight prosecutions between November 1915 and October 1922.[120] The tea shops' resilience was partly attributable to their system of management and partly because of the limits to the sentence that could be passed if a case was proved. In some cases the manager prosecuted was also the "proprietor," invariably a leaseholder, and so a successful prosecution could lead to the tea shop's closure or reform. In other cases, though, the proprietor remained at one remove from the tea shop's management and was therefore able to deny knowledge of illicit activity. Following the successful prosecution of manager Violet Winsor of the Ashanti Tea Rooms in October 1922, Magistrate Sir David Burnett commented that the real responsibility lay with tea shop proprietors, in this case Marian Tuke, who received the profits but escaped punishment.[121] Devolved management allowed proprietors to continue unscathed, even if this meant relocating and opening under a new name. This scenario was especially borne out in the case of Marian Tuke, whom *John Bull* named as the Marian Hawes, now divorced, implicated in the alleged indecent behavior of waitresses at the Ashanti in 1914. Hawes escaped prosecution when conduct at the Ashanti again came before the courts in October 1922 and remained, under this name, proprietor of the Tudor Tea Rooms, 303 High Holborn, which allegedly continued disorderly conduct even after the second Ashanti prosecution.[122] When shown a copy of *John Bull* making these evasions clear, the paper crowed, Tuke a.k.a. Hawes "paid off" all her waitresses, so distancing herself from disorderly conduct while allowing its continuation by new waitresses under the same management.[123]

It was even difficult to effectively prosecute those directly involved. At the time of Perryman's prosecution in 1915, only the manager could be held responsible for disorderly conduct; by 1922 waitresses could also be prosecuted for aiding and abetting, but the maximum penalty possible under Section 28 of the City Police Act was a five-pound fine per offense plus costs. While this penalty deterred those prosecuted from reoffending, and while the prosecutions had increasing effect after the City (Various Powers) Act of 1920, tea shop disorderly conduct continued sporadically until at least 1938, when waitresses at the Swan Café, Great Swan Alley, were prosecuted for kissing and cuddling customers.[124]

The post of tea shop commissionaire was the product of official fears over this kind of conduct and the fraught employment conditions encouraging it. Sourced from the Corps of Commissionaires, commissionaires were ex-servicemen available for temporary or permanent employment. Employers engaged commissionaires by visiting the corps' London headquarters, tucked away in narrow Exchange Court on 419 Strand, a ten-minute walk from Coventry Street Corner House, where Davidson was allegedly assaulted in 1910.[125] Pay and work prospects were good, but the conditions of employment punishing. Of the 2,503 commissionaires in London in 1910, 2,002 were in permanent employment and 167 temporarily employed.[126] The weekly rate from employers averaged twenty-eight shillings—sixteen shillings more than that of A.B.C. waitresses. But like tea shop waitresses, commissionaires faced steep deductions to their wages and even stricter discipline. A commissionaire joining the corps in 1911 paid two pounds on entrance, including one pound "caution money" as a guarantee of good conduct, then monthly contributions of seven shillings and sixpence toward uniform and general and sick funds. Single commissionaires lived in barracks, for which they paid extra, and although discharged from the armed services were subject to military discipline imposed by Division commanding officers.[127] This was valuable employment, especially for wounded ex-servicemen who may have struggled to find work elsewhere.[128] But some wondered, with its "exacting regulations and excessive fines," whether the corps—like tea shops—was more concerned with extraction from its members than charitable service.[129]

Commissionaires could be engaged for almost any task, and any length of time. Where employed in public, rather than domestic, situations, they were an advertisement for the corps, wearing a forage cap, greatcoat, and tunic with chevrons denoting rank and medals for previous service.[130] They might serve as day or night watchmen, timekeepers or gatekeepers at sporting events, messengers, porters, gymnastic or drill instructors, boatmen, or "ticket-" and "money-takers" at shows.[131] Commissionaires were especially favored for work in which their military experience made them ideal enforcement officials.[132] Harry Conniham, a music hall artist (whom we shall meet again in chapter 5), for example, alleged that shortly before his arrest for being a "suspected person" in January 1930, he and his companion were employed (illicitly) by a commissionaire overseeing a party on a ship moored at Embankment. Conniham was tasked with fetching taxis, his friend with guarding the cars parked opposite the ship.[133]

In the first two decades of the 1900s, demand for commissionaires exceeded supply, despite the corps' steady growth. This rising demand reflected the proliferation of commercial and leisure spaces in central London, and the need to regulate customer conduct within them. Department stores were regular employers, and, as film transitioned from music halls to auditoriums and increasingly demanded silent spectatorship, cinemas too.[134] Immediately before the outbreak of the Great War, when more than half of them volunteered to fight, commissionaires were especially useful to large tea shop chains such as Lyons, which employed them to regulate customer-waitress touch while basement tea shops were actively encouraging it.[135] Lyons subscribed the largest amount to the Corps of Commissionaires endowment fund in 1910—an annual subscription of five pounds, which had already acquired the company a "Life Governorship" of the corps and implies extensive use of its commissionaires.[136] As for the commissionaire who assaulted Davidson, the corps guaranteed employers the good conduct of its members up to a sum of one hundred pounds, depending on the commissionaire's rank and responsibility.[137] However, Lyons's regular use of and, albeit nominal, responsibility for the corps suggest that it may have settled Davidson's claim itself. In the same year as Davidson's alleged assault, forty-three commissionaires were dismissed from the corps.[138] Their names are listed in surviving enrollment registers, but not their offenses, and so we are left to rely on the corroboration of Lyons chief inquiry officer Frederick Stevens that Davidson was indeed assaulted, although the circumstances remain unclear.[139]

The commissionaire's assault of Davidson, ostensibly provoked by his overkeen interest in tea shop wages, showed Lyons's sensitivity to waitress employment conditions in 1910. But it also showed the perceived need to regulate the physical and affective touch between waitresses and customers shaped by those conditions. During Davidson's trial, Richard Levy raised the 1910 assault as part of an explanation for Lyons's antipathy toward Davidson, and of Davidson's alleged misconduct toward Dorothy Burn, a waitress at Lyons's tea shop at 15 Walbrook, in summer 1929. Burn claimed that on Davidson's first visit, he followed her around the tea shop, "got hold" of her, and told her she was "lovely" and "too good for the job." After this he became a daily visitor and refused service by anyone but her. Davidson showed Burn photographs of his actress friends, gave her a card with his London address, and frequently asked her out for tea.[140]

According to Levy, this behavior, although unusual, was part of Davidson's "campaign" to improve the working conditions of Lyons waitresses, of which his actions in 1910 were a part.[141] According to Roland Oliver, it was unwanted "pestering."[142] Lyons inquiry officer Frederick Stevens stated that he intervened when, on August 15, 1929, he followed Davidson out of the tea shop into Cannon Street and told him, as he had been told in 1910, to no longer visit.[143] It was not, Stevens claimed, ostensibly altruistic interfering to which Lyons objected, but Davidson's unwanted advances toward waitresses, particularly "trippies," or waitresses younger than eighteen.[144] But what Davidson's assault and Dorothy Burn's evidence revealed was that the employment conditions in which he interfered and the illicit touch for which he was accused were each a product of the other. Tea shop waitresses' straitened labor conditions and scanty representation, and the physical and affective touch between waitresses and customers, were inseparable, and they were jointly managed through company inquiry agents and the commissionaire's regulatory touch.

CONNECTED HISTORIES OF LABOR
UNREST IN BRITAIN AND INDIA

At around noon on October 29, 1931, Davidson caught the tube from Wood Lane to Charing Cross. On changing at Tottenham Court Road, he noticed two young women enter his car laden with luggage. The women, Davidson realized, had performed at a show he had seen at the Shepherd's Bush Empire the night before.[145] Taking advantage of the open car space, Davidson shifted over and struck up a conversation. According to Percival Butler, the Arrow's Agency detective trailing Davidson on behalf of the Bishop of Norwich, Davidson told the women about his own "theatrical experience." He mentioned performing in *Charley's Aunt*, an immensely popular farce that ran in London and toured Britain in multiple productions between December 1892 and December 1896, at the beginning of his brief acting career.[146] When the train reached Charing Cross, Davidson carried their luggage across the station and bundled them onto the train to Chatham, but not before taking their address in order to send them the Actor's Church Union lodging book "so that they would have nice lodgings on their tour."[147]

The ease with which Davidson could join the new passengers was made possible by the reordering of tube car space over the 1920s. By January 1929, the Northern Line had replaced its gate stock with more spacious "standard" stock, complete with automatic central doors.[148] As we saw in chapter 3, this change itself resulted from the transformation of the tube's capital base as it gradually entered public control after 1921. But at the same time, the postwar economic conditions stimulating this restructuring—and the corresponding economy of bodies in tube cars—also reshaped the bodily relations between tea shop waitresses and customers *above* ground. It was only incidental that the passengers Davidson met were stage performers. But there was nonetheless a symmetry between their career and the "acting" increasingly expected of tea shop waitresses—acting shaped by the same economic conditions enabling Davidson's conversation as he rattled along on the tube.

Like the tube, Lyons also benefited from rising spending power and customer numbers in 1919. Between June 1919 and June 1920, sales in Lyons tea shops were 50 percent higher than they had been the previous year. But also like the tube, Lyons struggled to profit from this increase because of rising costs.[149] The lifting of wartime price controls combined with materials shortages to cause rising inflation over 1919 and, to stem it, the increase of the bank rate to 7 percent by 1920.[150] Although Lyons enjoyed higher turnover, it also had to buy more stock at higher prices, foodstuff prices alone rising by 31.5 percent between June 1919 and June 1920. Consequently, by June 1920, gross annual profit was the lowest it had ever been in the company's history. Lyons chairman Montague Gluckstein partly blamed these conditions on the widespread postwar introduction of the eight-hour workday, which he claimed hindered production from matching demand and so reducing inflation.[151] Rising costs left Lyons with no option but to raise prices, the price of a cup of tea increasing from twopence halfpenny to threepence in July 1919 and that of a cup of coffee from threepence to threepence halfpenny in October 1920.[152] These increases drew considerable negative comment in the press.[153]

There was one commodity that did not suffer a rampant increase in wholesale price after the Great War: tea. Tea production in India, Britain's primary supplier, increased by sixty-four million pounds between 1914 and 1919; this increase, combined with the release onto the market of tea purchased by the British government during the war, resulted in a significant drop in wholesale prices to less than one shilling per pound of tea between May 1919 and December 1920.[154] Tea plantation owners subsequently attempted to limit the price drop by stopping picking across all plantations in India from November 15, 1920.[155] As one of the six largest purchasers of tea at the London auctions, Lyons surely benefited from the drop in wholesale prices. But the combination of inflation and rising wage costs—which increased by around one million pounds between June 1919 and June 1920—seem to have significantly outweighed any savings made.[156] In spring 1920, director Gluckstein began to look at the bottom line with some anxiety.

In this context of financial difficulty, and with national labor unrest at its height, rumors circulated. In May 1920, word spread that the pay of Lyons waitresses had been cut from thirty shillings to twenty-one shillings a week and commission from one shilling to sixpence on the pound.[157] For the first time since 1895, tea shop waitresses organized to counter the change with direct action. Former members of the International Caterers' Employees' Union joined unionist Tom Cann to form the United Catering Trade Union, which, like Tom Mann in 1895, offered logistical advice and support.[158] On May 21, 1920, an alleged three thousand Lyons waitresses crammed into Memorial Hall, Farringdon, to draw up their demands, including the payment of "union rates," a forty-eight-hour workweek, and the abolition of deductions from pay. Equally contentious was Lyons's alleged "victimization" of waitress union members, six of whom, Tom Cann told the *Daily Mail*, had been unfairly dismissed.[159] In response, Lyons flatly denied that there was any such thing as a "union rate" and that waitresses were paid anything less than thirty shillings or worked anything more than forty-eight hours a week.[160]

Despite protesting, by May 26, it seemed as though the agitation was over after Lyons agreed to most demands, excepting those concerning pay, and the waitresses agreed to work with Lyons to push for the creation of a trade board.[161] The proposed strike was called off.[162] But the peace was short-lived. Following the dismissal of kitchen hand F. Sparkes, a widow with three children, for wearing her union badge, hundreds of Lyons waitresses again met to discuss direct action. Voting to strike, the waitresses picketed every Lyons tea shop starting at 7:00 a.m. the following day, August 17, 1920.[163] Numbering over five hundred, they marched from the tea shops to join a procession through the West End.[164] But the strike was, the press wryly noted, a storm in a teacup. Because Lyons produced nearly all its food at Cadby Hall in Hammersmith, and because the cooks' and carmen's unions had not joined the strike, the supply of goods to Lyons tea shops was relatively unaffected.[165] Moreover, at a time when demobilization pushed the number of registered unemployed women to half a million, Lyons easily recruited replacements for strikers.[166] Two days after the strike began, Lyons director Alfred Salmon told the *Daily Mail* that three thousand women had applied for six hundred vacancies, one thousand of whom had been employed immediately.[167] Cook and syndicalist Wilf McCartney later wrote that he and Tom Cann had complained to the London Trades Council (LTC), with which the United Catering Trade Union was affiliated, about other unions failing to support the unionized waitresses, but apparently to no effect; the LTC rather claimed it had supported the campaign.[168] Wherever the responsibility lay, by August 19, the strike was effectively over.[169]

While lower wholesale tea prices failed to lessen Lyons's economic woes, they had comparable effects on labor at the other end of the commodity chain in Assam. The price drop meant that some tea plantation owners cut the wages of the laborers, or "coolies," picking tea. At the same time, inflation in India increased considerably over the war, so that tea plantation laborers were significantly worse off by 1920.[170] Most of these laborers were migrants on indenture contracts, driven to Assam since the 1860s by a combination of famines in other parts of India and the promise of full employment.[171] Working conditions were harsh. Wages were below subsistence level and supplemented by payment in kind, making economic independence impossible. Labor was gendered, women and children being given the more delicate but grueling work of plucking because of their ostensibly finer touch.[172] Laborers were compelled to remain within the gardens, monitored by watchmen, and subject to beatings; escapees could be arrested by locals who were paid bounties to return them.[173] The suppression of wages and rising cost of living in 1920 compounded these hardships, and on September 6, 1920, eighteen days after the strike of tea shop waitresses, tea plantation laborers launched their own series of strikes. These strikes continued across Assam from September 1920 until January 1922 and were severe enough to prompt the government of Assam to appoint an enquiry committee to report on tea plantation labor conditions in November 1921.[174] Although the historical verdict varies, the committee concluded that the strikes were caused by a combination of economic pressures and anticolonial agitation as noncooperation spread across India. Particular blame was placed on noncooperators who ostensibly stirred up discontent at tea plantation bazaars.[175]

Labor unrest in Assam's tea plantations did not influence that in London's tea shops, occurring shortly after. It also had, in part, a different economic cause: falling wholesale prices for tea, rather than rising wholesale prices of other products purchased by tea retailers. Nonetheless, the timing of strikes in Assam and London indicates how employers at both ends of the commodity chain faced comparable problems simultaneously because of their integration within a single global market. Postwar shortages and inflation in Britain and India resulted in higher costs, declining profits, real or anticipated wage cuts, and nationwide labor unrest. This connection between the economic conditions of tea plantation laborers and tea shop waitresses remained primarily correlative while Lyons purchased its tea by auction, at one remove from tea production. But it became stronger in 1924, when Lyons began to plant tea on its newly purchased Lujeri Estate in Nyasaland (present-day Malawi), thereby taking control of the entire commodity chain.

FIGURE 16 Tea pluckers on Lyons's Lujeri Estate, Nyasaland (present-day Malawi), ca. 1928–1938. ACC/3527/475, no. 87, from the J. Lyons & Company Ltd. collection.
© London Metropolitan Archives, City of London

This move into tea cultivation was driven by rising consumer demand and fears over fluctuating wholesale prices caused by anticolonial agitation in Assam.[176] Its effect was to more closely tie the economic conditions and bodily disciplining of tea shop waitresses to those of tea plantation laborers, many of them women and children, who were now part of the same operation. Ironically, it did not allow Lyons to escape the effects of anticolonial nationalism as its continuation of the *thangata* system, which required labor without pay in lieu of rent, made the Lujeri Estate the site of occasional labor unrest.[177] How much the connection between the supply and retail of tea translated into direct changes for tea shop waitresses is difficult to tell, but what is certain is that the global labor unrest of 1920 drove Lyons to gain more control over both its supply chain and the bodily behavior of its waitresses.

HABITS OF DISCIPLINE AND DESIRE

Lyons waitresses had received formal training ever since the company opened a training school at 396 Strand in 1912.[178] But in the years following the tea shop strike, Lyons redoubled its efforts to manage the professional conduct and public image of its waitresses. In December 1921, Lyons introduced its first post–training school examination for waitresses. Waitresses were tested on their general catering knowledge, the best then required to write a final paper covering the finer intricacies of tea shop service.[179] A year later, Lyons required tea shop kitchens to display weekly mottoes encouraging good service. Waitresses read such pithy advice as "Your temper is your own, never lose it."[180] In January 1925, Lyons completely relaunched the image of its waitresses. Renamed "Nippy," the Lyons waitress was no longer the recalcitrant striker but the obedient "symbol of public service."[181] A major uniform change signaled the shift: a shorter dress and apron, lower collar, and the replacement of a cap with a coronet approximated contemporary women's fashions and distanced waitresses from the popularly disparaged uniform and work of domestic service.[182] The Nippy image struck a careful "conservative modernity"; appealing enough to draw comment, but more modest than the avant-garde fashions of the "flapper."[183] It required waitresses to combine the independence of modern femininity with the efficiency of modern industry. The notebook kept by Nippy Ethel Fage in the 1930s, for example, gives detailed instructions concerning the correct preparation and service of tea (twenty-two separate points) as well as regulations governing nail manicures (staff may have their nails manicured for nine pence

All Ready for the First Customer

8
30

Just before the café is opened to the public. The final polish is being given, menus put on tables, napkins folded. The café opens at midday, does not close until 11 p.m.

FIGURE 17 Disciplined habitus in the metropole: "Nippies" set tables in a Lyons Corner House. From "Nippy," *Picture Post*, March 4, 1939, 30.
© The British Library Board

at 59 Shaftesbury Avenue on Tuesdays, Wednesdays, and Saturdays if they make an appointment through their manager).[184]

Decades later, former Nippies recalled how this image of industrious femininity was strictly enforced. As historian Judith Walkowitz notes, ex-Nippies reminiscing on their experience at Lyons nearly always remembered the severity of the preduty inspection.[185] Nippies were required to have clean collars and cuffs, flat shoes, black stockings without runs, and clean nails, and to have their coronet touching their eyebrows; no lipstick or jewelry were to be worn, except wedding and engagement rings.[186] The company publication, *Lyons Mail*, distributed monthly to the 18,700 employees subscribing to the Lyons Club, and its commissioned film *Noona Be Nippy* (1929) gave further direction on appropriate waitress habitus. Shot by Bertie Joseph, who introduced waitress examinations in 1921, *Noona Be Nippy* followed the form of *The Rake's Progress*, contrasting the rapid advancement of efficient waitress "Nora Swift" with the blunders of slipshod "Noona Sloe." This time, however, the story took an optimistic turn, showing how "patient training" could redeem even the most "unpromising pupil." The film acted as part instruction, part inducement for Nippy viewers, showing, for example, how to correctly serve a poached egg, how to set a table and "pack" a tray, and the heights to which the most skilled waitresses could advance.[187]

For the more jaundiced observer, Lyons's efforts to routinize waitress habitus was just one element of the wider routinization of everyday London life. In J. B. Priestley's novel *Angel Pavement* (1930), the Lyons Corner House became a bewildering place where waitress and customer behavior was reduced to a fine balance between service and erotic frisson: a "citadel" of industrial-scale organization and a magnet for young, spendthrift clerks like "Mr. Turgis" looking for love on a budget. Hidden among the forest of tables, Turgis was one of those men "juggling with fractions of a farthing" who knew exactly how long it took a waitress "to carry a tray of given weight from the kitchen lift to the table in the far corner." But despite the apparent opportunities for love, Turgis found himself crammed at a table with three other less-than-appealing customers, "shooting amorous glances" to indifferent girls at adjacent tables and served by a "snappy" waitress.[188]

By 1936, in line with his broader intellectual evolution over the 1930s, Priestley had sharpened his social critique.[189] Seen through Rose Salter's eyes in *They Walk in the City* (1936), London's chain tea shops lacked any human dimension, each appearing instead "nearly as severely business-like as a power-house." Waitresses "hastily and efficiently served mathematically regular portions of food and measures of drink," and "made you feel that you must have a train to catch outside."[190] Reading Ethel Fage's notebook, this depiction had a ring of truth about it. Even the entry on baked beans was intimidatingly precise: "Serve two ladles of Baked Beans in vegetable dish[,] a teaspoon of tomato sauce in centre[;] serve on 8¼ inch plate with four diamonds of toast round edge. Crust to be cut off."[191]

Priestley's account of tea shop regimentation was part of a wider critique of modern urban alienation.[192] But despite its polemical tone, it highlighted how closely Lyons had attempted to manage waitress, and correspondingly customer, behavior since the 1920 strike. Moreover, it indicated that even by the mid-1930s, tea shops were still haunted by the specter not only of disobedient waitresses but also disorderly ones. In the same year as *They Walk in the City* was published, commandant of the Women's Auxiliary Service Mary Allen reported a return of shady tea shops, where waitresses in "abbreviated musical comedy uniforms" accepted "gross familiarities from customers" and led them into back rooms for sex.[193] It was in this context that Lyons emphasized the Nippy's merits as an efficient worker and potential wife. In April 1927, for example, the *Lyons Mail* began to publish the names of Nippies married the previous month, encouraging readers to think of themselves as wives in training; desirable but also efficient and respectable, a contrast to the easy waitress of the basement tea shop.[194] While tea shops had long presented waitresses as potential wives, Lyons's focus on the idealized femininity *and* industrious propriety of the Nippy responded both to earlier labor disputes and continued anxiety over potential illicit touch.

Davidson's touch of waitresses exposed the tensions in this evolving routinization of tea shop labor. When not pulling managers aside for a word, Davidson alleged, he was "selecting" efficient waitresses to help him conduct business with his long-term business partner Arthur Gordon.[195] Upon entering a tea shop, Davidson would scan the floor for a waitress who looked "quick in her work," touch her shoulder to attract her attention, and, if she seemed amenable, ask her to deliver messages for himself and Gordon.[196] Some waitresses, such as Dorothy Burn, apparently agreed, although they were occasionally discouraged, Davidson claimed, by the "chipping" of other waitresses jealous of the generous tip given for this service.[197] Others, such as Kathleen Grant, a Nippy at Maison Lyons on Oxford Street whom Davidson tried to conscript in late August 1930, refused. Giving evidence on April 2, 1932, Grant complained that Davidson's constant chatter compelled her to wait at his table longer than necessary, something that was "against the rules."[198] With Nippies expected to maintain rapid customer turnover while serving smartly, and with the Oxford Street Corner House serving more than twenty-eight thousand meals in the last weekend of August 1930, Davidson's attempt to turn waitresses into personal messengers was both a product of and a problem for Lyons's Nippy service.[199]

Here the spatial arrangement of Lyons tea shops also mattered to changing customer behavior. Whereas basement City tea shops were small, intricately partitioned, and dimly lit, Lyons's flagship tea shops were vast, open-plan spaces illuminated by chandeliers and windows reaching up to fifteen feet. Maison Lyons, where Davidson pursued Grant, ranged over seven floors and three former shopfronts on Oxford Street, the basement alone accommodating three hundred customers.[200] On entering the ground floor, customers found themselves in a spacious chocolate shop decorated with palms and tiered displays, from which they descended via a generous marble staircase to the basement tearoom below.[201] From the tearoom entrance customers had a sweeping view of the entire space. To the right, one looked toward Oxford Street, from which light filtered down through pavement skylights running the length of the building. To the left, in the corner, one looked toward double swing doors giving access to the service room and "wash-up."[202] Tables were lined in rows divided into stations, each tended by a different waitress, and space was ample: even at full capacity, the basement provided fifteen feet per person.[203]

This arrangement allowed maximum efficiency of service, and therefore turnover, as well as surveillance by the floor superintendent. But although touch could be more easily regulated, this was at the cost of also making it easier for those enamored of a particular waitress or customer. When he entered the basement of Maison Lyons, Davidson would wait to see where Grant was serving and then make a beeline for her tables. Sometimes he even asked her superintendent where she was stationed.[204] If City tea shops offered spaces where intimacy was concealed, Maison Lyons left few spaces to hide. So persistent was Davidson that if Grant saw him arrive, she would rush to the service room or hide behind a pillar, of which the floor plan shows only two standing detached, to the right of the room.[205] The open-plan space of

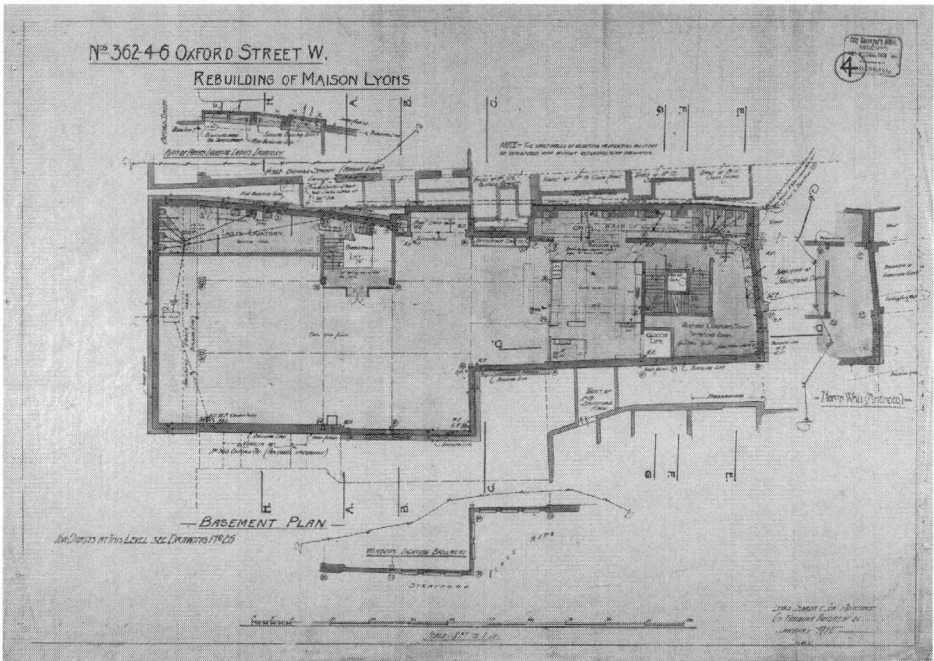

FIGURE 18 The basement of Maison Lyons, where Harold Davidson pursued Nippy Kathleen Grant. Hiding places were afforded by two freestanding pillars to the west of the room and the service room to the east. Nos. 362-4-6 Oxford Street W.: Rebuilding of Maison Lyons, January 1915. COL/SVD/PL/01/2711, Plan no.4, from the Corporation of London Collection. © London Metropolitan Archives, City of London

cavernous tea shops such as Maison Lyons allowed for more regulation of touch but also encouraged it through spectacularizing waitresses as objects of service and streamlining access between them and customers.

At the same time, Davidson's attentions toward waitresses were conditioned by the depiction of Nippies as ideal potential wives—notwithstanding his long-suffering wife, Molly, in Stiffkey. As with A.B.C. waitress Phyllis Holt, Davidson also periodically asked Kathleen Grant to the theater, ostensibly to talk about Kathleen's mother, who was, incidentally, one of Davidson's parishioners.[206] Davidson was able to extend such invitations liberally as his contacts in theater meant he was often given tickets to "paper the house"— that is, to distribute freely in order to pack audiences and generate interest in a play.[207] During shows he would slip backstage to mingle with the cast and sometimes force his way onstage, appearing, one former undergraduate friend remembered, as a "rather odd clerical shadow reflected by strong limelight, and marring perhaps a particularly beautiful scene."[208] The frequency with which Davidson invited waitresses to join him at the theater led to some joking about the number of "wives" he had acquired. The waitresses of the Lyons tea shop on St. James's Street even nicknamed Davidson "The Mormon"; Mormons, Davidson half-proudly, half-bitterly explained to Chancellor North, were "popularly supposed to have an enormous number of wives."[209] But if Davidson's invitations were motivated by his desire for vicarious wives, they were also an effect of the efforts Lyons and its competitors made to idealize their waitresses' femininity, a femininity to which many customers succumbed. When cross-examined, Phyllis Holt admitted that over three and a half years spent working for the A.B.C., she had had as many as one hundred conversations in which customers had invited her out to the cinema.[210] Although persistent, Davidson did not account for all of them.

Davidson's touch of waitresses "selected" as messengers, and his repeated theater invitations, were something more than the actions of a predatory tea shop customer, however unsettling. They were instances of physical and affective touch figured by the economic conditions governing interwar tea shops; forms of desire shaped by global shifts in labor and capital structuring tea shop life. Since at least the introduction of the Nippy, waitresses were expected to be both ideal potential wives and unobtainable blurs of efficiency. They were expected to at once engage in an increasingly emotional labor, blurring the affective boundaries between themselves and customers, and in a labor *of* emotion that carefully managed the elision. Unable to shape their conditions of labor through striking, and never entirely free from associations of illicit touch, waitresses were expected to achieve a particular mode of abstract exchange with customers—an emotional transaction that nonetheless avoided any tactile or emotional "investment"—that resulted from the abstraction of their own labor as itself an exchangeable commodity.[211]

Yet crucially, as Dorothy Burn's evidence and later positive recollections from former Nippies show, many waitresses were also aware of how this abstract exchange enhanced their desirability further. While for some it meant unwelcome advances from customers like Davidson, for others it could be used both as a way to repel these advances or, more positively, to develop friendships or find love. Nippy Edith Walker remembered how, when working at the Lyons tea shop in Oxford Street, Manchester, the "marvellous organist" who played the Wurlitzer at the local Gaumont Cinema would always sit at her station and give a generous tip of twopence.[212] Florence Wright, a Nippy at 10 Oxford Street, London, in the 1930s, similarly recollected the gifts she received and still treasured the record of the Gilbert and Sullivan operetta HMS Pinafore given her by one customer.[213] The expectation for Nippies to be desirable but detached could generate unwelcome responses from tea shop customers who, like Davidson, transgressed the emotional or physical boundaries it required. But it could equally be suspended by Nippies, often leading to more positive, if still ambiguous, relationships with customers.

The Nippy's incarnation in theater especially revealed this divergence between company expectations of waitresses and the more indeterminate relations of the tea shop floor. On October 30, 1930, producer Julian Wylie's new musical comedy Nippy opened at the Prince Edward Theatre in London. The play told the story of an ordinary Corner House Nippy caught between love and fame, social distinction and anonymity. When the celebrations of Boat Race night spill into Oxford Street Corner House, Oxford undergraduate and former Etonian Bob Dering abandons his student "ragging" for "the most charming and attractive of waitresses," Nippy Grey, played by Binnie Hale. The very same night, director Albert Crumpet also spots Nippy Grey's charms and offers her a starring role in his forthcoming film. Nippy Grey, however, opts for love. She kisses Bob, earning herself an immediate dismissal. But Bob's father, Sir William, predictably disapproves of the match and threatens to disinherit Bob, compelling Grey to abandon her newfound love and accept Crumpet's offer to become a Hollywood actress. The following year Grey returns to Britain a star and, with all social barriers to marriage removed, reunites with Bob.[214]

Nippy epitomized the ideal of what the Nippy was and of what she could become, both dissolving and reinforcing the difference between them. In the words of one reviewer, Binnie Hale, "in an exalted form [. . .] vitalises those swift and dainty girls who people our tea-shops and adorn the surroundings by the grace of their manner and the urbane adroitness of their service."[215] Or as the *Tatler* put it, Hale's performance of Nippy Grey "is not only the embodiment of professional nippiness behind the tea-tray, but the essence of Cockney wit, *savoir faire*, and independence."[216] What struck reviewers was how the ordinary glamour of the waitress invested her with the potential for the extraordinary glamour of the film star, as well as the urbanity and tact of the modern wife. The studied grace of Binnie Hale the dancer and film star elicited and enlarged that of ordinary waitresses: "She is never at rest; but her ubiquity is not irritating, it is entrancing, because in everything she does there is meaning and the imperceptible effect of study."[217]

Nippy developed this theme through a scene in the second act, when the audience is screened the opening announcement to the film in which Grey stars. The credits are an endless list of variations on similar-sounding names attached to similar-sounding jobs and announcing the imminence of a film that never arrives; a parody of the self-promoting American "hyper-super talkie" and foil to the ordinary glamour of its tea shop waitress star.[218] The film-within-a-play, revealingly produced by an "Otto Hogwasch," critiques the difference between British and American productions, musical comedy and film, the contrast echoing the contrast between the waitress's glamour and that of the conventional film star (which Grey herself also parodies).[219] Just as, it was implied, the British could do anything the Americans could but more honestly, and with irony, so the tea shop waitress could be a film star, keep her charm, and marry for love. And yet, the fact that only after *becoming* a film star could Grey marry her social better reinforced her ordinariness and the social distinctions that had precluded marriage in the first place. In *Nippy*, Nippy Grey's discovered talent as a film star amplified the grace of the tea shop waitress, while also enforcing the waitress's *difference* as an ordinary worker "behind the tea-tray" which that grace apparently suspended.

Nippy's self-referential form especially foregrounded this tension between what was possible and what was not for the average Nippy. The film in act 2 was—another pun—*The Lady of Lyons*, an adaptation of the romantic melodrama of the same name written by Edward Bulwer-Lytton and first performed in 1838. In its name the film reiterated to its Nippy viewers the common origins of its star actress. In the same way, *Nippy* featured in its chorus Viola Scott from Coventry Street Corner House, the real-life version of the ordinary Nippy who becomes an actress. Scott had auditioned for the part with twenty other Nippies and was ostensibly included in the production to ensure that the rest of the chorus behaved like real Nippies as closely as possible.[220] Those Nippies who saw the show, or who read about it in the *Lyons Mail*, were given a living example of the acting success to which they might aspire while also, through Scott's very involvement in the musical as the monitor of "reality," being reminded of the difference between the fictional and real Nippy.

There is no reference to Davidson attending *Nippy*. But given that he liked encouraging Nippies' acting aspirations, started his career in comedy acting, and was unlikely to pass over a musical devoted to Nippies, it would be surprising if he did not at least once attend, or invite waitresses to. Indeed, it was September 1930, just over a month before *Nippy* opened, that Davidson began asking Kathleen Grant to join him at the theater. Whether *Nippy* was suggested or not, Davidson's habit of inviting waitresses to the theater, and the tactile relations of which this was a part, responded to the trope running throughout the musical that Nippies were both potential wives and star actresses. Yet by acting on that trope, Davidson upset the balance between the ideal of waitresses as potential wives and actresses and as disciplined workers that Nippies were expected to hold in tension. Davidson turned the abstract exchange between waitress and customer into a *real*, tactile relation—even Nippy Grey, when she kissed Bob Dering, could not escape the consequences of that.

FILM STARS AND TENDENTIOUS JOKES

Nippy Grey's film success was not entirely beyond reach for the average waitress. In the last week of April 1928, director Anthony Asquith shot *Underground* at the Waterloo tube station between 1:30 and 4:30 a.m. every day. The Underground Electric Railways Company of London granted Asquith special permission to transform the station into a "miniature Hollywood." For a few hours each day, Waterloo filled with cables, arc lights, and extras dressed as commuters.[221] Ever the opportunist, Davidson, who somehow knew the lead actress Elissa Landi, visited the set each morning and brought along anyone interested in the production: his children, his children's school friends, a few girls selling fruit, and waitresses. For some of these Davidson secured "crowd work"; others had to settle for unpaid work and the benefit of a "cheap film test." For Davidson, who no doubt also thoroughly enjoyed the experience, the work was an opportunity for waitresses to fulfill their silver

MR. A. ASQUITH'S "UNDERGROUND" FILM

Actors and actresses on the escalators during the taking of the picture. Mr. Anthony Asquith is directing the operations with the help of a megaphone.

FIGURE 19 The film set of *Underground*, Waterloo Underground Station, in the early hours of April 27, 1928. The extras included "Nippies" for whom Harold Davidson secured "crowd work"; Davidson perhaps hovers somewhere behind the camera. From "Mr A. Asquith's 'Underground' Film," *Daily Mirror* (London), April 28, 1928, 16.
© Daily Mirror/Mirrorpix

screen dreams and supplement their incomes. Extras earned twenty-one shillings a day—a significant amount for Nippies earning between thirty-two and fifty shillings a week.[222]

As we saw in chapter 3, *Underground* made visible tacit norms of personal space emerging on the tube in the 1920s. By contrast, however, Davidson's involvement with the film transgressed similar codes of appropriate touch between customer and waitress then forming in the tea shops from which its waitress-extras were drawn. Indeed, Davidson's nighttime jaunts to Waterloo called attention to the very conditions underpinning those codes of conduct in tea shops. This became especially evident in the light of accusations made by A.B.C. waitress Winifred Barker at Davidson's trial. Barker alleged that, besides irritatingly always ensnaring her in conversation while she was busy serving, Davidson once told her she had "nice teeth," and then "patted her under the chin."[223] In a characteristically oblique response to the accusation,

Davidson replied that he found it unlikely that he would have done such a thing in a restaurant, but "should not in the least hesitate to do it if I wanted to look at their teeth, to see if they were uneven." Here, an incredulous Chancellor North interjected:

> Chancellor. Just attend, because I want you to do justice to yourself. Do you really say that you would pull her lips down and look at her teeth?—A. If a girl was asking me whether she was suitable for film work, and definitely seemed to be interested, supposing her teeth were all completely uneven, I should say: "No, you had better go to a dentist."
>
> Q. You would open her lips and look at her teeth, just as you would a horse?—A. Yes.

Davidson's emphasis on the importance of even teeth to the ideal of modern beauty was not matched by adherence to unspoken rules about public touch, though he did claim he would not examine a waitress's teeth unless the tea shop was "completely empty."[224]

If Davidson's actions were shocking for Chancellor North, who vigorously underlined this section of the trial transcript in red pencil, they were not wholly inexplicable. In part they replicated the discourse that tea shop waitresses were everyday stars: both actresses on the tea shop floor and talents waiting to be discovered. Indeed, less than two weeks after Barker gave evidence, the *Daily Express* ran an article framed in these very terms.[225] After a fruitless survey of "London's working girls" for "types" suitable to feature in British films, the *Express* correspondent hit upon the tea shop waitress as the next potential film star. Customers of Coventry Street Corner House, he wrote, often called waitress Barbara Coombes "Leila Hyams"—"because of her resemblance to the Hollywood actress"—and regularly told her "she ought to be on the screen." Capturing the same paradox as *Nippy*, he suggested that "perhaps balancing a tray of steak-and-kidney puddings is a girl who has just the personality that distinguishes film stars from ordinary mortals."[226] With a suspiciously immediate response, director Marmaduke Wetherell took the correspondent at his word. A day after reading the *Express* article, Wetherell visited Coventry Street Corner House, chatted with Coombes, and signed her up for his next film, *The Moorland Mystery*.[227] Although Winifred Barker did not visit the set of *Underground*, the treatment she received from Davidson, however unwelcome, resonated with encounters such as these, encounters encouraged by the papers, repeated in shows like *Nippy*, and in which Lyons likely had a hand.[228]

In many cases, Nippies did not even have to take the initiative to make their film debut. Around the time of Davidson's trial, Lyons regularly made its tea shops available for filming or lent props and Nippies to producers shooting a tea shop scene. On one of the same nights as waitresses sought crowd work in *Underground*, Albert Bramble was shooting *Chick* (1928), the story of a City clerk who inherits a marquisate and whose new identity is accidentally revealed in a tea shop. Bramble secured permission to film in Lyons's Westminster Bridge Station tea shop, across the river from where Asquith was shooting *Underground*, and borrowed Nippies from Coventry Street Corner House to work as extras.[229] And again on April 5, 1932, the seventh day of Davidson's trial, when Winifred Barker gave evidence, director Thomas Bentley recruited six Nippies to serve in the tea shop scenes of his film *After Office Hours* (1932). Lyons lent cutlery, tariffs, even hat racks, to help Bentley get every detail perfect in the Elstree Studios' reconstruction of a tea shop. While some Nippies felt the filming experience valorized their work as waitresses, others involved were less enchanted, one apparently claiming, "I think I would sooner be a Nippy than a film star."[230]

For one author this was the sensible response to the trend in Nippy acting. J. B. Priestley's *They Walk in the City* gave a very different message to directors offering Nippies a slice of stardom. As eccentric and inscrutable as Davidson, the character delivering this message provided the fictional counterpoint to Davidson's efforts to encourage waitresses as film actresses. One day when serving in the Copper Kettle, a tea shop just off the Strand, Rose Salter noticed "an untidy fattish man," with "thick eyebrows, a turned-up nose, and a loose comical mouth" enter. The customer, a despondent playwright, was initially unresponsive, but upon realizing that Rose was new to London, he launched into a warning on its perils. London was a "wilderness," he said, in which one easily became lost. When Rose returned with the bill, the playwright solemnly drew from her a promise: "'Promise me,' he said mournfully, 'you won't ever become an actress and have a temperament and a personality and a book of press cuttings and an agent and two big offers from Hollywood. Now promise!'"[231]

The warning captured the novel's theme that London threatened its inhabitants' sense of self and echoed established claims that the film industry enabled the economic and sexual exploitation of women dreaming of film stardom.[232] It was as much autobiographical commentary as criticism of the aspirations that Priestley believed tea shops foisted on their waitresses. The playwright's disheveled appearance recognizably recalled Priestley's, and his warning to Rose ventriloquized Priestley's own feeling of being adrift in the early 1930s. As the playwright gave his parting words, Rose "suddenly realized that though he was being clever and grand and patronizing [...], he was a desperately worried, unhappy man, as deeply lost as she could ever be in this ridiculous London he described." Here Priestley voiced through Rose his confused frustration at the decreasing popularity of his plays in the early 1930s and the, in his view, perverse unpredictability of those reviewing them.[233] Through critiquing the expectations placed on tea shop waitresses and their negative effect on waitresses' sense of self, Priestley also examined the expectations placed on his own work and the self-questioning that resulted—a self-questioning he sought to manage through the fictional tea shop scene.

The disheartened playwright in *They Walk in the City* shone a sidelight on Davidson's altogether more tactile relations with waitresses. Like the author he stood in for, the playwright had a peculiarly reflexive understanding of the disorientation London caused to an individual's sense of self. His plea that Rose Salter give up Hollywood aspirations was an attempt to reestablish the boundaries of the self, his and hers, that the trope of waitress film stars eroded. By contrast, every one of Davidson's defenders depicted him as a person who, however well intentioned, lacked any reflexivity, especially regarding his actions toward waitresses. Concluding his defense, Richard Levy described Davidson as "a man who is [...] utterly indifferent—not intentionally so, but by nature—to the way in which other people would regard his behaviour." Davidson had "gone about a work upon which he has set his heart which involves conduct which most of us, perhaps, would not be involved in, and he does not realize that that conduct might subject him to misunderstanding."[234]

This indifference was apparently borne out by the way in which Davidson's actions in court seemed to waver between the wry knowingness and mock innocence of the music hall performer. When accused of flashing one-pound notes in front of waitress Dorothy Burn during his dealings with Arthur Gordon, Davidson defended himself as if performing another variety show act, explaining how he evaded pickpockets by keeping money wrapped in his socks. Apparently oblivious to the effect it would have on his credibility, if not on the public gallery, Davidson offered to demonstrate how he could remove money with his boots still on. His defense counsel declined the offer.[235]

At other times Davidson's responses suggested a more serious tack but were made so pointedly as to undercut this, and to do so explicitly, for comedic effect. Accused by Roland Oliver of conspiring with the "swindler" Arthur Gordon, Davidson riposted that he was "being charged with sexual immorality, and not with financial immorality"; if the Bishop of Norwich would "frame another charge on that," Davidson would be "delighted to meet it." Upon Davidson pugnaciously asking Chancellor North whether it was possible to add "being a swindler" to the charge sheet, there was such a riotous response from the public that North ordered part of the gallery to be cleared.[236] Ever the performer, Davidson appeared both aware and unaware of the effects of his actions, both within and outside his trial. Yet while in music hall this equivocation between knowledge and ignorance was a secret shared with the audience—it depended on a common understanding—in court it was unclear to observers whether it really was intentional or the product of a more troubling naivete.[237]

Davidson's outrageous responses consequently drew frequent laughter whenever he took the stand. After he requested that swindling be added to the charges against him, the prosecution complained of "vociferous cheering and clapping" greeting the response. Later in Davidson's cross-examination, his long-suffering defense counsel again stopped proceedings to complain of the "great deal of laughter" permitted in court over the previous hour.[238] Laughter responded to Davidson's apparently intentional comic innocence. But it also reflected a deeper discomfort over what could be known about him and what his relations with waitresses revealed. In part, the public gallery's laughter was an uncomfortable response to Davidson's inscrutability: a product of epistemological uncertainty, or the inability to know what Davidson himself knew about the consequences of his actions.[239] Surely he *knew* that inspecting a waitress's teeth "as you would a horse" was indefensible, and that claiming otherwise undercut his credibility? Yet at the same time, the laughter reflected a discomfort not at knowing too little, but too much. Whatever his self-knowledge, Davidson's actions exposed a connection between the precarity of tea shop labor and the tactile desires of tea shop customers that was all too well known but rather forgotten.

In this way, Davidson's comic turns captured in microcosm the tendentious quality of his life overall: apparently innocent, but with an end potentially exceeding its superficial value. Just as Davidson's actions in tea shops and court appeared both innocent and knowing, so observers turned his whole life into that of the holy fool, the social nonconformist who was both risible and revelatory. Two days after Davidson was convicted, on July 10, 1932, his wife, Molly, granted an interview to the *Sunday Dispatch* in which she apparently exemplified this assessment of Davidson: "Mr Davidson is a very clever man who has made but poor use of the keen brain he possesses . . . People—perhaps because they are less limited than I—take off their hats to him. They say to me with bated breath: 'What a clever man your husband is' and I mentally register: 'What fools you are.'"[240] For C. L. R. James, newly arrived in London, Molly's interview epitomized the British public's obsession with sordid revelations—not the evidence of "high civilization" he sought for his audience back in Trinidad.[241] But at another level the article neatly shifted between the innocence and knowingness of observer and observed in the depiction of Davidson as holy fool. As the correspondent ventriloquized Molly, Davidson was both intelligent and ignorant, and Molly was both able and unable to discern between them. Ultimately it remained unclear where the knowledge, which the *Dispatch* deliberately phrased in religious terms, lay: "He has pirouetted through life on a single text, 'Thank God I am not like the rest of men,' and most devout is my reply—for the world's sake—'Thank God you're unique.'"[242]

If Davidson's actions seemed to some contemporaries to reveal more than superficially appeared, they did so in a way analogous to the tendentious joke.[243] Unwelcome and unsolicited, Davidson's poking and prodding nonetheless connected domains that were normally kept distinct but, through unexpected analogues and convergences, revealed a hidden complicity.[244] By responding to the trope that waitresses could be film stars, and by his touch of those hoping to fulfill it, Davidson exposed the limitations of waitress employment conditions—low wages and increasing emotional labor—and their relation to customer desire. His touch connected the circumspect emotional labor expected of tea shop waitresses, and the desire it stimulated in customers, with its economic underpinnings; it connected waitresses' abstract exchange with customers, and customers' correspondingly frustrated desire, to the abstraction of their own labor as workers. The merest graze, the slightest brush, rubbed against and exposed the capitalist conditions making it and the desire underpinning it possible.

CONCLUSION

Harold Davidson, his defense counsel Richard Levy suggested, had "nervous hands."[245] Lady Evelyn Waechter, governess of the Foundling Hospital and friend of Davidson's, agreed, confirming his irrepressible public displays of affection. Davidson often kissed people on the forehead, "lightly—almost childishly," or kissed his hand and touched them with it.[246] He kissed everyone, it seemed, including, according to his landlady at 85 Macfarlane Road, his landlord and the milkman.[247] Indeed, during his examination Davidson admitted that he had "constantly to restrain myself from touching the learned Chancellor," to which the chancellor replied, "You had certainly much better not."[248]

References to Davidson's nervous hands characterized his behavior in psychoanalytic terms popular in the 1930s. Nervousness implied a lack of bodily control, and therefore culpability, while not quite suggesting actions that might be considered pathological. Crucially, although Davidson's defenders described his touch as symptomatic of his mental state, they however avoided any etiological explanation provided by psychiatry. No one at his trial, for example, connected his nervousness with the diagnosis of anxiety or other psychological conditions forwarded by Sigmund Freud or his contemporaries.[249] These were attempts to explain while simultaneously suggesting that Davidson's actions were more complex than any explanation could account for.[250] For Davidson himself, nervousness stemmed from an impulse to communicate. As he explained, he "emphasize[d] things much more by the sense of touch." Davidson also touched to gain another's attention or give direction. He would not, he claimed, "hold a waitress's hand in public" but would certainly "touch her arm," perhaps

FIGURE 20 On having "nervous hands": Harold Davidson holds hands with Lady Waechter de Grimston on the steps of Church House, Westminster, after hearing the judgment delivered against him, July 8, 1932.
© PA Images/Alamy Stock Photo

"constantly." He explained, "If they are hurrying by, and you want to attract their attention, instead of letting them slip by [. . .] I would just touch their arm, so that they would have to stop."[251] In all of this, though, Davidson assured his defense counsel that he did not "intend to convey" anything immoral.[252]

When concluding the defense, Levy also explained Davidson's impulse to touch in theological terms. Levy elaborated Lady Waechter's evidence to argue that "when he [Davidson] puts his arm upon people and [k]isses them upon the forehead or upon the cheek [. . .] that is a sign, not of immorality, but of friendship, sometimes merely of kindness."[253] Levy framed this in a language of sensuous Christian discipleship. Citing the archbishop of York, he asserted that "Christianity does not consist in abstaining from doing things that no decent man would do, but in doing things that nobody would dream of doing but for the touch of the Spirit of Christ." A kiss, he claimed, was "enjoined" by the New Testament "not as a thing foul and indecent" but as "a sign of holiness and of friendship."[254] As Levy explained it, Davidson's touching derived from Christian love and, because of this, was both innocent and indiscriminate. Like the holy fool, Davidson's touch, sanctioned by divine touch, fulfilled Christian discipleship through its nonconformity.

Yet as the laughter at Davidson's defense reveals, it was precisely the irresolvability of these explanations—the *inscrutability* of Davidson—that made his case so eloquent.[255] Unable to know the reason behind his actions, or Davidson's ability to know it himself, it was impossible for observers to avoid the connection between touch, desire, and the capitalist conditions of tea shop labor that both his avowed "rescue work" and his misconduct made apparent. Davidson ostensibly chased after and grabbed managers to talk about their waitresses. He was assaulted for overzealous interest in waitresses' pay or waitresses themselves. Whatever the truth in these allegations, each time touch established a connection between the economies of labor and desire that transcended Davidson's eccentricity. Davidson's touch bodied forth decades of straitened labor relations as well as revealing, in the effect these relations had on the emotional and tactile labor of waitresses, the shifting conditions for customer desire. The labor in which he intervened, and the desire that his touch also expressed, were bound by the same mode of abstraction—one economic, the other social—characterizing the life of interwar tea shops. Davidson's touch, to adapt William Sewell's phrasing, gave *embodied* form to that economic and social abstraction, at the same time as being its libidinal effect: the materialization, as a squeeze of the arm or a kiss, of that which made it possible.[256]

As for Davidson, after his trial, he showed the same inscrutable "indifference" to the perception of others. Even before Chancellor North delivered his verdict on July 8, 1932, Davidson was performing music hall skits at the Embassy Skating Rink in Birmingham.[257] The performances, which included parodies of preaching and melodramatic acting, aimed at recouping Davidson's court expenses (£750 compared with the prosecution's £8,205) and continuing his defense through afternoon lectures on "Christian Ideals in Social Life."[258] Found guilty, deprived of his living, and with the prosecution's costs awarded against him, Davidson became ever more desperate to earn money and clear his name. Between summer 1932 and summer 1936, Davidson established himself as a Blackpool Beach entertainer, performing for the crowds and protesting his innocence with speeches and cartoon postcards. Beginning with a ten-day fast in a barrel in 1932, by 1936 he was performing in a re-creation of hell in which a mechanical devil appeared to jab him in the backside with a pitchfork.[259]

For summer 1937, Davidson contracted to perform in showman Fred Rye's lion cage at the Pleasureland amusement park in Skegness. Davidson would deliver a short speech before entering the cage and posing with the lions.[260] Whether aware of the irony or not, he would act the part of "Daniel in the Lion's Den," vindicating himself before the world with God's approval.[261] But Davidson was not so fortunate as Daniel. During the evening show on July 28, Davidson startled one of the lions, who set upon him and dragged him to the corner of the cage. Only after sixteen-year-old lion tamer Renee Somer beat the lion off with a whip and drove an iron bar into its mouth was Davidson freed.[262] Two days later, Davidson died at Skegness Cottage Hospital. Rye kept the show closed only three days. On August 1, the public was invited to return to "See the Lion that Mauled the Rector!"[263]

It is difficult to know whether Davidson convinced many people about his impulse to touch. He remains inscrutable, hard to explain, but harder to explain away. His troubling relations with waitresses reveal a wider story of shifting global commodity chains, intense commercial competition, and regulated labor. Yet they also reveal how such capitalist conditions became incarnated in, and contested through, new forms of desire, touch, and experiences of vulnerability and violability.

CHAPTER FIVE

Revelations of the London Fog

"It's only for love," Mary Jones told the arresting constable, "he is not pay-ing." Perhaps more savvy to the law on public indecency, her partner Albert Parker demurely said, "all right," and buttoned up his trousers.[1] The night of Tuesday, December 9, 1924, might have seemed a good time to have sex outside the Commercial Buildings in Southwark, south London. On Monday night an anticyclone from Germany had pushed westward into the British Isles, hanging a cloudless sky over a chilly London: ideal conditions for fog to grow by Tuesday afternoon. Tuesday night was the foggiest of the year, the beginning of three consecutive days' fog—the longest duration in Lon-don since Christmas 1916—and the occasion for new delights and dangers beneath the murky pall.[2] While burglars made the most of the opportunity, an anxious London General Omnibus Company posted fifty-four "fogmen" with hurricane lamps at street junctions "to pilot buses into their proper street." Even then, two 123B buses inching in opposite directions at only walking pace collided head-on in the gloom.[3]

Meteorologists lyricized the fog's sensory disorder. Describing his ascent in a kite balloon over Croydon Aerodrome on the Tuesday night, C. Biddle-combe recalled breaking through three hundred feet of fog into "brilliant moonlight." During the ascent "nothing was visible in any direction, and all sounds coming up from the ground were muffled to an indistinctness that made them appear very far away."[4] Meteorological observations intersected with a different kind of moonlighting that night: public sex. The record of the Meteorological Office's fog-filtering apparatus allows us, remarkably, to track hourly fog density during Jones and Parker's stolen intimacy. A circular card exposed to siphoned air at hourly intervals trapped fog particulates, fog density being marked by that of the spots staining the card.[5] The record

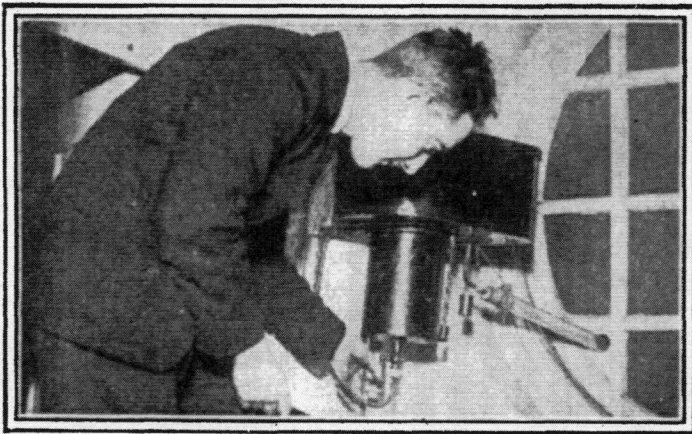

Measuring the fog at the Meteorological Office in Kensington yesterday. Air from outside is drawn through a tube into the instrument, where it is filtered through a card. The density of the fog is indicated by the amount of dirt deposited on the card during the process.

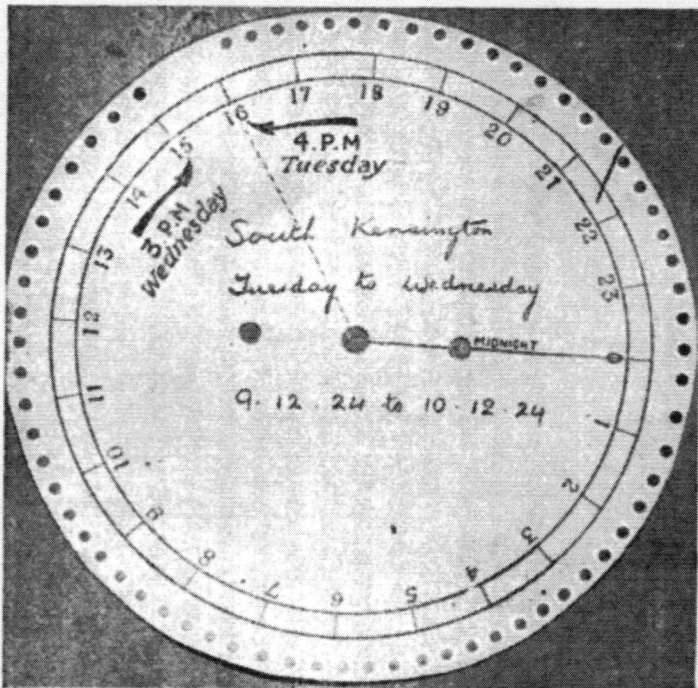

A record of London's fog from 4 p.m. on Tuesday to 3 p.m. yesterday, secured with the instrument. The ring of dirt spots on the edge show how the fog increased in density towards midnight, lifted slightly in the early morning, and gradually thickened again during the day.

between 4:00 p.m. December 9 and 3:00 p.m. December 10 showed fog density peaking around midnight, barely forty minutes after Jones and Parker were arrested. Yet as they unfortunately discovered, even bad weather can let you down.

Jones and Parker's fogbound rendezvous seems to bear out the contemporary trope of fog as a cover for illicit touch.[6] Indeed, newspapers widely represented the fog of December 1924 as encouraging a spate of Mayfair robberies by burglars who exploited the thickened night. Between December 10 and 11, 1924, at least six burglaries occurred on the mile-long walk between Norfolk Street in Bayswater and 37 Park Lane in Mayfair, a sweep of London's grandest Regency and Victorian property.[7] Three years later, Alfred Hitchcock's *The Lodger: A Story of the London Fog* (1927) appropriated fog as the "*mis-en-scène*" to the crime genre, an appropriation later inverted by newspaper reports of "cosh attacks" during the Great Smog of 1952, which described fog-shrouded assaults in filmic terms.[8] Yet to focus on representations of what fog concealed misses the more fundamental relationship between the sensory practices of the street and their regulation in law that fog *revealed*. Fog was not merely a "cover" or "setting" for illicit touch, both interpretations establishing binaries of nature and society, and passive objects and active causes.[9] Instead, to use Nead's and Latour's term, fog "translated" relations between the ostensibly autonomous "body" of law contained in legal discourse and the bodies that law regulated.[10]

London fog's mediation between law and the bodies it regulated arose through two intersecting changes over the nineteenth century. As London's population increased sixfold between 1800 and 1900, coal consumption dramatically increased from approximately one million tons in 1800 to fifteen million tons by 1913.[11] Rising smoke pollution encouraged the increasingly frequent formation of winter fogs by the last quarter of the century. Filling London's streets with eye-stinging vapor, fog caused widespread disruption and seemed to mark a new relationship between humans and their environment in the industrial age. For those parsing their way through the heavy air, fog constituted a disorienting new spatial reality in which things were not quite what they seemed. At the same time, the human origins of fog

FIGURE 21 A record of London's fog taken at the Meteorological Office in South Kensington between 4:00 p.m. Tuesday, December 9, and 3:00 p.m. Wednesday, December 10, 1924. Mary Jones and Albert Parker were arrested having sex outside the Commercial Buildings, Southwark, at 11:25 p.m. on December 10. From "London Held to Ransom by the Fog Fiend," *Daily Mirror* (London), December 11, 1924, 1.
© Daily Mirror/Mirrorpix

suggested to some observers, Taylor argues, that humans were not separate from the "natural" world but part of it, and contributed to its making.[12] Literally in front of one's eyes, fog was at once a material effect of this newfound participation of humans in their environment and a useful figure, in novels and newspapers, for interpreting it: both matter and metaphor.[13]

This duality of fog as both a physical thing and a means of interpreting relationships between things is what connects it to another, apparently unrelated, area of life: the workings of law. In London, this particularly meant the workings of the lowest courts, the police courts, which ruled on "lesser" crimes such as importuning (soliciting) or pickpocketing, and which witnessed a vast increase in caseloads over the late nineteenth century.[14] While fog offered a convenient way for explaining fluctuations in crime, the increasing frequency of fogs and volume of police court business was coincidental rather than causal. Instead, the significance of fog lay in how it physically affected the embodied experience of the street and connected this experience with the narration of bodies in court. Plunging streets into darkness, fog made visible the nature of the criminal suspect *as* a body and showed how this conceptualization was related to their prosecution during a time when police courts were increasingly stretched.[15]

Fog mediated this relation between the body "in" and "outside" of law in two ways. Rather than merely occupying space, or governing activity within it, fog engulfed it, making the bodily experience of being *within* space tangible. Through its sensorially disorienting effects, fog temporarily called attention to the streetgoer's fundamental, but easily forgotten, existence as a body-in-the-world.[16] The popular association of fog with crime connected this condition of embodiment with its narration and regulation in court. By materializing space, fog showed how what was sensorially possible on the street conditioned what was plausible in court, and how law converted that experience into a legal object, subsequently conditioning behavior on the street.[17] This chapter therefore connects the embodied experience of the street, particularly the relation between touch and obscured vision, with its discursive and embodied rendering in court. Contemporaries linked these embodied experiences through the figure of fog, or "atmosphere," both as a material thing that obscured vision and as a metaphor for the breakdown of legal procedure. The history of London fog is here told as a phenomenological "history of air" and of the work which air performed in figuring, on the street and in law, the body within it.[18]

We can glimpse this double role of fog in the case of Parker and Jones. When cross-examined, Constable Collyer claimed to have stood only five yards away from the couple, a distance from which he "could see perfectly," despite the fog. Constable Atkinson, however, stated that he and Collyer had stood twelve yards away, rescuing the contradiction with his claim that the couple was illuminated by a nearby lamp, which Collyer neglected to mention. In the court minutes there follows a line and a paraphrase of Parker's defense: he and Jones had not had sex but would have done—but no one would have seen in fog anyway.[19] At one level this was wrangling over the facts of the night; the distance, for example, at which the constables observed the couple. But it also highlights how the sensory possibilities of the street shaped whether those facts became *legal* facts—that is, facts insofar as they were instances of something defined within law—and, inversely, how law brought those sensory possibilities into being as legal facts in the first place.[20]

As with prostitution cases, police officers and magistrates depended on a ragbag of bylaws and public control orders in the absence of statutes specifically dealing with public indecency. Seeking to simplify, *Vincent's Police Code* for 1924 stressed the potential for the offense to affect others and the nature of the space in which it was committed as the variables determining the possibility of a charge. Whereas borough council bylaws did not necessarily require that the offense cause a nuisance to passersby, the Town Police Clauses Act (1847) only applied to those "who in any street *to the annoyance of residents or passengers* willfully and indecently exposes his person" (emphasis in original). A "street" was "any place of public resort or recreation ground belonging to or under the control of the Local Authority, and any unfenced ground adjoining or abutting upon any street in an urban district."[21]

Yet the Commercial Buildings, where Jones and Parker were arrested, resisted categorization: situated on an alley too minor to appear on maps, they seem to have been between Doon Street and Stamford Street, northeast of Waterloo Station, according to two indecency cases for 1927.[22] Described as a "cement passage" in 1899, the alley was neither unambiguously public nor private.[23] Johnston's *Metropolitan Police Guide* for 1922 also stated that indecency "must be committed in a public place," but this was not, confusingly, necessarily "a place open to the public; if many persons may be offended by it and several see the act it is sufficient."[24] But in Jones and Parker's case, the issue of visibility called this requisite into question and continued to do so even in clear weather: contrary to Constable Atkinson's claim, the alley was described by a policeman three years later as "a badly lighted thoroughfare," suggesting that multiple witnesses to indecency committed there were unlikely.[25] In such cases the police were hamstrung, and the *Metropolitan Police*

Guide knew it: "It appears to be still undecided whether or not an indictment for indecent exposure can be sustained by evidence of one actual witness, and of the fact that other persons might have seen the exposure."[26]

What an examination of fog reveals is the shifting "immanent" relationship between the law practiced in London's police courts and the bodies it regulated: how the "body" of law subsisted on and, through narratives performed in court, reified and subsequently shaped embodied behavior on the street.[27] Law did not stand in opposition to the material reality of the street, "inscribing" meaning onto it or "constructing" it from scratch.[28] Instead, law emerged *from* and rearticulated the sensory possibilities of the street, turning them into an object of knowledge and so constructing a fictional, ever-fragile distinction between itself and the bodies it ruled on.[29] The history of how touch and law were materialized in and through each other is therefore also that of the changing epistemological relationship between law and the material world during a period of intense pressure on London's police courts. London fog made this relationship visible, both as a physical thing that made bodies present and as a figurative device that connected embodied experience to its narration in law. For this reason, this chapter moves between the warren of south London's streets and its rendering in police courts, between law as discourse and as something bodily performed, and between fog as a thing and a figure that connected these domains in revealing, if evanescent, ways.

WEIGHING FOG

Although a regular occurrence, London's fogs varied wildly in severity between the 1870s and 1950s. Peaking around 1890, with December that year suffering twenty days' fog, the average annual number of foggy days declined in the 1900s.[30] Major fogs lasting several days were a seasonal expectation between the 1870s and 1890s but declined to the point of nostalgic connoisseurship by the 1920s: only 1916, 1924, 1948, and 1952 saw comparable spells.[31] The "elderly men" known for "button-holing friends, acquaintances, and total strangers to inflict upon them histories of [invariably worse] bygone London fogs" were nothing new, but by 1916 their tales contained just enough irritating truth to justify satirizing. One newspaper correspondent related how, during his two-hour train journey into the City, fellow passengers competed for the most fantastical account until one recollected a fog lasting from November 5, 1852, until February 26, 1853—the winter, perhaps not coincidentally, over which Charles Dickens's *Bleak House* (1853) was serialized—that "was so thick that the City Corporation had eventually to dynamite it, section by section."[32] In the face of a declining incidence of London fogs, storytellers had to make the most of dwindling opportunities to downplay present fogs in relation to those past.[33]

Meteorologists' attempts to trace variations in fog incidence concealed continuing uncertainty over when exactly a fog could be called a fog. Fog's ephemerality and tricksy nature seemed to some whimsical observers to make the causal relation between smoke and fog, like fog itself, beyond reach.[34] Even when meteorologists did, starting in the mid-1920s, narrow down the smoke-fog relation, they continued to emphasize its dependence on a plethora of contingencies.[35] Yet despite this uncertainty, at least since Harold des Voeux, president of the Coal Smoke Abatement Society, coined the term *smog* in 1904, reformers, journalists and council officers invariably connected smoke emissions with fog incidence: substituting coal with cleaner power sources therefore became crucial to reducing fog.[36]

Central to this goal were the related questions of energy use and London's traffic problem. In the same year as the term *smog* was coined, Alderman Henry Knight connected these issues in his evidence before the Royal Commission on London Traffic. According to Knight, Londoners' addiction to coal for domestic use was one of the main causes of the city's traffic congestion. At a time when London annually consumed approximately eighteen million tons of coal, the delivery of coal by trundling goods vehicles was alone enough to cause constant disruption. Coal deliveries snarled traffic and indirectly fueled London's fogs, which in turn worsened congestion: banning coal for domestic use, Knight claimed, would solve both problems.[37] Although the commissioners demurred from such a solution, they, too, connected energy use with traffic and, implicitly, London fogs. The commission welcomed the London Underground's new electric tube lines already under construction, both as a means of easing congestion for suburban travel and as a cleaner alternative to underground steam trains.[38] No explicit connection was made between the transition to electric tube trains and reduction of London fogs, in part because electrification was already underway, but commentators soon made this link after new electric lines opened.[39]

By the 1920s, the London County Council (LCC) sought to establish the direct causal connection between energy use, smoke, and fog. In 1923, the Council's Public Control Department calculated that between 1902 and 1922, the number of gas appliances sold or on hire by the three major London gas companies increased from about 623,000 to more than 2.1 million; roughly the same period saw the number of electric units sold for lighting, power, and heat increase from about 66.3 million to more than 449 million. Although gas and electricity production emitted smoke, this smoke was ostensibly more easily filtered at its source, and certainly less polluting in place of household coal fires. For the Public Control Department, these changes lessened, if not fog frequency, then the conditions for the formation of fog.[40] While the shift toward gas and electricity gave reason to be optimistic about decreasing fog incidence, it also highlighted the ongoing need to accurately measure and control smoke nuisances; still in 1923, London consumed an estimated eighteen million tons of coal a year.[41]

The LCC's effort to calculate the effect of smoke on fog formation emerged from earlier attempts to measure fog itself. This research meant that by the 1920s, LCC officials increasingly thought of fog in terms of its tangible qualities rather than only its visible effects: fog *as* matter, rather than the matter of fog. In the first official inquiry into the incidence of London fog, commissioned by the LCC in the winters of 1901–1902 and 1902–1903, fire-fighters across London recorded the degree to which fog obscured objects at a set distance from their stations. Recognizing the impossibility of achieving a common measure, in the second year they switched to measuring the degree to which fog impeded traffic, a change nevertheless maintaining emphasis on the effect fog had on visibility.[42] But beginning in 1912, and especially after the refinement of the Meteorological Office's fog-filtering apparatus in 1920, researchers increasingly attempted to capture samples of the particulates suspended in fog, and from them estimate the weight and concentration of fog itself.[43] Although smoke abatement inspectors continued to visually estimate the density of smoke, rather than gather samples to weigh, in 1931 the LCC attempted to establish for the first time a direct, statistical relation between the opacity of smoke and the quantity of its particulates, enabling inspectors to visually estimate the weight of smoke itself.[44] Increasingly, LCC researchers and inspectors conceptualized fog as an *object itself*, one that at once occupied and *displaced* space, rather than as a visual effect manifest only through its occlusion of other objects.

LINKBOYS AND PHANTOM OMNIBUS RIDES

Supposedly consigned to winters past, the midcentury return of fog threw London out of joint. Between December 5 and 9, 1952, fog suspended the capital in an earlier era, its association with the drab Victorian city juxtaposed with the Technicolor modernity of the forthcoming coronation of Elizabeth II.[45] As visibility dropped to less than forty yards in some places, "eighty-mile-an-hour police patrol cars, answering emergency calls, crept through the murk guided by constables walking with torches."[46] While such reports highlighted the anachronism of fog in an age of rapid-response cars, they also indicated its anachronistic effects: torch-bearing constables fumbling through the gloom hinted at how fog put bodies out of time and place. Fog caused the return of anachronistic figures such as linkboys, at the same time disrupting how the rhythms of the street intersected with the bodily rhythms of pedestrians.[47] The enduring importance of coal fires between the 1870s and 1950s meant that Londoners were doubly displaced by perennial fogs; first from their ostensible modernity and second from their own bodily perceptions of time and space.

Linkboys, employed by pedestrians to blaze a passage through the fog, united this double displacement. Formerly a common nocturnal sight until made redundant by gas lighting, linkboys reappeared during fogs throughout the early twentieth century, recalling an earlier, darker period. During bad fogs in the 1910s, the newspaper vendor near Somerset House relayed people across the Strand brandishing lit rolled newspapers; elsewhere, boys carrying naphtha torches charged a penny a journey.[48] The marked increase in speed and prevalence of motor buses after the Great War compelled the London General Omnibus Company to even create its own cohort of linkboys in 1919 to direct vehicles along key routes.[49] Commentators were struck by what Nead terms the temporal "uncanny" of this pre-Victorian spectacle.[50] James Bone, London correspondent of the *Manchester Guardian*, recorded how one night during the early 1900s a man returning home in fog saw Edward VII escorted by footmen and policemen bearing flaming torches. The king "had been dining with a Court lady in Portman Square, and, finding it impossible to go by carriage in the fog, had decided to summon torches and a guard and walk just as a Stuart king would have done."[51] Yet linkboys also embodied the perceptual uncanny of fog itself. "Phantom voices came from out the grey cloud," according to one correspondent during Christmas 1904;

> they were from human beings a few yards away but quite invisible. Feeling one's way through the greyness up what used to be the Strand, the wanderer became aware from the tramping feet and shouts and the clinking of harness that there was a confused mass of halted traffic. Boys carrying lighted candles or bull's-eye lanterns sprang out in front of pedestrians and said, "Light you home for a penny, sir."[52]

Out of place in historical time, linkboys also here exemplified fog's disturbance of the rhythms of everyday life intersecting in the sensate body. The reference point, or "measure," that the rhythm of omnibus traffic provided for pedestrians broke down within an acoustic and visual confusion that distorted the bodily perception of time and space: a discordance of unlocatable voices, indiscernible spaces, and surprising proximities.[53]

Knocked out of sync, pedestrians struggled to recover their bodily rhythms as fog intruded on every sense. One reporter described how fog "attacked people who were abroad in the streets, stinging their eyes and throat, causing headache and a general lassitude," a description strikingly similar to the reports of travel in the smoke-filled tunnels of the Metropolitan Railway.[54] In fact, commenting on fog five years earlier, one reporter described how "the whole of the great City was transformed into a species of gigantic underground railway tunnel, full of blinding, stifling vapour. Every one [sic] had smarting eyes and a raw throat."[55] And at the same time as the debilitating steamy atmosphere of the tube pervaded the street, thousands escaping the street flooded the tube—notably only two months after the first District and Metropolitan electric services began running in September 1905, clearing the tunnels of steam:

> Carriages were packed until passengers overflowed on to the guard's platform. The "straphanger" was a much-envied individual, for there were not enough straps to go round. [...]
>
> On the Metropolitan carriages which had no middle doors many passengers in the centre seats were carried past their stations because they were physically unable to get out. "I've played Association Football in my time," said a middle-aged passenger, "but I failed to get out at Blackfriars when I tried to. [...] I don't believe an ordinary Rugby player would have done it."[56]

The disordered rhythms of the street, and of the fog-choked pedestrians fleeing underground, intersected with new tactile dispositives forming on the tube. Amid the crush, straphangers adopted new tacit rules of standing space, while scrums in unrenovated Metropolitan carriages amplified calls for middle doors to ease passenger flow. Sensory displacement above ground alternately mirrored and propelled that below ground.

While tube passengers managed the squeeze, fog victims "groped about in the inky darkness."[57] Besides its temporal uncanny, fog also created a spatial one.[58] It made familiar space unfamiliar while, paradoxically, accentuating a pedestrian's sensory awareness. "Even the great arc-lamps were invisible at a distance of a few yards," reported the *Daily Mail* on October 28, 1901. "People blundered against omnibuses and cabs, retreated precipitately on to the pavement and found themselves on the wrong side of the road."[59] A few days later schoolteacher Ruth Mayhew, then courting the neurologist Henry Head (both of whom we met in chapter 1), described traveling across London in the fog. So thick was the fog that it appeared as if it were a "wall" through which came the disembodied voices of other enveloped travelers. Mayhew's cabman was compelled to lead the horse, and the sharp air pricked her eyes so badly that she "wept profusely," obscuring her vision even more.[60] With visibility gone, the experience of being a *body* within space, rather than a decorporealized viewer, was made immediate. This is glimpsed in the same winter, when blind people acted as street guides, aided, apparently, by their acuter awareness of body and place.[61]

Indeed, fog offered the chance to highlight blind people's greater embodied awareness of place in contrast to the metaphorical and, temporarily, physical "blindness" of sighted counterparts (as discussed in chapter 2). In March 1918, a blind resident of St. Dunstan's Hostel for Blind Soldiers and Sailors reported meeting a current officer hopelessly lost in Regent's Park during one of London's recent fogs. Unaware of his new acquaintance's impairment, the officer made a joke about their proximity to the hostel for blind ex-servicemen, which the St. Dunstanner indulged before leading the officer to his destination of York Gate without difficulty.[62] The St. Dunstanner shared this story with the *St Dunstan's Review*, which was read on publication to residents of the hostel and regularly featured anecdotes satirizing the ignorance of sighted people for presuming that of blind people. In this way, the St. Dunstanner shared an inside joke about the "blindness" of sighted people made, literally, visible by their comparable impairment during fog.

For sighted travelers, this newfound and hesitant bodily awareness applied on public transport too. In contrast to tube travel, where proximity forced passengers to improvise bodily boundaries, the near invisibility of other passengers during fog made the experience of omnibus travel eerily embodied. "Ghostly figures could be seen slipping past on omnibuses," commented one reporter, and the sensation of riding one was "that of moving slowly through space surrounded by impenetrable darkness." Suddenly passengers would be "aroused by a voice that came from the darkness demanding the fare."[63] Normally absent from consciousness, which is consumed with disembodied vision, in fog bodies were brought to presence once more. Because the body is the ground for the world, fog's transformation of the perceivable world in turn transformed the body as a ground for knowledge.

FIGURE 22 Phantom buses in the fog: Piccadilly Circus at noon on a foggy day, by George W. F. Ellis, 1924. SC/PH/CL/02/E2103.
© London Metropolitan Archives, City of London

By obscuring vision, fog returned the body to itself, reminding travelers of their existence both as objects within space and as embodied subjects perceiving it.[64]

What is more, by recalling the absent body, fog also made present the space of the street. Rather than concealing the space between buildings, by recorporealizing the body, fog made that space a tangible presence, literally casting the street into relief. "Stung they ever so sharply your eyes and lungs," James Bone remembered in 1925, "their chemistry precipitated your sense of London anew [. . .]. There is a rough, fantastic, Gargantuan goblin London lying waiting for these fogs, taking corporal [sic] existence only when the hour comes; a London's Particular makes visible a certain world whatever it may obscure."[65] Fog made visible a world that was, like a photographic negative, the negative of the world it materialized. Its immaterial presence accentuated the *material* nature of the street and experience of being a body within it. "In whichever direction the bewildered pedestrian turned," reported one newspaper in December 1904, "he was confronted at a distance of four feet by a solid grey wall which his eyes could never penetrate and which his hands could never touch. It was no longer real London with tangible objects in it, but just a grey, level desert with no obstructions and nothing real except the ground beneath one's feet."[66]

Presenting a "solid grey wall" that nevertheless remained intangible, fog revealed the impossible duality of the air it filled: at once coterminous with space and a form of matter, fog was both the ground of being for people within it and an object itself. It was an absence to be in and a presence to contend *with*, the self-erasing ground for being and implicated *in* being.[67] As one reporter hinted in 1904, this duality made fog both a "solid" imprint of the buildings it surrounded and a nebulous "cloud" effacing them: "London had suddenly become a strange new city. [. . .] The spacious streets had become a solid mass of grey, just as solid as the mass of grey which hid the buildings on each side. The world was suddenly an intangible, invariable grey cloud, through which one saw pin-points of light."[68] By bringing the body and the space it occupied to presence simultaneously, fog made pedestrians acutely conscious of their locality yet unable to perceive it. For the phrenologically minded—those who believed mental faculties were deducible from a skull's contours—fog was therefore "the chance for the Londoner proud of a 'bump for locality'":

> Feeling his way by the house-walls he perceived that his conviction that the tube station was the fifth on the left was gradually oozing. [. . .] When the fifth turning to the left failed for the first time in a dozen years to produce a tube station and he found an unknown street in a quarter where he supposed "every brick" familiar, he began discounting his topography.[69]

Even those with a "bump for locality" resorted to the equally hopeless tack of bumping into things. The most habituated commuter was outwitted by the experience of being a body newly sensitive to its locality but maddeningly ignorant of it—all because of the intangible tangibility of fog.

PHENOMENOLOGY OF CRIME
AND ITS PROSECUTION

Throughout the late nineteenth and early twentieth century, commentators associated the baffling sensory effects of fog with crime. Reports of robberies and murders that directly or indirectly attributed these crimes to the cover provided by fog became stock features of winter newspapers.[70] For several days in November 1909, the *Daily Mail* carried the story of Florence Staples, shot dead by a former stoker of the HMS *Pembroke*, Luke Brannan, after allegedly refusing him sex without payment.[71] Brannan shot Staples as she walked away after an argument on the street, apparently then escaping "under the cloak of fog."[72] These connections between crime and the sensory disorder of fog continued into the 1950s. In December 1952, reporters frequently enrolled fog as both a metonym for and explanation of crime, the *Daily Mail* connecting an apparent spate of "cosh" (beating) attacks with the Great Smog then gripping London.[73] Published five months earlier, Margery Allingham's novel *The Tiger in the Smoke* (1952) similarly conscripted fog as the pathetic fallacy for blackmail and as the cause of criminal deception within the plot.[74] For innumerable reporters, novelists, and film directors, fog was a meteorological metonym for crime—the specter haunting the Big Smoke—and the cause of crime itself.[75]

Such accounts highlighted the importance of the senses—particularly sensory disruption—to committing crime: fog disoriented victims and allowed perpetrators to escape unseen. Yet they overlooked the more fundamental nature of street crime and its policing as *always* an embodied event, one which subsequent narratives in court sought to contain. What made London fog significant was not the cover it temporarily provided for crime but the way its ethereal presence made the embodied experience of the street, and the dependence of credible courtroom narratives of crime on it, visible. By associating a spatial uncanny with crime, fog revealed, or, in Nead's terms, "translated," the way in which the ability to see, move, and touch in a particular area conditioned what narratives of crime were viable in court. These narratives in turn reshaped the embodied experience of the street.[76] Fog revealed, in short, an ineluctable entanglement of touch "in" and "outside" law.

This entanglement was especially evident in south London in the early twentieth century, and with crimes subject to police court law. It was not that south London was markedly foggier, though that was a common claim of novelists and social investigators.[77] Rather, its confusion of streets exemplified the close interdependence of *specific* embodied experiences of the street and the stories told about them in court. The shooting of Florence Staples, for example, occurred in a knot of narrow streets, the idiosyncrasies of which shaped how the act could be made into a legal case in court. Etham Street, where Staples lived, was "one of the darkest in the Borough," Constable Sommersgill told Charles Booth ten years earlier. A narrow, cobbled street of two-storied houses, it was the haunt of "thieves, prostitutes, [and] ticket-of-leave men"—of whom Brannan was evidently one.[78] The shooting occurred where Great Dover Street intersected Tabard Street through Black

Horse Court, a small street with a pub on one side, two houses and a shop on the other. Tabard Street was notorious for a series of houses owned by a local widow and "let out in rooms for single nights and short periods," mainly to prostitutes and "shady people."[79] The "character" of these streets was clearly important to legal arguments made in court. But Booth's descriptions also indicate how every physical difference in the street might shape those arguments too. While fog was central to the legal narratives in this case, it revealed the more basic relation between those narratives and the particularity of space that it filled.

The tangle of south London streets intersected with a defining feature of police court law: summary jurisdiction. If legal narratives were contingent on particular embodied experiences of the street, then they also depended on the potential for magistrates to recognize those experiences. This was more likely in London police courts, where a single, permanent magistrate, often with intimate knowledge of his district, passed judgment, rather than a panel of jurors.[80] Magistrates accumulated this knowledge through "surprise visits" and comments from the police, warrant officers, court missionaries, and, after 1907, probation officers.[81] During the trial of Giovanni and Salvatore Grassi, charged in March and April 1930 with managing the Empress Hotel at 54–60 Waterloo Road, Lambeth, as a brothel, Sergeant Harold Parker gave evidence tying Waterloo's warren of streets with the problems of policing the area and making cases in court. Waterloo Road, he told the magistrate of Lambeth Police Court, was "a difficult neighbourhood." Prostitutes frequented the road nearest the train station, where there was "considerable traffic" and cheap hotels charging around seven shillings and sixpence a night, mainly to those who missed their trains.[82] The constant flow of travelers provided a regular customer turnover and the hotels inexpensive accommodation, and the fact that many who missed their trains lacked luggage meant prostitutes could pose as the partners of their similarly empty-handed clients. This meant it was difficult to determine the incidence of prostitution *and* to turn it into a credible case in court. Only after fifteen nights' observation, during which time Parker and Constable Alexander Kinkaid saw 180 couples enter, including forty-two women known as prostitutes, did the police prosecute.[83]

Parker's account of Waterloo did more than admit the qualified nature of evidence possible in such a case—the identification of known prostitutes, the unstocked hotel "kitchen," guestbook discrepancies, fleeting stays, and absent luggage of hotel guests. It asked the magistrate to excuse these weaknesses on the basis of his knowledge of the physical *locale* and the type of fugitive intimacies possible within it. "All great railway stations," the *London Perambulator* corroborated, "surround themselves with a sort of debatable land that is neither residential, commercial, industrial, trading, nor theatrical. It has shabby hotels and makeshift lodgings, bawdy houses, pawnbroker's shops, second-hand dealers [. . .]. A strange temporary look hangs about the place as though the denizens were always packing up, many of them moving on, [. . .] and the place was organized for the immediate disposal of their goods." Waterloo in 1925 exemplified this "sinister side of the drama of coming and going, [. . .] with its shabby confusion of railway arches and rows of dark little houses lying in ambush in its intricacies, its second-rate music-hall rendezvous, and a particular South London blight near the river suggesting wharfland."[84]

The "South London blight" fastened on the railway station, spreading out far beyond. Walking north under the arches of the South Eastern Railway on Waterloo Road, the streetgoer came to the aptly named Elbows Corner on York Road, where, since at least the 1890s, "the poorer music hall artists loaf[ed] in hope of a job."[85] One of these was Harry Fowler, out of work since mid-December 1919 and arrested for importuning men on January 5, 1921. During his trial, Fowler claimed he had spent the evening drinking in the Hero pub opposite the station until 10:00 p.m., when he left and walked up the road toward Waterloo Bridge to a coffee stall, possibly the same one that worked outside 17 Waterloo Road just before the war. He claimed to have been waiting for a bus to Victoria.[86] Constable Ernest King recounted a different story, detailing Fowler's encounter with a sailor outside the Hero. "'Hello Jack you seem lonely.' The sailor said 'Just a bit.' Prisoner said 'I'm looking for one of you for the night' and he touched the sailor in his private parts. The sailor put himself in a fighting attitude." Fowler allegedly hurried toward Waterloo Bridge and tried his luck with two other sailors before King arrested him on the corner of York Road.[87]

Besides unemployed music hall artists, York Road accommodated many of their agents, as well as a rash of brothels.[88] Narrow streets connected York Road with Belvedere Road, lined with "low, dirty, and half-derelict wharves looking on to a welter of black mud except at the high tide."[89] Here in January 1921, Constable King arrested Jean Campbell and Thomas McEleney for indecency. McEleney, one of those travelers who "hadn't got a train for some time," met Campbell near the new Victory Arch entrance to Waterloo Station on York Road: "I'd been told by Dr to mix with opposite sex to help me to talk as I was suffering from neurasthenia."[90] Back on York Road, and only a week later, two constables noticed Charles Warnham accosting men between the Duke of York saloon bar and a urinal in adjacent York Street. On entering the bar they allegedly heard him ask another man, "Come on, old sport, aren't you going to have a blow through down the hole in the wall?" The Hole in the Wall bar squatted beneath the railway arches running up to Waterloo East Station on the opposite side of Waterloo Road. One of the constables made its alternative meaning, and possibly alternative purpose, clear when he gave evidence that, upon his arrest, Warnham was "wearing a pair of trousers with a large split over the backside." Warnham alleged a police setup: he did not go to any bar of that name and had received the hole at the police station, where the station officer told him to bend down, put his hand to the trousers, and ripped them. His mother, Eliza, who had patched them up previously, corroborated.[91] Whatever the truth of the matter, the magistrate had to be alert to the way that the topology of south London not only created possibilities for illicit encounters but also became a local lexicon *of* those encounters as well.

Heading back to Elbows Corner and turning north toward the Thames, the streetgoer approached the Empress Hotel, let by Giovanni Grassi since November 1918. Outside the hotel one January evening in 1923, Elsie Leonard allegedly grabbed the arm of a passerby and flashed an insinuating question. Constable Marshman arrested her and her companion Peggy Robinson for soliciting—"Damn it, kid, give us a chance." Leonard, who lived on the notorious Oakley Street between Blackfriars Road and Waterloo Road, claimed she didn't touch the man and was only waiting for a bus over Waterloo Bridge; the man had approached her asking for twopence, which she refused.[92] Constable Charles Barber had arrested Florence Lucock and Lily May for the same offense at the same spot almost exactly two years previously. Lucock and May had come arm in arm from Stamford Street, at the intersection of York and Waterloo Roads.[93] Stamford Street was "one of the ugliest and most sordid streets in London," according to Walter Besant in 1912. This was another haunt of prostitutes, music-hall agents, and "poverty-stricken actors waiting for engagements."[94] Just off it ran the passage where Mary Jones and Albert Parker were arrested for indecency in 1924. It also gave onto Coin Street, where Lewis Hodgkinson and Nellie Smith were arrested for indecency in February 1914. Allegedly caught in the act, Smith bombarded Constable Walter Rake with all possible extenuating circumstances. "I'm hard up, it's my first night out, he didn't do it but he tried to feel me." But the place, as much as the evidence itself, was against her: Hodgkinson was fined only ten shillings, Smith five pounds, far more than even the usual inequality required by a law that penalized female prostitutes rather than their male clients.[95]

Had Constable Rake kept to Waterloo Road, "a broad road flanked by bad architecture, and noisy with omnibuses, trams, cabs, and heavy vans," his task would not have been easier.[96] Walking south toward St. George's Circus, the streetgoer passed the Aubin Street lodgings of railway porters, known for their variable earnings and reputedly heavy drinking. The whole street was swallowed up by station redevelopment, completed in 1922.[97] To the east, the streetgoer passed the Union Jack Club, opened in 1907. Located at 91 Waterloo Road, opposite the station, the club provided a library, billiard and coffee rooms, and 204 guest rooms for noncommissioned servicemen visiting London. In theory, the club closed at 12:30 a.m., "after which hour no one except those staying at the Club or wishing to occupy a bedroom [we]re admitted"; in practice, the individual rooms made it a good place for guests to bring back partners met outside.[98] Like the Empress Hotel 31 doors down, the Union Jack Club's street front was also popular with those soliciting the passing trade, especially its footloose armed services constituent. As the locus for servicemen thronging London during and immediately after the Great War, it subtly shifted the nature and geography of prostitution as the seasoned "professional" of the West End, increasingly targeted by the police, gave way to the more youthful, and more dispersed, "amateur." This increasingly prevalent "type" ostensibly did not ply out of necessity but for "an evening out," and was found "around the bus-stops and in the tea-lounges of the cheap-rich hotels," Thomas Burke alleged. "It began in khaki-mania, but it is now for many a settled course of life."[99]

Whatever her motivations, Sibyl Thomas was spotted soliciting outside the Union Jack Club in January 1921. She had been testing the waters with sailors outside the Fire Station—150 Waterloo Road, and another hot spot for soliciting since it opened in 1910—before crossing to the club and the Hero pub fifty yards up.[100] The large number of servicemen passing through its doors—forty-two thousand alone using its sleeping accommodation in the first nine months—also made it one of London's most important queer cruising grounds.[101] In mid-January 1927, Joseph Phillips, his face "covered with powder, eyebrows penciled, lips rouged," accosted four men outside the club before walking down to Wellington House, opened in 1928 as the David Grieg department store at 133–155 Waterloo Road, where he approached another. He was arrested in Cornwall Road when, mistaking the plainclothes constable shadowing him for a potential client, he angled again: "Well Jack would you like to spend a night with me. [. . .] I want love and affection—not money so much, altho' I could do with a little."[102]

"Misery Junction," people called it.[103] Here, in acute form, space mattered—both to the possibility for illicit touch and to the parameters of legal narratives possible in court and the effect those narratives had on subsequent illicit encounters on the street. If fog revealed the relation between embodied experiences of the street and the actual and legal existence of illicit touch, then north Lambeth and Southwark in the early twentieth century exemplified this relation. Its warren of streets *enabled* fleeting sexual encounters at the same time as it *constituted*, through the magistrate's local knowledge and summary jurisdiction, the law governing and shaping them. Rather than existing in a relationship "with" police court law, specific embodied experiences of the street—the ability to touch, be touched, and get away with it without being seen—were stitched into that law, while that law was stitched into those experiences of the street and brought into being through them.

MAKING SENSE IN THE POLICE COURT

It was 11:30 p.m. on Christmas Eve, 1920. Constables Armstrong and Northcote were standing outside the Rockingham pub at Elephant and Castle, a junction just south of St. George's Circus. Glancing across the street, Armstrong saw what he called a "scuffle'" within the crowd clamoring around the tram, or streetcar—but nothing requiring immediate attention. Minutes later, he was approached by William Beckwith, who alleged that he had been punched as he attempted to board the tram. "What the f—g hell are you looking at?" demanded the man blocking his entry, who with two others pushed Beckwith back and gave him a "nasty clout" on the mouth. When Beckwith returned to the tram with the two constables, he later claimed at the trial in Tower Bridge Police Court, he identified his assailant—a costermonger named Samuel Rowen—and his two accomplices, one of whom was Albert Bentley.

Here the story presented in court frayed at the edges. After Beckwith identified the men, he claimed, "Rowen broke away and I could not hold him"; he was chased and arrested in Tarn Street, where a large bus company was located. But Constable Armstrong gave a different account. Instead, he shifted the magistrate's attention away from Rowen and onto Bentley. He stated that even before he left the Rockingham, he had noticed Bentley blocking the footboard of the number 56 tram, thereby allowing fellow pickpockets to work among the tumble of bodies pressed against the entrance. When he approached, Bentley was repeating the ruse for another tram. Armstrong put his hand on Bentley's shoulder; Bentley threw his overcoat at him and bolted, Rowen covering his escape by tripping up the pursuing constable. Only at this point did Rowen come to his attention, not, apparently, because Beckwith had identified him as a culprit. Yet this contradicted Beckwith's evidence that it was *Rowen* initially blocking the tram entrance—the cause of their fracas and the assault—and that when he returned to the tram, it was the third man "not in custody" holding the rails, *not* Bentley. It also contradicted Armstrong's own evidence that when he first saw the defendants across the street, they were not doing anything for which they could be arrested.[104]

If this sounds confusing, then it should. These contradictions indicate the messy reconciliation between the embodied experience of the street and police court law. They show how a street's physical constraints on sight and touch conditioned not only possibilities for criminal touch but also the plausibility of narratives about that touch in court and therefore its existence as a legal "fact." When Beckwith reported his assault to the constable, he later recounted, he was asked whether he had "felt any hands in my pockets." He replied that he had not and was "merely charging Rowan [*sic*] with hitting me in [the] face," to which the constable responded bluntly, "All you can do is to summon him." As this was an arrest and not a summons, the constable was implying, the police, not Beckwith, would define the charge.

This marked a redirection from Beckwith's original claim of assault to a police charge of pickpocketing, with assault as a subordinate charge: an easier case to make stick given the timing of the tram tussle during the return home of last-minute Christmas shoppers, with their presents and extra provision of cash. This redirection developed into a contested geography of the street as each witness tried to jam the sensory experience possible within it into a different charge that made sense—literally and figuratively—in law. According to Beckwith, he walked one hundred yards to the Rockingham from the tram, which stopped outside a fruiterer's on Walworth Road; he couldn't recall whether there was a lamp standard by the shop. But Armstrong claimed that the tram ran short of the fruit shop, stopping only twenty yards from where he had stood. He further added that there was a lamp standard directly opposite where the tram stopped, strengthening his claim to have detected Bentley's obstructionism from a distance. The contradictions reached a head when Constable Northcote alleged that the defendants had tried pickpocketing Beckwith after assaulting him—which Beckwith flatly denied.[105]

These tensions between the street and its incarnation in law were only resolved through tensions in law itself, which shifted between registers of formality during the trial. Legal formality and minute book form shifted in tandem. After Beckwith rejects Northcote's evidence, there is a line in the minute book, followed by the court clerk's interpolation. The clerk records that the magistrate refuses to admit evidence of Rowen and Bentley's previous convictions, but there then follows a long list of exactly that, along with a marginal note that the magistrate "raises no objection to this informal method of bringing the evidence of previous convictions before the Court." It was then short work for the magistrate to disregard Beckwith's narrative of the street and convict the defendants as "rogues and vagabonds" rather than for assault.[106]

What this episode highlights is the often uneven fit between the embodied experience of the street and its existence in law—and the tricky search for their immanent relation. "The magistrate is often not over-punctilious in his regard for the rules of evidence," wrote Hugh Gamon, a social investigator for the Toynbee Trust, in 1907. "They are exceedingly technical, and somewhat unreasonable at certain points. They have been devised more for the regulation of trial by jury than for the magistrate of legal knowledge and practical experience." In a "drunk and disorderly" case, for example, the magistrate might simply ask the assistant jailer or clerk if they recognized the defendant in order to confirm suspicions of guilt.[107] And yet, for indictable cases sent to a higher court, "the evidence is more strictly guarded against a breach of the technical rules of Law" and "the depositions of evidence are more carefully written down by the clerk, and signed by the witness."[108]

The particular nature of the case against Rowen and Bentley meant that *both* these statements were true. The list of their previous convictions was long: nine for Rowen between July 1908 and August 1920, including three for assault and two for loitering, and nine for Bentley between December 1913 and March 1920, including five for successful or attempted larceny and two for being a suspected person.[109] Rowen lived at 27 Millcot [Milcote] Street, Blackfriars; Bentley, a stone's throw away at 140 Blackfriars Road, part of the Peabody Estate social housing opened in 1871.[110] These details suggest that Rowen and Bentley were both well known at Tower Bridge, probably as accomplices, long before their convictions were "informally" presented in court. What was an offense for the police court (being "rogues" and "vagabonds") therefore also had potential as one for a higher court—being "incorrigible rogues," which required the judgment of a jury.[111] Potentially referable to quarter sessions, the "technical" accuracy of evidence had added importance. Yet at the same time, the impossible contortions of the street sensescape into credible *legal* accounts of the street compelled the magistrate to abandon that accuracy in order, paradoxically, to preserve it; in order to make possible a legal case which could subsequently reappear at sessions before a jury.[112] Precisely because the rules of evidence were stricter in higher courts, they had to be bent in police courts when the embodied experience of the street translated poorly into a case in law. As J. A. R. Cairns, Thames Police Court magistrate, cautioned in 1923, "in indictable offences a prisoner should not be committed for trial unless the evidence is such that a jury would probably convict."[113] But to establish that evidence, rules had to be broken. Magistrate Henry Waddy Turner was strongly of this opinion:

> It is simply futile to keep on telling a garrulous woman in the witness-box, whose burning passion is to interject every few seconds to the man in the dock, "Oh, you scoundrel!" that she must give the precise words that were used, use the first person and not the third, not make statements that are hearsay, and so on.
>
> The very next moment she exclaims, "All the neighbours know him; he only came out of prison last week!"
>
> If a magistrate insists in this matter on the standard of the High Court of Justice, he may easily miss the truth. It is often from some aside, in itself wholly inadmissible, that the thread appears by means of which an apparently hopeless tangle may be undone.
>
> After all, a magistrate is a lawyer, and he sits without a jury; he must learn to discard.[114]

An aside revealing a defendant's previous conviction might be just what the magistrate needed to judge a case adequately concrete for indictment.

Consequently, Detective Inspector Webber presented the list of previous convictions *before* Rowen and Bentley gave evidence or a judgment was reached, enabling the magistrate to settle on a charge that allowed for conflicting narratives of the touch and vision possible in the street: both were tried under Section Four of the Vagrancy Act as "suspected persons and thieves."[115] They were convicted as rogues and vagabonds and committed to quarter sessions at Newington where, on January 13, 1921, Justice Allan Lawrie and twelve jurors convicted them as incorrigible rogues and suspected persons, sentencing Rowen and Bentley to nine and six months' hard labor, respectively; the assault charge had fallen out of the picture.[116] When the street could not be converted into a narrative in law, then law had to accommodate the street by suspending its own rules of evidence.

Yet it worked the other way around, too: while embodied experience conditioned the making of law, law also brought that experience into being as an object through narratives woven in court. Crucially, though, these narratives were not wholly discursive but themselves existed only through the material workings of the court: through tangible paperwork and embodied practices that materially conditioned the reproduction of the street in legal form. The legal objectivity of the street, of its embodied experience, still existed only through files that could be circulated, compared, and collated, connecting the particulars of a case with the general, and through bodies that could be arranged into a particular habitus and spatial relationship that allowed those connections to emerge as legal "truths."[117] Rather than bringing into being the "Law" which, as it was understood by contemporary jurisprudence, already existed, these objects and practices brought Law into being *as a concept itself* through each instance of their use, thus collapsing its ostensible autonomous existence *as* "Law."[118]

The case of Harry Conniham, a twenty-three-year-old music hall artist, and Robert Wright, a twenty-one-year-old hairdresser, charged together with being suspected persons in January 1930, is an example. To prevent police narratives of the street being incorporated into one another, so unfairly invalidating his own, Conniham requested that each constable present his evidence without the presence of the other in court. In a system where, only two decades previously, clock-watching magistrates seldom bothered to exclude other witnesses from court and defendants were "seldom aware" of their right to do so, this request was strikingly astute.[119] Remarkably, Conniham drafted questions with which to quiz each constable independently, thereby precluding corroborating evidence that might challenge his own account of events. But more remarkable is the way he presented this evidence: as, appropriate to his profession, a play. "The Night Patrol," submitted in a blue exercise book framed with flowers, was a play of two acts, the second of which exhaustively outlined Conniham's movements in the predawn hours of January 12. Accompanying the play was a sketch map of the route he took from Embankment to Southwark Street, along with arrival times at each location.

The action began with an offer of work. At 10:30 p.m. on Saturday, January 11, Conniham got to talking with a commissionaire who offered him "a chance to earn a few shillings fetching taxis for people attending a party on his ship when they started going home at one o'clock." Wright was to guard the cars parked nearby. Performing their duties until the ship's pier closed at 4:30 a.m., they ambled along the Embankment until reaching Waterloo Bridge, where they had a cup of tea at The Welcome, an all-night traveling café.[120] The Welcome, later known as The Silver Lady, was a coffee van providing tea, coffee, bread, and dripping, as well as socks and mufflers, for down-and-outs. Run and financed by Betty Baxter, the twentysomething granddaughter of the founder of the *Christian Herald*, it began operating in August 1929 and became increasingly important as the Great Depression bit harder and a growing tide of unemployed people from distressed areas flooded London.[121] The van opened on the Embankment at 1:00 a.m. before driving to Trafalgar Square, up to Bayswater Road, and then back to its pitch opposite Cleopatra's Needle on the Embankment sometime between 5:00 and 6:00 a.m. Each area attracted its own "colony" of drifters, with young men like Conniham and Wright preferring Embankment; older men settled themselves farther away, under the covered section of Craven Steps off the Strand, but still close to the van.[122]

From the month it began operating, the superintendent of "A" Division, H. Martin, took a negative view of The Welcome café. Martin believed the van attracted "undesirables," whom the police had been trying to clear from Embankment.[123] Implicit in his and others' remarks on the case was the

FIGURE 23 The Welcome all-night traveling café serving tea, coffee, bread, and dripping to down-and-outs on Embankment. The photo featured in Betty Baxter's advertisement of *The Night Patrol* film in *The Sunday at Home* in 1930. 1983-5236/308.
© Daily Herald Archive/Science Museum Group

assumption that those receiving unofficial charity were by definition undesirables because they refused to use the Metropolitan Asylum Board Night
Office at Charing Cross, which served as "a clearing house for all 'helpable'
destitute persons."[124] However, Martin saw no way to prevent the van from
operating except through a charge of obstruction, which was near impossible in the spacious hours of early morning.[125] Two years after Conniham
and Wright's arrest, with two hundred people being served each night, Martin finally took action and ordered his officers to "drive the vagrants away
and not let them congregate."[126] This action sparked a furious reaction in
the press, with the *Star* reporting that those who frequented the van were
"in danger of arrest."[127] After concerned constituents wrote to Member of
Parliament for Hendon Sir Philip Cunliffe-Lister, Metropolitan Police Commissioner Lord Trenchard issued a directive on December 1, 1931 that the
order should not be enforced.[128] Into the 1930s, The Welcome was associated
with loitering and "unhelpables" whom the police disliked congregating but
lacked legal pretext to arrest.[129]

Conniham claimed that he and Wright chatted at the van between 4:35
and 4:40 a.m. and then walked along Embankment; the clock on the new
Lever House read 4:43 a.m. Crossing Blackfriars Bridge, they stopped at
another coffee stall on Blackfriars Road, where they had tea, doughnuts,
and cream. They then turned into Southwark Street and, after five hundred
yards, paused to count the five strikes of Big Ben ringing out across the city
from the clock tower of the Houses of Parliament. Both being interested in
football, they bought copies of the *News of the World* and *Sunday Express* at
a nearby newspaper depot and then continued toward London Bridge.[130]
Constables Hormaid and Woolf arrested them outside a "closed refreshment
house" opposite St. Saviour's Public Baths.[131]

Through these narratives Conniham sought to control the law's formulation of the embodied experience of the street. His to-the-minute timings
and detailed topography of Southwark aimed at shaping how law extracted
the exemplary from the incidental. In magistrate's discourse, he introduced
new *facts in issue*, "facts which are alleged by the prosecution and denied by
the accused," and precluded others by meticulously providing additional *relevant facts*, facts close enough to facts in issue that they make them "probable
or improbable."[132] He said, for example, that when the constables arrested
him, they claimed to have started their observations from Embankment,
where The Welcome stood, but when they arrived at the police station, they
claimed they had only done so "from a doorway in Southwark Street." Conniham asked which of the two was correct. Disputing this point implied a

suspicion of police tactics to wait for coffee van loitering, which was suspect but not arrestable, to become "loitering with intent," which was. Conniham continued:

> You also said that you saw us stop at a coffee stall in Blackfriars Road yet you watched our approach from a doorway in Southwark Street which is the first turning from the Bridge on the left of Blackfriars Road and the first shop doorway is three or four hundred yards from that corner. May I ask you how you could have seen us at the coffee stall from the position stated.[133]

By multiplying facts in issue and delimiting the possibility for others through a precise urban topology, Conniham constricted how law could reproduce the embodied experience of the street. He constricted how law knitted together different accounts of that experience into a single narrative, matching it up with the existing body of legal files in order to make it a particular instance of a general *case* within law; in this instance, being a suspected person.[134]

But the material differences in his narratives—a map, a play, a list of questions—highlight how narrating the street was not only a matter of abstracting the general from the particular but turning that particular back *into matter*: into files that could be assembled and reassembled, circulated, and toward which it was necessary to take a particular bodily attitude.[135] If law necessitated the knitting together of files, then material variations between and tactile practices toward those files counted as much for the law's making of the street as the narrative content they materialized.[136]

Conniham's play, penciled in a standard lined exercise book but pinned with the court minutes, was caught between sincerity and whimsy. On one level, it was an earnest plea for acquittal; on another, a tongue-in-cheek suggestion that truth was staged, rather than simply related, in court. By providing a transcript for his evidence in court, it scripted him as an actor who bodily *performed* truth on the witness stand. Yet "The Night Patrol" was even more intriguing than this. The title referenced a film of the same name, shot by Norman Lee for H. B. Parkinson Productions at The Welcome exactly four months prior to Conniham and Wright's arrest. The film, now lost, worked in a vein of nighttime travelogues established by Harry Parkinson through his *London after Dark* (1926) series, which dwelled lovingly in the darker spaces of London's underside.[137] In similar tones of charity and exposé, *The Night Patrol* featured down-and-outs receiving refreshments from The Welcome café. One segment was shot over twenty minutes on the morning of September 12, 1929, but it is impossible to know who was present.[138] Conniham might have heard about the film through chatting at the van, or he might even have featured in it.

A month after Conniham and Wright's trial, *The Night Patrol* made it into national papers when an incensed George Bernard Shaw wrote to the *Times* complaining of its denial of a license by the British Board of Film Censors. Shaw revealed more of the film's content: it told two stories, one of a miner who travels to London in search of better prospects but finds himself jobless and adrift on the Embankment; another of a young woman lured to London by a bogus "White Slaver's advertisement" who is drugged, smuggled onto a ship for the Continent, escapes, and finally is rescued by charity workers.[139] The film attempted to dissuade economic migrants from traveling to London and to fundraise for Baxter's Welcome café and the Elizabeth Baxter Hostel for Stranded Women and Girls at 52 Lambeth Road established by her grandmother.[140] But *The Night Patrol* was denied a license, initially, Shaw was told, because it "might discourage" girls from traveling to London when they were "badly wanted" as domestic servants, and then, when he wrote directly to the censor, because it depicted the forbidden topic of the white slave traffic.[141] The denial, and Shaw's letter to the *Times*, triggered a prickly debate in the press about the inadequacies and necessity of film censorship and, ultimately, the truthfulness of documentary representation: how could it be wrong, Baxter asked, to depict real cases if they educated viewers of the dangers to which down-and-outs were prone?[142] The National Vigilance Association, by contrast, argued that although *The Night Patrol* was doubtless "harmless," licensing it would allow similar films to be made that were not and were "made with a winking eye on the box office."[143] By March 13, 1930, the Home Secretary was asked in the House of Commons why "extraordinarily fine educational British films [were] being banned for political reasons" while American films bordering on "indecency" were waved through.[144]

Conniham presented his version of *The Night Patrol* five weeks before it became national news, possibly coinciding with Baxter's private screenings of the film and tussles with the censor.[145] Whether he featured in it or had merely heard of it, titling his evidence after the film conveyed the importance of convincingly *acting* the part of down-and-out, both on the street and in court. This performance passionately countered the cultivated "indifference" toward files adopted by every magistrate's habitus: what Magistrate Cairns called the "judicial temper." It was essential, Cairns wrote, to resist forming an opinion until the last possible moment, essential to hesitate at every opportunity: only then might judgments ultimately be given unequivocally and peremptorily.[146] Hesitation, and the justice dependent on it, stemmed from mental and bodily self-control and a calculated "equable" habitus toward other bodies in court: "An unfortunate prisoner should not be made the victim of a disordered digestion."[147] Through a comportment of disinterest, magistrates *embodied* that hesitation essential to sifting the relevant from the irrelevant. Explaining why he easily cried at the theater but never at the police court, Marylebone magistrate Alfred Plowden mused that "the stage to me is the world of reality—the world, nothing but a stage. In the one I feel, because I am *free* to feel. In the other, being just an actor like all around me, I have learnt [. . .] how to conceal every natural emotion."[148] "The Night Patrol" responded to this truth, confirming that law was not only performed in the translation of "documents" into "files" but in the embodied performance of, and toward, those documents themselves—in each postural stance and grip and shun of *paper*.

But accompanying the play were very different documents: an address card—5 Sloane Court, in affluent Chelsea—and letter to the court clerk from Lady Clodagh Anson, daughter of the Marquis of Waterford. Anson volunteered at The Welcome and had served Conniham and Wright on the morning of January 12. She knew Conniham as "Charlie Chaplin," an alias he acquired by copying the comedian "in pit queues or in the smaller cinemas when one of the Chaplin films was being shown."[149] Anson's letter, however, failed to fit Conniham's account. As a character testimonial that even mistook his name—"Harry Calindale"—it could not support Conniham's intervention in law's linking of documents in order to extract a case. The letter gave no information on the morning encounter and closed with Anson's assertion that she had "never known him expect money in exchange for his services" or to "cadge for money," a hair's breadth from contradicting his account of fetching taxis for partygoers.[150] The first act of the play, crossed out, was in fact a defense against this charge made by a constable on a separate occasion—"I saw a gentleman having a little difficulty in opening a cab door from the inside so I offered assistance by opening the door from outside. He then offered me some coins for my help so I did not refuse them."[151] Anson did not know Conniham well. Her letter ineffectively shaped how documents were chained together to reproduce the embodied experience of the street and assess its possibility as a case in law.

Anson's memoirs revealed the ineffectiveness of her intervention, and the fact that this was concealed from her, all too clearly. In parts her account, published a year later, accorded with Conniham's careful delineation of the street; what was sensorially possible and factually probable within it. She wrote that when Conniham and Wright left the coffee van, "they were walking slowly, as they meant to get to the fish market about five." Billingsgate was a magnet for down-and-outs seeking work, and because Conniham and Wright were arrested at 5:00 a.m. walking toward London Bridge, which abutted the market, this supposition was highly likely. But when it came to events in court, which she did not attend, she claimed that the "kind-hearted" magistrate, finding that the defendants had not been carrying any implement with which to break and enter, acquitted them and rebuked the constables for suspecting guilt simply on the basis of the state of their clothes.[152] In reality, the magistrate found both defendants guilty of being suspected persons and sentenced them to one day's hard labor.[153]

What this contradiction showed was not only the weakness of Anson's corroboration but, more important, how it conflicted with the play *as a letter*. Contrary to the play, which scripted Conniham's performance, the letter apologized for Anson's absence in court: it stood in for that absence, situating the truth of its narrative not in its performance but in the status behind it. If the play countered the magistrate's bodily indifference to files, Anson's decision to send a letter ignored it altogether, failing to influence how it was turned into a case through a process of embodied doubt. Which is strange, given that she, like Cairns, similarly worried about the magistrate's bowel movements. "The magistrate," she decried, "is a complete law unto himself." If he was sympathetic, then he could do much good, "but if he suffers from indigestion, or has allowed himself to get strong and very unreasonable prejudices," then he might turn "perfectly harmless human beings into bitter criminals."[154]

The ordering of bodies and documents shaping the extraction of a case depended on a proper ordering of court space. Through enclosures, elevations, paneling, and thresholds, court space materialized the logic of the legal process reproducing the embodied experience of the street.[155] A collocation of bodies and documents, it circumscribed the way in which the embodied experience of the street emerged in law; became part of the body *of* law. Tower Bridge Police Court, where Conniham and Wright were tried, was the "culmination of police-court building ideals" when it opened on 211 Tooley Street, just east of London Bridge Station, in 1906.[156] Entering beneath a colonnaded balcony via a flight of shallow stone steps, the litigant passed into "a spacious and lofty hall, panelled in oak, with benches set against the walls." Here congregated applicants for summonses, heard when the court opened at 10:00 a.m., "prosecutors, witnesses, complainants, defendants, friends and loafers," all pacing restlessly, talking in "eager knots," or seated against the wall, "dull, listless, and silent." The hall gave onto the principal courtroom, a large, square room "with a clerestory of wood and glass rising out of the roof." Despite its famously poor acoustics, which threatened both the giving and receiving of evidence, Gamon felt it possessed an "unostentatious grandeur" conducive to the sober exactitude of law.[157]

The court floor was "as full of partitions as the bottom of a fishing cobble." At the far end of the room, "on a carpeted dais and beneath a canopy," stood the magistrate's oak and red leather "throne." Running in front of the dais was "a paling of finished woodwork, cutting his worship off from all contact with the common herd." This physical distance aimed at preserving the objective one underpinning the magistrate's judicial temper.[158] To the magistrate's left and right were "solemn cupboards, devoted to the repose of heavy legal tomes," while before him was "a writing-table, piled with reference books and papers."[159] With the law, quite literally, at his side, the magistrate confronted a heap of jostling depositions, each requiring reconciliation with one another and with the law of which they aspired, or refused, to be a case.

This spatial mediation situated the magistrate at the center of a legal one. Unique to petty courts, where one or both sides often lacked solicitors, magistrates played a "double part," cross-examining witnesses on behalf of unrepresented litigants at the same time as assessing the viability of the extracted case within law.[160] The magistrate acted as "counsel and judge," turning the embodied experience of the street into a legal object while simultaneously judging the final product.[161] This shift was spatially marked if the defendant chose to step down from the "narrow iron dock," raised in the center of the room on a wooden platform, and walk across the room to instead give evidence as a witness under oath in the box adjacent to the magistrate and facing the clerk.[162]

Both the clerk's bodily disposition and spatial position kept the magistrate's dual role in creative tension. For the magistrate, Gamon wrote, "the Law is elastic"; for the clerk, "it is red tape." Compared with the magistrate's cultivated indifference, the clerk had "an air of critical precision about his mouth and garments."[163] His desk was "in a little pen at the feet of the magistrate, but outside the pale": "The clerk sits on a little elevation of his own, facing the left wall of the court, his desk at right angles to the magistrate's table, and his chair a little to the left of the magistrate but within a few feet of him; so that at the signal he can get up, lean over the magistrate's desk, and confer with him without being overheard by any one."[164] This ability to confer was essential to the clerk's role as assistant and check on the magistrate's balancing act as counsel and judge. If the magistrate was "on the wrong path,"

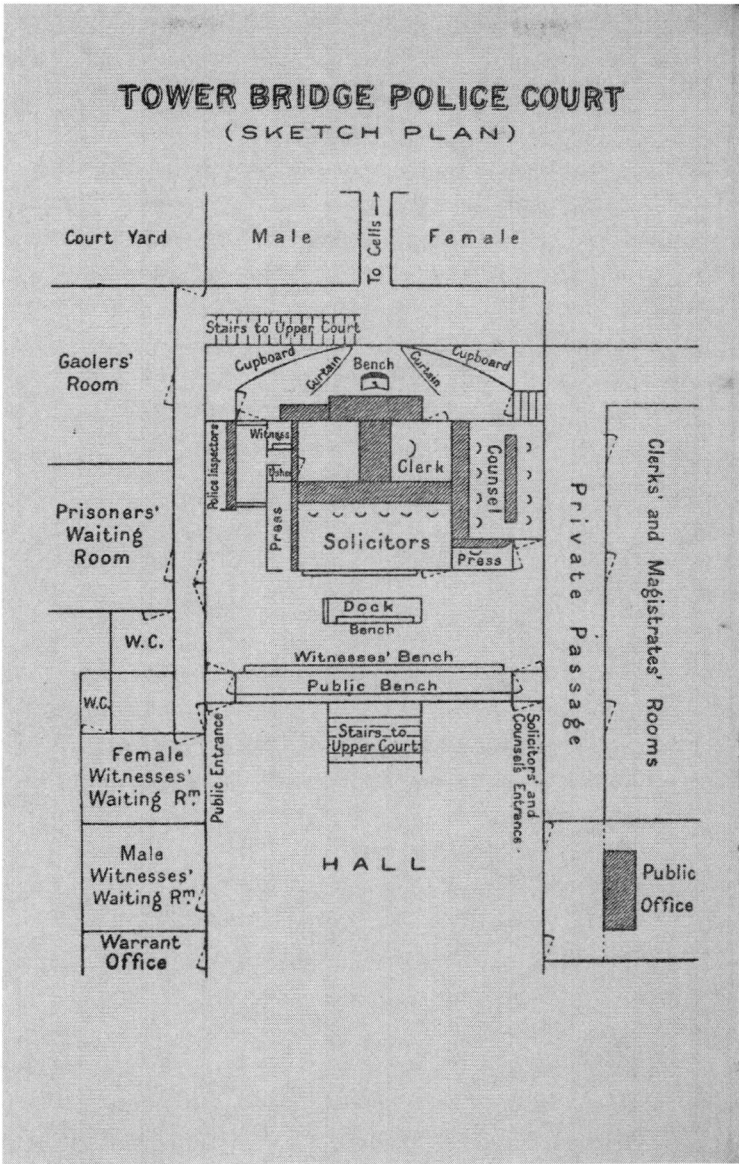

TOWER BRIDGE POLICE COURT

(SKETCH PLAN)

Court Yard | Male | To Cells → | Female

Stairs to Upper Court

Cupboard | Bench | Cupboard

Curtain | Curtain

Gaolers' Room

Police Inspectors

Witness

John

Clerk

Counsel

Press

Press

Solicitors

Prisoners' Waiting Room

Clerks' and Magistrates' Rooms

Private Passage

W.C.

Dock
Bench

W.C.

Witnesses' Bench

Public Bench

Female Witnesses' Waiting Rᵐ

Public Entrance

Stairs to Upper Court

Solicitors' and Counsels' Entrance

Male Witnesses' Waiting Rᵐ

HALL

Public Office

Warrant Office

FIGURE 24 Legal process materialized through courtroom layout: ground floor sketch plan of Tower Bridge Police Court in 1907. From Hugh R. P. Gamon, *The London Police Court: To-day and To-morrow* (London: J. M. Dent, 1907), xviii.
© The British Library Board

it was "for the clerk to get up quietly and by a whisper arrest his steps"; or the magistrate might "apply to him for the law," or ask the clerk's opinion on "what he thinks the proper punishment should be."[165] Where we see the clerk's parenthetical appearance in the minutes to Rowen and Bentley's trial, any of these occurrences might have taken place. Equally, the clerk might have gotten up to consult the magistrate on the admissibility of Anson's letter as evidence. While the magistrate mediated between the extraction of a case and its judgment in law, the clerk's attitudinal and physical perpendicularity regulated "the legal sanity of his decisions."[166]

Clodagh Anson's letter was not a one-off. She and others often sent letters to police courts intervening in the extraction of a case.[167] More than only discursive interventions, these were part of the stuff and substance of law: of law's subsistence on the embodied experience of the street, an experience that at once conditioned the legal narratives that could be told, was reproduced through those narratives, and was judged as a case within law by the configuration of bodies and papers embodying law in court. Proceedings at Tower Bridge, the model police court in the heart of Southwark, reveal this immanent, ongoing relation of touch and law; the public, standing at the back with "staring eyes, puckered brows, and parted lips," confirming its reproduction through its spectatorship.[168] In the London police court, the hand conjured up *through* law, and accepted as an instance of a case within it, constituted the hand *of* the law, and it was this that the public came to see—and vicariously feel.

THE ATMOSPHERE OF LAW

Harry Conniham and Robert Wright's dramatic appearance in the paperwork of Tower Bridge Police Court reveals the dependence of legal narratives about touch on the sensory habits and objects of the courtroom. Yet throughout the late nineteenth and early twentieth century many of those involved in police court trials were persistently concerned about the proper functioning of those very sensory habits, and therefore of law itself. In their fretting about the threat to legal process, magistrates, solicitors, and journalists associated the breakdown of sensory practices on which law depended with fog, both as a direct physical cause of that breakdown and as a means of interpreting and describing it. By the late 1920s, when fogs became increasingly uncommon, the word most frequently used to bemoan legal process—"'atmosphere'"— denoted a procedural environment more than a physical one, though it retained this double meaning. Fog, or atmosphere, not only revealed the relationship between the body in and outside law: it also became associated with the cause and conceptualization of that relationship's collapse.

The trouble began with a death. In early March 1878, an unfortunate reporter named Mr. C. Radford died of "cold and inflammation" allegedly caused by the poor ventilation of Marylebone Police Court. On a Saturday afternoon sitting following the death, solicitors practicing at the court made a representation to its magistrate, Mr. Mansfield, complaining of the "extreme danger" in which the ventilation of the court placed them, and the consequent poor health they had suffered the past winter. Mansfield could only agree: fireplaces filled the court with smoke, requiring windows to be open, while ventilators admitted smoke and "blacks," or soot particles, from outside and were consequently sealed.[169] The winter of 1877–1878 was particularly foggy, London seeing days of continuous fog three weeks before Radford's death, and the court's ventilation did little to protect its attendees from exposure to choking air from within or without.[170] Magistrate Mansfield's comments, published in the *Daily Telegraph* that Monday, drew swift response in the House of Commons. When questioned about the article, the first commissioner of works, Gerard Noel, claimed that, upon visiting the court on Wednesday and ordering the reopening of the sealed ventilators the following morning, the court's ventilation was "all that could be desired."[171] Pressed again three days later, however, Noel conceded that a full investigation into the ventilation of London's police courts had been ordered.[172]

The special commission on police court ventilation conducted by the *Lancet* medical journal revealed an architectural malaise far worse than had been imagined. The commission visited four police courts and meticulously measured the volume of their rooms in order to calculate the "fresh" air available based on the average number of people present and current ventilation system. At each court the commissioners found the ventilation woefully inadequate—at Marylebone most of all. There, the commissioners estimated the volume of the courtroom to be 14,000 cubic feet and the average number of attendees one hundred. Based on this calculation, they recommended that "the *entire* volume of air within the Court should be exchanged for outside street-air every eight, or, at most, every ten minutes."[173] Yet nothing approaching this recommendation was achieved. Three fireplaces in the court admitted smoke and dirt from outside but failed to expel polluted air from inside. Windows either created an "unendurable" draft or were sealed, and doorways admitted "the foulest air" from those crowded into charge rooms.[174]

The *Lancet*'s comments on police courts' polluted air reflected a wider practice of signifying class distinctions through one's smell or ability to smell others.[175] The "rough and often dirty crowd" that frequented police courts was blamed for the corruption of their air, which affected the ostensibly more refined olfaction of middle-class solicitors and magistrates more acutely.[176] But these comments were also about how polluted "atmosphere" disturbed the bodily comportment of those making and evaluating cases, and therefore threatened the functioning of law. "The very day following" Gerard Noel's "confident assertion" about the adequacy of Marylebone's ventilation, the *Lancet* spikily reported, "the atmosphere became so foul that a young attorney was taken ill and had to leave the Court, while a solicitor [...] had to abandon the trial four times, to refresh himself with a little external air. Mr Mansfield was also powerfully affected."[177] If, as Magistrate J. A. R. Cairns later asserted, the proper functioning of law in police courts depended on the magistrate's "judicial temper," then the physical, even foggy, atmosphere of police courts such as Marylebone directly threatened the legal order.[178]

In the following decades, concerns about the atmosphere of police courts, like the winter fogs connected to it, periodically resurfaced. In 1905, the *Lancet* again reported the enervating atmosphere of police courts, conceiving of this in terms of tactile as well as aerial pollution. At the "crowded police court," where litigants and lawyers pressed together, "the person of clean habits" was "bound to 'rub shoulders' with the unclean." Inadequate ventilation also meant that many courts suffered from "frowsiness [stuffiness] in the air."[179] The new Tower Bridge Police Court, opened that year, was a marked exception to this general state of affairs. Here the innovation of two courtrooms in the same building allowed "criminals" and "non-criminals"— criminal and civil cases, but the elision of criminality with the working class was telling—to be segregated. Aerial pollution was mitigated by inlets at each radiator that drew in a "flow of fresh air from the outside"—if, that is, there was no fog.[180]

Yet while court construction and the steady decline of fog lessened fears about the physical atmosphere of police courts, concerns remained about the proper functioning of the material and bodily practices through which cases were made. Fifty years after the commission on police court ventilation, press attention was again drawn to the health and habitus of London's magistrates. Although the term *atmosphere* had lost some of its literal meaning, still commentators used it to describe and explain an apparent breakdown in the sensory habits through which law was enacted. The first disquieting signs came with a series of sentences passed by London magistrates that were subsequently quashed on appeal. In August 1927, Magistrate Frederick Mead convicted Major Graham Bell Murray for drunk and disorderly conduct, while shortly after, Magistrate Chartres Biron convicted Frank Champain for importuning; both convictions were overturned by the London Sessions. What might have been seen as the proper functioning of law was, owing to the high status of the defendants, the spark for public outcry over its perceived decrepitude. Commentators were split over whether it was more worrying that the convictions depended on uncorroborated evidence, itself conditional on a police officer's "physical and moral vision," or that this evidence was accepted by two of London's most experienced magistrates.[181]

For the *Law Journal* the problem was one of law: because victims of offensive public behavior typically refused to testify, and the charge of soliciting, for example, required evidence of annoyance caused, magistrates necessarily relied on uncorroborated statements.[182] Consequently, police officers, unable to prove that a defendant caused annoyance and perhaps unable to see the whole encounter, used stereotypical phrases; the victim "seemed to be annoyed" was a favorite.[183] This argument encouraged Home Secretary Sir William Joynson-Hicks to appoint a Street Offences Committee on October 14, 1927, to investigate.[184] But for the *Law Times*, the magistrates' judicial oversight was less because of problems in the law than that magistrates were "overworked."[185] In January 1928 it reported that no fewer than five magistrates were indisposed by sickness, apparently work-related, leaving only twenty to cover the whole metropolitan area.[186] A Law Society deputation brought this to the Home Secretary's attention on March 28, 1928, highlighting intolerable delays in London's police courts and requesting the appointment of additional magistrates. Seven months later Joynson-Hicks appointed a Committee on Metropolitan Police Courts and Juvenile Courts.[187] Rather than examining the difficulties of obtaining corroborated evidence on the street, this inquiry shifted attention to the breakdown in embodied procedures eliciting and assessing that evidence in court.

There was much similarity in the reports of ailing magistrates before and during the committee's sitting to those half a century before. Now, however, "atmosphere" was not only a physical cause but also a metaphorical description of police courts' apparent malfunctioning. Two months after the Law Society deputation, J. A. R. Cairns—of the judicial temper—began a sitting with an excoriating attack on the Home Office complaining of how magistrates were "overworked." Magistrates were, he vented, "the scullions of the judiciary, without status and without consideration."[188] One month later Cairns suffered a nervous breakdown and took leave for a fortnight.[189] Further stress-induced illnesses continued among his colleagues on the bench.[190]

Despite the innovations of Tower Bridge Police Court, regular court attendees and witnesses to the committee continued to blame such illnesses on court "atmosphere," the meaning of which wavered between the physical, situational, and moral. According to the secretary of the Church of England Temperance Society, police courts had a "peculiar, nauseating acridity," their stale air producing a feeling of "frowsy stuffiness."[191] Such conditions made it difficult to concentrate, but concentration was particularly important in a court of summary jurisdiction. Magistrates had to complete long lists of cases, constantly switching from one point of law to another. Director of Public Prosecutions Sir Archibald Bodkin thought this especially hard on magistrates as although clerks took notes, during the trial a magistrate had to "memorise the evidence and keep his mind absolutely fixed all the time."[192] This was not easy if his mind was not rested. Magistrates were supposed to preside between 10:00 a.m. and 5:00 p.m. for only three days a week during the period when annual leave was not taken, and to cover for colleagues when it was. But unplanned absences, combined with the statutory requirement that the courts remain open every day except Sundays, Christmas Day, and Good Friday, meant that by 1929 some magistrates worked up to six days a week.[193] This placed a heavy strain on magistrates already performing a taxing task. Accounting for the ongoing illness of one-fifth of the magistrates, Acting Chief Magistrate R. F. Graham Campbell bleakly summarized their work as "a strenuous life in an atmosphere which is none too good."[194]

Atmosphere-induced absences exacerbated congestion in the courts still further. Magistrates trying to keep up with their lists already struggled to grant complicated cases much time, resulting in repeated adjournments.[195] This struggle was even more marked where magistrates covered absent colleagues at other courts and were unable to hear cases over successive days.[196] It could take weeks before enough time was found to conclude a complex case. Archibald Bodkin had "heard," he testified, "the most woeful jeremiads about the overpressure on certain of the London Police magistrates, terrible breakdowns now and again, and never being able to get through their lists."[197] Under such conditions, it became nearly impossible for magistrates to maintain the mental attitude, performed through a careful bodily disposition toward documents and other bodies, required for the judicious examination of a case.

The inability of magistrates to complete their lists arose from the growing list of statutes supplying them. Here, too, atmosphere permeated the crisis in police court procedures, this time as an object of law itself. Although severe fog outbreaks were rare by the 1920s, the London County Council continued to press local sanitary authorities to prosecute industries for high levels of smoke pollution.[198] Following a Departmental Committee on Smoke and Noxious Vapours in 1921, new smoke abatement legislation considerably widened the terms under which offenders could be prosecuted. Under the 1926 Public Health (Smoke Abatement) Act, a smoke nuisance was defined for the first time in terms of its measurable quantity and not just, as with previous legislation, its visual appearance.[199] At the same time as LCC researchers began measuring fog in terms of its matter rather than appearance, police courts also increasingly rendered smoke a tangible object. New smoke abatement legislation did not significantly increase the number of prosecutions brought before magistrates.[200] But it did represent a broader trend whereby the increasing volume, scope, and complexity of interwar legislation placed increasing demands upon the bench.

The primary culprit behind the increasing caseload faced by magistrates in the late 1920s was rising motorcar ownership. Crimes associated with automobiles—smash-and-grab robberies, obstruction, traffic offenses— significantly increased the number of time-consuming cases coming before magistrates.[201] This was especially so after the 1930 Road Traffic Act required all private cars to be insured, thereby guaranteeing lengthy wrangling over compensation claims.[202] Entries in court minute books over these years change from often parsimonious summaries to apparently interminable accounts of who struck whom at the intersection. The increasing procedural distinction between police and juvenile courts, in which magistrates also presided, and the growing number of statutes concerning offenses by and against children also demanded increased specialization within a struggling bench.[203] A 1929 inquiry into the police and juvenile courts noted the growing strain this dual system placed on magistrates but could find no way of relieving the pressure.[204] Combined, these and other changes meant an increasing number and complexity of cases over which magistrates struggled to maintain their careful performance of embodied doubt.

By the 1930s, the increased caseload and complexity of police court business pushed magistrates to breaking point. The situation was so bad, wrote one anonymous solicitor in 1932, that there was widespread and dangerous "discontent" among the working class with the condition of "English Justice."[205] In a scathing attack on the English legal system, the pseudonymous "Solicitor" alleged that Parliament continued adding laws to the statute book without concern for the burden these laws placed on magistrates. Legislators treated courts of summary jurisdiction "as a kind of legal Woolworths, supplying cheap brands of justice suitable for the lower classes" to the point that the law was in danger of being "brought into contempt."[206] Citing Dickens and alluding to the fog with which *Bleak House* famously opens, the solicitor claimed that only Parliament was "equally obsolete in its atmosphere and procedure" as the criminal law courts.[207] Such atmospheric allusions continued in 1937, with author Robert Sinclair alleging that the bench was populated by "aged and tired-looking men" dispensing justice "in an atmosphere that would kill a miner's canary." Indeed, several of these had "died in harness—worn out, according to Mr Cairns," by the need to continue working because of "poverty and an inadequate pension."[208]

In the same year as Sinclair's complaint, the Home Office took note of these canaries of police court atmosphere and launched another inquiry. This committee revealed even more than the last the threat posed by the breakdown of tactile habits on which law in police courts depended. It reported that congestion in the courts sometimes meant that the delay between applications for summonses and hearings could reach three months, meaning that witnesses often related half-remembered events in a piecemeal or stylized manner.[209] Magistrates burdened with time-consuming cases might have to rush to complete their lists, making it difficult for litigants to "keep up with what is being said and done" and for magistrates themselves to discern the "distinguishing features" of a case.[210] The fact that clerks had to write in longhand compounded these problems further since cases were becoming more rushed but the importance of recording them, notably where insurance companies were involved, only increased. The clerk's handwriting, already "the terror of judges" (and historians) in the case of Mr. Nairn of Tower Bridge, was pushed to the limit.[211] Together these pressures made it increasingly difficult for magistrates to maintain a studied embodied hesitation and to extract a case from the mounting piles of paper.

The metaphorical conception of law in terms of fog or "atmosphere" was not incidental to the fogs permeating London in the late nineteenth and early twentieth centuries. It emerged from the historical, sensory experience of these fogs by reporters, magistrates, and solicitors who stumbled through ethereal streets and steeped in smoky courtrooms. By 1937 the protracted fogs of the 1870s had, with notable exceptions, long passed, and *atmosphere* denoted legal procedure more than the environment in which it occurred. But still the metaphor, with its residual physical connotations, captured the way in which law was threatened by the breakdown of tactile practices through which it subsisted. Describing law in terms of fog couched the strains of legal process in terms of ailing bodies, occluded vision, and fumbling hands and, inversely, reinforced these as the physical perception of fog itself. Metaphor emerged from this tactile experience of the world and shaped the conception of law—and perception of fog—within it.[212]

CONCLUSION

While police courts groaned under pressure, contemporary jurisprudence offered little to explain or solve their problems. As defined by University of London chair of jurisprudence John Austin in 1832, and how it continued to be defined in the 1930s, jurisprudence purported to elucidate the tenets of an autonomous domain of "Law," without regard to the beliefs and social conditions of a particular era.[213] Jurisprudence did not examine Law as the sum of its parts—laws—but the "rules of law or legal principles" subtending them, reiterated University of Adelaide professor of law John Salmond in 1893.[214] In most textbooks, any suggestion that law, whether "applied" or as a domain of knowledge itself, had a contingent, sensory basis in the world in which it was practiced was erased as the condition of its existence. Instead, jurisprudence reified Law as a discrete domain, perpetuating this distinction through the fiction that change in the law, or divergent "interpretations" of it, merely represented the "discovery" of principles always already extant within it.[215]

In the police courts the reality was quite different. Here, the construction of a case in law emerged through each particular configuration of bodies and documents in court. Rather than, as Bruno Latour has suggested, this configuration maintaining the fiction of law's self-founding existence, the dependence of a case also on the sensory possibilities of the street *beyond* the court—what glimpses and glances were possible in Waterloo's tangled streets—dissolved it.[216] While engulfing the streets, London's fogs revealed those sensory possibilities, associating them not only with the ability to illicitly touch but also to formulate credible narratives of illicit touch in court. At the same time, the way in which the tactile possibilities of the street were turned into an object in court shaped how police and suspects acted on those possibilities beyond it.[217] Not only did police and defendants play language games in court, thereby contesting the credibility of a charge through their narration of the street, they *acted out* those games on the street, seeking or avoiding those actions which might fit what sensory possibilities were required for a case to stick. The Royal Commission on Police Powers and Procedures reported in 1929 that police witnesses occasionally tried to secure convictions "in charges of a vague character, such as 'loitering with intent to commit a felony,'" by presenting evidence in "stereotyped phrases" that had "an air of sameness and unreality."[218] In turn, defendants such as Harry Conniham, charged with that very offense nine months later, meticulously narrated the embodied experience of the street to preclude such stereotyping.

To adapt Yan Thomas's phrasing, touch was the integument of law—that which delimited and contained it, and within which it lived—and law that of touch.[219] In the police court, with its creative interpretation of the rules of evidence and its magistrate strung between counsel and judgment, each existed *insofar* as they were part of the other. This made the enactment of law in police courts particularly susceptible to changes in magistrates' caseloads: the increasing complexity, delays, and rush of trials all put increasing pressure on the tactile production of cases and the legal reproduction of touch. But rather than representing a breakdown in the application "of" Law, these pressures were instead another instance of changes in law's simultaneous subsistence on touch and construction of it, and of itself, as distinct objects.[220] This was a relationship between law and touch illuminated by fog and changing once again by the time that physical fog was, almost, a thing of the past.

Tender

What happens to our grasp of nineteenth- and twentieth-century Britain when it comes through our subjects' hands? How does the touch of that bewildered traveler, buffeted on the human tide of Liverpool Street Station one morning at the beginning of the twentieth century, change our histories of this period, or of our present? The history of touch reveals transformations in what it meant to be a body over the last two centuries, as well as broader histories in which the body played a central part. Mandatory elementary education, state provision for blind children, and the return of disabled soldiers after World War I intensified efforts to understand how vision and touch were related, and how knowledge came through feel. The rise of experimental psychology, imperial ventures of anthropology, and the influence of aesthetic literature reshaped understandings of the relationship between mind, body, and world. And changing norms for touch in crowded public spaces such as "tube cars" of the London Underground and tea shops in the city reflected new understandings of how the self could and should relate to others.

These histories underpin some of the most important transformations in nineteenth- and twentieth-century Britain. Changing understandings of the relationship between touch and vision contributed to the historical production and opposition of "able-bodiment" and disability, as well as an assumed connection between sensory, intellectual, and political ability. This history of touch traces the shifting sensory basis of citizenship: the changing horizons of who was or was not "perceptible" to politics because of differing abilities to perceive. New scientific ideas about the relationship between mind, body, and world, themselves resulting from changes in what scientists did with their hands, reshaped beliefs about where ideas and feelings came from. The changing uses of touch in experiments and law courts reveal the shifting sensory origins of scientific and legal knowledge and the contingent distinction of those fields from the phenomenal world. Finally, new kinds of urban public space, such as the refreshment bar on Liverpool Street Station's concourse, its layout, and the managed behavior of those within it, encouraged new desires to touch and formulations of personal space to avoid it. These changes constituted a history, shared but unique to every individual, of what it meant to be a body available to and able to affect others, and how this experience structured power relations of race, class, age, and gender and sexuality. The history of touch was also, in short, one of disability, scientific and legal reasoning, urban life, capitalism, and the potential for violence or tenderness at the heart of every embodied encounter.

What was perceived through touch, and thought about touch, emerged through these individual embodied encounters. Touch, including its history, was inseparable from the lived entanglements through which it was enacted. By tracing these entanglements in nineteenth- and twentieth-century Britain, I have argued that, contrary to representations of the mind as separate from the world sensed and of sensory change as linear, the experience and understanding of touch were enacted through ongoing, situated, and intertwined embodied encounters. Tactile perception, and understandings of touch, emerged through active, embodied *involvement* in the world touched, an involvement veined with multiple temporalities.

This argument suggests a different understanding of sensation and sensory change from that implicit in much sensory history. Theories of modernity from the late nineteenth and early twentieth centuries have proven surprisingly tenacious in framing our accounts of sensation in the same period in which those theories were formulated. From these theories, and the nineteenth- and twentieth-century mind sciences on which they were based, we have derived a model of the mind as independent from the world perceived and of the perceivable world as preexisting the act of perception. The task of the person perceiving—that passenger dodging traffic and hawkers outside Liverpool Street Station—was to represent a world that preceded them and from which they remained always apart.[1] Small wonder that when theorists such as Georg Simmel thought about the effect of social and technological transformations on sensory life, they thought in terms of an individual overwhelmed by and desensitized to the stimuli they experienced, lost in spectacle, and required to manage their senses or have their sensory environment managed for them. These ways of thinking continue to shape how we think about touch, both in our histories and our present.

Yet the early twentieth century was also a time in which an alternative understanding of sensation began to be formulated that we might use to examine sensory change in this and other periods. Already latent in Henry Head and Gordon Holmes's concept of cognitive "schemata," derived from later work extending Head's self-experiment, was a theory of perception as emerging through the perceiver's active, embodied, and situated involvement in the world perceived. This idea was radically extended by mid-twentieth-century phenomenology and, most recently, by theorists of embodied cognition into a theory of the perceiving subject as inherent within, and the originator of, the world perceived.[2] Head and Holmes's work, while hewing to a representationist model of the mind, gestured toward an alternative understanding in which the perceiver was not independent of the world perceived but part of it, and both brought that world into being and was brought into being by it through their ongoing interaction. This understanding points toward a different history of touch in Britain's cerebral age. With only contingent distinctions between mind and body, perceiver and world perceived, this was a history of endless, and endlessly ramifying, embodied encounters and their intersecting temporalities. Touch—what was perceived and what it meant—was made and remade through particular embodied interactions varying between spaces and over disparate times.

The model of perception intimated by Head and Holmes is more than a theory of touch: it is also one of how touch changes and, therefore, of history. Thinking of touch as ceaselessly emergent across countless interactions questions attempts to understand sensory change as linear—as more or less stimulation, or sensitivity to it. This assumption of linearity was central to accounts of modernity and pioneering sensory histories and still underpins accounts of contemporary sensory life.[3] The idea that touch was distinct from the mind and could be measured in rises and falls over history was fundamental to the literary impressionism of authors such as Virginia Woolf but also established by that archcritic of modernity, D. H. Lawrence. In a trio of poems published in 1929, Lawrence bemoaned the advance of what he saw as the world of the mind at the expense of touch.[4] In the first, Lawrence adopts the injunction "noli me tangere," recalling the moment when a resurrected Jesus told Mary Magdalene not to touch him, to enjoin those "creatures of mind, don't touch me!" In modernity touch has become attenuated, abstracted, so that individuals touch with "mental fingers" and "mental bodies"—touch that Lawrence wants no part of. "Great is my need to be chaste / and apart," Lawrence writes with aching irony, "in this cerebral age."[5] In another poem, titled simply "Touch," Lawrence reprises the

theme, writing that "Since we are so cerebral | we are humanly out of touch."
And knowing this is also its cause, "For if, cerebrally, we force ourselves
into touch, | into contact | physical and fleshly, | we violate ourselves, | we
become vicious."[6] Violation here comes not from unwanted touch but from
the attempt to reestablish touch without shedding its subordination to the
mind. In these poems touch has become a habit of the mind so that "human"
touch, unmediated by thought, has dwindled.

Yet these poems prelude a third in which Lawrence envisions another
kind of touch and another potential history. "Touch comes when the white
mind sleeps | and only then," the poem begins. It is a vital force which
"seeps | slowly up in the blood of men | and women":

> Soft slow sympathy
> of the blood in me, of the blood in thee
> rises and flushes insidiously
> over the conscious personality
> of each of us
> with a soft one warmth, and a generous
> kindled togetherness, so we go
> into each other as tides flow
> under a moon they do not know.[7]

Touch here is not subordinated to the mind but rises and falls, like water
beneath the ocean's surface, outside consciousness. Change is less the linear
advance of modernity than the cyclical turn of the tides. The fluctuation
of touch is slow, in contrast to the "white[-hot]" frenzy of the mind, and
permeates bodies as if blood. The sibilant, alliterative susurration of words
conveys a sympathy of states in which touch not only permeates individual
bodies but penetrates their distinctions, gathering those bodies into a shared
"togetherness." Lawrence imagines a preconscious togetherness in which
the touch of one is inseparable from that of another, each made possible
by their shared corporeal existence in, and as part of, the world. In short: a
shared condition of tenderness.[8] Jacques Derrida later imagined something
similar when writing on the caress, which in its giving, its tendering, is also
an opening or exposure to a shared tenderness: "hold, take what I do not possess, nor you, what we do not and shall never possess."[9] To touch is to reach
out, which is also to expose one's shared, inalienable capacity to be reached.

Lawrence and Derrida, and Merleau-Ponty, too, understood this shared
tenderness in almost utopian terms. Tenderness returns us to our common

condition, to a universal, foundational state in which differences between bodies, existential as well as physical, dissolve.[10] Everybody hurts. Everybody longs for a unity that is, after all, and as psychoanalysis claims, our original state.[11] For many writers, tenderness is what unites us as humans and consoles us as bodies. Yet this book has also shown how such unity and consolation are also marked by difference and violence. If Lawrence anticipated the ecstasy that would come through regaining our "kindled togetherness"—an implicitly queer, sexual union expressed in heterosexual, gendered terms— later critics point to the inequalities and dangers of tenderness. "But what am I for you," writes Luce Irigaray to an imagined man in her feminist critique of the caress, "other than that place from which you subsist? Your subsistence. Or substance." A caress can appropriate, reify gendered and sexual differences of identity, embodiment, and agency, rather than reunite bodies that were, except for the vicissitudes of modernity, never really apart.[12] Think of twenty-year-old waitress Alice Farrell, pulled in to kiss her sometime customer from the A.B.C. tea shop in an empty train compartment, a first-class "smoking," on her way home from work (as described in chapter 4).[13] We might all be tender, but not, as power differences of race, class, age, ability, and gender and sexuality ensure, in the same way. Tenderness might relieve us of our painful isolation from one another, but it is also what makes us subject to pain at others' hands. Tender, tenderness: to offer, to be gentle, to be injurable, to be raw.

This book has explored what a history of tenderness—the shared condition of all care and violence—might look like. It has shown the constant emergence of touch and the world touched through their mutual entanglement over particular spaces and domains of knowledge. Throughout the nineteenth and early twentieth century, attempts to train blind children's sense of touch reinforced beliefs that other senses compensated for the lack of sight, while simultaneously defining those children by what they lacked. The extent to which touch could substitute for vision marked the extent to which blind people might be involved in economic and political life, a concept that became the prime target of activists rethinking disability by the mid-twentieth century. Since at least the 1870s, the increasingly accessible and indeterminate spaces of public transport and commercial leisure intensified anxieties about inappropriate touch but also sharpened experiences and conceptions of bodies *as* violable and requiring personal space. Where, when, and whom one could touch—and understandings of what inappropriate touch meant—emerged from changing embodied encounters in early twentieth-century tube cars, tea shops, and other public spaces, themselves shaping and shaped by flows of local and global capital. And in courtrooms and neurological experiments, touch was the means by which it was also defined, located, and reconstructed in legal or scientific cases. As the twentieth century wore on, the shifting sensory relationship of magistrates and neurologists to their object—how they used touch—remade the boundaries between science and law and the phenomenal world observed.

These themes converged in a series of "experiments" into the education of blind children and adults conducted in Sunderland, England, from 1907 into the 1920s. In a "chance remark" to the director of Sunderland Museum and Art Gallery, G. I. Walker, a teacher at the city's School for the Blind, noted the difficulties his students faced with developing an accurate sense of the form, texture, or scale of things. Sympathetic and intrigued, Director J. A. Charlton Deas invited children from the school to handle some of the museum's taxidermy animals so that they might form mental images of these animals along "correct lines." The exercise soon expanded into a "systematic course of demonstrations" at the museum for Sunderland's blind adults and children. The demonstrations consisted of five three-hour sessions, taught separately to adults on Sunday afternoons and to children on Monday mornings, covering art, natural history, and miscellaneous objects at the museum.[14]

Each session took the same form: after a brief "lecturette" on the topic, sighted guides helped pass the fingers of blind visitors over specimens of animals and other objects while providing an accompanying description.[15] Blind visitors were introduced to, among other things, paintings, polar bears, sharks, starfish, flamingos, flintlocks, swords, and a plaster cast of Lord Leighton's life-size *An Athlete Wrestling with a Python*, the "more venturesome" men climbing stepladders to get a closer feel. One girl was "placed in a giant clam shell" while six boys were "mounted" on a stuffed lion, the better to aid their "mental visualisation" of size.[16] In one photograph taken on a natural history Monday, the subject is hands: as many hands as could spread over the walrus's bulk as possible. With twelve children pressing both hands on the model from every angle, this was not a record of seeing by touch—individual, sequential, dexterous—but a visual representation of it for sighted viewers. Other photographs show a large freestanding screen behind the specimens that framed even more clearly for sighted viewers the tactile observation occurring in front. In these ways, photography reassimilated tactile perception into visual terms, even at the point of its occurrence.

Deas kept these "experiments" going after the initial series through occasional demonstrations at the museum or local trips to the seaside, into

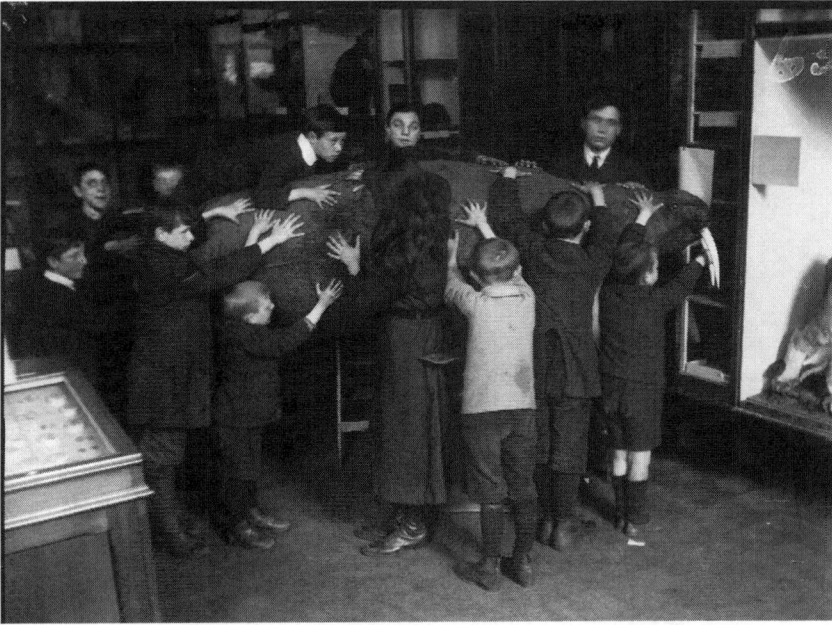

FIGURE 25 Children from Sunderland School for the Blind studying a taxidermy walrus at Sunderland Museum and Art Gallery, June 1913. TWCMS: 2006.7978.
© Sunderland Museums/Bridgeman Images

hayfields, or up the River Wear.[17] By 1929 the museum offered two summer courses of twenty demonstrations each for blind children and adults.[18] A century later, Deas's endeavors for blind people stand out for their remarkable foresight and earnest solicitousness. Over three decades, alongside the museum demonstrations, Deas also lobbied for other museums to open their collections to blind visitors, organized experiments in pottery making, began a reading circle of novels (rather than dull didactic literature), and arranged for radios to be delivered to blind listeners.[19] His work was suffused with sympathy and care, as well as understandings of blindness that distanced him from those he worked for and are now discomforting after five decades of disability activism. Tenderness, then, is here both my subject and my attitude toward it—with all its conflicting feelings.

From his first experiment, Deas started from the realist belief, held also by Walker, that there was a singular, preexisting reality from which the mind was detached and which it perceived indirectly through constructing "mental pictures" (Walker's words). Accurate perception of the world depended on the development of mental pictures that followed "correct mental standards," even for objects perceived by touch.[20] Like other educationists in the early twentieth century, Deas therefore saw blindness as a deficiency, the task of touch being to compensate for this deficiency so that blind people could gain a more accurate approximation of a shared singular reality: "To them, their fingers are eyes; fingers which are much more capable than the less sensitive ones of sighted people."[21] Yet even with such powers of compensation, the implication was that blind people's conceptualization of the world was, literally, an incomplete picture.

A letter from Walker, himself blind, to Deas put the point more bluntly. Since the demonstrations, Walker wrote, discussions at the Blind Institute had "become varied and interesting, and show that the minds of those attending have been awakened and stimulated, and made to understand that they are indeed deficient, and sadly ignorant of what is around them."[22] Walker meant this positively, as such knowledge fed the hunger to learn and appreciation of those who taught, but it underscored the paradoxical disablement that concepts of tactile compensation caused. While the museum demonstrations sought to lessen the distinctions between blind participants and sighted visitors, they simultaneously reified the sighted as sources of economic, moral, and political possibility to which blind people might aspire but never quite achieve. "It is the want of vivid and approximately correct mental standards or mental pictures which makes it so difficult for the blind [. . .] to enter intelligently into the many questions affecting their own economic and ethical condition," Walker wrote.[23] The museum demonstrations sought to overcome this "want of [. . .] correct mental standards" but were also premised on the assumed impossibility of fully doing so, at once promising and compromising the opportunity for blind participants to become, in Walker's words, efficient "workers and citizens."[24]

At the same time, the museum demonstrations were studies of where bodies, or an awareness of one's body, ended and of how this awareness changed over time. As more reliant on touch, and less able to control how they were touched, blind visitors to the museum might have contributed to wider discussions about vulnerability—violability—in public space. Many of the adults traveled unaccompanied to the museum by tram (streetcar), of which they had free use.[25] But the fact that the demonstrations were held when the museum was closed, and that blind participants were taught in mixed-gender groups as a class apart, meant there was apparently no discussion of how their experience of public space differed from that of sighted people, among themselves, or across spaces. Nevertheless, the demonstrations did encourage thinking about how varying sensory capabilities resulted in a variable awareness of one's body and its place in space. At the beginning of the art demonstration, the dimensions of the gallery were given in paces, its arrangements of lighting and hanging pictures described, so that blind visitors could orient themselves to the art observed, something done unconsciously by sighted visitors.[26] Conversely, in a later lecture on the demonstrations, Deas cited Maria Montessori's practice of blindfolding sighted schoolchildren so that they could better perceive objects through touch, "the first sense which a child develops."[27] Implicit in such discussions was an understanding of touch, proprioceptive awareness, and bodily boundaries as individually variable and subject to change.

Finally, the museum demonstrations were not only experiments into the education of blind people but also a way of tactilely examining the relation between mind and body analogous to Henry Head's self-experiment in the same year. The focus of the demonstrations was on their practical and moral benefit to participants, but Deas also saw them as tactile studies of how touch and the mind were related. Five weeks after the demonstrations, Deas asked children at the School for the Blind to model in clay the objects they had touched. Nine children aged eight to fifteen obliged, and these models were displayed to museum visitors in glass cabinets along with framed photographs of the demonstrations.[28] It is striking how closely the children's models resembled what sighted observers would recognize as the intended animals, one model vividly capturing the tangled ruff of a lion's mane, another the tension of a coiled snake. The models irresistibly invite such a comparison but in so doing continue the ableist measurement of blind people's perception in visual terms. A photograph of the display later featured in a talk Deas gave on "What the Blind May 'See': Some Museum and Other Experiments in Tactile Sight" (1929).[29] Through these visual reproductions of "tactile sight," what the children perceived of the museum's exhibits became itself an exhibit. The models ostensibly materialized—made tangible—the children's "mental pictures" and powers of touch which, when displayed, became a tool for examining how such pictures were created—for blind and sighted alike. "Object-lessons" at the museum became a lesson in how objects were perceived, and therefore reflected on and enacted the very boundary between perceivers and the "objective" world.[30]

Historicizing emergent experiences and meanings of touch similarly raises questions about its contemporary ethics and politics. The conceptual shift, in the 1960s, toward disability as an effect of one's social and material environment rather than of impairment set the terms, and the tensions, for how it would be debated into the present. Since then, disability studies has wrestled with how to recognize the contingency of disability on the environment while accounting for the particular lived reality and experience of physical impairment.[31] While productive, this distinction between disability and impairment failed to unsettle that between perceivers and the world perceived, or between disability and ability. In this framework, all perceivers continue to be understood as separate from the world, and the sensorially impaired therefore hindered by "incomplete" access to it.

One question arising from these enduring binaries is whether disability might be conceptualized outside a framework of ability altogether, a framework that inevitably reinscribes disability as a "problem."[32] This book has emphasized its subjects' embodied involvement in the world perceived but maintained that such involvement also entailed, at least for those subjects, a contingent separation. But if, combining recent scholarship in science and technology studies and cognitive science, we think of humans as entangled with nonhuman entities and of perception as occurring "in" the thing perceived, how does this reconceptualization change understandings of the "human" that are implicitly tied to perceptual ability?[33] How does reexamining the relation between perceiving subjects and the world perceived trouble distinctions between perceiving subjects themselves—between ability and disability—and the ostensible "fullness" of life each implies? A more radical rethinking of the limits of the body, of touch *as* limit, offers a way to question the assumed limits of particular ways of perceiving.

An equally pressing question concerns the relationship between vulnerability, personal autonomy, and consent. Long before the legal definition of *sexual harassment* in the 1970s, the articulation in the early twentieth century of bodies, especially women's bodies, as violable in public space established an ideal of personal autonomy and the concept of consent as the core issues of sexual ethics. The concept of autonomy recognized—and was opposed against—the ever-present vulnerability of one body to the touch of another, with consent figuring as a way to manage the relation. As Gilson argues, the consequence of this thinking in subsequent feminist scholarship was a focus on the unequal distribution of vulnerability along gendered lines, the association of vulnerability with "harm," and the solution to vulnerability—consent—required from an individual potentially unable to grant it as a result of their already "compromised" status.[34]

The century-long formulation of the opposition between autonomy and vulnerability has thus generated several questions among present-day feminist scholars about a more effective political response to the risks of touch. How can we account for unequal experiences of vulnerability—for example, in terms of race, class, gender, and age—while maintaining its underlying universality and contingency for all?[35] How can we respond politically to these unequal experiences without reproducing the problem by suggesting such experiences—and powerlessness—are "inherent" to particular identities that are therefore in need of external intervention? How can we manage the risk of harm intrinsic to vulnerability without seeing the solution in a fictive autonomy that places the burden, impossibly, on the individuals concerned?[36]

These questions played out in the Transport for London (TfL) 2021–2024 campaign against sexual harassment, which brings the nineteenth-century story of Alice Farrell, whom we met in the introduction, into the present. The campaign displayed posters on buses, tube trains, and stations identifying specific types of sexual harassment, each with an accompanying definition. Although the campaign press release noted that, in a 2019 study, "women were nearly twice as likely as men to mention personal safety as a barrier to walking and using public transport," the campaign did not target any specific group.[37] The posters were directed at potential perpetrators and bystanders rather than victims, aiming to change consensus about what behavior could go unchallenged rather than encourage victims to change their behavior prior to or after harassment.

Despite this approach, the word-definition format of the posters implicitly recognized that both the meaning of the words displayed and the acceptability of their associated actions remained ambiguous. Indeed, the definitions often took a tautological form: "Touching: touching someone inappropriately is sexual harassment and is not tolerated." The continuing ambiguity was reflected in responses to the campaign, in which commuters called attention to the difficulty of defining the offense—despite the definition—or criticized TfL for incorrectly defining sexual assault as sexual harassment, thereby undermining its credibility for prosecuting offenses correctly.[38] On one poster about "pressing," an angry passenger crossed out its definition as "harassment" and wrote in "ASSAULT" to make the meaning of the action crystal clear. By centering its sexual harassment campaign around the question of definition, TfL highlighted the fraught ambiguity of both the words defining the offense and the autonomy of the bodies offended against. We are left with a question no less urgent now than it was for Lawrence and his critics: how should we be tender, in this bruising life?

· · ·

Passing through Liverpool Street Station today presents a very different experience of touch from that of 1900. Gone is the grand turreted south entrance and its sweeping approach roads jammed with carriages and pedestrians; gone is the long, Gothic western wing of lofty mainline booking office, first- and second-class waiting rooms, with adjoining ladies' waiting rooms, refreshment room, general and ladies' dining rooms, and Great Eastern Railway Company offices connecting with the G. E. R. Hotel on Liverpool Street.[39] In their place are a small pedestrianized forecourt connecting Liverpool Street with a single sunken glassed concourse giving onto the platforms and ringed by a two-tiered retail arcade. The renovation of the station between 1985 and 1991 marked the enclosure and privatization of public space, as well as of the touch formerly occurring within it. The insistent touch of hawkers and itinerant flower sellers of the early twentieth century has been replaced by regulated relations between retailer and customer, who now purchases a bouquet from the prim *Flower Station* inside.

The remaining public space, by contrast, has been opened up and desegregated, physically and socially, to improve surveillance, maximize movement, and minimize waiting. Without waiting rooms and cloakrooms, there is less opportunity to linger without cost, or need to police illicit touch: a new architecture of visibility governs behavior. Travelers are encouraged to move on, or else move into retail spaces where they might pass time productively. The reorganization of space at Liverpool Street Station, and with it the kinds of touch possible, is also one of time—specifically of waiting— whereby waiting is discouraged to reduce the waste of time, crowding, and undesirable kinds of touch accompanying it, or diverted into economically productive activities such as shopping.[40]

After exiting through the stone pillars skirting the station perimeter, relics from the former layout, you see to your right the square glass canopy of the Liverpool Street entrance to the new Elizabeth Line, opened in May 2022. Built on the site of the London and North Western Railway booking office of the former Broad Street Station, long ago demolished, the Elizabeth Line Station seeks to realize the ideal of frictionless travel. In place of the stairs, booking offices, and staffed ticket barriers of the former station, the Underground station minimizes physical barriers that cause delays and reduce accessibility. Spacious tunnels, contactless payments, and "step-free access"—that is, access via ramps, elevators, or both rather than stairs or escalators—aim toward a touch-free transition from train to street, and less potential touch of others en route.[41] Frictionless travel elides the ideal of accessibility with that of economic exchange: unhindered movement below ground at once removing disabling barriers and mirroring an ideal of frictionless transactions in the City above.

Turning left and walking to the end of Liverpool Street, you at last come upon, like the traveler of 1900, Devonshire House. Not a shabby hotel anymore, it is actually the rebuilt adjacent Devonshire Chambers at 142–146 Bishopsgate, but the name remains, given to a building now housing a luxury patisserie and cocktail bar.[42] Here, and in the neighboring complex, differences in access maintain distances between people, tactile as well as social. In the space once occupied by the original Devonshire House, set back a block behind a new public plaza, now stands a forty-three-story, Singaporean-owned tower, housing 160 "sky residences" and a five-star hotel complete with subterranean ballroom. One Bishopsgate Plaza captures, in spatial form, the dramatic increase in inequality and new configurations of global capital reshaping touch in contemporary Britain. The widening extremes of wealth over the last century, themselves a product of the City, materialize here as a separation of spaces, which is also a tactile separation of those on the street from those high above. Standing on the site of the former Devonshire House hotel, you perhaps look up to gaze at today's hotel guests floating in the fourth-floor infinity pool, suspended, as it were, above the city.

The history of touch, as one of countless entanglements and constant emergence, does not allow for a final statement. But that is also one of its strengths as a mode of critique, and an ethics, today. As the changes around Liverpool Street Station over the past century demonstrate, historicizing touch could not be more important for understanding the capitalist reordering of time and space, reification of ability, and crisis of inequality in contemporary Britain and, perhaps, for cultivating our tenderness amid it all.

Acknowledgments

There is a wonderful phrase in Japanese that captures my feelings while writing these acknowledgments. *Mono no aware* is tricky to translate—that is part of the feeling—but roughly means the experience of being affected by something and the insight derived from this. When used in discussions of Japanese literature, it typically refers to a combined sense of pathos and sharpened understanding arising from awareness of the passing of time. This book can only exist because of the ideas, inspiration, and almost stubborn belief given by friends, loved ones, and teachers. Writing these words on a rainy November day, the leaves of the London plane trees thick on the ground, I am deeply grateful to the many people who have shaped my thoughts and sustained me in my search to understand touch.

This book started at the University of Oxford many years ago, and I owe friends and colleagues there for their stimulation across all kinds of history. My research was made possible by an Arts and Humanities Research Council studentship and, later on, by a Vice-Chancellor's Fund/Andrew Smith Memorial Foundation Award, Bryce Research Studentship, and Magdalen College's Angus Macintyre Scholarship. I could not have contemplated undertaking the project without this support; thank you to those who believed I was worth supporting, and supporting to the end. My life at Oxford was enriched by a group of dear friends who also happened to be brilliant historians. Although I was unaware at the time, my reading group discussions with Ilya Afanasyev, Charlotte Greenhalgh, Erika Hanna, Matt Hollow, Matt Houlbrook, Eloise Moss, and Will Pooley kept my horizons broad and reminded me why history mattered. Thank you for welcoming this novice into the fold, and for invigorating conversations in cozy pub corners. Dave Pigott, Dean Sheppard, and James Golding, by contrast, reminded me that there were other things to life, too; for bonfire nights, adventures abroad, and fabulous home-cooked meals, thank you. At Oxford, I was fortunate to have many conversations with faculty who gave their unhesitating support for this odd topic: Craig Clunas, Pietro Corsi, Christina de Bellaigue, Siân Pooley, and Selina Todd. Thank you especially to Laurence Brockliss and Nick Stargardt: you gave me confidence in my early days of study to aspire to be a historian. Midway through this project, Dan Healey provided remarkably generous comments on the entire manuscript.

My research has been significantly helped by the deep knowledge of archivists and librarians. I owe every one of them a debt but particularly acknowledge Wendy Hawke, at London Metropolitan Archives, who helped secure access to uncatalogued material and decipher handwriting, and Sean Wilcox, at RNIB, who responded patiently to endless requests. An earlier, shorter version of chapter 3 first appeared as "How We Came to Mind the Gap: Time, Tactility, and the Tube" in *Twentieth-Century British History* 27, no. 4 (December 2016): 524–54. I am grateful to Oxford University Press for permission to use parts of this article in a revised form.

A visiting fellowship at Princeton University changed not only the way I thought about the project but also what history could be for me. The History Department provided a home away from home while testing me with its unstinting rigor. Angela Creager, Michael Gordin, Katja Guenther, Erika Milam, Jennifer Rampling, and Keith Wailoo engaged me with generous conversations and teaching; Katja also read an early draft of chapter 1. Gyan Prakash balanced eye-opening readings of *Capital* with wit and infectious bonhomie. I am especially grateful to Emily Thompson, who offered sensory studies fellowship (and homemade apple pie) and made all this possible. I also found some wonderful intellectual fellow travelers and friends along the way. Tom Clayton was and is a constant outpost and literary companion. Francis Dennig reached out across disciplines with generosity and enduring warmth. Devika Shankar and Alastair McClure: thank you for your easy humor, joyful chaos, and wry critique whenever we meet, in Hong Kong and beyond. While I was living in New Jersey, the Del Valley British History Group offered an anchor, and companionship, to a scholar adrift. Lynn Hollen Lees, Andrew Lees, and Seth Koven opened their homes, shared work, and made me feel embedded in a community.

I completed this book while a lecturer at the University of Bristol and could not ask for a more caring and supportive group of colleagues and friends. I am lucky to find myself in a department where so many prioritize kindness, collegiality, and intellectual curiosity. There are too many colleagues to mention here, but thank you to those who have nurtured me as a teacher and trusted that good things take time, especially Tim Cole, Josie McLellan, Simon Potter, James Thompson, Karen Skinazi, and Vanda Zajko. Thank you especially, Robert Bickers, for your gentleness and friendship, and for variously nudging me and keeping me afloat in rough waters. To my fellow historians of senses, science, sexuality, and cities, I am constantly inspired—sometimes overawed—by your drive and intelligence, while keeping it all together; Victoria Bates, Hannah Charnock, Andy Flack, Erika Hanna, Sarah Jones, Stephen Mawdsley, and Will Pooley, you make me think harder about my work whenever we talk. Thank you, Ruth Glynn and Erika, for keeping the urban studies fire burning, and Amy Edwards, Grace Huxford, Saima Nasar, and Shaun Wallace, for comradeship. Vivian Kong and Ray Yep (and Robert), our conversations and gastronomic explorations of Bristol's finest Sichuanese and Cantonese food inspire me to keep looking beyond the horizon of modern Britain. I especially give thanks to Su Lin Lewis and Sean Fox, for uplifting me with your openheartedness, real advice, and deep care. Friends in other departments have kept my world wide and interesting. Thank you, Michael Benson, for listening and for outings at home and abroad; Emma Cole, for being the exemplary colleague (and person) to live up to; Tim Gao, for your wry humor and deep heart; Will Kynan-Wilson, for talks in the garden; Shuangyi Li, for pulling me out of work with your great spirit; Michael Malay, for tenderhearted attention and mulberry picking, and Andreas Schönle, for teaching me to stay curious.

Over the years of writing this book I have been sustained by countless conversations with colleagues who have encouraged me and sharpened my thinking. The book would not be anything close to what it is without their help. A brief time as a visiting scholar at Johns Hopkins University gave me just the boost I needed to reexamine several chapters. Shane Butler, Tamer el-Leithy, Mary Fissell, H. Yumi Kim, John Marshall, Todd Shepard, and Liz Thornberry made me think very hard, as well as showing me a good time. Katie Hindmarch-Watson was an all-around friend, critic, and host extraordinaire. Many others have shared ideas and sources and invited me to present my own. I cannot do justice to the kindnesses offered me, but I thank Fredrik Albritton Jonsson, Chris Bischof, Stephen Brooke, Deborah Coen, Tom Crook, Santanu Das, Lucy Delap, Laura Doan, Margot Finn, Christine Grandy, Simon Gunn, Rhodri Hayward, Richard Hornsey, Kate Imy, Erik Linstrum, Peter Mandler, Ben Mountford, Lynda Nead, Barbara Pohl, Simon Schaffer, Joan Scott, Michal Shapira, and Chris Waters. James Vernon and Deborah Cohen gave critical advice and encouragement on the project at just the right time and have buoyed me up throughout. Thank you to Guy Orto-lano for providing me with the model of prose and academic friendship, and for reminding me to follow my instincts and heart. I am especially grateful to Guy and Susan Pedersen for allowing me to present a draft introduction at the Columbia University Modern British History Seminar and for the patient, extraordinarily generous comments with which they and Sarah Cole followed up. I am grateful to the Warner Fund of the University Seminars, Columbia University, for supporting the publication of this work.

I have been fortunate to meet scholars and friends who have made a particularly significant impression on my thinking, even before this project began. It was my great good fortune to have met Tom Simpson on the steps of a Cambridge auditorium, myself giddy after a talk by Natalie Zemon Davis and Amitav Ghosh; ten years of sharing a love of history, literature, and the films of Satyajit Ray with Tom and Jude Simpson have followed. My work has also been indelibly shaped by Sujit Sivasundaram. Sujit, your teaching has left an itch to think globally that has only become more persistent over time; thank you for your unbounded generosity and confidence in me. I am glad, too, that I gathered the nerve to introduce myself to Tom Johnson and Erin Maglaque in the Bodleian café one autumn afternoon; both after the historian's heart, they set a high standard for what historical work can be and provided respite and intellectual fuel when needed. Hilary Buxton, I can still remember our first fateful cup of tea together; for always getting to the heart of things, and for the best company over roti canai, thank you.

This book has benefited from the eyes of some extraordinary editors and readers. Doug Mitchell embraced the project with zest and attentiveness from the beginning. He generously engaged not only with my ideas but also with me, and our conversations soon ranged across the films of Wong Kar Wai and Michael Haneke, jazz, and Seamus Heaney. It is my considerable sadness that we could not meet in person. Priya Nelson and Mary al-Sayed kept the ship steady during the COVID-19 pandemic, giving me reassurance and encouragement when most needed. Thank you to Dylan Montanari and Fabiola Enríquez Flores for so enthusiastically taking the baton and guiding me wisely in the final stages. Thank you also to Tamara Ghattas and Lori Meek Schuldt for your great rigor and professionalism. I was lucky to have two readers whose meticulous comments spanned the smallest detail to the biggest conceptual aspirations of the book and enabled me to make it much better. Chris Otter and my anonymous second reader read the manuscript with honesty and care, and they gave some of the most thoughtful, theoretically interesting comments that I received over the whole project. Any shortcomings and errors remain entirely my own.

My journey as a historian owes most to the kindness of three teachers who have, in their own ways, set for me the benchmark for historical scholarship. William Whyte brought gentleness, lightness of perspective, and a knowledge of modern history that is positively biblical. His theoretical sophistication and curiosity have shaped the direction of my work, especially my fondness for phenomenology and buildings, although he is too self-effacing to admit it. Ever since giving me an intellectual home while I was in the States, Seth Koven has been a constant and passionate interlocutor. He has read and heard the whole manuscript several times and kept me going when times got tough. Seth helped me understand that this book was about tenderness, in its multiple meanings; he has taught me the largeness of the heart and the historical imagination, and their inseparable relation. My longest debt is owed to Matt Houlbrook, who has guided me on the intellectual road for close to a decade and a half. Matt has been an unwavering source of inspiration and support, his compassion and dedication to his historical subjects ramifying through all that he also does professionally. I owe more of my intellectual development to him than I can say, and I can only hope this book lives halfway up to the example he sets.

This book would not have lifted off the ground without the support of my friends and loved ones. Roeland Verhallen, our conversations and collaborations remind me who I am and where I come from; thank you for joyfully sharing so much. Giles Colclough and Mo Turner, you somehow bring an equal amount of sanity and extravagant fun to my life; for your sensitivity, impossible style, and for our adventures together, thank you. Joe Delo and Jamie Arberry, thank you for always knowing what to say, and for so freely opening your home and lives to me in London. Almost fifteen years' of gallery visits and conversations on art with KV Duong have nourished me; thank you, KV, for your irrepressible desire to learn and experiment. Tony and Hazel Park, you teach me what true generosity looks like, and to linger over good food shared. For our river walks and KBBQ feasts at home and away, thank you. Kin-Fung Ting, thank you for being a fellow old soul and lover of old things. To others in my crew of friends in London and beyond—Jack and Stella Fitzgerald, Chris Bowland, Henry and Alex Curr, James Golding, Edy Chandra, Izak Nel, Kentaro Tani, Ralph Mont.—spending time with you has deepened my life and brought great joy. I owe much also to Florian and Anna Ganzinger, with whom conversation about philosophy and real life effortlessly flows. I am especially grateful to James Ma. James, thank you for sitting through more conversations about Henry and Ruth than can be imagined, for helping me understand what embodied mind was really about, and for making me believe that what I wrote mattered during the dark winter days of lockdown.

Above all, thank you to my family, which has encouraged me, lifted me up, and been an unwavering source of love. To my sister Han, you are the model of joy and perfect twin; thank you for embracing every circumstance, and for always seeking the light. Even before becoming my brother-in-law, Dave, you have taught me how to combine thought with fun; thank you for your endless enthusiasm and commitment to connection. To my brother Dom, thank you for understanding me and what I need, and for always being there. Deb, if I could choose my sister-in-law, I would choose you; thank you for your uncompromising dedication to joy, and for always knowing what to prioritize, right now. To my nieces and nephew Sophie, Maddie, and Josh, thank you for the unexpected pleasures of chaos, and for having no patience with the past. My gran, Mavis, was a fellow soul in her love of history and responsible for my first fascination with London. It brings me great pleasure that she lives on in this book, through another that I cite from her father's, and my great-grandfather's, collection. I dedicate this book to my parents, whose love and dedication surpass any words that I can write here. Thank you to my mum, Liz, and my dad, Pieter, for making everything possible while reminding me what matters. Together they, more than anyone else, have helped me understand tenderness.

Source Abbreviations

BBC	BBC Written Archives
CRL	Cadbury Research Library Special Collections, University of Birmingham
LEP	Library of Experimental Psychology, University of Cambridge
LMA	London Metropolitan Archives
LPL	Lambeth Palace Library
LSE	British Library of Political and Economic Science, London School of Economics
LTM	London Transport Museum Archives
NCW	New College Worcester Archives
NRO	Norwich Record Office
RLHA	Royal London Hospital Archives
RNIB	Royal National Institute of Blind People Archives
TFLA	Transport for London Archives
TNA	The National Archives
TWAM	Tyne & Wear Archives and Museums
WCAR	Wolfson Centre for Archival Research, Library of Birmingham
WL	Wellcome Library

Notes

INTRODUCTION

1 "The Monster Station at Liverpool Street," *Westminster Gazette*, January 12, 1894, 6; "Overcrowded Trains," *Daily Mail* (London), October 29 1902, 3; Karl Baedeker, *London and Its Environs: Handbook for Travellers*, 14th ed. (Leipzig: Baedeker, 1905), 58.

2 "Overcrowded Trains," 3; *Liverpool Street Station: interior* (1905), London Metropolitan Archives (hereafter cited as LMA), SC/PHL/02/0629/76/18710.

3 Henri de Noussanne, "London's Human Tide: Liverpool Street from 7 till 9 a.m.," *Daily Mail*, August 28, 1902, 4.

4 "Liverpool Street Railway Station," in *The Descriptive Album of London: A Pictorial Guide Book* (London: Descriptive Album Publishing Co., 1896), n.p.

5 *Pictorial and Descriptive Guide to London and its Environs*, 27th ed. (London: Ward, Lock, 1906), 275.

6 *View looking west down Liverpool Street, c. 1884*, London Transport Museum Archives (hereafter cited as LTM), 1998/84925; "Obstructions in Liverpool-Street," *Globe*, December 19, 1894, 7.

7 "Railway Station Crime," *Daily Mail*, August 30, 1905, 3.

8 *Devonshire House in Bishopsgate* (1920), LMA, SC/PHL/01/003/WN314.

9 The following scene is reconstructed using, in addition to sources cited in notes 10–12, Charles E. Goad, *Insurance Plan of London* (1887), Vol. 3, Sheets 308 and 311, LMA, q8973050, and LMA, O.S.map/VII.56/1894–1896.

10 Walter Besant, *London City* (London: A. & C. Black, 1910), 181, 188; Harold Clunn, *The Face of London: The Record of a Century's Changes and Development*, 7th ed. (London: Simpkin Marshall, 1937), 36–38, 246.

11 George R. Sims, "London Street Corners," in *Living London: Its Work and Its Play, Its Humour and Its Pathos, Its Sights and Its Scenes*, 3 vols., ed. George R. Sims (London: Cassell & Co., 1901–1903), 2:91.

12 "Railway Station Crime," 3; "The King of Pickpockets," *Hackney and Kingsland Gazette*, September 29, 1890, 3; "Police Intelligence," *Morning Post* (London), June 13, 1892, 8.

13 "Guildhall," *London Evening Standard*, June 30, 1890, 3.

14 *Post Office London Directory: Part III; Commercial and Professional Directory* (London: Kelly, 1899), 852.

15   "Overcrowded Trains," 3.

16   "Not a Very Ancient Mariner," *Reynolds's Newspaper* (London), January 5, 1890, 8.

17   Georg Simmel, "The Metropolis and Mental Life" [1903], in *The Blackwell City Reader*, ed. Gary Bridge and Sophie Watson (Oxford: Blackwell, 2002), 11–15.

18   Walter Benjamin, "Paris, the Capital of the Nineteenth Century" [1935], in *Walter Benjamin: Selected Writings*, vol. 3, ed. Howard Eiland and Michael W. Jennings, trans. Edmund Jephcott (Cambridge, MA: Belknap Press of Harvard University Press, 2002), 32–49.

19   The foundational work on this is Alain Corbin, *The Foul and the Fragrant: Odor and the French Social Imagination*, trans. Miriam L. Kochan, Roy Porter, and Christopher Prendergast (Cambridge, MA: Harvard University Press, 1986). See also Wolfgang Schivelbusch, *Disenchanted Night: The Industrialization of Light in the Nineteenth Century*, trans. Angela Davies (Berkeley: University of California Press, 1988); James Winter, *London's Teeming Streets, 1830–1914* (London: Routledge, 1993), esp. 1–15 and 42–49; Richard Sennett, *Flesh and Stone: The Body and the City in Western Civilization* (London: Faber, 1994), 317–49. Sennett sees the ostensible "mutual indifference" that nineteenth-century city dwellers adopted toward one another and attempts to plan cities to reduce contact between bodies, as comprising an era of "urban individualism" (323).

20   "The Enlargement of Liverpool-Street Station, Great Eastern Railway: No. 1," *Engineer*, June 8, 1894, 493.

21   I depend on and diverge from Chris Otter's argument that the history of vision is typically told as one of discipline or capital. Otter instead tells this story as a material history of liberalism and its limitations. Chris Otter, *The Victorian Eye: A Political History of Light and Vision in Britain, 1800–1910* (Chicago: University of Chicago Press, 2008), 2.

22   Norbert Elias, *The Civilizing Process: The History of Manners* and *State Formation and Civilization*, trans. Edmund Jephcott (Oxford: Blackwell, 1994), 42–47; Pierre Bourdieu, *Distinction: A Social Critique of the Judgement of Taste*, trans. Richard Nice (London: Routledge, 2010); Corbin, *Foul and Fragrant*.

23   There is a small but wide-ranging historiography on touch, especially in the history of medicine and literature. For works that particularly inspired me, see Shigehisa Kuriyama, *The Expressiveness of the Body and the Divergence of Greek and Chinese Medicine* (New York: Zone Books, 1999); Elizabeth Harvey, ed., *Sensible Flesh: On Touch in Early Modern Culture* (Philadelphia: University of Pennsylvania Press, 2002); Santanu Das, *Touch and Intimacy in First World War Literature* (Cambridge: Cambridge University Press, 2005); Mark Paterson, *The Senses of Touch: Haptics, Affects and Technologies* (Oxford: Berg, 2007); Mark Jenner, "Tasting Lichfield, Touching China: Sir John Floyer's Senses," *Historical Journal* 53, no. 3 (September 2010): 647–70; Elizabeth Harvey, "The Portal of Touch," *American Historical Review* 116, no. 2 (April 2011): 385–400; Constance Classen, *The Deepest Sense: A Cultural History of Touch* (Urbana: University of Illinois Press, 2012); Abbie Garrington, *Haptic Modernism: Touch and the Tactile in Modernist Writing* (Edinburgh: University of Edinburgh Press, 2013); Joe Moshenska, *Feeling Pleasures: The Sense of Touch in Renaissance England* (Oxford: Oxford University Press 2014); David Parisi, *Archaeologies of Touch: Interfacing with Haptics from Electricity to Computing* (Min-

neapolis: University of Minnesota Press, 2018); Alex Purves, ed., *Touch and the Ancient Senses* (London: Routledge, 2018), esp. intro. For more literary musings, see Gabriel Josipovici, *Touch* (New Haven, CT: Yale University Press, 1996); Pablo Maurette, *The Forgotten Sense: Meditations on Touch* (Chicago: University of Chicago Press, 2018).

24 D. H. Lawrence, "Noli Me Tangere," in *Complete Poems*, ed. Vivian de Sola Pinto and Warren Robert (Harmondsworth, UK: Penguin, 1993), 468–69.

25 Thomas Burke, *The London Spy* (London: Thornton Butterworth, 1922), 40–41, 54.

26 Karl Marx, "Economic and Philosophical Manuscripts (1844)," in *Early Writings*, trans. Rodney Livingstone and Gregor Benton (London: Penguin, 1992), 353. For a discussion, see David Howes, *Sensual Relations: Engaging the Senses in Culture and Social Theory* (Ann Arbor: University of Michigan Press, 2003), ch. 8.

27 As history became reconceived as a singular temporality with temporally specific planes of experience, it became possible to think of sensation, too, as historical. In Koselleck's words, the "temporalization of history" enabled the historicization of experience—the experience of time, but also of sensation. Reinhart Koselleck, "Historia Magistra Vitae: The Dissolution of the Topos into the Perspective of a Modernized Historical Process," in *Futures Past: On the Semantics of Historical Time*, trans. Keith Tribe (New York: Columbia University Press, 2004), 37.

28 Corbin, *Foul and Fragrant*, 4, unpaged references to Robert Mandrou, *Introduction to Modern France, 1500–1640: An Essay in Historical Psychology*, trans. R. E. Hallmark (London: Edward Arnold, 1975); Lucien Febvre, "Smells, Tastes, and Sounds" [1942], in *The Problem of Unbelief in the Sixteenth Century: The Religion of Rabelais*, trans. Beatrice Gottlieb (Cambridge, MA: Harvard University Press, 1982), 423–31.

29 Georg Simmel, "Sociology of the Senses," in *Simmel on Culture: Selected Writings*, ed. David Frisby and Mike Featherstone (London: Sage, 1997), 118.

30 Indeed, in his subsequent survey of the history of the senses, Corbin identified the 1860s as marking "the emergence of the *modernity* evoked by Baudelaire" and later described by Simmel. This modernity entailed above all a somatic and sensory transformation, including a new attention to bodily appearance, hygiene, and the regulation of intimacy, and "new thresholds of the tolerable." Alain Corbin, *Time, Desire, and Horror: Towards a History of the Senses*, trans. Jean Birrell (Cambridge: Polity, 1995), viii–ix.

31 Lynda Nead, *Victorian Babylon: People, Streets and Images in Nineteenth-Century London* (New Haven, CT: Yale University Press, 2000), 58–62, 101–8; Richard Dennis, *Cities in Modernity: Representations and Productions of Metropolitan Space, 1840–1930* (Cambridge: Cambridge University Press, 2008), esp. 129–34, 309–12; James Vernon, *Distant Strangers: How Britain Became Modern* (Berkeley: University of California Press, 2014). See also Isobel Armstrong, *Victorian Glassworlds: Glass Culture and the Imagination, 1830–1880* (Oxford: Oxford University Press, 2008), 133–41.

32 The key work on this, with a focus on smell, is Corbin's *The Foul and the Fragrant*. For introductions, see Kate Flint, "The Social Life of the Senses: The Assaults and Seductions of Modernity," and Alain Corbin, "Urban Sensations: The Shifting Sensescape of the City," both in *A Cultural History of the Senses in the Age of Empire*, ed. Constance Classen (London: Bloomsbury, 2014), 25–45 and 47–67, respectively. For key sensory histories exploring the nineteenth- and twentieth-century city as a space of sensory

excess, see John M. Picker, *Victorian Soundscapes* (Oxford: Oxford University Press, 2003); Emily Thompson, *The Soundscape of Modernity: Architectural Acoustics and the Culture of Listening in America, 1900–1933* (Cambridge, MA: MIT Press, 2004); Nicholas Kenny, *The Feel of the City: Experiences of Urban Transformation* (Toronto: University of Toronto Press, 2014); Aimée Boutin, *City of Noise: Sound and Nineteenth-Century Paris* (Urbana: University of Illinois Press, 2015); James G. Mansell, *The Age of Noise in Britain: Hearing Modernity* (Urbana: University of Illinois Press, 2017).

33   Virginia Woolf, "Oxford Street Tide" [1932], in *The Essays of Virginia Woolf*, vol. 5, *1929–1932*, ed. Stuart N. Clarke (London: Vintage, 2009), 284.

34   Virginia Woolf, "Street Haunting: A London Adventure" [1927], in *The Essays of Virginia Woolf*, vol. 4, *1925–1928*, ed. Andrew McNeillie (London: Hogarth, 1994), 481.

35   Virginia Woolf, "An Unwritten Novel," in *Monday or Tuesday* (London: Harcourt, Brace, 1921), 18. Thanks to Matt Houlbrook for this reference.

36   The narrative of the city as a consumerist spectacle which might also be consumed is indebted to Benjamin, "Paris, the Capital of the Nineteenth Century." For works exploring the intensification of vision and visibility in the city, see Kate Flint, *The Victorians and the Visual Imagination* (Cambridge: Cambridge University Press, 2000); Peter Bailey, *Popular Culture and Performance in the Victorian City* (Cambridge: Cambridge University Press, 1998), 128–50; Erika D. Rappaport, *Shopping for Pleasure: Women in the Making of London's West End* (Princeton, NJ: Princeton University Press, 2000); Erika D. Rappaport, "The Senses in the Marketplace: Stimulation and Distraction, Gratification and Control," in Classen, *Cultural History of the Senses*, 69–88. See also Vanessa R. Schwartz, *Spectacular Realities: Early Mass Culture in Fin-de-siècle Paris* (Berkeley: University of California, 1998); Peter Gurney, *The Making of Consumer Culture in Modern Britain* (London: Bloomsbury, 2017), ch. 5.

37   Otter, *Victorian Eye*. See also Jonathan Crary, *Suspensions of Perception: Attention, Spectacle, and Modern Culture* (Cambridge, MA: MIT Press, 1999); Lynda Nead, *The Haunted Gallery: Painting, Photography, Film, c. 1900* (New Haven: Yale University Press, 2007), ch. 3.

38   Woolf, "Street Haunting," 485.

39   Woolf, "Street Haunting," 486.

40   Woolf, "Oxford Street Tide," 285.

41   Woolf, "Street Haunting," 490–91; Vernon, *Distant Strangers*, 49. On the changing performativity of selfhood and its relation to cultures of trust and authenticity, see Matt Houlbrook, *Prince of Tricksters: The Incredible True Story of Netley Lucas, Gentleman Crook* (Chicago: University of Chicago Press, 2016).

42   This idea was at the heart of Corbin's argument in *The Foul and the Fragrant* and was central to Georg Simmel's "Sociology of the Senses" and, from another angle, Pierre Bourdieu's *Distinction*, which understood taste in gustatory as well as aesthetic terms. The historiography developing Corbin's argument on social distinction is too lengthy to cite in full, but for representative examples, see Mark M. Smith, *Listening to Nineteenth-Century America* (Chapel Hill: University of North Carolina Press, 2001); Mark M. Smith, *How Race Is Made: Slavery, Segregation, and the Senses* (Chapel Hill: University of North Carolina Press, 2006); Laura Gowing, *Common Bodies: Women, Touch, and Power in Seventeenth-Century England* (New Haven, CT: Yale University Press,

2003); Jonathan Reinarz, *Past Scents: Historical Perspectives on Smell* (Urbana: University of Illinois Press, 2014); Adam Mack, *Sensing Chicago: Noisemakers, Strikebreakers, and Muckrakers* (Urbana: University of Illinois Press, 2015); William Tullett, *Smell in Eighteenth-Century England: A Social Sense* (Oxford: Oxford University Press, 2019); Erica Fretwell, *Sensory Experiments: Psychophysics, Race, and the Aesthetics of Feeling* (Durham, NC: Duke University Press, 2020).

43 Virginia Woolf, "Street Music" [1905], in *The Essays of Virginia Woolf*, vol. 1, 1904–1912, ed. Andrew McNeillie (London: Hogarth, 1986), 28. Although Woolf recognized the nuisance that street musicians and other noise caused to fellow Londoners, her later writing instead celebrated the potential for noise to spark associative thinking or to connect a community of listeners: Kate Flint, "Sounds of the City: Virginia Woolf and Modern Noise," in *Literature, Science, Psychoanalysis, 1830–1970: Essays in Honour of Gillian Beer*, ed. Helen Small and Trudi Tate (Oxford: Oxford University Press, 2003), 181–94.

44 Tim Edensor, "The Social Life of the Senses: Ordering and Disordering the Modern Sensorium," in *A Cultural History of the Senses in the Modern Age*, ed. David Howes (London: Bloomsbury 2014), 31–54; see also Helen Rees Leahy, *Museum Bodies: The Politics and Practices of Visiting and Viewing* (Farnham, UK: Ashgate, 2012); Constance Classen, *The Museum of the Senses: Experiencing Art and Collections* (London: Bloomsbury, 2017); Brian Ladd, *The Streets of Europe: The Sights, Sounds, and Smells That Shaped Its Great Cities* (Chicago: University of Chicago Press, 2020), ch. 4. This argument intersects with a much larger historiography on attempts to order the space of the nineteenth- and twentieth-century city and the subjectivity of its inhabitants. Although only sometimes concerned with sensory change, these works explore the material transformations of the urban environment from which it is inseparable. For representative examples, see Patrick Joyce, *The Rule of Freedom: Liberalism and the Modern City* (London: Verso, 2003); Tom Crook, *Governing Systems: Modernity and the Making of Public Health in England, 1830–1910* (Oakland: University of California Press, 2016); Katie Hindmarch-Watson, *Serving a Wired World: London's Telecommunications Workers and the Making of an Information Capital* (Oakland: University of California Press, 2020).

45 Otter, *Victorian Eye*; Elaine Hadley, *Living Liberalism: Practical Citizenship in Mid-Victorian Britain* (Chicago: University of Chicago Press, 2010). See also Dell Upton, *Another City: Urban Life and Urban Spaces in the New American Republic* (New Haven, CT: Yale University Press, 2008).

46 For a critique of the representational model of the mind, see Mark Johnson, *Embodied Mind, Meaning, and Reason: How Our Bodies Give Rise to Understanding* (Chicago: University of Chicago Press, 2017), esp. ch. 3.

47 Corbin, *Foul and Fragrant*, 229.

48 Henry Head and Gordon Holmes, "Sensory Disturbances from Cerebral Lesions," *Brain*, 34, no. 2–3 (November 1911), 102–254, reprinted in Henry Head, *Studies in Neurology*, 2 vols. (London: Hodder & Stoughton, 1920), 2:604–8.

49 Maurice Merleau-Ponty, *Phenomenology of Perception*, trans. Colin Smith (London: Routledge, 2002), 112–15. Merleau-Ponty cites Head and Holmes's "Sensory Disturbances of Cerebral Lesions" on 113.

50 Merleau-Ponty, *Phenomenology of Perception*, 235–39.

51 Merleau-Ponty, *Phenomenology of Perception*, 240–51.

52 The pioneering work in this field, which is in conversation with *Phenomenology of Perception*, is Francisco J. Varela, Evan Thompson, and Eleanor Rosch, *The Embodied Mind: Cognitive Science and Human Experience* (Cambridge, MA: MIT Press, 1991). Later work elaborating and contesting this book, and which has particularly stimulated me, includes Evan Thompson, *Mind in Life: Biology, Phenomenology, and the Sciences of Mind* (Cambridge, MA: Belknap Press of Harvard University Press, 2007), pt. 1; Tim Ingold, *The Perception of the Environment: Essays on Livelihood, Dwelling, and Skill* (London: Routledge, 2011), esp. 157–71, 243–87; Alva Noë, *Action in Perception* (Cambridge, MA: MIT Press, 2004); Lambros Malafouris, *How Things Shape the Mind: A Theory of Material Engagement* (Cambridge, MA: MIT Press, 2013); Shaun Gallagher, *Enactivist Interventions: Rethinking the Mind* (Oxford: Oxford University Press, 2017); M. Johnson, *Embodied Mind*; Shaun Gallagher and Dan Zahavi, *The Phenomenological Mind*, 3rd ed. (London: Routledge, 2020). For an introduction to debates on embodied cognition, see Albert Newen, Leon De Bruin, and Shaun Gallagher, "4E Cognition: Historical Roots, Key Concepts, and Central Issues," in *The Oxford Handbook of 4E Cognition*, ed. Albert Newen, Leon De Bruin, and Shaun Gallagher (Oxford: Oxford University Press, 2018), 3–16.

53 Noë, *Action in Perception*, 1–2.

54 Gallagher, *Enactivist Interventions*, 9–12.

55 Gallagher and Zahavi, *Phenomenological Mind*, 130–32.

56 James J. Gibson, "The Theory of Affordances," in *The Ecological Approach to Visual Perception* (Dallas: Houghton Mifflin, 1979), 119–35. For a useful interpretation of Gibson's work in relation to Merleau-Ponty's, see Ingold, *Perception of the Environment*, 157–71; 243–87.

57 Malafouris, *How Things Shape the Mind*, 4–6, 8–9, 166–167.

58 For reflections on this question from the perspective of political philosophy, see Erin Manning, *Politics of Touch: Sense, Movement, Sovereignty* (Minneapolis: University of Minnesota Press, 2006).

59 Gallagher, *Enactivist Interventions*, 115, 174.

60 Reinhart Koselleck, *Sediments of Time: On Possible Histories*, ed. and trans. Sean Franzel and Stefan-Ludwig Hoffmann (Stanford, CA: Stanford University Press, 2018), chs. 1, 10.

61 Michel Serres, *The Five Senses: A Philosophy of Mingled Bodies*, trans. Margaret Sankey and Peter Cowley (London: Bloomsbury Academic, 2016 [1985]), 59.

62 Serres, *Five Senses*, 81.

63 This approach is stimulated by Giorgio Agamben's rethinking of Western philosophical understandings of being as substance and proposal for an "ontology of immanence." In this proposal, the self is not an a priori substance but subject to, and constituted by, its ongoing use of the body and world: "The living being uses-itself, in the sense that in its very life and in its entering into relationship with what is other than the self, it has to do each time with its very self, feels the self and familiarizes itself with itself. *The self is nothing other than use-of-oneself.*" Agamben's theory of an emergent, self-constituting subject elaborates Michel Foucault's understanding of

one's self as the result of a "relationship with oneself." In Agamben's interpretation, citing Foucault, "The practice of the self is that operation in which the subject
adequates itself to its own constitutive relation and remains immanent to it: 'the
subject puts itself into play in taking care of itself.'" There is no better example—
and history—of this constitution of the self through use of oneself, than that of the
ever self-referential sense of touch. See Giorgio Agamben, *The Use of Bodies*, trans.
Adam Kotsko (Stanford, CA: Stanford University Press, 2016), esp. 29–30 ("ontology of
immanence" at 29), 54–56 ("The living being" quotation at 54), 100–106 ("The practice
of the self" quotation at 104); Giorgio Agamben, "On Potentiality," in *Potentialities:
Collected Essays in Philosophy*, ed. and trans. Daniel Heller-Roazen (Stanford, CA: Stanford University Press, 1999), 177–84; Michel Foucault, *The Hermeneutics of the Subject:
Lectures at the Collège de France, 1981–1982*, ed. Frédéric Gros, trans. Graham Burchell
(New York: Palgrave Macmillan, 2005).

64 For a critique of the figure of the "hypothetical blind man" as a "prop for philosophical theories of mind," see Georgina Kleege, *More than Meets the Eye: What Blindness
Brings to Art* (New York: Oxford University Press, 2018), ch. 2.

65 As Merleau-Ponty argued in his preface to *Phenomenology of Perception*, no reasoning,
including phenomenological reasoning, can be fully abstracted from the world it
examines. An examination of being-in-the-world is also a product of it, the history
of which might also be traced, if never completed. Merleau-Ponty, *Phenomenology of
Perception*, xxiii–xxiv.

66 Parisi, *Archaeologies of Touch*, 102–3, 108–9.

67 Here I diverge from Parisi's important argument: Parisi, *Archaeologies of Touch*, 4.

68 Louise Jackson, "Making Sexual Harassment History: The UK Context," Gender Equalities at Work, June 24, 2021, https://www.genderequalitiesat50.ed.ac.uk/2021/06/24
/making-sexual-harassment-history-the-uk-context/.

69 Jacqueline Rose, *On Violence and On Violence Against Women* (London: Faber, 2021),
38–39, 46–49.

70 Merleau-Ponty, *Phenomenology of Perception*, pt. 1, chs. 1 and 2.

71 This genealogy is traced in the notes to the recent translation of *Phenomenology of
Perception* by Donald A. Landes: Maurice Merleau-Ponty, *Phenomenology of Perception*,
trans. Donald A. Landes (London: Routledge, 2012), 101–3, 516n4, 516n5, 516n7. In addition to those by Head, key works cited include Jean Lhermitte, *L'Image de Notre Corps*
(Paris: Nouvelle Revue Critique, 1939); Paul Schilder, *Das Körperschema: Ein Beitrag
zur Lehre vom Bewusstsein des Eigenen Körpers* (Berlin: Springer, 1923). See Donald A.
Landes, *The Merleau-Ponty Dictionary* (London: Bloomsbury, 2013), 32–33.

72 Mark Paterson, *How We Became Sensorimotor: Movement, Measurement, Sensation* (Minneapolis: University of Minnesota Press, 2021), 11.

73 Simon Kuper, "Don't Touch Me, I'm British," *Financial Times*, March 5–6, 2011, 170.

74 Juulia T. Suvilehto, Enrico Glerean, et al., "Topography of Social Touching Depends
on Emotional Bonds Between Humans," *Proceedings of the National Academy of Sciences*
112, no. 45 (October 2015): 13814–15; Juulia T. Suvilehto, Lauri Nummenmaa, et al.,
"Cross-Cultural Similarity in Relationship-Specific Social Touching," *Proceedings of
the Royal Society B* 286, no. 1901 (April 2019): 8.

75 On the psychological and social importance of touch, see David J. Linden, *Touch: The*

Science of Hand, Heart, and Mind (London: Viking, 2015), esp. ch.1; Adam Phillips, *On Kissing, Tickling, and Being Bored* (London: Faber, 2016).

76 Erik Linstrum, *Ruling Minds: Psychology in the British Empire* (Cambridge, MA: Harvard University Press, 2016), ch. 1.

77 Stefan Höhne, *Riding the New York Subway: The Invention of the Modern Passenger* (Cambridge, MA: MIT Press, 2021).

78 Andreas Malm, *Fossil Capital: The Rise of Steam Power and the Roots of Global Warming* (London: Verso, 2016), 253–54; Henry James, "London," *Essays in London and Elsewhere* (London: James R. Osgood, McIlvaine, 1893), 29–33; Chiang Yee, *The Silent Traveller in London* (London: Country Life, 1938), 55–64. See also B. R. Mitchell, *International Historical Statistics: Europe 1750–2005*, 6th ed. (Basingstoke, UK: Palgrave Macmillan, 2007), 465–66.

79 Joyce, *Rule of Freedom*; James Vernon, *Hunger: A Modern History* (Cambridge, MA: Belknap Press of Harvard University Press, 2007); Otter, *Victorian Eye*; Hadley, *Living Liberalism*.

80 Judith R. Walkowitz, *City of Dreadful Delight: Narratives of Sexual Danger in Late-Victorian London* (London: Virago, 1992); Judith R. Walkowitz, "Going Public: Shopping, Street Harassment, and Streetwalking in Late-Victorian London," *Representations* 62 (Spring 1998): 1–30; Nead, *Victorian Babylon*, ch. 4. On the growing presence of unaccompanied women as consumers, workers, and philanthropists in Victorian and Edwardian London and its cultural implications, see also Rappaport, *Shopping for Pleasure*; Seth Koven, *Slumming: Sexual and Social Politics in Victorian London* (Princeton, NJ: Princeton University Press, 2006); Hindmarch-Watson, *Serving a Wired World*. On historical debates about the rise of sexual harassment, see Robin J. Barrow, "Rape on the Railway: Women, Safety, and Moral Panic in Victorian Newspapers," *Journal of Victorian Culture* 20, no. 3 (September 2015): 341–56; Michal Shapira, "Indecently Exposed: The Male Body and Vagrancy in Metropolitan London before the Fin de Siècle," *Gender & History* 30, no. 1 (March 2018): 52–69.

81 Karen Barad, "On Touching—The Inhuman That Therefore I Am," *differences* 23, no. 3 (2012): 206. A similar approach is developed by Sara Ahmed and Jackie Stacey, for whom thinking and writing about skin might be itself a kind of skin: Sara Ahmed and Jackie Stacey, "Introduction: Dermographies," in *Thinking Through the Skin*, ed. Sara Ahmed and Jackie Stacey (London: Routledge, 2001), 1.

82 Michael Rembis, "Challenging the Impairment/Disability Divide: Disability History and the Social Model of Disability," in *Routledge Handbook of Disability Studies*, ed. Nick Watson and Simo Vehmas, 2nd ed. (London: Routledge, 2019), 377–78.

83 Dan Goodley et al., "Provocations for Critical Disability Studies," *Disability & Society* 34, no. 6 (2019), 986. I borrow the concept "minor history" from Ann Laura Stoler, *Along the Archival Grain: Epistemic Anxieties and Colonial Common Sense* (Princeton, NJ: Princeton University Press, 2009), 7.

84 The dual conceptual and activist history of disability history is addressed by Michael Rembis, Catherine Kudlick, and Kim E. Nielsen, introduction to *The Oxford Handbook of Disability History*, ed. Michael Rembis, Catherine Kudlick, and Kim E. Nielsen (Oxford: Oxford University Press, 2018), 3–4.

85 Ben Whitburn and Rod Michalko, "Blindness/Sightedness: Disability Studies and the

Defiance of Di-Vision," in *Routledge Handbook of Disability Studies*, ed. Nick Watson and Simo Vehmas, 2nd ed. (London: Routledge, 2019), 225.

86 Rosemarie Garland-Thompson, "Misfits: A Feminist Materialist Disability Concept," *Hypatia* 26, no. 3 (Summer 2011): 594.

87 Tanya Titchkosky, "The Ends of the Body as Pedagogic Possibility," *Review of Education, Pedagogy, and Cultural Studies* 34, no. 3–4 (2012): 82–93.

88 My thinking here has been influenced by recent attempts to write the conceptual history of consent through that of the legal or political subject able to grant it. See Elizabeth Thornberry, *Colonizing Consent: Rape and Governance in South Africa's Eastern Cape* (Cambridge: Cambridge University Press, 2018); Emily A. Owens, "Consent," *differences* 30, no. 1 (2019): 148–56. See also Estelle B. Freedman, *Redefining Rape: Sexual Violence in the Era of Suffrage and Segregation* (Cambridge, MA: Harvard University Press, 2013). On the interpretive challenges posed by changing legal and social understandings of consent, see Shani D'Cruze, *Crimes of Outrage: Sex, Violence, and Victorian Working Women* (London: UCL Press, 1998), 19–20.

89 This rethinking of vulnerability, and the related concept of precarity, can be traced to Judith Butler's *Precarious Life: The Powers of Mourning and Violence* (London: Verso, 2004) and has been developed by Ann V. Murphy, *Violence and the Philosophical Imaginary* (Albany: State University of New York Press, 2012); Catriona Mackenzie, Wendy Rogers, and Susan Dodds, eds., *Vulnerability: New Essays in Ethics and Feminist Philosophy* (New York: Oxford University Press, 2014), in which see esp. Catriona Mackenzie, "The Importance of Relational Autonomy and Capabilities for an Ethics of Vulnerability," 34–59; Erinn Gilson, "Vulnerability and Victimization: Rethinking Key Concepts in Feminist Discourses on Sexual Violence," *Signs* 42, no. 1 (2016): 71–98; Judith Butler, Zeynep Gambetti, and Leticia Sabsay, eds., *Vulnerability in Resistance* (Durham, NC: Duke University Press, 2016).

90 The examination of touch as exemplifying one's being-in-the-world, and the vulnerability that is its consequence, is founded on Maurice Merleau-Ponty's famous account of two hands touching in his essay "The Intertwining—The Chiasm," in *The Visible and the Invisible*, ed. Claude Lefort, trans. Alphonso Lingis (Evanston, IL: Northwestern University Press, 1968), 130–55. For a later exploration, see Judith Butler, "Merleau-Ponty and the Touch of Malebranche," in *Senses of the Subject* (New York: Fordham University Press, 2015), 36–62. On how differences in gender, sexuality, race, and bodily ability variably affect an individual's experience of their corporeal exposure to others, see Gail Weiss, *Body Images: Embodiment as Intercorporeality* (New York: Routledge, 1999); Gail Weiss, "The Normal, the Natural and the Normative: A Merleau-Pontian Legacy to Feminist Theory, Critical Race Theory, and Disability Studies," *Continental Philosophy Review* 48 (2015): 77–93; Iris Marion Young, *On Female Body Experience: "Throwing Like a Girl" and Other Essays* (Oxford: Oxford University Press, 2005), 27–45; Sara Ahmed, *Queer Phenomenology: Orientations, Objects, Others* (Durham, NC: Duke University Press, 2006); Helen Ngo, *The Habits of Racism: A Phenomenology of Racism and Racialized Embodiment* (Lanham, MD: Lexington Books, 2017).

91 Walkowitz, "Going Public," 2; Walkowitz, *City of Dreadful Delight*. "Individuation is an accomplishment, not a presupposition, and certainly no guarantee": Butler, *Precarious Life*, 27.

92   Jennifer C. Nash, "Pedagogies of Desire," *differences* 30, no. 1 (2019): 197–217; Eva
      Cherniavsky, "#MeToo," *differences* 30, no. 1 (2019): 15–23; Gilson, "Vulnerability and
      Victimization," 75–76.

93   This argument has its roots in Edmund Husserl's *The Crisis of European Sciences and
      Transcendental Phenomenology* (1936) and the preface to Maurice Merleau-Ponty's *Phe-
      nomenology of Perception*. For both, scientific knowledge—indeed, all cognition and
      its results—is conditional on the *particular intentionality* (the particular situated,
      embodied involvement in the world) of those producing it. David Woodruff Smith,
      "Science, Intentionality, and Historical Background," in *Science and the Life-World:
      Essays on Husserl's* Crisis of European Sciences, ed. David Hyder and Hans-Jörg Rhein-
      berger (Stanford, CA: Stanford University Press, 2010), 6–8; Hans-Jörg Rheinberger,
      On Historicizing Epistemology: An Essay, trans. David Fernbach (Stanford, CA: Stanford
      University Press, 2010), 41.

94   On the constitution of law, and legal objects, through material practices, see Alain
      Pottage and Martha Mundy, eds., *Law, Anthropology, and the Constitution of the Social:
      Making Persons and Things* (Cambridge: Cambridge University Press, 2004); Cornelia
      Vismann, *Files: Law and Media Technology*, trans. Geoffrey Winthrop-Young (Stanford,
      CA: Stanford University Press, 2008); John Brigham, *Material Law: A Jurisprudence of
      What's Real* (Philadelphia: Temple University Press, 2009); Bruno Latour, *The Making
      of Law: An Ethnography of the Conseil d'Etat*, trans. Marina Brilman and Alain Pottage
      (Cambridge: Polity, 2010); Alain Pottage, "The Materiality of What?" *Journal of Law
      and Society* 39, no. 1 (March 2012): 167–83; Christopher Tomlins, "Historicism and
      Materiality in Legal Theory," in *Law in Theory and History: New Essays on a Neglected
      Dialogue*, ed. Maksymilian Del Mar and Michael Lobban (Oxford: Hart, 2016), 57–83;
      Tom Johnson, "Legal History and the Material Turn," in *The Oxford Handbook of Legal
      History*, ed. Markus D. Dubber and Christopher Tomlins (Oxford: Oxford University
      Press, 2018), 497–513. This body of work is in occasional dialogue with the vast lit-
      erature on the material constitution of science and scientific knowledge, although
      the latter also derives from a tradition of historical epistemology. Key works include
      Bruno Latour and Steve Woolgar, *Laboratory Life: The Construction of Scientific Facts*, 2nd
      ed. (Princeton, NJ: Princeton University Press, 1986); Peter Galison, *Image and Logic: A
      Material Culture of Microphysics* (Chicago: University of Chicago Press, 1997), esp. 827–
      40; Lorraine Daston and Peter Galison, *Objectivity*, 2nd ed. (New York: Zone, 2010);
      Hans-Jörg Rheinberger, *An Epistemology of the Concrete: Twentieth-Century Histories of
      Life* (Durham, NC: Duke University Press, 2010). For a work especially relevant to my
      investigation of the sensory entanglement of body and world, see Karen Barad, *Meet-
      ing the Universe Halfway: Quantum Physics and the Entanglement of Matter and Meaning*
      (Durham, NC: Duke University Press, 2007).

95   T. Johnson, "Legal History and the Material Turn," 504.

CHAPTER ONE

1   Henry Head to Ruth Mayhew, January 16, 1903, Wellcome Library (hereafter cited as
      WL), PP/HEA/D.4/13.

2   Henry Head and W. H. R. Rivers, "A Human Experiment in Nerve Division," *Brain* 31, no. 3 (November 1908): 325–26.

3   Head and Rivers, "Human Experiment," 327–28.

4   For the broader intellectual and institutional context of these experiments within neurology, see Stephen T. Casper, *The Neurologists: A History of a Medical Speciality in Modern Britain, c. 1789–2000* (Manchester: Manchester University Press, 2014). See also J. C. Stevens and B. G. Green, "History of Research on Touch," in *Pain and Touch*, ed. Lawrence Kruger (San Diego, CA: Academic Press, 1996), 1–23; F. C. Rose, *History of British Neurology* (London: Imperial College Press, 2012).

5   "Sir Henry Head: Pioneer in Neurology," *Times* (London), October 10, 1940, 7. See also "Sir Henry Head, M.D., F.R.C.P., F.R.S., 1861–1940. Editor of 'Brain,' 1910–1925," *Brain* 63, no. 3 (1940): 205–8, WL, PP/HEA/A.4.

6   Gordon Holmes, "Sir Henry Head. 1861–1940," *Obituary Notices of Fellows of the Royal Society* 3, no. 10 (December 1941): 683.

7   For invaluable accounts of Head's research and relationship, see L.S. Jacyna, *Medicine and Modernism: A Biography of Sir Henry Head* (London: Pickering & Chatto, 2008); Tiffany Watt Smith, *On Flinching: Theatricality and Scientific Looking from Darwin to Shell Shock* (Oxford: Oxford University Press, 2014), ch. 3.

8   Henry Head to Ruth Mayhew, May 6, 1903, WL, PP/HEA/D.4/14.

9   Head to Mayhew, May 6, 1903.

10   Parisi, *Archaeologies of Touch*, 99–101.

11   Parisi, *Archaeologies of Touch*, 102.

12   A similar claim about the uses of experimental physiology to determine the correspondence between stimuli and neurological structures and psychological processes was made by Hermann von Helmholtz in 1850. Helmholtz used touch, in the form of electric current applied to his subject's skin, to measure the time elapsed between stimulus and sensation. Henning Schmidgen, *The Helmholtz Curves: Tracing Lost Time*, trans. Nils F. Schott (New York: Fordham University Press, 2014), 132–35.

13   Kurt Danziger, *Constructing the Subject: Historical Origins of Psychological Research* (Cambridge: Cambridge University Press, 1990), 27.

14   Henry Head, typescript autobiography, November 1926, WL, PP/HEA/A.1, 18, 23–24; Henry Head to Ruth Mayhew, March 6, 1903, WL, PP/HEA/D.4/13.

15   Henrika Kuklick, "Fieldworkers and Physiologists," in *Cambridge and the Torres Strait: Centenary Essays on the 1898 Anthropological Expedition*, ed. Anita Herle and Sandra Rouse (Cambridge: Cambridge University Press, 1998), 173–74; Linstrum, *Ruling Minds*, 19.

16   Fretwell, *Sensory Experiments*, 13–18.

17   Andrew J. Rotter, *Empires of the Senses: Bodily Encounters in Imperial India and the Philippines* (Oxford: Oxford University Press, 2019), 33. On experimental psychology's challenge to the assumption of racial differences in sensory acuity, see Linstrum, *Ruling Minds*, 26, 31–36.

18   Maria Montessori, cited in Parisi, *Archaeologies of Touch*, 142.

19   Michael Pettit, *The Science of Deception: Psychology and Commerce in America* (Chicago: University of Chicago Press, 2013), 55–56, 58–59.

20 Parisi, *Archaeologies of Touch*, 102. Parisi terms the outcome of this process where touch was concerned a "haptic subject": 18–20.

21 There is an extensive literature on the emotional and embodied constitution of scientific knowledge. See Christopher Lawrence and Steven Shapin, eds., *Science Incarnate: Historical Embodiments of Natural Knowledge* (Chicago: University of Chicago Press, 1998); Steven Shapin, "The Philosopher and the Chicken: On the Dietetics of Disembodied Knowledge," in *Never Pure: Historical Studies of Science [. . .]* (Baltimore: Johns Hopkins University Press, 2010), 237–58; see also Ulinka Rublack, *The Astronomer and the Witch: Johannes Kepler's Fight for His Mother* (Oxford: Oxford University Press, 2015). I have especially drawn inspiration from Kuriyama, *Expressiveness of the Body*.

22 Deborah R. Coen, *Vienna in the Age of Uncertainty: Science, Liberalism, and Private Life* (Chicago: University of Chicago Press, 2007); Staffan Bergwik, "An Assemblage of Science and Home: The Gendered Lifestyle of Svante Arrhenius and Early Twentieth-Century Physical Chemistry," *Isis* 105 (2014): 265–91; Donald L. Opitz, Staffan Bergwik, and Brigitte Van Tiggelen, eds., *Domesticity in the Making of Modern Science* (Basingstoke, UK: Palgrave Macmillan, 2016). For a useful overview of this work, see Deborah R. Coen, "The Common World: Histories of Science and Domestic Intimacy," *Modern Intellectual History* 11, no. 2 (2014): 417–38.

23 On the late nineteenth- and early twentieth-century entanglement of literature and neurology, see Laura Salisbury and Andrew Shail, introduction to *Neurology and Modernity: A Cultural History of Nervous Systems, 1800–1950*, ed. Laura Salisbury and Andrew Shail (Basingstoke, UK: Palgrave Macmillan, 2010), 1–40. See also Anne Stiles, *Popular Fiction and Brain Science in the Late Nineteenth Century* (Cambridge: Cambridge University Press, 2012); Ulrika Maude, "Modernism, Neurology, and the Invention of Psychoanalysis," in *The Bloomsbury Companion to Modernist Literature*, ed. Ulrika Maude and Mark Nixon (London: Bloomsbury, 2018), 267–84.

24 Ruth Mayhew, rag book, October 1902, 29, WL, PP/HEA/E.3/4.

25 Henry Head, rag book, October 1902, 29, WL, PP/HEA/E.3/4.

26 Walter Pater, *The Renaissance: Studies in Art and Poetry*, 6th ed. (1901; repr., London: Macmillan, 1904), viii, 234–36.

27 On the entangled relation between the scientist's lifeworld and "world-making," see Jerome Bruner, "Possible Castles," in *Actual Minds, Possible Worlds* (Cambridge, MA: Harvard University Press, 1986), 44–54.

28 This idea is in conversation with Gaston Bachelard's concept of "phenomenotechnique," which informs Hans-Jörg Rheinberger's phenomenological history of science: Rheinberger, *Epistemology of the Concrete*, 27–31, 218–20.

29 This draws on Karen Barad's argument that "intra-actions" between phenomena, which includes scientists and their objects, causes their contingent differentiation from one another and between scientific concepts and the phenomenal world. I, however, retain a phenomenological rather than posthumanist perspective in this chapter. Barad, *Meeting the Universe Halfway*, 139–40.

30 Danziger, *Constructing the Subject*, 28–35.

31 Ernst Heinrich Weber, "De Subtilitate Tactus" (1834), in *E. H. Weber on the Tactile Senses*, ed. and trans. Helen E. Ross and David J. Murray, 2nd ed. (Hove: Erlbaum UK, 1996), 29–30, 32–33, 48.

32   Charles Scott Sherrington, "Cutaneous Sensations," in *Text-Book of Physiology*, vol. 2, ed. E. A. Schäfer (Edinburgh: Pentland, 1900), 928–31.

33   Johannes Müller, *Elements of Physiology*, 2 vols., trans. William Baly (London: Taylor and Walton, 1838–1842), 1:766.

34   Müller, *Elements of Physiology*, 2:1065–67.

35   Müller, *Elements of Physiology*, 2:1072.

36   Sherrington, "Cutaneous Sensations," 969–970. For a return to this idea, see H. H. Price, "Touch and Organic Sensation: The Presidential Address," *Proceedings of the Aristotelian Society*, n.s., 44 (1943–1944): i–xxx. On touch and common sensibility in relation to muscular sensation, see Roger Smith, "'The Sixth Sense': Towards a History of Muscular Sensation," *Gesnerus* 68, no. 1 (2011): 218–71.

37   Müller, *Elements of Physiology*, 2:1059, 1087.

38   See Müller himself: Müller, *Elements of Physiology*, 2:1069; Ulf Norrsell, Stanley Finger, and Clara Lajonchere, "Cutaneous Sensory Spots and the 'Law of Specific Nerve Energies': History and Development of Ideas," *Brain Research Bulletin* 48, no. 5 (1999): 457.

39   Ernst Weber, "Tastsinn und Gemeingefühl," in *E.H. Weber on the Tactile Senses*, 213.

40   Weber, "Tastsinn und Gemeingefühl," 158–159, 163.

41   Norrsell, Finger, and Lajonchere, "Cutaneous Sensory Spots," 458; David C. Sinclair, *Cutaneous Sensation* (Oxford: Oxford University Press, 1967), 4–5.

42   Sherrington, "Cutaneous Sensations," 945–46; Edwin G. Boring, *Sensation and Perception in the History of Experimental Psychology* (New York: D. Appleton-Century, 1942), 466–67.

43   E. G. B., "Max von Frey, 1852–1932," *American Journal of Psychology* 44, no. 3 (July 1932): 584–86; Boring, *Sensation and Perception*, 469.

44   Sherrington, "Cutaneous Sensations," 921.

45   As Rheinberger argues, experimental instruments set the conditions under which "epistemic objects" can emerge: Rheinberger, *Epistemology of the Concrete*, 218.

46   James Sully, "Recent Experiments with the Senses," *Westminster Review* 42, no. 1 (July 1872): 165–98, reprinted in James Sully, *Sensation and Intuition: Studies in Psychology and Aesthetics* (London, 1874), citation 72.

47   See especially the confusion over pain: Sherrington, "Cutaneous Sensations," 966.

48   Kuriyama, *Expressiveness of the Body*, 77, 95–96.

49   Sherrington, "Cutaneous Sensations," 976–77.

50   James Sully, *An Essay on Laughter: Its Forms, Its Causes, Its Development and Its Value* (London: Longmans, 1902), 56–62. See also Havelock Ellis, *Studies in the Psychology of Sex*, vol. 4, *Sexual Selection in Man* (Philadelphia: F. A. Davis, 1905), 12–15; Louis Robinson, "Ticklishness, and the Phenomena of Tickling," in *A Dictionary of Psychological Medicine* [. . .], vol. 2, ed. D. H. Tuke (London: J. & A. Churchill, 1892), 1295–96.

51   Herbert Spencer, *The Principles of Psychology*, 2nd ed., vol. 1 (London: Williams and Norgate, 1870), 67.

52   G. York, "Hughlings Jackson's Evolutionary Neurophysiology," in *A Short History of Neurology: The British Contribution, 1660–1910*, ed. F. C. Rose (Oxford: Butterworth-Heinemann, 1999), 157–58; James Taylor, revised by Walton of Detchant, "Jackson, John Hughlings (1835–1911)," in *Oxford Dictionary of National Biography*, Oxford Uni-

versity Press, 2004; online ed., September 23, 2004, https://doi.org/10.1093/ref:odnb/34137.

53 Sherrington, "Cutaneous Sensations," 970, 984.

54 G. S. Hall and A. Allin, "The Psychology of Tickling, Laughter, and the Comic," *American Journal of Psychology* 9, no. 1 (October 1897): 12.

55 Robinson first outlined this experiment in a paper read before the British Association for the Advancement of Science in 1894: Louis Robinson, "On the Anthropological Significance of Ticklishness," *Report of the Sixty-Fourth Meeting of the British Association for the Advancement of Science held at Oxford in August 1894* (London: BAAS, 1894), 778. There is no record of the experiment in the Council or Garden Committee minutes of the Zoological Society of London for the previous decade, suggesting that it was conducted without permission.

56 Louis Robinson, "The Science of Ticklishness," *North American Review* 185, no. 617 (June 21, 1907): 413–14.

57 Robinson, "Science of Ticklishness," 414–18. Charles Darwin devoted only a page to ticklishness in his *The Expression of the Emotions in Man and Animals* (London: John Murray, 1872), 201.

58 See Nick Hopwood, *Haeckel's Embryos: Images, Evolution, and Fraud* (Chicago: University of Chicago Press, 2015).

59 Kuklick, "Fieldworkers and Physiologists," 168.

60 W. H. R. Rivers, introduction to *Reports of the Cambridge Anthropological Expedition to Torres Straits*, vol. 2, *Physiology and Psychology*, Pt. 1, ed. A. C. Haddon (Cambridge: Cambridge University Press, 1901), 2.

61 W. H. Winch, "Review: *Reports of the Cambridge Anthropological Expedition to Torres Straits: Volume II*: [. . .], 1901, 1903," *Mind*, n.s., 13, no. 50 (April 1904): 274; Simmel, "Metropolis and Mental Life." Francis Galton made similar investigations in the 1880s, concluding that the sensory acuity of "wild races" was not superior to that of "white men." Francis Galton, *Inquiries into Human Faculty and Its Development*, 2nd ed. (London: Dent, 1907), 22.

62 Rivers, introduction to *Reports*, 6; Graham Richards, "Getting a Result: The Expedition's Psychological Research, 1898–1913," in Herle and Rouse, *Cambridge and the Torres Strait*, 139.

63 W. McDougall, "Cutaneous Sensations," in *Reports of the Cambridge Anthropological Expedition to Torres Straits*, vol. 2, *Physiology and Psychology*. Pt. 2, ed. A. C. Haddon (Cambridge: Cambridge University Press, 1903), 193–94.

64 McDougall, "Cutaneous Sensations," 189–92.

65 Kuklick, "Fieldworkers and Physiologists," 173.

66 Kuklick, "Fieldworkers and Physiologists," 166–67.

67 William Rivers cited in Kuklick, "Fieldworkers and Physiologists," 174.

68 Winch, "Review," 277. For a more critical review drawing attention to the problem of language in self-reporting, see E. B. Titchener, "On Ethnological Tests of Sensation and Perception [. . .]," *Proceedings of the American Philosophical Society* 55, no. 5 (1916): 211.

69 W. H. R. Rivers, "Observations on the Senses of the Todas," *Journal of Psychology* 1, no. 1 (December 1905): 321–96.

70 D. Sinclair, *Cutaneous Sensation*, 4–5.

71 See the interview of would-be patients by the Out-Patient Hall Inquiry Officer described in E. W. Morris, *A History of the London Hospital* (London: Edward Arnold, 1910), 10.

72 Hubert Llewellyn Smith, "Influx of Population (East London)" [written in 1888], in *Life and Labour of the People in London*, vol. 3, *Poverty: Blocks of Buildings, Schools, and Immigration*, ed. Charles Booth, 1st ser. (London: Macmillan, 1902), 102–3, 106, 113. See also Beatrice Potter, "The Jewish Community," 166–92, in the same volume. For a visualization of the estimated preponderance of Jews in the streets surrounding the London Hospital, see the map "Jewish East London" (1899) in C. Russell and H. S. Lewis, *The Jew in London: A Study of Racial Character and Present-Day Conditions* (London: T. Fisher Unwin, 1900).

73 Henry Head to Ruth Mayhew, September 5, 1902, WL, PP/HEA/D.4/12.

74 Morris, *History of the London Hospital*, 17; Head and Rivers, "Human Experiment," 324.

75 Head and Rivers, "Human Experiment," 324.

76 See William E. Evans-Gordon, *The Alien Immigrant* (London: Heinemann, 1903). See also Daniel Pick, *Faces of Degeneration: A European Disorder, c. 1848–c. 1918* (Cambridge: Cambridge University Press, 1989).

77 Fretwell, *Sensory Experiments*, 17–18. This conclusion continued Francis Galton's claims that sensory acuity was greatest among men and increased with intelligence. Galton, *Inquiries into Human Faculty*, 20.

78 Head and Rivers, "Human Experiment," 324.

79 Henry Head to Ruth Mayhew, April 3, 1903, and n.d. (envelope postmarked April 11, 1903), WL, PP/HEA/D.4/14.

80 "The War," *Times*, November 6, 1901, 8.

81 See, for example, the case of Jamaican soldier L. G. H., wounded by a bullet at the Battle of Tweefontein (Groenkop) on July 22, 1901, and examined by Head and Sherren at University College Hospital on January 26, 1902. Henry Head and James Sherren, "The Consequences of Injury to the Peripheral Nerves in Man," *Brain* 28, no. 2 (November 1905): 316–19.

82 Head to Mayhew, April 3, 1903.

83 Head and Rivers, "Human Experiment," 325–26, 340; Lett's Rough Diary and Almanac for 1903 (hereafter cited as Day Book), April 26, 1903, and loose insert at May 7, 1903, Library of Experimental Psychology (hereafter cited as LEP; uncataloged).

84 Day Book, May 23, 1903; May 27, 1903, LEP; Head and Rivers, "Human Experiment," 328.

85 See the exemplary irony of Head's weekly schedule, stuck onto the rear of a photograph of Head relaxing with his family, stamped 1902, WL, PP/HEA/B.5. Also, Henry Head to Ruth Mayhew, October 25, 1902, WL, PP/HEA/D.4/12.

86 Head and Rivers, "Human Experiment," 342.

87 Henry Head to Ruth Mayhew, May 15, 1903, WL, PP/HEA/D.4/14.

88 Head and Rivers, "Human Experiment," 347–51.

89 Henry Head, rag book, October 1903, WL, PP/HEA/E.3/5; Head to Mayhew, September 5, 1902.

90 Head and Rivers, "Human Experiment," 342.

91 Head and Rivers, "Human Experiment," 342.

92 On the theatricality of Head's relation to Rivers during the experiment, see Watt Smith, *On Flinching*, 149–50.

93 Head and Rivers, "Human Experiment," 343; Henry Head to Ruth Mayhew, November 27, 1903, WL, PP/HEA/D.4/16.

94 Head to Mayhew, November 27, 1903.

95 Head to Mayhew, May 15, 1903.

96 Head and Rivers, "Human Experiment," 345, 353.

97 Head and Rivers, "Human Experiment," 353–54.

98 Head and Rivers, "Human Experiment," 343.

99 Head and Rivers, "Human Experiment," 343, 345.

100 Henry Head cited in Jacyna, *Medicine and Modernism*, 123.

101 Henry Head, introduction to Head, *Studies in Neurology*, 1:3–4.

102 Head, introduction to Head, *Studies in Neurology*, 1:6.

103 Watt Smith, *On Flinching*, 144–46.

104 Head, introduction to Head, *Studies in Neurology*, 1:9–10.

105 Henry Head, W. H. R. Rivers, and James Sherren, "The Afferent Nervous System from a New Aspect," *Brain* 28, no. 2 (1905): 99–116, reprinted in Head, *Studies in Neurology*, 1:58. Subsequent page references are from the reprint edition.

106 Head and Rivers, "Human Experiment," 340–42.

107 Head, Rivers, and Sherren, "Afferent Nervous System," 58–59.

108 Head and Rivers, "Human Experiment," 340–42.

109 Head, Rivers, and Sherren, "Afferent Nervous System," 61.

110 Head, Rivers, and Sherren, "Afferent Nervous System," 61–63.

111 Head, Rivers, and Sherren, "Afferent Nervous System," 63; Head and Rivers, "Human Experiment," 442–43.

112 Schmidgen, *Helmholtz Curves*, 137.

113 Head and Rivers, "Human Experiment," 444–45.

114 Head, introduction to Head, *Studies in Neurology*, 1:11.

115 See Gül Inanç and Michael Walsh, "Amongst the Nerves of the World: C. R. W. Nevinson's Visions of Post-war London, 1919–1929," *London Journal* 32, no. 2 (2007): 172–74.

116 The phrase was established at least since the opening of London's Central Telegraph Office in 1876, when journalist John Munro claimed that "telegraph lines are the nerves of the world": Hindmarch-Watson, *Serving a Wired World*, 18.

117 *Brain*, collection of volumes owned and annotated by John Hughlings Jackson, subsequently owned and annotated by Henry Head, 1879–1894, Royal London Hospital Archives (hereafter cited as RLHA), RLHPP/HEA/2/1–16; Head, epilogue to Head, *Studies in Neurology*, 2:801. See also Charles S. Sherrington, *The Integrative Action of the Nervous System* (New Haven, CT: Yale University Press, 1906), 2, 8.

118 Head, introduction to Head, *Studies in Neurology*, 1:10–11.

119 Head and Rivers, "Human Experiment," 446–49.

120 Day Book, loose insert at May 7, 1903 (dated April 29, 1903); May 11, 1903; May 19, 1903, LEP.

121 Ludwig Wittgenstein, *Philosophical Investigations*, trans. G. E. M. Anscombe, P. M. S. Hacker, and Joachim Schulte, 4th ed. (Chichester, UK: Wiley-Blackwell, 2009), sec. 258.

122 Jürgen Renn and Tilman Sauer, "Errors and Insights: Reconstructing the Genesis of

General Relativity from Einstein's Zurich Notebook," in *Reworking the Bench: Research Notebooks in the History of Science*, ed. Frederic L. Holmes, Jürgen Renn, and Hans-Jörg Rheinberger (Dordrecht, Neth.: Kluwer Academic, 2003), 261–64; Rheinberger, *Epistemology of the Concrete*, 244–45.

123 Henry Head and Theodore Thompson, "The Grouping of Afferent Impulses within the Spinal Cord," *Brain* 24 (1905): 116–340; Henry Head and Gordon Holmes, "Sensory Disturbances from Cerebral Lesions," *Brain* 34 (1911–12): 102–271; Henry Head, "Sensation and the Cerebral Cortex," *Brain* 41 (1918): 57–253, all reprinted in vol. 2 of Head, *Studies in Neurology*.

124 Holmes, "Sir Henry Head," 674–76. See also Holmes's defense of these findings in Gordon Holmes, "Disorders of Sensation Produced by Cortical Lesions," *Brain* 50 (1927): 413–27, reprinted in *Selected Papers of Gordon Holmes*, ed. Charles G. Phillips (Oxford: Oxford University Press, 1979), 278–92.

125 Head, introduction to Head, *Studies in Neurology*, 1:3.

126 Day Book, May 17, 1903, LEP.

127 Head and Rivers, "Human Experiment," 345–46, 350. On Wilson, see "Mr Ernest Wilson," *Times*, March 4, 1911, 11.

128 Henry Head, "Appendix: Some Criticisms of Our Work," in Head, *Studies in Neurology*, 2:831.

129 Carlo Ginzburg, "Clues: Morelli, Freud, and Sherlock Holmes," in *The Sign of Three: Dupin, Holmes, Pierce*, ed. Umberto Eco and Thomas A. Sebeok (Bloomington: Indiana University Press, 1983), 81–118.

130 Daston and Galison, *Objectivity*, 120–21.

131 F. M. R. Walshe, "The Anatomy and Physiology of Cutaneous Sensibility: A Critical Review," *Brain* 65, no. 1 (1942): 54–55.

132 Major Greenwood Jr., *Physiology of the Special Senses* (London: Edward Arnold, 1910). See also the first edition of Walter R. Brain and Eric B. Strauss's *Recent Advances in Neurology* (London: J. & A. Churchill, 1929), 237–73; John S. B. Stopford, *Sensation and the Sensory Pathway* (London: Longmans, 1930); Martin Flack and Leonard Hill, *A Textbook of Physiology* (London: Edward Arnold, 1919), 591–92.

133 Walshe, "Anatomy and Physiology," 54–55.

134 Walshe, "Anatomy and Physiology," 59.

135 Jacyna, *Medicine and Modernism*, 167.

136 Jacyna, *Medicine and Modernism*, 154–59.

137 Ruth Mayhew to Henry Head, May 4, 1903, and June 29, 1903, WL, PP/HEA/D.4/14.

138 Ruth Mayhew to Henry Head, March 24, 1903, WL, PP/HEA/D.4/13. Thirteen years later Mayhew (by then Ruth Head) gathered together her favorite sections from James's novels and published them as *Pictures and Other Passages from Henry James* (London: Chatto & Windus, 1916). She wrote that, of all the qualities of the heroines in James's novels, for her the one that had the most enduring influence was "their capacity for receiving mental impressions"—a capacity Henry Head equally treasured (v–vi).

139 James composed prefaces for each of his novels when they were collected in a New York edition published between 1907 and 1909. Henry James, "Preface to 'The Wings of the Dove,'" in *The Art of the Novel: Critical Prefaces* (New York: Scribner, 1934), 303.

140 Henry James, *The Wings of the Dove* (Westminster, UK: Archibald Constable, 1902), 51.

141 James, *Wings of the Dove*, 54.

142 Henry Head to Ruth Mayhew, November 6, 1903, WL, PP/HEA/D.4/16.

143 Ruth Mayhew to Henry Head, November 7, 1903, WL, PP/HEA/D.4/16.

144 On letters as a means by which writers and recipients mutually constitute one another, especially bodily, see Seth Koven, *The Match Girl and the Heiress* (Princeton, NJ: Princeton University Press, 2014), 184–85, 230–37. Koven significantly draws attention to the ways that narratives of bodies establish intimate relationships at the same time as intimacy transforms those narratives. For an essential account of Head and Mayhew's correspondence as a "process of mutual representation," see Jacyna, *Medicine and Modernism*, 169–84.

145 Liz Stanley, "The Epistolarium: On Theorizing Letters and Correspondences," *Auto/Biography* 12 (2004): 209.

146 Kate Thomas, *Postal Pleasures: Sex, Scandal, and Victorian Letters* (Oxford: Oxford University Press, 2012), 4–9. This accounts for the historical and critical interest, beginning in the late eighteenth century, in the gendered erotics of epistolary exchange: Carolyn Steedman, "A Woman Writing a Letter," in *Epistolary Selves: Letters and Letter-writers, 1600–1945*, ed. Rebecca Earle (Aldershot, UK: Ashgate, 1999), 126.

147 Stanley, "Epistolarium," 203, 208.

148 Michael Roper, "Splitting in Unsent Letters: Writing as a Social Practice and a Psychological Activity," *Social History* 26, no. 3 (October 2001): 318–39. For an account of letter writing as a "performance" that nonetheless remains open-ended, see Houlbrook, "'A Pin to See the Peepshow': Culture, Fiction, and Selfhood in Edith Thompson's Letters, 1921–1922." *Past and Present* 207, no. 1 (May 2010): 221, 226–28.

149 See also Thomas, *Postal Pleasures*, 30; Michael Roper, *The Secret Battle: Emotional Survival and the Great War* (Manchester: Manchester University Press, 2009), 49.

150 On letter writing as a substitute for absence that simultaneously reestablishes it, as well as the social difference it mediates, see Koven, *Match Girl and Heiress*, 251–52.

151 Henry Head to Ruth Mayhew, May 22, 1903, WL, PP/HEA/D.4/14.

152 "The Theatres," *Daily News* (London), April 10, 1899, 8.

153 "'The Gay Lord Quex,' at the Globe," *Pall Mall Gazette*, April 10, 1899, 1. See also "Pinero's New Play," *Lloyd's Illustrated Newspaper*, April 9, 1899, 1; "Globe Theatre," *Morning Post*, April 10, 1899, 6; "The Morality of Lord Quex," *Era*, May 13, 1899, 17.

154 John Russell Stephens, *The Censorship of English Drama, 1824–1901* (Cambridge: Cambridge University Press, 1980), 150.

155 "The Institute of Journalists," *Times*, September 4, 1902, 8. For the ensuing exchange, see "Sir Edward Russell and 'The Gay Lord Quex,'" *Times*, September 5, 1902, 6; September 9, 1902, 8; September 10, 1902, 10; September 12, 1902, 5; September 13, 1902, 14.

156 On the enthusiasm for "household gods," see Deborah Cohen, *Household Gods: The British and Their Possessions* (New Haven, CT: Yale University Press, 2006).

157 Jacques Derrida, *Copy, Archive, Signature: A Conversation on Photography*, trans. J. Fort (Stanford, CA: Stanford University Press, 2010), 23–25.

158 Mayhew to Head, October 7, 1902, WL, PP/HEA/D.4/12. See also Koven, *Match Girl and Heiress*, 229–30.

159 Mayhew to Head, October 7, 1902.

160 Ruth Mayhew to Henry Head, November 30, 1902, WL, PP/HEA/D.4/12.

161 Mayhew to Head, November 30, 1902.

162 Roland Barthes, *A Lover's Discourse: Fragments*, trans. Richard Howard (London: Vintage, 2002), 216–17.

163 Mayhew to Head, October 7, 1902.

164 Marjorie Stone, "Browning, Elizabeth Barrett (1806–1861)," *Oxford Dictionary of National Biography*, Oxford University Press, 2004; online ed., October 4, 2008, http:// www.oxforddnb.com/view/article/3711.

165 This repeats the hermeneutic "distanciation" of the text itself: Paul Ricoeur, "The Hermeneutical Function of Distanciation," in *Hermeneutics and the Human Sciences: Essays on Language, Action, and Interpretation*, trans. John B. Thompson (Cambridge: Cambridge University Press, 1981), 131–41.

166 Mayhew to Head, October 7, 1902.

167 Henry Head, rag book, August 1902, WL, PP/HEA/E.3/4.

168 Ruth Mayhew, rag book, August 1902, WL, PP/HEA/E.3/4.

169 Henry Head to Ruth Mayhew, January 9, 1903, WL, PP/HEA/D.4/13.

170 Barthes, *Lover's Discourse*, 93.

171 Head to Mayhew, January 9, 1903.

172 Jacyna, *Medicine and Modernism*, 185.

173 Jacyna, *Medicine and Modernism*, 214–22.

174 For the exchange and discussion of literature through correspondence, see Houlbrook, "'A Pin to See the Peepshow,'" 236–39.

175 Ruth Mayhew to Henry Head, November 10, 1902, WL, PP/HEA/D.4/12. Hugo's statement came at the beginning of his *The Last Day of a Condemned Man* (1829), a novel narrating the thoughts of a man sentenced to execution. Victor Hugo, *The Last Day of a Condemned Man*, trans. Christopher Moncrieff (Richmond: Oneworld Classics, 2009), 42.

176 Mayhew to Head, November 10, 1902.

177 Pater, *Renaissance*, 238.

178 Henry Head to Ruth Mayhew, November 14, 1902, WL, PP/HEA/D.4/12.

179 Ruth Mayhew to Henry Head, November 17, 1902, WL, PP/HEA/D.4/12. Pater derived some of his material on Winckelmann from Eckermann's *Conversations with Goethe in the Last Years of His Life* (1836), first published in English in 1839. See Pater, *Renaissance*, 185, and the relevant passage in Johann Eckermann, *Conversations of Goethe with Eckermann*, trans. John Oxenford (London: J. M. Dent & Sons, 1930), 173.

180 Mayhew to Head, November 17, 1902.

181 Houlbrook, "'A Pin to See the Peepshow,'" 236.

182 Ruth Mayhew to Henry Head, May 16, 1903, WL, PP/HEA/D.4/14.

183 Head to Mayhew, May 22, 1903. The lines, paraphrased by Head, are from Yeats's "Down by the Salley Gardens," first published under this title in his *Poems* (1895).

184 Head to Mayhew, May 22, 1903.

185 Mayhew to Head, May 4, 1903.

186 Barthes, *Lover's Discourse*, 71.

187 Barthes, *Lover's Discourse*, 57–58.

188 Ruth Mayhew to Henry Head, October 8, 1903, WL, PP/HEA/D.4/16. Mayhew was responding to Head's letter of October 5, 1903.

189 Henry Head to Ruth Mayhew, October 9, 1903, WL, PP/HEA/D.4/16.

190   Head and Rivers, "Human Experiment," 343.

191   Barthes, *Lover's Discourse*, 73–74.

192   Rhodri Hayward, "Neurology and the Resurgence of Demonology in Edwardian Britain," *Bulletin of the History of Medicine* 78, no. 1 (2004): 37–58.

193   On this subject-object position in Head's self-experiment, see Watt Smith, *On Flinching*, 149–50.

194   Henry Head to Ruth Mayhew, July 21, 1903, WL, PP/HEA/D.4/15.

195   Record for July 20, 1903, in Head and Rivers, "Human Experiment," 340.

196   Ruth Mayhew to Henry Head, July 22, 1903, WL, PP/HEA/D.4/15.

197   Mayhew to Head, July 22, 1903.

198   Head to Mayhew, November 27, 1903. The full stanza, drawn from the poem "À Clymène" in the anthology *Fêtes Galantes* (1869), is: "Puisque ta voix, étranger / Vision qui derange / Et trouble l'horizon / De ma raison." Norman R. Shapiro provides a more poetic translation than my own: "Strange vision that upsets / The distant silhouettes / Lined up against the sky / Of my mind's eye." Both citations from Paul Verlaine, *One Hundred and One Poems by Paul Verlaine: A Bilingual Edition*, trans. Norman R. Shapiro (Chicago: University of Chicago Press, 1999), 52, 53.

199   Head derived the concept "Dämmer zustand" from German psychiatry, especially that of Richard von Krafft-Ebing, who outlined the concept in his *Lehrbuch der Psychiatrie* (1888). Krafft-Ebing described it as a "psychical twilight" in which the conscious individual's senses became dim and consciousness of time and space was thrown into confusion. D. Hack Tuke, ed., *A Dictionary of Psychological Medicine* [. . .], vol. 1 (London: J. & A. Churchill, 1892), 325. See also Hugo Lang, *A German-English Dictionary of Terms Used in Medicine and the Allied Sciences*, ed. Bertram Abrahams (London: J. & A. Churchill, 1905), 90.

200   On the erotic subtext of Head's citation of Verlaine, see Watt Smith, *On Flinching*, 150. See also Susan Taylor-Horrex, *Verlaine: "Fêtes Galantes" and "Romances Sans Paroles"* (London: Grant & Cutler, 1988), 38–40.

201   Head to Mayhew, November 27, 1903.

202   Head and Rivers, "Human Experiment," 374.

203   Henry Head to Ruth Mayhew, March 8, 1904, WL, PP/HEA/D.4/18.

204   This exemplifies the "body biographies" theorized in Koven, *Match Girl and Heiress*, ch. 4.

205   Day Book, May 23, 1903; May 25, 1903, LEP.

206   Head and Rivers, "Human Experiment," 328–30.

207   Henry Head to Ruth Mayhew, May 24, 1903, WL, PP/HEA/D.4/14.

208   Sherrington, "Cutaneous Sensations," 966–69, 1000.

209   Head and Rivers, "Human Experiment," 422–29.

210   Head to Mayhew, May 24, 1903.

211   Henry Head, *Destroyers and Other Verses* (London: Humphrey Milford, 1919).

212   Ruth Head, *A History of Departed Things* (London: Kegan Paul, 1918).

213   Jacyna, *Medicine and Modernism*, 191. For an account of the novel, see 190–94.

214   William Wordsworth, *The Excursion*, ed. Sally Bushell, James A. Butler, and Michael C. Jaye, with the assistance of David García (Ithaca, NY: Cornell University Press, 2008), lines 50–51.

215 Stanley, "Epistolarium," 214.

216 As Liz Stanley argues, "counter-epistolaria," or unordinary letters such as open or draft letters, entail a different form of address that also implicitly disrupts that which authors use in "ordinary" letters. In the case of Mayhew's fictional love letters, the disruption occurs retrospectively and toward the author rather than the addressee. Liz Stanley, "The Epistolary Gift, the Editorial Third-Party, Counter-Epistolaria: Rethinking the Epistolarium," *Life Writing* 8, no. 2 (June 2011): 145.

217 Head and Rivers, "Human Experiment," 342.

218 Henry Head to Ruth Mayhew, April 27, 1904, WL, PP/HEA/D.4/18.

219 See, for example, Walshe, "Anatomy and Physiology," 67, 74, 78; Harvey Carr, "Head's Theory of Cutaneous Sensibility," *Psychological Review* 23, no. 4 (July 1916): 262–78; Wilfred Trotter, "The Insulation of the Nervous System [1926]," in *The Collected Papers of Wilfred Trotter, F.R.S.* (Oxford: Oxford University Press, 1941), 47–70.

220 Alan J. McComas, *Galvani's Spark: The Story of the Nerve Impulse* (Oxford: Oxford University Press, 2011), 64–65.

221 McComas, *Galvani's Spark*, 69–71; M. J. G. Cattermole and A. F. Wolfe, *Horace Darwin's Shop: A History of The Cambridge Scientific Instrument Company, 1878–1968* (Bristol, UK: Hilger, 1987), 62–63. The Whipple Museum of the History of Science, Cambridge, holds the original instrument (Wh.2723) also described in the Cambridge Scientific Instrument Company's List No.124, "Some Physiological Apparatus," July 1913 (CSI.150).

222 E. D. Adrian, "The Activity of the Nerve Fibres: Nobel Lecture, December 12, 1932," in Nobelstiftelsen, *Nobel Lectures: Physiology or Medicine, 1922–1941* (Amsterdam: Elsevier, 1965), 295; Yngve Zotterman, *Touch, Tickle, and Pain*, 2 vols. (Oxford: Oxford University Press, 1969–71), 1:219–21; McComas, *Galvani's Spark*, 102–3.

223 Walshe, "Anatomy and Physiology," 84.

224 Walshe, "Anatomy and Physiology," 90.

225 Zotterman, *Touch, Tickle, and Pain*, 2:68–74.

226 John Paul Nafe, "A Quantitative Theory of Feeling," *Journal of General Psychology* 2 (January 1, 1929): 199–211.

227 David C. Sinclair, "Cutaneous Sensation and the Doctrine of Specific Energy," *Brain* 78, no. 4, (December 1, 1955): 609. This seemed supported by later histology, which revealed that touch "spots'" were in fact clusters of nerve endings that produced patterns of impulses convening on a single nerve fiber: G. Weddell, "The Anatomy of Cutaneous Sensibility," *British Medical Bulletin* 3, no. 7–8 (1945): 171.

228 George Holman Bishop, "Neural Mechanisms of Cutaneous Sense," *Physiological Reviews* 26, no. 1 (January 1946): 78.

229 Barad, *Meeting the Universe Halfway*, 139–40.

CHAPTER TWO

1 "Weather Report—Monday," *Yorkshire Post & Leeds Intelligencer*, September 2, 1873, 7; "The Crops in Ryedale," *York Herald*, August 30, 1873, 10.

2 Alfred Hirst, *My Dark World* (London: British & Foreign Blind Association, 1898), 3–5.

3 "English Shipping," *Age* (London), October 18, 1881, 1 (supplement); "Shipping and

Commerce," *Leader* (Melbourne), January 7, 1882, 22; "Mr Alfred Hirst," *Times* (London), August 30, 1913, 9.

4 Hirst, *My Dark World*, 5.

5 See, for example, "About the Blind," *Advertiser* (Adelaide), October 26, 1898, n.p. Hirst remained a folk legend in the Australian press until at least his death in October 1913: "The Early Days of the Sydney Wool Trade," *Sydney Wool and Stock Journal*, August 21, 1908, 6–7; "Colonial Wool Trade," *Sydney Morning Herald*, October 18, 1913, 9.

6 G. Thomas Couser, *Recovering Bodies: Illness, Disability, and Life-Writing* (Madison: University of Wisconsin Press, 1997), 10; Koven, *Match Girl and Heiress*, ch. 4.

7 On photography as a "contract" requiring its subject's tacit agreement, see Ariella Azoulay, *The Civil Contract of Photography* (New York: Zone, 2008), ch. 2.

8 This chapter uses the term *blind* because although it overlooks the considerable variation in visual impairment among those legally categorized as blind, it highlights the political implications of the homogenization of a diverse group of people as "the blind." Using this term also highlights its pervasiveness throughout the nineteenth and twentieth centuries as a word for both physical and metaphorical impairment, where each implied the other. For modern-day medical and legal definitions of blindness, see Mark Paterson, *Seeing with the Hands: Blindness, Vision, and Touch after Descartes* (Edinburgh: Edinburgh University Press, 2016), 12–15. On the shifting conceptualization of blindness, see D. A. Caeton, "Blindness," in *Keywords for Disability Studies*, ed. Rachel Adams, Benjamin Reiss, and David Serlin (New York: NYU Press, 2015), 34–37.

9 On the intrinsic "plurality" of relations opened up by a photograph, see Azoulay, *Civil Contract*, ch. 2.

10 For similar debates about the relationship between vision, hearing, and independence surrounding the introduction of talking books in the 1930s, see Matthew Rubery, "From Shell Shock to Shellac: The Great War, Blindness, and Britain's Talking Book Library," *Twentieth Century British History* 26, no. 1 (2015): 1–25.

11 Hirst, *My Dark World*, 6, 14.

12 H. J. Wagg, *A Chronological Survey of Work for the Blind: From the Earliest Records up to the Year 1930* (London: Sir Isaac Pitman & Sons, 1932), 58; Alfred Hirst, *Types for the Blind* (London: Elliott and Sons, 1894).

13 Jacques Derrida, *Of Grammatology*, trans. Gayatri Chakravorty Spivak (Baltimore: Johns Hopkins University Press, 1976), 144–45, 154, 314.

14 Vanessa Warne, "'So That the Sense of Touch May Supply the Want of Sight': Blind Reading and Nineteenth-Century British Print Culture," in *Media, Technology, and Literature in the Nineteenth Century: Image, Sound, Touch*, ed. Colette Colligan and Margaret Linley (Farnham, UK: Ashgate, 2011), 43–64; Paterson, *Seeing with the Hands*, ch. 6. See also Heather Tilley, *Blindness and Writing: From Wordsworth to Gissing* (Cambridge: Cambridge University Press, 2017), 3–5.

15 Jan Eric Olsén, "Vicariates of the Eye: Blindness, Sense Substitution, and Writing Devices in the Nineteenth Century," *Mosaic* 46, no.3 (September 2013): 75–91; Heather Tilley and Jan Eric Olsén, 'Touching Blind Bodies: A Critical Inquiry into Pedagogical and Cultural Constructions of Visual Disability in the Nineteenth Century," in *The Edinburgh Companion to the Critical Medical Humanities*, ed. Anne Whitehead and

Angela Woods (Edinburgh: Edinburgh University Press, 2016), 260–75. For the *longue durée* history of educational provision for blind children in Britain, see Gordon Phillips, *The Blind in British Society: Charity, State and Community, c. 1780–1930* (Aldershot, UK: Ashgate, 2004).

16 This connection between bodily, economic, and political independence was further strengthened by a growing culture of physical self-improvement and, after the Great War, the rehabilitation of disabled soldiers. See Ina Zweiniger-Bargielowska, *Managing the Body: Beauty, Health, and Fitness in Britain, 1880–1939* (Oxford: Oxford University Press, 2010); Julie Anderson, *War, Disability, and Rehabilitation in Britain: "Soul of a Nation"* (Manchester: Manchester University Press, 2011); Seth Koven, "Remembering and Dismemberment: Crippled Children, Wounded Soldiers, and the Great War in Britain," *American Historical Review* 99, no. 4 (October 1994): 1167–1202; Deborah Cohen, *The War Come Home: Disabled Veterans in Britain and Germany, 1914–1939* (Berkeley: University of California Press, 2001).

17 On the mutual constitution of ability and disability in a contemporary context, see Dan Goodley, "The Dis/ability Complex," *DiGeSt: Journal of Diversity and Gender Studies* 5, no. 1 (2018): 6–7.

18 Here and throughout I make this argument with reference to Jacques Rancière's understanding of the "distribution of the sensible": Jacques Rancière, *The Politics of Aesthetics: The Distribution of the Sensible*, ed. and trans. Gabriel Rockhill (London: Continuum, 2004), 7–8, 89; Davide Panagia, *The Political Life of Sensation* (Durham, NC: Duke University Press, 2009), 2–3, 6–7.

19 Hirst, *My Dark World*, 10.

20 The new understanding of disability became known as the "social" model and defined itself against what it saw as an earlier "medical" model. For overviews, see Rod Michalko, *The Difference That Disability Makes* (Philadelphia: Temple University Press, 2002), 50–60; Colin Barnes, "Understanding the Social Model of Disability," in *Routledge Handbook of Disability Studies*, ed. Nick Watson, Alan Roulstone, and Carol Thomas (London: Routledge 2012), 12–29; Paul K. Longmore, *Why I Burned My Book and Other Essays on Disability* (Philadelphia: Temple University Press, 2003), 1–11. For calls for a more historical attitude toward disability, and the value of disability as a critical tool, see Beth Linker, "On the Borderland of Medical and Disability History: A Survey of the Fields," *Bulletin of the History of Medicine* 87, no. 4 (Winter 2013): 499–535; Koven, "Remembering and Dismemberment"; Catherine J. Kudlick, "Disability History: Why We Need Another 'Other,'" *American Historical Review* 108, no. 3 (June 2003): 763–93. I am grateful to Hilary Buxton and Kate Imy for their expertise in this area.

21 London Institute for Massage by the Blind prospectus, 1901, Royal National Institute of Blind People Archives (hereafter cited as RNIB), P/2/2/C, Box 3, 1.

22 London Institute for Massage by the Blind minute book, January 27, 1902, RNIB, RS/10/7/B; "Massage by the Blind," *British Journal of Nursing* 29 (1902): 526; "Teaching the Blind and Deaf in Japan," *Quiver*, January 1901, 701–4; "An Ancient Profession," *Review of Reviews* 49, no. 292 (April 1914), 311; "Massage by Blind Soldiers," *Times*, November 2, 1920, 117.

23 "New Profession for the Sightless," *London Journal* 12, no. 296 (December 23, 1911), 203.

24 W. H. Broad, "The Blinded Soldier as a Masseur," *Beacon* 4, no. 37 (January 1920): 11.

25 Henshaw's Blind Asylum in Manchester began training blind masseurs in 1895, but this was only one element of its vocational training. J. Barclay, *In Good Hands: The History of the Chartered Society of Physiotherapy, 1894–1994* (Oxford: Butterworth Heinemann, 1994), 44–45; Wagg, *Chronological Survey*, 83.

26 National Institute of Massage by the Blind minute book, March 31, 1914, RNIB, RS/10/7/B.

27 London Institute of Massage by the Blind minute book, RNIB, RS/10/7/B, loose insert: Balance Sheet and Report (1910), 1; "Massage by Blind Operators at a London Hospital," *Daily News*, August 17, 1910, 7.

28 National Institute of Massage by the Blind minute book, July 30, 1912, RNIB, RS/10/7/B.

29 National Institute of Massage by the Blind minute book, November 26, 1912, RNIB, RS/10/7/B.

30 Barclay, *In Good Hands*, 20–22.

31 Incorporated Society of Trained Masseuses Council minutes, WL, SA/CSP/B.1/1/1, 1.

32 See, for example, the minor infringement by one member who advertised in a railway timetable and was subsequently struck off the roll of members and blacklisted by the society in five medical journals in March 1899. Barclay, *In Good Hands*, 30.

33 Barclay, *In Good Hands*, 14–16.

34 Barclay, *In Good Hands*, 50.

35 Metropolitan Police Report, October 18, 1895, The National Archives (hereafter cited as TNA), MEPO 2/460, 1–2.

36 Social Purity Department of the National British Women's Temperance Association to police, April 30, 1897, and enclosed article of *London Figaro*, April 22, 1897, TNA, MEPO 2/460, both 1.

37 "Massage Houses Unmasked," *John Bull*, April 24, 1920, TNA, HO 45/17371, 6. The London County Council responded with bylaws in 1915 and 1920 attempting to tighten regulation of massage establishments.

38 Barclay, *In Good Hands*, 44–45, 52.

39 See, for example, the strict expectations for the "costume" of masseuses outlined in the ISTM's training manual: M. Pireau, *Massage Manual: Intended for the Use of Students for the I.S.T.M. Examination* (London: Scientific Press, 1912), 2–3.

40 W. H. Illingworth, *History of the Education of the Blind* (London: S. Low, Marston, 1910), 53.

41 National Institute for Massage by the Blind minute book, May 28, 1912, RNIB, RS/10/7/B.

42 Incorporated Society of Trained Masseuses Council minutes, WL, SA/CSP/B.1/1/1/8–15.

43 National Institute for Massage by the Blind minute book, January 28, 1913, RNIB, RS/10/7/B.

44 Arthur Pearson, *Victory Over Blindness: How It Was Won by the Men of St Dunstan's and How Others May Win It* (London: Hodder & Stoughton, 1919), 18.

45 Pearson, *Victory Over Blindness*, 19.

46 Luke McKernan, "Pearson, Sir (Cyril) Arthur, first baronet (1866–1921)," in *Oxford Dictionary of National Biography*, Oxford University Press, 2004; online ed., last modified May 26, 2016, https://doi.org/10.1093/ref:odnb/35441; Sidney Dark, *The Life of*

Sir Arthur Pearson (London: Hodder & Stoughton, 1922), 139; Pearson, *Victory Over Blindness*, 18–19.

47 Pearson, *Victory Over Blindness*, 35, 37; "The House of Miracles," *Illustrated London News*, December 25, 1915, 19.

48 "Future of Blind Soldiers," *Evening Mail* (London), April 21, 1915, 6; Arnold Bennett, "The Under-side: A Hospital and a Hostel," *Daily News*, July 2, 1915, 4.

49 Pearson, *Victory Over Blindness*, 119.

50 Pearson, *Victory Over Blindness*, 122.

51 Pearson, *Victory Over Blindness*, 147–48, 151.

52 See, for example, Richard King, "A Pictorial Appeal for the Blind Soldier," *Sphere* (London), December 30, 1916, 16. On the changing politics of care of disabled ex-servicemen, see Koven, "Remembering and Dismemberment," 1182–84; D. Cohen, *War Come Home*, 29–37.

53 [Percy Way], "Physiotherapy by the Blind: A Short Account of the Early History of the Movement," RNIB 4/10/47, 2–3; Wagg, *Chronological Survey*, 125. On the later history of the NIB School of Massage, see Percy L. Way, "Choosing a Career: The Future of the Blind Child," *Beacon* 9, no. 102 (June 1925): 12–15.

54 Incorporated Society of Trained Masseuses Council minutes, July 27, 1917, WL, SA/CSP/B.1/1/12.

55 Incorporated Society of Trained Masseuses Council minutes, November 23, 1917, WL, SA/CSP/B.1/1/12. See also Incorporated Society of Trained Masseuses Council minutes, July 11, 1919, WL, SA/CSP/B.1/1/14.

56 [Way], "Physiotherapy by the Blind," 3–4.

57 "Massage by the Blind," *Times*, June 23, 1934, 9.

58 Paterson, *Seeing with the Hands*, 9.

59 Tom Hulme, "'A Nation Depends on Its Children': School Buildings and Citizenship in England and Wales, 1900–1939," *Journal of British Studies* 54 (April 2015): 406–32; Vernon, *Hunger*, 161–64.

60 College of Teachers of the Blind, *The Education of the Blind: A Survey* (London: Edward Arnold, 1936), 1–3; G. Phillips, *Blind in British Society*, 200–208, 214.

61 G. Phillips, *Blind in British Society*, 244–251.

62 Koven, "Remembering and Dismemberment," 1173.

63 Thomas Armitage, *The Education and Employment of the Blind: What It Has Been, Is, and Ought to Be* (London: Harrison & Sons, 1871).

64 Koven, "Remembering and Dismemberment," 1176; G. Phillips, *Blind in British Society*, 392–393; Wagg, *Chronological Survey*, 71.

65 College of Teachers of the Blind, *Education of the Blind*, 4–5.

66 Illingworth, *History*, 121–22. For an account of a large workshop employing up to one hundred blind workers in Tottenham Court Road, London, in around 1900, see R. Austin Freeman, "Afflicted London," in Sims, *Living London*, 3:28–31.

67 Illingworth, *History*, 149–50.

68 John Welshman, "Physical Education and the School Medical Service in England and Wales, 1907–1939," *Social History of Medicine* 9, no. 1 (1996): 31–48.

69 Zweiniger-Bargielowska, *Managing the Body*, 85.

70 College of Teachers of the Blind, *Education of the Blind*, 20.

71 G. Phillips, *Blind in British Society*, 395–396.

72 See Ian Hacking, "Making Up People," in *Historical Ontology* (Cambridge, MA: Harvard University Press, 2002), 100, 105–6.

73 Hulme, "'A Nation Depends on Its Children,'" 412–13.

74 College of Teachers of the Blind, *Education of the Blind*, 4–5.

75 Bernard Harris, "Eichholz, Alfred (1869–1933)," in *Oxford Dictionary of National Biography*, Oxford University Press, 2004; online ed., January 3, 2008, https://doi.org/10.1093/ref:odnb/63806.

76 Zweiniger-Bargielowska, *Managing the Body*, 72, 68.

77 James Cantlie, *Physical Efficiency: A Review of the Deleterious Effects of Town Life upon the Population of Britain, with Suggestions for their Arrest* (London: G. P. Putnam's Sons, 1906).

78 Zweiniger-Bargielowska, *Managing the Body*, 72.

79 Zweiniger-Bargielowska, *Managing the Body*, 87; George Newman, *The Building of a Nation's Health* (London: Macmillan, 1939), 269–71.

80 Newman, *Building of a Nation's Health*, 254–56.

81 M. Davidson, "Physical Training for the Blind," letter to editor, *Teacher of the Blind* 9, no. 1 (May 1921): 15–19. The adoption of new board thinking is also evident in E. Evans, "Physical Activity Exercises for the Blind," *Teacher of the Blind* 8, no. 4 (February 1921): 81–83, which commented on the "lack of elasticity of movement" of blind children and recommended daily exercises derived from the 1919 Syllabus of Physical Training. See also articles by G. M. Campbell in the October, November, and December 1914 issues of *Teacher of the Blind* as well as the photographs of model postures for the physical exercise of blind children in G. M. Campbell, "Physical Training of the Blind," *Teacher of the Blind* 3, no. 1 (January 1915): 20–21. Combined with this was an increasing emphasis on the recreational aspect of exercise, as Newman had stressed: A. Burke, "Games as a Regular Part of the Equipment of the Classroom," *Teacher of the Blind* 20, no. 2 (November 1931): 45–51.

82 "A New Development in Dalcroze Eurhythmics," *Teacher of the Blind* 11, no. 4 (February 1924): 65.

83 "The System of Training in Rhythm and Rhythmic Movement," *Beacon* 4, no. 43 (July 1920): 4.

84 M. Meredyll, "Eurhythmics and the Blind!" *Teacher of the Blind* 5, no. 5 (September 1917): 55.

85 Alfred Hollins, *A Blind Musician Looks Back: An Autobiography* (Edinburgh: W. Blackwood & Sons, 1936), 38.

86 Meredyll, "Eurhythmics and the Blind!" 55.

87 Émile Jaques-Dalcroze, "Eurhythmics and the Education of the Blind," trans. E. R. Hutchinson, *Teacher of the Blind* 4, no. 2 (March 1918): 26–27; "Eurhythmics for the Blind," *Beacon* 7, no. 77 (May 1923): 11–12.

88 "Eurhythmics for the Blind," 11.

89 Jaques-Dalcroze, "Eurhythmics," 28–29; K. C., "The Sense of Rhythm and the Blind Child, letter to the editor, *Teacher of the Blind* 7, no. 1 (February 1919): 8–9.

90 Meredyll, "Eurhythmics and the Blind!" 56.

91 College of Teachers of the Blind, *Education of the Blind*, viii–ix; F. M. Earle, "Principles

Underlying the Teaching of Blind Children," *Teacher of the Blind* 15, no. 4 (June 1927): 106; F. M. Earle, "Principles Underlying the Teaching of Blind Children," *Teacher of the Blind* 16, no. 1 (September 1927): 5; "The Psychology Course," *Teacher of the Blind* 16, no. 4 (March 1928): 82–83.

92   College of Teachers of the Blind, *Education of the Blind*, x.

93   Pierre Villey, *The World of the Blind: (A Psychological Study)*, trans. A. H. Ward (London: Simpkin, Marshall, 1922), 16, 24, 98; John M. Ritchie, *Concerning the Blind: Being a Historical Sketch of Organised Effort on Behalf of the Blind of Great Britain* [. . .] (Edinburgh: Oliver & Boyd, 1930), 195–97.

94   College of Teachers of the Blind, *Education of the Blind*, 57–58.

95   G. Phillips, *Blind in British Society*, 256.

96   College of Teachers of the Blind, *Education of the Blind*, 101.

97   College of Teachers of the Blind, *Education of the Blind*, 69–71. The Royal Normal College even had an old bus standing in its grounds to provide its students with the opportunity to become tactilely familiar with public transport. M. Ward, "At School with the Blind," *Beacon* 1, no. 5 (May 1917): 8.

98   College of Teachers of the Blind, *Education of the Blind*, 133–34.

99   College of Teachers of the Blind, *Education of the Blind*, 6–7.

100   For example, E. F. Benson, "The House-Party" (*Pall Mall Gazette*), W. L. George, "If I Were Blind" (*Evening Standard*), E. Le Breton Martin, "Sing a Song of Sunshine," all in *A Little Book of Sunshine: A Collection of Articles, Stories and Poems on Sunshine House, the Blind Babies' Home at Chorley Wood, Herts.* (n.p., n.d., ca. 1918), 13, 17, 41.

101   "For Sightless Children," in *A Little Book of Sunshine*, 92–93.

102   This remained true of Sunshine Homes into the 1950s. M. S. Colborne Brown, "The Care, Training and Education of Blind Young Children in the Royal National Institute for the Blind's Sunshine Home Residential Nursery Schools," n.d., ca.1953, RNIB, RS/7/3/E/ Box 1, 7–8.

103   When Montessori offered a training course and supplementary lectures on her teaching method in London in early 1920, there were more than two thousand applications for 250 places. S. B. P., "Childhood's Royal Road to Learning: The Montessori Methods of Education," *Beacon* 4, no. 38 (February 1920): 3; Colborne Brown, "Care, Training and Education of Blind Young Children," 3–4.

104   S. B. P., "Childhood's Royal Road to Learning," 3–4. The method was subsequently recommended by C. W. Kimmins, former chief inspector of the London County Council Education Department, at a speech to a joint meeting of the College of Teachers of the Blind and Association of Teachers of the Blind in March 1923. C. W. Kimmins, "Special Features in the Training of the Blind," *Beacon* 7, no. 76 (April 1923): 13–14.

105   A. Maccheroni, "The Montessori Method," *Beacon* 4, no. 43 (July 1920): 8.

106   College of Teachers of the Blind, *Physical Education of the Blind: Being the Report of the Summer Course, July, 1933, at the School for the Blind, Swiss Cottage, Under the Auspices of The College of Teachers of the Blind* (n.p., n.d., ca. 1933), Education Library, University of Birmingham (uncataloged), 7–8.

107   College of Teachers of the Blind, *Physical Education of the Blind*, 8.

108   College of Teachers of the Blind, *Physical Education of the Blind*, 13.

109   College of Teachers of the Blind, *Physical Education of the Blind*, 15.

110 College of Teachers of the Blind, *Physical Education of the Blind*, 26–27.

111 College of Teachers of the Blind, *Physical Education of the Blind*, 60–61.

112 College of Teachers of the Blind, *Education of the Blind*, 190–91.

113 College of Teachers of the Blind, *Education of the Blind*, Appendix. A contemporaneous report by the Board of Education suggested that schools for partially sighted children dealt with similar problems in posture through specially adapted Bishop Harman desks. Board of Education, *Report of the Committee of Inquiry into the Problems Relating to Partially Sighted Children* (London, 1934), 107–9.

114 College of Teachers of the Blind, *Physical Education of the Blind*, 62–63.

115 College of Teachers of the Blind, *Education of the Blind*, 69–70.

116 College of Teachers of the Blind, *Education of the Blind*, 49–50.

117 College of Teachers of the Blind, *Education of the Blind*, 57–58.

118 College of Teachers of the Blind, *Education of the Blind*, 183–88.

119 Vanessa Warne, "Between the Sheets: Contagion, Touch, and Text," *19: Interdisciplinary Studies in the Long Nineteenth Century* 19 (2014): 4; Houlbrook, "'A Pin to See the Peepshow.'" On the broader contemporary anxiety over masturbation, see Thomas Laqueur, *Solitary Sex: A Cultural History of Masturbation* (New York: Zone, 2003).

120 College of Teachers of the Blind, *Education of the Blind*, 187–88.

121 See prospectuses of Chorleywood College under headmistresses Phyllis Monk and D. A. McHugh: Chorleywood prospectuses, New College Worcester Archives (hereafter cited as NCW), NCW 2/1, both 3. Freestanding chairs were, however, used in both instances.

122 College of Teachers of the Blind, *Education of the Blind*, 45–46.

123 College of Teachers of the Blind, *Education of the Blind*, 42–43.

124 College of Teachers of the Blind, *Education of the Blind*, 39–41.

125 College of Teachers of the Blind, *Education of the Blind*, 62–63.

126 Armitage, *Education and Employment of the Blind*, 22.

127 Entry for August 19, 1902, Log book 1901–1939, Royal Victoria School for the Blind, Newcastle-upon-Tyne, Tyne & Wear Archives and Museums (hereafter cited as TWAM), E.NC18/10/1.

128 Tilley and Olsén, "Touching Blind Bodies," 268.

129 Tilley and Olsén, "Touching Blind Bodies," 270; Wagg, *Chronological Survey*, 89.

130 Ritchie, *Concerning the Blind*, 204.

131 John M. Ritchie, "The Mental Life of a Person Born Blind," *Teacher of the Blind* 19, no. 3 (January 1931): 61–62; Ritchie, *Concerning the Blind*, 175. This argument referred specifically to congenitally blind people; those who lost their sight some years after their birth, Ritchie argued, could develop mental "images" from their memory of the world when sighted. On John Locke's understanding of blindness, see Paterson, *Seeing with the Hands*, ch. 2.

132 Ritchie, *Concerning the Blind*, 176–77.

133 Ritchie, *Concerning the Blind*, 178–79.

134 Ritchie, *Concerning the Blind*, 177–78.

135 Villey, *World of the Blind*, 188.

136 College of Teachers of the Blind, *Education of the Blind*, 124.

137 W. Eager to Leonard Hardcastle, May 8, 1932, RNIB, RNIB/4/17/223.

138   Leonard Hardcastle to W. Eager, May 20, 1932, RNIB, RNIB/4/17/223.

139   J. M. Ritchie to W. Eager, March 6, 1936, RNIB, RNIB/4/17/223.

140   Report by Linden Lodge on the use of relief maps, 1936, RNIB, RNIB/4/17/223, 1.

141   Leonard Hardcastle's response to reports from Swiss Cottage and Linden Lodge, n.d., RNIB, RNIB/4/17/223, 2.

142   The distinction between "functional" and "absolute" equivalence is Paterson's: Paterson, *Seeing with the Hands*, 56.

143   College of Teachers of the Blind, *Handbook for School Teachers of the Blind* (Bristol, UK: College of Teachers of the Blind, 1956), 243.

144   Reports by Myfanwy Williams, RNIB, RS/7/4/D Box 6.

145   D. G. Pritchard, *Education and the Handicapped, 1760–1960* (London: Routledge, 1963), 209–12.

146   College of Teachers of the Blind, *Handbook*, 8–9.

147   College of Teachers of the Blind, *Handbook*, 232.

148   Report by William Bickley, n.d., ca.1960, RNIB, RS/7/2/E Box 1, 1–3.

149   Report by William Bickley, 7; Hannah Gay, *The History of Imperial College London, 1907–2007: Higher Education and Research in Science, Technology, and Medicine* (London: Imperial College Press, 2007), n.101, 375.

150   R.C. Fletcher, introduction to Nuffield Report (proposed), RNIB, RS/7/4/E Box 7, 4–5. See also Careers of ex-pupils of Chorleywood College, September 1947, RNIB, RNIB/4/5/9, 1; Donald Bell, *An Experiment in Education: The History of Worcester College for the Blind, 1866–1966* (London: Hutchinson, 1967), 43.

151   Fletcher, introduction to Nuffield Report, 6–7.

152   Fletcher, introduction to Nuffield Report, 5. The National Institute for the Blind became the Royal National Institute for the Blind in 1953.

153   Abraham Wexler, *Experimental Science for the Blind: An Instruction Manual* (Oxford: Pergamon, 1961), 5–7.

154   Fletcher, introduction to Nuffield Report, 7.

155   Mary Waring, *Social Pressures and Curriculum Innovation: A Study of the Nuffield Foundation Science Teaching Project* (London: Routledge, 1979).

156   Report justifying funding application to the Nuffield Foundation, April 1965, RNIB, RS/7/2/E Box 1, 3; Fletcher, introduction to Nuffield Report, 7.

157   Report justifying funding application, 7.

158   Fletcher, introduction to Nuffield Report, 8.

159   W. J. Pickles, "Surface Representation," in Nuffield Report (proposed), RNIB, RS/7/4/E Box 7, 72.

160   Pickles, "Surface Representation," 74.

161   Pickles, "Surface Representation," 77.

162   Pickles, "Surface Representation," 80.

163   Pickles, "Surface Representation," 103.

164   Pickles, "Surface Representation," 117–19.

165   For a discussion of contemporary blind self-portraiture, see Kleege, *More than Meets the Eye*, ch. 9.

166   Pickles, "Surface Representation," 116.

167   Philip Donnellan, "Parker, (Hubert) Charles (1919–1980)," in *Oxford Dictionary of*

National Biography, Oxford University Press, 2004; online ed., October 3, 2013, https://doi.org/10.1093/ref:odnb/59626.

168   Audience Research Report for *BD8*, November 2, 1967, BBC Written Archives (hereafter cited as BBC), M 34/2, 1; typescript of telephone calls reacting to *BD8* Part 1, BBC, M 34/2, 1; Charles Parker to Lee Farmer, February 14, 1969, Wolfson Centre for Archival Research (hereafter cited as WCAR), MS 4000/2/124B.

169   *No Longer Alone*, British Pathé, Film ID 2717.04, 1961, video, 17:47, https://www.britishpathe.com/asset/196064/.

170   Script of *BD8 Part Two: Independence of the Blind*, WCAR, MS 4000/2/124A, 14.

171   Script of *BD8 Part Two*, 4.

172   *BD8: 2; The Independence of the Blind*, directed by Philip Donnellan (London: BBC, 1967).

173   Lee Farmer, interview, January 25, 1967, WCAR, MS 4000/6/1/54/87/C-88/C.

174   Victor Horsley, interview, January 25, 1967, WCAR, MS 4000/6/1/54/89/C.

175   Charles Parker, "The Blind Set: Declaration of Intent," April 14, 1968, WCAR, MS 4000/2/124B, 1.

176   Philip Donnellan to Walter Thornton, October 11, 1967, BBC, M 34/2. For earlier uses of canes to aid navigation, see memo from B.O.B. to Colborne Brown, October 9, 1956, and unsigned memo, probably by Colborne Brown, October 12, 1956, RNIB, "Worcester College," RS/7/2/C Box 1, both 1; F. R. Marriott, "How the Blind Travel," *Beacon* 4, no. 38 (February 1920): 7–8.

177   Parker, "The Blind Set," 1–2.

178   This suggestion echoes Cohen's argument that strong philanthropic support for disabled ex-servicemen both responded to and enabled the withdrawal of state support after the Great War: D. Cohen, *War Come Home*, 4–5.

179   Anne Lapping, "How Do We Treat the Blind as People?" *New Society*, March 14, 1968, WCAR, MS 4000/2/124B, 374.

180   *The Blind Set: An Encounter with Prejudice*, recording of first half, October 9, 1968, WCAR, MS 4000/6/1/54/179/C.

181   *The Blind Set* production script, "As Broadcast," WCAR, MS 4000/2/124B, 3–4. Saint George was a member of the Praetorian Guard of the Roman army, executed for his Christianity in 303. He was popular among crusaders as a protector saint in the eleventh and twelfth centuries, and around this time he became associated with a legend in which he killed a dragon that had been extracting human tributes from a terrified village. Although he was from Cappadocia, in modern-day Turkey, he became increasingly claimed as patron saint of England in the sixteenth century, encapsulating "Englishness" and the virtues of overcoming difficulties and protecting the defenseless.

182   WCAR, MS 4000/6/1/54/179/C.

183   Charles Parker to J. A. Leonard, October 1, 1968, WCAR, MS 4000/2/124B.

184   Audience Research on "Blind Set," n.d., 1–3; L. A. Brown to Charles Parker, October 11, 1968; Clarence Gilbert to Charles Parker, October 11, 1968; Keith Brace, *Birmingham Post* radio review, October 12, 1968, 1; all WCAR, MS 4000/2/124B.

185   Audience Report for *The Blind Set*, n.d., WCAR, MS 4000/2/124B, 1. F. Brace, a retired secretary, was "disgusted" at the presentation of the insensitivity of the sighted and the apparent dependence of the blind. See Audience Research on "Blind Set," 2.

186 H. Dudley to Charles Parker, October 10, 1968, WCAR, MS 4000/2/124B.

187 Charles Parker to H. Dudley, October 23, 1968, WCAR, MS 4000/2/124B.

188 H. Dudley to Charles Parker, October 28, 1968, WCAR, MS 4000/2/124B.

189 D. Lineham to Charles Parker, n.d., WCAR, MS 4000/2/124B.

190 J. Gilbey to BBC and RNIB, enclosed in letter to Charles Parker, October 10, 1968, WCAR, MS 4000/2/124B.

191 Charles Parker to S. Wilson, October 25, 1968, WCAR, MS 4000/2/124B.

192 S. Wilson to Charles Parker, October 14, 1968, WCAR, MS 4000/2/124B.

193 Anonymous note attached to 2 shillings 6 pence, October 6 [16?], 1968, WCAR, MS 4000/2/124B.

194 Charles Parker, "Analysis of HPM memo, 30/10/68, referring to C.R4, strictures on 'The Blind Set,' 30/11/68, 'Strictly Confidential,'" WCAR, MS 4000/2/124B, 2–3.

195 Charles Parker, "Analysis HPM memo 30/10/68 contd," November 3[0?], 1968, WCAR, MS 4000/2/124B, 6–7.

196 Parker, "Analysis of HPM memo, 30/10/68, referring to C.R4, strictures on 'The Blind Set,'" 8.

197 Parker, "Analysis of HPM memo, 30/10/68, referring to C.R4, strictures on 'The Blind Set,'" 4.

198 Parker, "Analysis of HPM memo, 30/10/68, referring to C.R4, strictures on 'The Blind Set,'" 2.

199 Parker, "Analysis HPM memo 30/10/68 contd," 1.

200 Charles Parker to A. R. Hay, October 28, 1968, WCAR, MS 4000/2/124B.

201 Parker to Farmer, February 14, 1969.

202 Parker, "Analysis of HPM memo, 30/10/68, referring to C.R4, strictures on 'The Blind Set,'" 6.

203 Blind American writer Hector Chevigny made a similar point: Hector Chevigny, *My Eyes Have a Cold Nose* (London: Michael Joseph, 1947), 83–85.

204 Paul Hunt, ed., *Stigma: The Experience of Disability* (London: Chapman, 1966).

205 "Royal Normal College for the Blind," *Times*, June 29, 1901, 19.

206 J. F., *The Law of Compensation: Blind, but Self-Reliant* (London: printed by the author, 1904), 8–11.

207 F., *Law of Compensation*, 4–5.

208 For a critique of the social model, see Christopher A. Riddle, "The Ontology of Impairment: Rethinking How We Define Disability," in *Emerging Perspectives on Disability Studies*, ed. Matthew Wappett and Katrina Arndt (New York: Palgrave Macmillan, 2013), 23–39. See also Simo Vehmas, "What Can Philosophy Tell Us About Disability?" in *Routledge Handbook of Disability Studies*, ed. Nick Watson, Alan Roulstone, and Carol Thomas (London: Routledge, 2012), 298–309.

209 For a twenty-first-century theoretical example, see Titchkosky, "Ends of the Body," 92.

CHAPTER THREE

1 "Murder of Polish Countess," *Times*, May 27, 1957, 6; "18,000 Interviewed in Murder Hunt," *Times*, August 20, 1957, 4.

2 Emanuel Olu Akinyemi, statements of May 24 and May 29, 1957, in Unsolved Murder

of Countess Teresa Lubienska at Gloucester Road Underground Station, Kensington, on May 24, 1957, Statements Material to Report, TNA, MEPO/2/11018.

3   Vivian Russell Devan, statement of May 30, 1957, in Unsolved Murder, Statements Material to Report, TNA, MEPO/2/11018.

4   Kazimerz Krzyzanowski, statements of May 25 and May 29, 1957, in Unsolved Murder, Statements Material to Report, TNA, MEPO/2/11018.

5   "18,000 Interviewed in Murder Hunt."

6   Walkowitz, *City of Dreadful Delight*; Nead, *Victorian Babylon*, ch. 4.

7   Barrow, "Rape on the Railway," 342–43.

8   The pioneering discussion of this reformulation of social relations, in dialogue with Georg Simmel, is Wolfgang Schivelbusch's *The Railway Journey: The Industrialization of Time and Space in the 19th Century* (Berkeley: University of California Press, 1986), esp. 73–76. For later elaborations, see Peter Bailey, "Adventures in Space: Victorian Railway Erotics, or Taking Alienation for a Ride," *Journal of Victorian Culture* 9, no. 1 (2004): 1–21; Vernon, *Distant Strangers*, 35–37.

9   Philip Vann, *Cyril Power Linocuts: A Complete Catalogue* (Farnham, UK: Lund Humphries, 2008), 22–23.

10   James Vernon's *Distant Strangers* uses *The Tube Train* as its cover image. On tube cars as sites for the emergence of "modern" social relations, see also David Welsh, *Underground Writing: The London Tube from George Gissing to Virginia Woolf* (Liverpool: Liverpool University Press, 2010), ch. 3; Haewong Hwang, *London's Underground Spaces: Representing the Victorian City, 1840–1915* (Edinburgh: Edinburgh University Press, 2013), ch. 2. For New York, see Höhne, *Riding the New York Subway*, 10–14.

11   Vernon, *Distant Strangers*, xi, 8, 35–37; David Ashford, *London Underground: A Cultural Geography* (Liverpool: Liverpool University Press, 2013), ch. 1. For a comparable reading of a contemporaneous painting of the New York Subway, see Christoph Lindner on James W. Kerr's *7th Avenue Subway*, 1931, in Christoph Lindner, *Imagining New York City: Literature, Urbanism, and the Visual Arts, 1890–1940* (Oxford: Oxford University Press, 2015), 163–65; on the emotional and social "containerization" of New York Subway passengers caused by "a numbing of the senses," see Höhne, *Riding the New York Subway*, 137–38. The similarity of Lindner's reading to Vernon's suggests a greater equivalence between representations of American and British modernity than Vernon's emphasis on British peculiarity allows. It does, however, support Vernon's critique of the pluralization of modernity as an analytic category. James Vernon and Simon Gunn, "What Was Liberal Modernity and Why Was It Peculiar in Imperial Britain?" in *The Peculiarities of Liberal Modernity in Imperial Britain*, ed. James Vernon and Simon Gunn (Berkeley: University of California Press, 2011), 5–6, 12.

12   For a critique of present-day representations of commuting, see Tim Edensor, "Commuter: Mobility, Rhythm, and Commuting," in *Geographies of Mobilities: Practices: Spaces, Subjects*, ed. Tim Cresswell and Peter Merriman (Farnham, UK: Ashgate, 2011), 189–202.

13   Arthur Tribe, statement of July 25, 1957, in Unsolved Murder of Countess Teresa Lubienska at Gloucester Road Underground Station, Kensington, on 24 May 1957, Statements Non-material to Report, TNA, MEPO/2/11019.

14 For key histories of the tube taking these various approaches, see Christian Wolmar, *The Subterranean Railway: How the London Underground Was Built and How It Changed the City Forever*, rev. ed. (London: Atlantic Books, 2012); Richard Dennis, "Making the Underground Underground," *London Journal* 38, no. 3 (November 2013): 223. See also Stephen Halliday, *Underground to Everywhere: London's Underground Railway in the Life of the Capital* (Stroud, UK: Sutton, 2004).

15 June Kitchin, statement of May 27, 1957, in Unsolved Murder, Statements Material to Report, TNA, MEPO/2/11018.

16 Joyce, *Rule of Freedom*, 4. See also Patrick Joyce, *The State of Freedom: A Social History of the British State since 1800* (Cambridge: Cambridge University Press, 2013), 5–6. For examples of such an approach, though not from an explicitly governmentality perspective, see Richard Hornsey, "'He Who Thinks, in Modern Traffic, Is Lost': Automation and the Pedestrian Rhythms of Interwar London," in *Geographies of Rhythm: Nature, Place, Mobilities and Bodies*, ed. Tim Edensor (Farnham, UK: Ashgate, 2010), 101; Richard Dennis, "The Architecture of Hurry," in *Cityscapes in History: Creating the Urban Experience*, ed. Katrina Gulliver and Heléna Tóth (Farnham, UK: Ashgate, 2014), 132–33.

17 J. B. Priestley, "Man Underground," in *Self-Selected Essays* (London: William Heinemann, 1932), 75. The analogy between passengers and parcels became especially appealing once the Post Office opened an underground railway between sorting offices in Paddington and Whitechapel in December 1927. This expanded on an earlier underground pneumatic tube for post that operated between Eversholt Street and Euston Station between 1863 and 1874. Ashford, *London Underground*, 22; Postal Museum, "The Story of Mail Rail," accessed September 7, 2023, https://www.postalmuseum.org/collections/story-of-mail-rail/.

18 Priestley, "Man Underground," 78.

19 Joyce, *State of Freedom*, 54; Otter, *Victorian Eye*; Tom Crook, "Secrecy and Liberal Modernity in Victorian and Edwardian England," in Vernon and Gunn, *Peculiarities of Liberal Modernity*, 72–90. Quotation from Joyce, *State of Freedom*, 29–30.

20 Michel Foucault, "1 February 1984: First Hour," in *The Courage of Truth: The Government of Self and Others II: Lectures at the Collège de France, 1983–1984*, ed. Frédéric Gros, trans. Graham Burchell (New York: Palgrave Macmillan, 2012), 7. For a discussion of these lectures, see Stuart Elden, *Foucault's Last Decade* (Cambridge: Polity, 2016), 201–4.

21 This argument is in contrast to recent governmentality theory, which still assumes, to differing degrees, a preexistent autonomy for the human subject in its relation "with" the nonhuman world—a dualism readily admitted as problematic. See Patrick Joyce and Tony Bennett, "Material Powers: Introduction," in *Material Powers: Cultural Studies, History, and the Material Turn*, ed. Patrick Joyce and Tony Bennett (London: Routledge, 2010), 11. For a critique of this problem through a historicization of "habit," see Tony Bennett, "Habit, Instinct, Survivals: Repetition, History, Biopower," in Vernon and Gunn, *Peculiarities of Liberal Modernity*, 102–18.

22 See, e.g., Vernon, *Distant Strangers*, xi.

23 Walter Benjamin, *The Arcades Project*, ed. Rolf Tiedemann, trans. Howard Eiland and Kevin McLaughlin (Cambridge, MA: Belknap Press of Harvard University Press, 2002), 116, Da, 4.

24 See Bruno Latour, *We Have Never Been Modern*, trans. Catherine Porter (New York: Harvester Wheatsheaf, 1993).

25 Wolmar, *Subterranean Railway*, 219.

26 London Traffic, 1919, LMA, ACC/1297/MET/10/381, 5; T. C. Barker and Michael Robbins, *A History of London Transport: Passenger Travel and the Development of the Metropolis*, 2 vols. (London: Allen and Unwin, 1974), 2:193–94.

27 Wolmar, *Subterranean Railway*, 119–20.

28 London Traffic, 1919, LMA, ACC/1297/MET/10/381, 8.

29 London Traffic Enquiry, 1919, LMA, ACC/1297/MET/10/381, 4.

30 "Thieving on the Tube: Put Ferrets in the Holes," *John Bull*, April 10, 1915, 12.

31 London Traffic Enquiry, 1919, LMA, ACC/1297/MET/10/381, 9.

32 London Traffic, 1919, LMA, ACC/1297/MET/10/381, 10.

33 W. E. Blake, "The Traffic Problem of the 'UndergrounD,'" January 15, 1918, LMA, ACC/1297/UER/4/73, 8.

34 Graeme J. Bruce, *The London Underground Tube Stock* (Surrey: Ian Allen, 1988), 45.

35 Frank Pick, "Growth and Form in the Modern City," January 3, 1926, LTM, PA16, 21.

36 Lord Ashfield, "London's Traffic Problem Reconsidered," *The Nineteenth Century and After*, XCVI, 570 (August 1924), LTM, PE11, 171.

37 Albert Stanley [Lord Ashfield], "London Traffic in 1913," September 1915, LTM, PE1, 38.

38 London Traffic, 1919, LMA, ACC/1297/MET/10/381, 12.

39 Frank Pick, "Passenger Movement in London," n.d. (c.1923), LTM, PA12, 3.

40 Bruce, *Tube Stock*, 53–57; Lord Ashfield, "London's Traffic Problem," May 1920, LTM, PE10, 10.

41 Bruce, *Tube Stock*, 49, 53–59.

42 Albert Francis, statement of May 25, 1957, TNA, MEPO/2/11019.

43 Bruce, *Tube Stock*, 57.

44 Francis, statement of May 25, 1957.

45 Benjamin, *Arcades Project*, 119, D10a, 5.

46 *Underground*, directed by Anthony Asquith (British Instructional Films, 1928). For a synopsis, see Winn Stephens, "Underground," *Film Weekly*, April 15, 1929, 14–15.

47 Reviewers agreed, however, that the film lingered too long on explication, suggesting that norms of personal space were established enough to not deserve extended treatment: "'Underground,'" *Bioscope*, August 1, 1928, 41; "'Underground,'" *Kinematograph Weekly*, August 2, 1928, 41–42.

48 *Rich and Strange*, directed by Alfred Hitchcock (British International Pictures, 1931).

49 David L. Pike, "London on Film and Underground," *London Journal* 38, no. 3 (2013): 229.

50 I am indebted to Amy Smith's superb discussion of this topic in her MA project, "Eroticised Representations of Open-Topped 'Buses and Trams, 1881–1930" (University of Bristol, 2019). See also Brian Stokoe, "Viewing the Metropolis: The Experience of London by Bus," *London Journal* 41, no. 2 (2016): 150–69.

51 A. Smith, "Eroticized Representations," 11–12.

52 Arthur St. John Adcock, *London from the Top of a Bus* (London: Hodder & Stoughton, 1906); *London Old and New*, dir. Harry B. Parkinson and Frank Miller (H. B. Parkinson Productions, 1924).

53 On representations of shopgirls as simultaneously sellers of consumer objects and

objects to consume, see Lise Shapiro Sanders, *Consuming Fantasies: Labor, Leisure, and the London Shopgirl, 1880–1920* (Columbus: Ohio State University Press, 2006); Katherine Mullin, *Working Girls: Fiction, Sexuality, and Modernity* (Oxford: Oxford University Press, 2016), ch. 3. On the economic and cultural entanglement of West End department stores and East End "sweated" labor, see William M. Meier, "Going on the Hoist: Women, Work, and Shoplifting in London, ca. 1890–1940," *Journal of British Studies* 50, no. 2 (April 2011): 410–33.

54 Report, Enquiry into Ventilation, 1897, LMA, ACC/1297/MET/10/250/002, vi, ix-x, 1–6.

55 Barker and Robbins, *History of London Transport*, 2:115.

56 Barker and Robbins, *History of London Transport*, 2:106.

57 Thomas Way, *Turbines, Lots Road, Chelsea* (1911), LTM, 1983/4/8124.

58 Henry Mayhew, "Metropolitan Railway," in *The Shops and Companies of London and the Trades and Manufactories of Great Britain*, vol. 1, ed. Henry Mayhew (London, 1865), 150.

59 Bruce, *Tube Stock*, 13, 26.

60 Barker and Robbins, *History of London Transport*, 2:111.

61 Blake, "Traffic Problem of the 'UndergrounD,'" 1918, LMA, ACC/1297/UER/4/73, 6.

62 Operating Manager's Personal Letter No.8, November 29, 1929, LMA, ACC/1297/UER/4/077, 6.

63 Report, A.C. Ellis, February 22, 1906, LMA, ACC/1297/MET/10/163, 1.

64 *Daily Telegraph*, October 31, 1883, LMA, ACC/1297/MET/10/38/2.

65 Minutes of a Meeting of London MPs, May 12, 1919, LMA, ACC/1297/MET/10/381, 17.

66 Stanley [Lord Ashfield], "London Traffic in 1913," 1915, LTM, PE1, 30.

67 Valerie Thompson, statement of May 27, 1957; Dorothy Baker, statement of June 4, 1957; Patricia Rowan, statement of June 12, 1957; all in Unsolved Murder, Statements Non-material to Report, TNA, MEPO/2/11019.

68 Mabel Petley, statement of May 27, 1957, in Unsolved Murder, Statements Non-material to Report, TNA, MEPO/2/11019. A "Teddy boy" was a youth dressing in clothing characteristic of young men in the reign of Edward VII (1901–1910), typically a velvet-collared jacket and "drainpipe" trousers, and wearing sideburns. Some elements of the British press associated them with threatening behavior.

69 Register of Accidents and Special Occurrences No.7, 1921–1928, February 13, 1928, LMA, ACC/1297/MET/4/003.

70 Wolmar, *Subterranean Railway*, 86–88, 98; Desmond F. Croome, *The Circle Line, Including the Hammersmith and City Line* (Harrow Weald, UK: Capital Transport, 2003), 24; Barker and Robbins, *History of London Transport*, 2:116.

71 Register of Accidents and Special Occurrences No.7, 1921-1928, LMA, ACC/1297/MET/4/003; Register of Accidents and Special Occurrences No.9, 1932–1933, LMA, ACC/1297/MET/4/005.

72 For the new pace of tube travel after electrification, see Edwin Pugh, *The City of the World: A Book about London and the Londoner* (London: Thomas Nelson & Sons, 1912), 116–18.

73 Physician Karl von Vierordt first formulated this inverse relation between the perception of time intervals and their duration in his *Der Zeitsinn nach Versuchen* (1868). On "Vierordt's Law," see John Wearden, *The Psychology of Time Perception* (London: Palgrave Macmillan, 2016), 12–13. See also Helga Lejeune and J. H. Wearden, "Vierordt's

The Experimental Study of the Time Sense (1868) and its Legacy," *European Journal of Cognitive Psychology* 21, no. 6 (August 2009): 941–60.

74 Paul Virilio, *The Original Accident*, trans. Julie Rose (Cambridge: Polity, 2007), 10.

75 For the increasing attention given to short time intervals from the late nineteenth century onward, see Stephen Kern, *The Culture of Time and Space, 1880–1918*, rev. ed. (Cambridge, MA: Harvard University Press, 2003), 110–11.

76 Frank Pick, "The Place of the Motor Bus in Urban Passenger Transport," October 1920, LTM, PA5, 4; Ashfield, "London's Traffic Problem Reconsidered," 1924, LTM, PE11, 176.

77 Pick, "Place of the Motor Bus," 1920, LTM, PA5, 4; Ashfield, "London's Traffic Problem," 1920, LTM, PE10, 7–8.

78 Pick, "Place of the Motor Bus," 1920, LTM, PA5, 7–8.

79 Pick, "Place of the Motor Bus," 1920, LTM, PA5, 5.

80 Blake, "Traffic Problem of the 'UndergrounD,'" 1918, LMA, ACC/1297/UER/4/73, 1–2.

81 This individual, temporal, and cultural variability of "being-in-time" is discussed in Michael Jackson, *The Varieties of Temporal Experience: Travels in Philosophical, Historical, and Ethnographic Time* (New York: Columbia University Press, 2018), esp. xviii–xxi.

82 See also the introduction of automatic ticketing: Operating Manager's Personal Letter No.14, LMA, ACC/1297/UER/4/077, November 16, 1932; Report on Automatic Ticket Machines by Messrs. Holt, Ballingall and Fiske, July 24, 1919, LMA, ACC/1297/MET/10/355.

83 Wolmar, *Subterranean Railway*, 154.

84 "London's New Amusement: Up and Down the Escalator," *Illustrated London News*, October 14, 1911, 593; Operating Manager's Personal Letter No.8, November 29, 1929, LMA, ACC/1297/UER/4/077, 9.

85 W. Y. Lewis to Mr. Agnew and Mr. Baker, February 28, 1930, Transport for London Archives (hereafter cited as TfLA), (NEW) LT/150/014.

86 Statement by London Transport employee (anon.), n.d. (c. June 1963), TfLA, (NEW) LT1455/1276.

87 "London's New Amusement"; *Underground*, dir. Asquith (1928).

88 I am grateful to Lynda Nead for this comment.

89 Susan Haynes, statement of May 31, 1957, in Unsolved Murder, Statements Non-material to Report, TNA, MEPO/2/11019.

90 Bruce, *Tube Stock*, 49; Colin Curtis, *Buses of London: An Illustrated Review*, 2nd ed. (London: London Transport Executive, 1979), 145–48; Ken Blacker, *Routemaster*, 2nd ed., vol. 1 (Harrow Weald, UK: Capital Transport, 1995), 84–86.

91 Bruce, *Tube Stock*, 50.

92 Ashfield, "London's Traffic Problem," 1924, LTM, PE11, 167.

93 For horse-powered forerunners of the "pirate" motor bus, operating in the 1890s, see Shaw Desmond, *London Nights of Long Ago* (London: Duckworth, 1927), 41.

94 LGOC bus drivers occasionally responded in equal measure: see the traffic accident case before Lambeth Police Court: Lambeth Police Court minute book, April 20, 1926, LMA, PS/LAM/B/01/006.

95 Barker and Robbins, *History of London Transport*, 2:222–227.

96 Ashfield, "London's Traffic Problem," 1920, LTM, PE10, 7–10.

97   The term *rush hour* was coined in the United States in the 1870s, entering British usage by 1898, although it only became a commonly discussed experience after the First World War: *Oxford English Dictionary*, s.v. "rush hour, n.,". accessed October 1, 2022, https://www.oed.com/view/Entry/169041. See Richard Dennis, Phillip Gordon Mackintosh, and Deryck W. Holdsworth, "Architectures of Hurry: An Introductory Essay," in *Architectures of Hurry: Mobilities, Cities, and Modernity*, ed. Richard Dennis, Phillip Gordon Mackintosh, and Deryck W. Holdsworth (London: Routledge, 2018), 8. For the new experience of "rush hour," see Robert Lynd, "The Morning and Evening Rush," in *Wonderful London: The World's Greatest City Described by its Best Writers and Pictured by its Finest Photographers*, vol. 2, ed. Arthur St. John Adcock (London: Amalgamated Press, 1926), 580–91; Charles G. Harper, *More Queer Things about London* (London: Cecil Palmer, 1924), 15–16. For the reordering, albeit uneven, of social time, see Vanessa Ogle, *The Global Transformation of Time, 1870–1950* (Cambridge, MA: Harvard University Press, 2015), ch. 2; Jürgen Osterhammel, *The Transformation of the World: A Global History of the Nineteenth Century*, trans. Patrick Camiller (Princeton, NJ: Princeton University Press, 2014), 71–75.

98   H. Cunningham, "Leisure and Culture," in *The Cambridge Social History of Britain, 1750–1950*, vol. 2, ed. F. M. L. Thompson (Cambridge: Cambridge University Press, 1990), 281–83.

99   Stanley [Lord Ashfield], "London Traffic in 1913," 1915, LTM, PE1, 23, 30.

100 For a long-term contextualization of this shift, see Simon Abernethy, "Moving Wartime London: Public Transport in the First World War," *London Journal* 41, no. 3 (2016): 243.

101 Stanley [Lord Ashfield], "London Traffic in 1913," 1915, LTM, PE1, 22–23.

102 Pick, "Place of the Motor Bus," 1920, LTM, PA5, 9–10.

103 Barker and Robbins, *History of London Transport*, 2:218n.

104 Pick, "Place of the Motor Bus," 1920, LTM, PA5, 9–10.

105 Ashfield, "London's Traffic Problem," 1920, LTM, PE10, 11.

106 Arnold Palmer, *Straphangers* (London: Selwyn & Blount, 1927), ix.

107 Ann Pilcher, statement of June 18, 1957, in Unsolved Murder, Statements Non-material to Report, TNA, MEPO/2/11019.

108 Patricia Miatt, statement of June 1, 1957, in Unsolved Murder, Statements Non-material to Report, TNA, MEPO/2/11019.

109 Weiss, "Normal, Natural, and Normative," 85–86, 89.

110 Frederick Ayres to Superintendent of Kensington Police Station, June 7, 1957, TNA, MEPO/2/11019.

111 Thomas Burke, *Out and About: A Note-book of London in War-time* (London: Allen & Unwin, 1919), 99.

112 Mary Eastwood, statement of June 3, 1957, in Unsolved Murder, Statements Non-material to Report, TNA, MEPO/2/11019.

113 This argument moves away from an understanding of queerness as a form of being and toward one of queerness as a temporarily disruptive relation *to* the temporal and spatial conditions under which identities cohere. I draw here on work on queer temporality: Lee Edelman, *No Future: Queer Theory and the Death Drive* (Durham, NC: Duke University Press, 2004), 3–6; Elizabeth Freeman, *Beside You in Time: Sense Methods*

& *Queer Sociabilities in the American 19th Century* (Durham, NC: Duke University Press, 2019), 7–8. I am also inspired by Matt Houlbrook's and Laura Doan's development of queer as a method of thinking outside a genealogy of identity: Matt Houlbrook, "Thinking Queer: The Social and the Sexual in Interwar Britain," in *British Queer History: New Approaches and Perspectives*, ed. Brian Lewis (Manchester: Manchester University Press, 2013), 135–64; Laura Doan, *Disturbing Practices: History, Sexuality, and Women's Experience of Modern War* (Chicago: University of Chicago Press, 2013).

114　This argument has been especially advanced by critical phenomenologists in dialogue with Franz Fanon's *Black Skin, White Masks* (1952), itself responding to the original 1945 edition of Maurice Merleau-Ponty's *Phenomenology of Perception*: Linda Martín Alcoff, *Visible Identities: Race, Gender, and the Self* (Oxford: Oxford University Press, 2006), ch. 7; Ahmed, *Queer Phenomenology*, 135–39; Weiss, "Normal, Natural, and Normative," 86–89.

115　Ahmed, *Queer Phenomenology*, 136.

116　Frank Pick, "The Design of Modern Railway Stations in Europe and America," *Journal of the Royal Institute of Architects* 37, no. 10 (March 1930), LTM, PB21; "The New Piccadilly 'Tube' Station: 'The Best in the World,'" *Illustrated London News*, December 15, 1928, 1145.

117　Eve Kosofsky Sedgwick, *Tendencies* (London: Routledge, 1994), xii.

118　On tube stations as meeting places of would-be lovers first acquainted via "'Companionship' Columns," see T. Burke, *Out and About*, 110–11.

119　Michael Griffin, statement of June 8, 1957, in Unsolved Murder, Statements Non-material to Report, TNA, MEPO/2/11019. Piccadilly Circus and its tube station was a particularly popular site for men to meet other men, especially for working-class "queans": Matt Houlbrook, *Queer London: Perils and Pleasures in the Sexual Metropolis, 1918–1957* (Chicago: University of Chicago Press, 2005), 153–58.

120　Mark O'Mahony, statement of June 8, 1957, in Unsolved Murder, Statements Non-material to Report, TNA, MEPO/2/11019.

121　Houlbrook, *Queer London*, 243, 254–61. Ironically, Peter Wildeblood, one of three self-identified "homosexual" witnesses to the Wolfenden Committee and partly responsible for the construction of the "respectable" homosexual who confined his practices to private spaces, picked up Royal Air Force Corporal Edward McNally at Piccadilly Circus Station: Houlbrook, *Queer London*, 260. See Frank Mort, *Capital Affairs: London and the Making of the Permissive Society* (New Haven, CT: Yale University Press, 2010), 176.

122　Griffin, statement of June 8, 1957; O'Mahony, statement of June 8, 1957.

123　Frederick Williams, statement of June 7, 1957, in Unsolved Murder, Statements Material to Report, TNA, MEPO/2/11018.

124　Franz Fanon, cited in Alcoff, *Visible Identities*, 187. Concerns about interracial sex between Black male students and white women were acute enough twenty years earlier to result in police surveillance of the West African Student Union House in August 1937: Marc Matera, *Black London: The Imperial Metropolis and Decolonization in the Twentieth Century* (Oakland: University of California Press, 2015), 210–11.

125　Williams, statement of June 7, 1957.

126　Williams, statement of June 7, 1957.

127 Griffin, statement of June 8, 1957.

128 Quentin Skinner, "Meaning and Understanding in the History of Ideas," in *Visions of Politics: Regarding Method*, vol. 1 (Cambridge: Cambridge University Press, 2002), 84–86.

129 Kazimerz Krzyzanowski, statements of May 25, May 29, and July 1, 1957, in Unsolved Murder, Statements Material to Report, TNA, MEPO/2/11018.

130 See Hadley, *Living Liberalism*, 5, 8–9, 12–17; Butler, *Senses of the Subject*, esp. introduction.

131 Joyce, *State of Freedom*, 3–6, 27–28.

132 Giorgio Agamben, *Homo Sacer: Sovereign Power and Bare Life*, trans. Daniel Heller-Roazen (Stanford, CA: Stanford University Press, 1998), 1–5.

CHAPTER FOUR

1 Norwich Consistory Court minutes: Bishop of Norwich vs. Revd H. F. Davidson, April 5, 1932, Norwich Record Office (hereafter cited as NRO), DN/ADR/15/8/9/4, 663–69; 628–40.

2 "Yesterday's Law, Police, etc.," *Reynolds's Newspaper*, September 23, 1888; "The Cost of a Kiss," *Lloyd's Weekly Newspaper*, September 30, 1888.

3 "Stiffkey's Rector Cheered by His Flock," *Daily Express* (London), February 8, 1932, 11.

4 For accounts of Davidson's life and trial, see Jonathan Tucker, *The Troublesome Priest: Harold Davidson, Rector of Stiffkey* (Wilby, UK: Michael Russell, 2007); Tom Cullen, *The Prostitutes' Padre: The Story of the Notorious Rector of Stiffkey* (London: Bodley Head, 1975); Rob Baker, *Beautiful Idiots and Brilliant Lunatics: A Sideways Look at Twentieth-Century London* (Stroud, UK: Amberley, 2015), ch. 22.

5 Court minutes, Bishop of Norwich vs. Davidson, April 5, 1932, NRO, DN/ADR/15/8/9/4, 663.

6 Court minutes, Bishop of Norwich vs. Davidson, May 23, 1932, NRO, DN/ADR/15/8/9/4, 996.

7 Court minutes, Bishop of Norwich vs. Davidson, March 29, 1932, NRO, DN/ADR/15/8/9/3, 7.

8 Court minutes, Bishop of Norwich vs. Davidson, March 29, 1932, 33. Compare this with the criticism the Reverend A. Pitt received in 1891 for defending A.B.C. shareholders who accepted 28 percent dividends while waitresses' wages languished at ten shillings a week. "A.B.C. Girls' Wages," *Star* (London), November 10, 1891, 2, and November 12, 1891, 4; Sidney Thomson, letter to the editor, *Pall Mall Gazette*, November 2, 1891.

9 Koven, *Slumming*.

10 See Louise A. Jackson, *Women Police: Gender, Welfare and Surveillance in the Twentieth Century* (Manchester: Manchester University Press, 2006).

11 Walkowitz, *City of Dreadful Delight*, 46–47; Rappaport, *Shopping for Pleasure*, 75, 102–3.

12 Judith R. Walkowitz, *Nights Out: Life in Cosmopolitan London* (New Haven, CT: Yale University Press, 2012), 195.

13 On the rise of tearooms, tea shops, and temperance restaurants within the wider context of West End consumption, see Walkowitz, *City of Dreadful Delight*, 46–50; Rappaport, *Shopping for Pleasure*, 102–3; Walkowitz, *Nights Out*, 195–207; Brenda Assael,

The London Restaurant, 1840–1914 (Oxford: Oxford University Press, 2018), 28–36. See also Rohan McWilliam, *London's West End: Creating the Pleasure District, 1800–1914* (Oxford: Oxford University Press, 2020), 257–59.

14 Erika D. Rappaport, *A Thirst for Empire: How Tea Shaped the Modern World* (Princeton, NJ: Princeton University Press, 2017), 237–39. See also Ian Miller, "A Dangerous Revolutionary Force Amongst Us: Conceptualizing Working-Class Tea Drinking in the British Isles, c. 1860–1900," *Cultural and Social History* 10, no. 3 (2013): 419–38; Markman Ellis, Richard Coulton, and Matthew Mauger, *Empire of Tea: The Asian Leaf That Conquered the World* (London: Reaktion, 2015), 250, 255–57.

15 Rappaport, *Thirst for Empire*, 239.

16 Robin Douglas, *Well, Let's Eat* (London: Cassell, 1933), 105, 140.

17 Steven C. Topik and Allen Wells, "Commodity Chains in a Global Economy," in *A World Connecting, 1870–1945*, ed. Emily S. Rosenberg (Cambridge, MA: Belknap Press of Harvard University Press, 2012), 793–95; Rana P. Behal, *One Hundred Years of Servitude: Political Economy of Tea Plantations in Colonial Assam* (New Delhi: Tulika Books, 2014), 259 and Appendix Table 6.6.

18 This argument takes inspiration from Julia Laite, "Immoral Traffic: Mobility, Health, Labor, and the 'Lorry Girl' in Mid-Twentieth-Century Britain," *Journal of British Studies* 52 (2013): 693–721, and Koven, *Match Girl and Heiress*, ch. 2, in which similar connections are made between otherwise socially or physically distanced labor groups.

19 Koven, *Match Girl and Heiress*, ch. 2.

20 Walkowitz, *City of Dreadful Delight*, 80.

21 Walkowitz, *City of Dreadful Delight*, 41.

22 Walkowitz, *City of Dreadful Delight*, 80; Rappaport, *Shopping for Pleasure*, 109.

23 Work in these commercial leisure spaces contrasted with women's clerical work, where gender differences were spatially enforced by separate offices and staircases: Meta Zimmeck, "Jobs for the Girls: The Expansion of Clerical Work for Women, 1850–1914" in *Unequal Opportunities: Women's Employment in England, 1800–1918*, ed. Angela V. John (Oxford: Blackwell, 1986): 160; Hindmarch-Watson, *Serving a Wired World*, 59.

24 Rappaport, *Shopping for Pleasure*, 198; Sanders, *Consuming Fantasies*, 85; Mullin, *Working Girls*, 110, 120.

25 Peter Bailey, "Parasexuality and Glamour: The Victorian Barmaid as Cultural Prototype," *Gender & History* 2, no. 2 (Summer 1990): 148, 168.

26 Walkowitz, *Nights Out*, 207–8.

27 Walkowitz, *Nights Out*, 182, 11.

28 Walkowitz, *Nights Out*, 224.

29 The focus on spectacle and social performance depends, in part, on theories of performativity derived from the work of Michel de Certeau, Michel Foucault, and Erving Goffman: Rappaport, *Shopping for Pleasure*, 6; Sanders, *Consuming Fantasies*, 201n1; Walkowitz, *Nights Out*, 182, 213.

30 Joanna Bourke, *Disgrace: Global Reflections on Sexual Violence* (London: Reaktion, 2022), 8; Ruth Beecher and Stephanie Wright, "Historicizing the Perpetrators of Sexual Violence: Global Perspectives from the Modern World," *Women's History Review*, April 19, 2023, https://doi.org/10.1080/09612025.2023.2197790: 8.

31   My thinking about the historicity of desire is inspired by Deleuze and Guattari but understands this from a phenomenological perspective. See Eugene W. Holland, *Deleuze and Guattari's "Anti-Oedipus": Introduction to Schizoanalysis* (London: Routledge, 1999); Lauren Berlant, *Desire/Love* (New York: Punctum Books, 2012), esp. 64–65.

32   Beecher and Wright, "Historicizing the Perpetrators of Sexual Violence," 5.

33   Court minutes, Bishop of Norwich vs. Davidson, June 2, 1932, NRO, DN/ADR/15/8/9/2, 1950; March 31, 1932, NRO, DN/ADR/15/8/9/1, 292.

34   Walkowitz, "Going Public," 18.

35   Writing in 1998, Walkowitz saw these representations persisting in contemporary feminist accounts of street encounters; eighteen years later, Gilson made a similar assessment of discourses of victimhood: Walkowitz, "Going Public," 21; Gilson, "Vulnerability and Victimization," 81–87.

36   Gilson, "Vulnerability and Victimization," 78.

37   Here I am indebted to Butler's argument about shared ontological precariousness but focus on how this materializes differently in each embodied encounter: Butler, *Precarious Life*; Weiss, *Body Images*, 3; Ann Cahill, *Overcoming Objectification: A Carnal Ethics* (New York: Routledge, 2011), 23.

38   This argument builds on Emily Owens's historical critique of consent discourse as predicated on the presumed autonomy of the liberal subject: Owens, "Consent," 150. See also Murphy, *Violence and the Philosophical Imaginary*, 69; Mackenzie, "Importance of Relational Autonomy," 43–44.

39   Bourke, *Disgrace*, 9.

40   Harold Davidson to Mr Sheppard, C/o Messrs. Glynn Barton & Co., 4 January 1934, LPL, MS 4873.

41   See Anna Davin, "City Girls: Young Women, New Employment, and the City, London, 1880–1910," in *Secret Gardens, Satanic Mills: Placing Girls in European History, 1750–1960*, ed. Mary Jo Maynes, Birgitte Søland, and Christina Benninghaus (Bloomington: Indiana University Press, 2005), 209–23.

42   Desmond, *London Nights*, 70, 52; C. S. Peel, *A Hundred Wonderful Years: Social and Domestic Life of a Century, 1820–1920* (London: John Lane, 1926), 19; George R. Sims, *Glances Back* (London: Jarrolds, 1927), 194; quotation from Talbot Coke, "Tea-Rooms," *Hearth and Home*, July 11, 1895, 313.

43   "Where to Lunch When Shopping," *Hearth and Home*, March 3, 1892, 502; Coke, "Tea-Rooms," 313; Frances H. Low, "Profitable Employments for Educated Women," *Woman at Home*, n.d., 63.

44   Desmond, *London Nights*, 70.

45   Desmond, *London Nights*, 70; "The Café in London: An Appeal to Common Sense," *Pick-Me-Up*, November 24, 1894, 114.

46   Coke, "Tea-Rooms," 313.

47   Report by Eliza Orme on the Conditions of Work of Barmaids, Waitresses, and Book-Keepers, February 1893, *Royal Commission on Labour*, Cmd. 6894-XXIII, 200–204.

48   Board of Trade (Labour Department), Second Annual Report on Changes in Wages and Hours of Labour in the United Kingdom, 1894, Cmd. 8075, 177–77.

49   Report by Eliza Orme, 209.

50   "Waitress's Wages," *Pall Mall Gazette*, November 19, 1895. For the "New Girl," see Sally

Mitchell, *The New Girl: Girls' Culture in England, 1880–1915* (New York: Columbia University Press, 1995). See also Sally Mitchell, "Retrospective: The New Girl," *Victorian Periodicals Review* 46, no. 4 (Winter 2013): 554–61.

51 Report by Eliza Orme, 209.

52 "The A.B.C. Girls," *Woman's Herald*, November 28, 1891, 921; "Occasional Notes," *Pall Mall Gazette*, November 3, 1897.

53 Thomson, letter to the editor; "The Aerated Bread Company," *Standard*, November 1 1892, 7; "London, Wednesday, November 1, 1893," *Morning Post*, November 1 1893, 4.

54 "Aerated Bread Company," *Standard*.

55 "The A.B.C. Girls," *Woman's Herald*, November 21, 1891, 905, November 28, 1891, 921, December 5, 1891, 9, December 12, 1891, 9; "A.B.C. Girls' Wages," *Star*, November 10, 1891, 2. For the *Star*'s campaign on behalf of the Bryant & May match girls, see Koven, *Match Girl and Heiress*, 88n4.

56 "A.B.C. Girls' Wages," 4; letters to the editor, *Star*, November 14, 1891, 2; November 16, 1891, 4; November 19, 1891, 4; November 24, 1891, 4; December 8, 1891, 2; December 10, 1891, 4.

57 "The Aerated Bread Company," *Pall Mall Gazette*, November 21, 1889.

58 "Aerated Bread Co. and Their Work Girls," *Reynolds's Newspaper*, November 3, 1895.

59 Report by Eliza Orme, 207.

60 Nell Bacon, "My Days with Lyons," n.d., LMA, ACC/3527/231, n.p.

61 "Waitress's Wages," *Pall Mall Gazette*, November 19, 1895.

62 "The Strike of Waitresses," *Daily News*, October 24, 1895.

63 For New Unionism among Bryant & May match girls, see Koven, *Match Girl and Heiress*, 85–95. See also Louise Raw, *Striking a Light: The Bryant & May Matchwomen and Their Place in Labour History* (London: Continuum, 2009).

64 Tom Mann, *Tom Mann's Memoirs* (London: Labour Publishing, 1923), 101.

65 William Abraham, Michael Austin, James Mawdsley, and Tom Mann, *Minority Report of the Royal Commission on Labour*, 1894, Cmd. 7421, 127.

66 See J. E. Skuse, letters to the editor, *Woman's Herald*, November 28, 1891, 921; *Star*, December 10, 1891, 4.

67 "The Strike of Waitresses," *Times*, October 25, 1895, 6.

68 "To-day," *Standard*, 24 October 1895, 3.

69 *Standard*, 25 October 1895, 3. Erik Olssen, "Belcher, William," in *Dictionary of New Zealand Biography* (1993); online ed., *Te Ara—the Encyclopedia of New Zealand*, accessed September 11, 2023, http://www.TeAra.govt.nz/en/biographies/2b15/belcher-william.

70 Peter Bird, *The First Food Empire: A History of J. Lyons & Co.* (Chichester, UK: Phillimore, 2000), 45–46.

71 Bird, *First Food Empire*, 46.

72 Charles Booth and Jesse Argyle, "Household Service, &c.," in Charles Booth, ed., *Life and Labour of the People in London*, 2nd ser., vol. 4, *Industry: Public, Professional and Domestic Service, Unoccupied Classes, Inmates of Institutions* (London: Macmillan, 1903), 240–43.

73 "Barmaids and Waitresses in Restaurants: Their Work and Their Temptations," *Girl's Own Paper*, February 22, 1896, 329.

74 Booth and Argyle, "Household Service, &c.," 239.

75 Court minutes, Bishop of Norwich vs. Davidson, May 21, 1932, NRO, DN/ADR/15/8/9/4, 890.

76 Court minutes, Bishop of Norwich vs. Davidson, May 21, 1932, 892, 1002.

77 Court minutes, Bishop of Norwich vs. Davidson, April 1, 1932, NRO, DN/ADR/15/8/9/1, 411–12. The commissionaire would most likely have been prosecuted through a summons rather than directly after an arrest, especially if Lyons was sued for as much as two hundred pounds. Searches through daily newspapers and the summonses registers of Marlborough Street and Bow Street Police Courts, the principal West End courts, have, however, revealed no trace of the prosecution. Court registers, Marlborough Street Police Court, LMA, PS/MS/A/02/002–003, 1909–1912; Bow Street Police Court, LMA, PS/BOW/A/04/025–028, 1909–1911.

78 See Hannu Salmi, "Cultural History, the Possible, and the Principle of Plenitude," *History and Theory* 50, no. 2 (May 2011): 171–87.

79 Court minutes, Bishop of Norwich vs. Davidson, May 20, 1932, NRO, DN/ADR/15/8/9/4, 821–22.

80 "The Newsboys' Club," *Times*, June 7, 1910, 12; "The Newsboys' Club," *Times*, October 17, 1911, 6; T. Vezey Strong, "The Newsboys' Club," *Times*, October 25, 1911, 15.

81 "The Newsboys' Club," *Times*, April 3, 1912, 14; "The Newsboys' Club," *Times*, April 18, 1912, 14; "The Newsboys' Club," *Times*, May 9, 1912, 4.

82 Hubert Llewellyn Smith, ed., *The New Survey of London Life and Labour*, vol. 8, *London Industries III* (London: P. S. King and Son, 1934), 211.

83 Barbara Drake, "The Waiter," in *Seasonal Trades: By Various Writers*, ed. Sidney Webb and Arnold Freeman (London: Constable, 1912), 93–95.

84 Booth, *Life and Labour*, 4:244n; *Times*, May 4, 1898, 10; January 21, 1901, 4. See also Amalgamated Waiters' Society Rules c. 1896, British Library of Political and Economic Science, London School of Economics (hereafter cited as LSE), BOOTH/F/2/5/18.

85 "Amalgamated Waiters Society (London)," in *Historical Directory of Trade Unions*, vol. 5, ed. Arthur Marsh and John B. Smethurst (Aldershot, UK: Ashgate, 2006), 252.

86 Drake, "Waiter," 97.

87 Drake, "Waiter," 95.

88 "Training English Waiters," *Daily Mail*, February 15, 1910, 5; "Teaching British Boys to be Waiters," *Daily Mirror*, April 21, 1910, 9; "London's Foreign Waiters," *Daily Mirror*, August 30, 1910, 5.

89 "Waiters and Patriotism," *Daily Mail*, September 20, 1910, 5.

90 Wilf McCartney, *Dare to Be a Daniel! A Revolutionary Union in the Catering Trade, AKA The French Cooks' Syndicate*, 3rd ed. (1945; repr., London: Kate Sharpley Library, 2013), 14, 16, 22; "Waiters' Tips," *Daily Mail*, October 14, 1911, 5; "Waiter's 90-Hour Week," *Daily Mail*, April 1, 1912, 5; "International Caterers Employees Union," in Marsh and Smethurst, *Historical Directory of Trade Unions*, 259.

91 Drake, "Waiter," 92n.

92 Drake, "Waiter," 101. Tea shops also often charged waitresses for breakages, though this practice varied considerably between companies. Clementina Black, *Sweated Industry and the Minimum Wage* (London: Duckworth, 1907), 70.

93 Barbara Drake, *Women in Trade Unions* (London: Labour Research Department, 1920), 47.

94 Drake, *Women in Trade Unions*, 46.

95 "The Woes of the Waitress: Hard Lot of Women Workers in Teashops," *John Bull*, December 23, 1916, 12.

96 Barbara Drake, "The Tea-Shop Girl, being a Report of an Enquiry Undertaken by the Investigation Committee of the Women's Industrial Council," *Women's Industrial News* 17, no. 61 (April 1913): 125–26.

97 Arlie Russell Hochschild, *The Managed Heart: Commercialization of Human Feeling*, 2nd ed. (Berkeley: University of California Press, 2012), 7n. See also Amy S. Wharton, "The Sociology of Emotional Labor," *Annual Review of Sociology* 35 (2009): 147–65.

98 Hochschild, *Managed Heart*, 13.

99 A similar argument is made by Katie Hindmarch-Watson in her description of "bodied labour." However, my point is that the tactility of tea shop waitresses—their paradoxically distanced intimacy from customers in which touch was promised but, unless paid for, deferred—literally embodied their abstraction from their own labor, even while taking different forms in each encounter. Hindmarch-Watson, *Serving a Wired World*, 4.

100 "The Ashanti Tea Rooms," *Daily Mail*, December 23, 1914, 2. Lord Mayor Sir Charles Johnston sentenced Hawes to a fine of ten pounds and 23 shillings costs or one month's imprisonment per offense for the insurance fraud; Hawes paid. Court register, December 22, 1914, Mansion House Justice Room, LMA, CLA/004/04/076; gaoler's register, December 22, 1914, Mansion House Justice Room, LMA, CLA/004/05/006.

101 "In City Tea-Shops," *Sunderland Daily Echo and Shipping Gazette*, December 23, 1914, 2.

102 "In City Tea-Shops," 2; See also "Two City Tea Shops," *Daily Mail*, December 23, 1914, 2.

103 "A City Tea-Room," *Daily Mail*, July 19, 1915, 7.

104 Guildhall Justice Room minutes, July 16, 1915, LMA, CLA/005/06/149.

105 Guildhall Justice Room minutes, July 16; Guildhall Justice Room minutes, July 26, 1915, LMA, CLA/005/06/149.

106 Guildhall Justice Room minutes, July 26, 1915; "City Idlers," *Daily Mail*, July 27, 1915, 3.

107 Guildhall Justice Room court register, July 26, 1915, LMA, CLA/005/02/064; City Solicitor to The Worshipful The General Purposes Committee of Aldermen, September 17, 1915, Solicitor's Office report books, LMA, COL/CCS/SO/04/029.

108 Fawcett was fined thirty-three pounds and six shillings, and Newton twenty-five pounds and five shillings. Solicitor's Office report books, November 11, 1915, LMA, COL/CCS/SO/04/029. For Newton, see Guildhall Justice Room court register, November 10, 1915, LMA, CLA/005/02/064; Guildhall Justice Room minutes, November 10, 1915, LMA, CLA/005/06/152; Guildhall Justice Room gaoler's register, November 11, 1915, LMA, CLA/005/07/002; "City Tea-Shop Scandal," *Daily Mail*, November 11, 1915, 3.

109 Guildhall Justice Room minutes, July 16, 1915.

110 Guildhall Justice Room minutes, July 26, 1915.

111 "A City Tea Shop," *Portsmouth Evening News*, September 26, 1922, 5.

112 "Tea with Kisses," *Daily Mail*, December 10, 1920, 4. See City Solicitor to The Worshipful The General Purposes Committee of Aldermen, January 13, 1921, Solicitor's Office report books, LMA, COL/CCS/SO/04/031; Mansion House Justice Room court register, LMA, CLA/004/04/088, December 9 and 22, 1920, Mansion House Justice Room gaoler's register, December 22, 1920, LMA, CLA/004/05/008.

113 "Women's Conduct in Tea Rooms," *Daily Mail*, September 27, 1922, 6. Mansion House Justice Room court register, September 26 and October 11, 1922, LMA, CLA/004/04/091; Mansion House Justice Room gaoler's register, October 11, 1922, LMA, CLA/004/05/008; City Solicitor to The Worshipful The General Purposes Committee of Aldermen, September 14 and October 25, 1922, Solicitor's Office report books, LMA, COL/CCS/SO/04/032.

114 "Tea with Kisses," 4; "Women's Conduct in Tea Rooms," 6.

115 "Tea Shop Temptresses: Dimly Lighted Dens of Delilahs," *John Bull*, August 19, 1922, 12.

116 "Tea-Room Kisses," *Daily Mail*, January 1, 1919, 3. Mansion House Justice Room court register, December 31, 1918, LMA, CLA/004/04/084; Mansion House Justice Room gaoler's register, January 15, 1919, LMA, CLA/004/05/007.

117 Guy Cuthbertson, *Peace at Last: A Portrait of Armistice Day, 11 November 1918* (New Haven, CT: Yale University Press, 2018), 207–11.

118 "City Idlers."

119 Journalist Sydney Mosely gave a detailed exposé of postwar tea shop misconduct in his *The Night Haunts of London* (London: Stanley Paul, 1920), 34–39.

120 The tea shops prosecuted included the Carlton Tea Rooms, Café Bean, Club Tea Rooms (twice), Empire Café, Walbrook Café, Royal Exchange Tea Rooms, Mocha Café, and Ashanti Tea Rooms. See Westminster Police Court registers, March 15 and 22 and April 4, 11, 15, and 25, 1918, LMA, PS/WES/A2/038–039; "Police and a Tea Room," *Daily Mail*, March 18, 1918, 4; "Teashop Peck on the Cheek," *Daily Mail*, March 23, 1918, 4; "Far and Near," *Daily Mail*, April 26, 1918, 4 (all regarding Club Tea Rooms, spring 1918). Also, City Solicitor to The Worshipful the General Purposes Committee of Aldermen, May 12, 1916, Solicitor's Office report books, LMA, COL/CCS/SO/04/029; Mansion House Justice Room register, May 2 and 5, 1916, LMA, CLA/004/04/078; "Undesirable Tea-Shops," *Daily Mail*, May 3, 1916, 3 (all regarding Empire Café). Also, City Solicitor to The worshipful the General Purposes Committee of Aldermen, October 18, 1918, Solicitor's Office report books, LMA, COL/CCS/SO/04/030, (regarding Walbrook Café).

121 "Disorderly London Tea Rooms," *Yorkshire Post & Leeds Intelligencer*, October 12, 1922, 3.

122 "Tea Shop Delilahs: The Real Offender Who Goes Scott Free," *John Bull*, December 16, 1922, 9.

123 "Tea Shop Temptresses: The Real Offender Takes Flight," *John Bull*, December 30, 1922, 8.

124 Section 15 of the City of London (Various Powers) Act, 1920, amended Section 28 of the City of London Police Act, 1839. For the prosecution in 1927 of Ivene Piper and four other waitresses of the Carlton Café, see Guildhall Justice Room register, July 23, 1927, LMA, CLA/005/02/081; Guildhall Justice Room minutes, July 23, 1927, LMA, CLA/005/06/241; City Solicitor to The Worshipful The General Purposes Committee of Aldermen, September 1, 1927, Solicitor's Office report books, LMA, COL/CCS/SO/04/034. For the prosecution of Mollie Robinson and two waitresses of the Swan Café in 1938, see "P.C. Tells of 'Cuddling Noises,'" *Daily Mail*, May 11, 1938, 5; "City Café Kisses Bring £50 Fine," *Daily Mail*, May 13, 1938, 3.

125 *Annual Circular and Illustrated Advertiser Corps of Commissionaires*, No. 90, July 1911, LMA, uncatalogued (AC/77/040/D), 2.

126 *Annual Circular*, 12.

127 *Annual Circular*, 3; Peter Reese, *Our Sergeant: The Story of the Corps of Commissionaires* (London: Cooper, 1986), 35.

128 The Corps of Commissionaires accepted 241 ex-servicemen wounded during the Boer War between 1899 and 1903. Commanding Officer's Report for the Past Year, May 30, 1903, LMA, uncataloged (ACC/70/040/AE), 69.

129 "The Corps of Commissionaires," *John Bull*, November 14, November 28, and December 5, 1908, LMA, uncataloged (ACC/70/040/U), n.p.

130 *Rules and Regulations of the Corps of Commissionaires*, (1912), LMA, uncataloged (AC/77/040/E), 55.

131 *Annual Circular*, 2.

132 W. G. Clifford, *The Ex-Soldier: By Himself* (London: A. & C. Black, 1916), 74–76.

133 "The Night Patrol," loose insert in Tower Bridge Police Court minutes, January 13, 1930, LMA, PS/TOW/B/01/198.

134 Department stores also increasingly employed female private detectives to prevent shoplifting. See Annette Kerner, *Woman Detective* (London: Werner Laurie, 1954); Annette Kerner, *Further Adventures of a Woman Detective* (London: Werner Laurie, 1955). See also Louise Jackson, "The Unusual Case of 'Mrs Sherlock': Memoir, Identity and the 'Real' Woman Detective in Twentieth-Century Britain," *Gender and History* 15, no. 1 (April 2003): 114. On the increasing demand for cinema attendants, see National Council of Public Morals, *The Cinema: Its Present Position and Future Possibilities* (London: printed by the author, 1917), xxviii–xxix and evidence of A. E. Newbould, 267; Lise Shapiro Sanders, "'Indecent Incentives to Vice': Regulating Films and Audience Behaviour from the 1890s to the 1910s," in *Young and Innocent? The Cinema in Britain, 1896–1930*, ed. Andrew Higson (Exeter: University of Exeter Press, 2002), 97–110.

135 Reese, *Our Sergeant*, 110.

136 *Annual Circular*, 8.

137 "The Corps of Commissionaires," *Harmsworth Magazine*, n.d., LMA, uncataloged (AC/77/040/O), 544.

138 "Dismissed" implied misconduct, being distinguished from "discharged" ("men found to be unsuitable for the Corps") and "resigned." *Annual Circular*, 12.

139 The names of commissionaires who were suspended while inquiries were made into misconduct were entered into a "log book," of which I have found no trace. *Rules and Regulations*, 15. For enrolment registers, see LMA, ACC/3313/1/1–17.

140 Court minutes, Bishop of Norwich vs. Davidson, April 1, 1932, NRO, DN/ADR/15/8/9/1, 386–90.

141 Court minutes, Bishop of Norwich vs. Davidson, April 1, 1932, 411.

142 Court minutes, Bishop of Norwich vs. Davidson, April 1, 1932, 407–408.

143 Court minutes, Bishop of Norwich vs. Davidson, April 1, 1932, 409–10.

144 Court minutes, Bishop of Norwich vs. Davidson, April 1, 1932, 412–13.

145 Court minutes, Bishop of Norwich vs. Davidson, May 21, 1932, 981–82.

146 Court minutes, Bishop of Norwich vs. Davidson, April 6 and 7, 1932, NRO, DN/ADR/15/8/9/4, 771–74, 791.

147 Court minutes, Bishop of Norwich vs. Davidson, May 21, 1932, 981–82.

148 Mike Horne, *The Northern Line*, 3rd ed. (Middlesex, UK: Capital Transport, 2009), 36.

149 Report of the Annual Shareholder's Meeting, June 17, 1920, *Lyons Mail* (supplement)

(July 1920), LMA, ACC/3527/270, 1; Director's Office diary, October 2, 1920, LMA, ACC/3527/011.

150 Matthias Morys, "Cycles and Depressions," in *The Cambridge Economic History of Modern Britain*, ed. Roderick Floud, Jane Humphries, and Paul Johnson, 2nd ed., vol. 2 (Cambridge: Cambridge University Press, 2014), 229–54.

151 Report of the Annual Shareholder's Meeting, 3.

152 "3d. Cups of Tea," *Daily Mail*, July 29, 1919, 7; "3½d. Cup of Coffee," *Daily Mail*, October 4, 1920, 5.

153 "3½d. for a Cup of Coffee!" *Daily Express*, October 2, 1920, 1; "Why Not Cheaper Cups of Tea?" *Daily Express*, October 4, 1920, 1; "Coffeeteering," *Daily Express*, October 4, 1920, 4; "Coffee and High Finance," *Daily Express*, 5 October 1920, 1.

154 Percival Griffiths, *The History of the Indian Tea Industry* (London: Weidenfeld & Nicholson, 1967), 178–79. See also Denys Forrest, *Tea for the British: The Social and Economic History of a Famous Trade* (London: Chatto and Windus, 1973), 205.

155 Griffiths, *History of the Indian Tea Industry*, 178–79.

156 Report of the Annual Shareholder's Meeting, June 17, 1920, LMA, ACC/3527/270, 2.

157 "Demands of Lyons Girls," *Daily Mail*, May 22, 1920, 5.

158 McCartney, *Dare to be a Daniel!* 25–26. "Amalgamated Union of Hotel Club and Restaurant Workers," in Marsh and Smethurst, *Historical Directory of Trade Unions*, 252.

159 "Demands of Lyons Girls," 5.

160 "Lyons's Tea Girls," *Daily Mail*, May 24, 1920, 6.

161 "Lyons's Offer to Waitresses," *Daily Mail*, May 26, 1920, 3.

162 "No Lyons Strike," *Daily Mail*, May 27, 1920, 3.

163 "Teashop Strike," *Daily Mail*, August 17, 1920, 5.

164 "May a Tea-Girl Wear a Badge?" *Daily Mail*, August 18, 1920, 3; *Teashop Strike*, British Pathé, Film ID 218.29, August 19, 1920, video, 0:47, https://www.britishpathe.com/asset/48432/.

165 McCartney, *Dare to be a Daniel!* 27–28.

166 Keith Laybourn, *Unemployment and Employment Policies Concerning Women in Britain, 1900–1951* (Lewiston, NY: Edwin Mellen, 2002), 8.

167 "Lyons's Strike," *Daily Mail*, August 19, 1920, 3.

168 McCartney, *Dare to be a Daniel!* 28; London Trades Council, *London Trades Council, 1860–1950: A History* (London: Lawrence & Wishart, 1950), 114.

169 "Teashop Strike," *Daily Mail*, August 20, 1920, 3.

170 Griffiths, *History of the Indian Tea Industry*, 308.

171 Jayeeta Sharma, *Empire's Garden: Assam and the Making of India* (Durham, NC: Duke University Press, 2011), 73–75.

172 Behal, *One Hundred Years of Servitude*, 259.

173 Sharma, *Empire's Garden*, 75–77; Rana Pratap Behal, "Forms of Labour Protest in Assam Valley Tea Plantations, 1900–1930," *Economic and Political Weekly* 20, no. 4 (January 1985): PE19.

174 *Report of the Assam Labour Enquiry Committee, 1921–22* (Shillong [India], 1922), British Library, Mss Eur F174/974, 6; Behal, "Forms of Labour Protest," PE21.

175 *Report of Assam Labour Enquiry Committee*, 20.

176 Thomas Harding, *Legacy: One Family, a Cup of Tea, and the Company that Took on the

World (London: William Heinemann, 2019), 259–60; Rappaport, *Thirst for Empire*, 242–43.

177 Harding, *Legacy*, 262–63.

178 "Training Lyons' Waitresses," *Lyons Mail*, October 1920, LMA, ACC/3527/270, 15–16.

179 "Examinations for Waitresses," *Lyons Mail*, December 1921, LMA, ACC/3527/271, 189.

180 "Wisdom for Waitresses," *Daily Mail*, December 20, 1922, 5. Nippy Helen McCrae gave a radio talk for 2LO, the BBC's predecessor, on April 7, 1926, in which she mentioned some of the mottoes still in use. "'Nippy' at 2LO," *Daily Mail*, April 8, 1926, 7; "'Nippy' Calling," *Lyons Mail*, May and June 1926, LMA, ACC/3527/276, 41.

181 *The Perfect Nippy*, n.d., illustration of correct Nippy presentation, LMA, ACC/3527/565.

182 Bird, *First Food Empire*, 114–15; Bacon, "My Days with Lyons." For a balanced appraisal of how domestic servants themselves interpreted their work, see Lucy Delap, *Knowing Their Place: Domestic Service in Twentieth-Century Britain* (Oxford: Oxford University Press, 2011), 41–47.

183 Bird, *First Food Empire*, 119. On "conservative modernity," see Alison Light, *Forever England: Femininity, Literature, and Conservatism between the Wars* (London: Routledge, 1991), ch. 2.

184 Nippy Ethel Fage's notebook, 1930s, LMA, LMA/4306/A/001, n.p.

185 Walkowitz, *Nights Out*, 205.

186 Letters of reminiscence from former Nippies: Joy Hadson, March 1, 1990; R. Dobner, n.d.; Nellie Jouney, January 9, 1990; D. Hughes, January 7, 1990; Kathleen Pittman, February 10, 1990; L. Docwra, February 19, 1990, all LMA, ACC/3527/235.

187 "Noona be Nippy" and "An All-Staff Film," *Lyons Mail*, November 1929, LMA, ACC/3527/278, 164–65 and 166, respectively. No complete copy of the film survives, but the British Film Institute holds a section (parts 7 and 8 of 8): 18791. Bertie Joseph directed Lyons's training school for Nippies and also Outdoor Catering, to which Nora and Noona finally progress at the end of the film. "Joseph, Bertie," J. Lyons & Co., accessed September 12, 2023, http://www.kzwp.com/lyons.pensioners/obituary2J.htm.

188 J. B. Priestley, *Angel Pavement* (London: William Heinemann, 1930), 171–74.

189 John Baxendale, *Priestley's England: J. B. Priestley and English Culture* (Manchester: Manchester University Press, 2007), 46–56, 63–64.

190 J. B. Priestley, *They Walk in the City: The Lovers in the Stone Forest* (London: William Heinemann, 1936), 184–85. See also Paul Cohen-Portheim, *The Spirit of London* (London: B. T. Batsford, 1935), 90–91.

191 Ethel Fage notebook, n.p.

192 For Priestley's conceptualization of the novel, see J. B. Priestley, *Midnight on the Desert: A Chapter of Autobiography* (London: William Heinemann, 1937), 49–50.

193 Mary S. Allen, *Lady in Blue* (London: Stanley Paul, 1936), 236–37.

194 "78 Happy Brides," *Lyons Mail*, April 1927, LMA, ACC/3527/277, 292.

195 For a detailed investigation into Davidson's business relations with Gordon, see W. Barker, Criminal Intelligence Department report, February 29, 1932, TNA, MEPO 3/750.

196 Court minutes, Bishop of Norwich vs. Davidson, May 21, 1932, 874–75.

197 Court minutes, Bishop of Norwich vs. Davidson, May 25, 1932, NRO, DN/ADR/15/8/9/4, 1257–58.

198 Court minutes, Bishop of Norwich vs. Davidson, April 2, 1932, NRO, DN/ADR/15/8/9/1, 448–50.

199 Account book: number of meals served each day at the Oxford Street Corner House, 1928–1952, August 30 and 31, 1930, LMA, ACC/3527/058.

200 LCC Inspection Dept Case Copy, October 7, 1914, LMA, GLC/AR/BR/07/2551.

201 Ground floor of Maison Lyons, October 1916, Historic England, BL23645.

202 Maison Lyons basement plan, December 15, 1915, LMA, COL/SVD/PL/01/2711.

203 Superintending Architect's Department, Escape Section. Report to the Theatres etc. Committee, July 22, 1914, LMA, GLC/AR/BR/07/2551.

204 Court minutes, Bishop of Norwich vs. Davidson, April 2, 1932, 449.

205 Court minutes, Bishop of Norwich vs. Davidson, April 2, 1932, 450; Maison Lyons basement plan.

206 Court minutes, Bishop of Norwich vs. Davidson, April 2, 1932, 445.

207 Court minutes, Bishop of Norwich vs. Davidson, May 21, 1932, 978.

208 Reginald Kennedy-Cox, *Reginald Kennedy-Cox: An Autobiography* (London: Hodder & Stoughton, 1931), 51.

209 Court minutes, Bishop of Norwich vs. Davidson, April 1, 1932, 412–13; Court minutes, Bishop of Norwich vs. Davidson, May 24, 1932, NRO, DN/ADR/15/8/9/4, 1104.

210 Court minutes, Bishop of Norwich vs. Davidson, April 5, 1932, 637–38.

211 Here I draw on William Sewell's brilliant argument that the abstracting forces of capitalism in eighteenth-century France, and the subsequent development of "abstract forms of social relations," made it easier to accept new discourses of civic equality during the 1789 revolution. William H. Sewell Jr., "Connecting Capitalism to the French Revolution: The Parisian Promenade and the Origins of Civic Equality in Eighteenth-Century France," *Critical Historical Studies* 1, no. 1 (Spring 2014): 11.

212 Letter of reminiscence from Edith Walker, December 18, 1989, LMA, ACC/3527/235.

213 Letter of reminiscence from Florence Wright, n.d., LMA, ACC/3527/235.

214 The opening to act 2, scene 1 was captured on newsreel: *Nippy*, British Pathé, Film ID 1024.20, February 9, 1931, https://www.britishpathe.com/asset/64379/. "'Nippy,'" *Stage*, September 18, 1930; "'Nippy,'" *Era*, September 17, 1930, *Nippy*: press and magazine clippings of reviews, Cadbury Research Library Special Collections, University of Birmingham (hereafter cited as CRL), MS38/4305, both n.p.

215 J. T. G., "'Nippy,' at the Prince Edward," *Sketch*, November 12, 1930, CRL, MS38/4305, n.p.

216 Trinculo [pseud.], "'Nippy' at the Prince Edward Theatre," *Tatler*, November 19, 1930, CRL, MS38/4305, n.p.

217 J. T. Grein, "The World of the Theatre," *Illustrated London News*, November 15, 1930, 878. See also "The Playhouses," *Illustrated London News*, November 8, 1930, 848. Hale was already one of the stars of musical theater by 1930, having achieved widespread recognition for title roles in *No, No, Nanette* (1925) and *Sunny* (1926). Stanley Green, "Hale, Binnie," in *Encyclopaedia of the Musical* (London: Cassell, 1977), 168–69. On her film roles, see Rachael Low, *The History of British Film 1929–1939: Film Making in 1930s Britain* (London: Routledge, 1997), 332, 349, 371, 394, 398.

218 Harris Deans, "'Nippy' (Prince Edward)," *Sunday Graphic*, November 2, 1930; D.C.F., "'Nippy.'" *Theatre World*, December 1930, CRL, MS38/4305, both n.p.

219 "'Nippy,'" *Observer*, November 2, 1930, CRL, MS38/4305, n.p.

220 "A Wylie Scott," *Lyons Mail*, October 1930, LMA, ACC/3527/280, 133.

221 "Mr A. Asquith," *Daily Mail*, March 17, 1928, 13; "Film of Strube's 'Little Man,'" *Daily Express*, April 28, 1928, 3.

222 Court minutes, Bishop of Norwich vs. Davidson, May 23, 1932, 997–98. *Picture Post* estimated that Corner House Nippies earned around fifty shillings a week in 1939— twenty-five shillings in wages and twenty-five shillings in tips—whereas ordinary tea shop Nippies, though earning higher wages, received less in total because of fewer tips: thirty-two shillings was a "fair average." "A Day in the Life of a Nippy," *Picture Post* 2, no. 9 (March 4, 1939): 31.

223 Court minutes, Bishop of Norwich vs. Davidson, April 5, 1932, 642–43.

224 Court minutes, Bishop of Norwich vs. Davidson, May 23, 1932, 998–99.

225 On the fantasy of "overnight film stardom" and its cultivation by newspaper searches for future stars, see Chris O'Rourke, *Acting for the Silent Screen: Film Actors and Aspiration between the Wars* (London: I. B. Tauris, 2017), 99, 106–9.

226 "Teashop Girls with Poise of Film Stars," *Daily Express*, April 21, 1932. For a retrospective account of Coventry Street Corner House in the 1920s and 1930s, see Maurice Gorham, *Londoners* (London: Percival Marshall, 1951), 102–3.

227 The completed film was titled *A Moorland Tragedy* (1933). "Waitress to be Film Star," *Daily Express*, April 22, 1932, 11.

228 *Lyons Mail* reported the "coincidence." "Lyons in the News," *Lyons Mail*, May 1932, LMA, ACC/3527/282, 3. The *Tatler* strongly suspected that Lyons's publicity department was behind the production of *Nippy*. Trinculo [pseud.], "'Nippy' at the Prince Edward Theatre."

229 "'Nippy' on the Films," *Lyons Mail*, May 1928, LMA, ACC/3527/278, 19.

230 "'Nippy' on the Films," *Lyons Mail*, May 1932, LMA, ACC/3527/282, 10–11; also, "MacHinery: Film Star," *Lyons Mail*, September 1928, LMA, ACC/3527/278, 107.

231 Priestley, *They Walk in the City*, 172–74.

232 O'Rourke, *Acting for the Silent Screen*, 81–86.

233 *Dangerous Corner* (1932) only continued through Priestley's own financial backing; *Eden End* (1934) folded after a few weeks on Broadway. J. B. Priestley, *Margin Released: A Writer's Reminiscences and Reflections* (London: Heinemann, 1962), 198; Vincent Brome, *J. B. Priestley* (London: Hamilton, 1988), 164. On Priestley's distaste for critics, see *Margin Released*, 206. Priestley later wrote about the maddening inconsistencies in the critical reception of his work in Priestley, *Midnight on the Desert*, 7–10, 48–49.

234 Court minutes, Bishop of Norwich vs. Davidson, June 2, 1932, 1950.

235 Court minutes, Bishop of Norwich vs. Davidson, March 29, 1932, 28; April 1, 1932, 388; May 21 1932, 881–82.

236 Court minutes, Bishop of Norwich vs. Davidson, May 23, 1932, 1042–44.

237 Bailey, *Popular Culture and Performance*, 137.

238 Court minutes, Bishop of Norwich vs. Davidson, May 25, 1932, 1338.

239 Matt Houlbrook provides a different interpretation of laughter in court as expressing complicity between parties, and hence reasserting exclusivist social norms, in his unpublished manuscript "Songs of Seven Dials: An Intimate History of London in the 1920s and 1930s," an excerpt from which he kindly shared with me. Matt Houlbrook, email message to author, August 22, 2022.

240 Molly Davidson cited in the *Sunday Dispatch*, July 10, 1932, in Tucker, *Troublesome Priest*, 110.

241 C. L. R. James, *Letters from London*, ed. Nicholas Laughlin (Oxford: Signal Books, 2003), 119–21.

242 Molly Davidson, in Tucker, *Troublesome Priest*, 110.

243 My thinking of tendentious jokes comes from Sigmund Freud, as deployed by Gilles Deleuze and Félix Guattari. See Holland, *Deleuze and Guattari's "Anti-Oedipus,"* 24. For a critique of Freud's *Jokes and Their Relation to the Unconscious*, see Michael Billig, *Laughter and Ridicule: Towards a Social Critique of Humour* (London: Sage, 2005), ch. 7.

244 Holland, *Deleuze and Guattari's "Anti-Oedipus,"* 24.

245 Court minutes, Bishop of Norwich vs. Davidson, March 31, 1932, 292.

246 Court minutes, Bishop of Norwich vs. Davidson, June 1, 1932, 1879.

247 Court minutes, Bishop of Norwich vs. Davidson, May 27, 1932, NRO, DN/ADR/15/8/9/2, 1517.

248 Court minutes, Bishop of Norwich vs. Davidson, May 21, 1932, 877.

249 Allan V. Horwitz, *Anxiety: A Short History* (Baltimore: Johns Hopkins University Press, 2013), ch. 5.

250 This suggestion contrasts with attempts to make defendants wholly knowable through psychoanalysis: Houlbrook, *Prince of Tricksters*, 74–83.

251 Court minutes, Bishop of Norwich vs. Davidson, May 21, 1932, 877.

252 Court minutes, Bishop of Norwich vs. Davidson, May 21, 1932, 877.

253 Court minutes, Bishop of Norwich vs. Davidson, June 2, 1932, 1952.

254 Court minutes, Bishop of Norwich vs. Davidson, June 2, 1932, 1958–61.

255 Houlbrook, *Prince of Tricksters*, 80.

256 Sewell, "Connecting Capitalism," 16.

257 "Stiffkey Rector in Rink Recitals," *Daily Express*, July 6, 1932, 1.

258 "Stiffkey Rector Gives a 'Turn,'" *Daily Express*, July 7, 1932, 9; Harold Davidson to the Archbishop of Canterbury, January 22, 1937; Harold Davidson, letter to the editor, *Sunday Referee*, June 4, 1936, both in Lambeth Palace Library (hereafter cited as LPL), MS 4873.

259 "From Pulpit to Barrel," *Daily Express*, September 6, 1932, 9; Tucker, *Troublesome Priest*, 127; "Can Nothing Be Done About It?" *Blackpool Gazette and Herald*, April 18, 1936, LPL, MS 4873.

260 Tucker, *Troublesome Priest*, 141–43.

261 Mass Observation founder Tom Harrisson made the analogy in *Britain Revisited* (London: Victor Gollancz, 1961), 150.

262 "Lion Mauls Ex-Rector of Stiffkey," *Daily Express*, July 29, 1937, 1.

263 "Ex-Rector Dies, Show is Still to Go On," *Daily Express*, July 31, 1937, 1.

CHAPTER FIVE

1 Tower Bridge Police Court (TBPC) minute book and TBPC register, December 10, 1924, LMA, PS/TOW/B/01/139 and PS/TOW/A/01/158, respectively.

2 "The Worst Fog of the Year," *Manchester Guardian*, December 11, 1924, 9; "The Weather of December, 1924," *Meteorological Magazine* 59, no. 708 (January 1925): 295–97.

3   "Jewel Thieves' Coups in Great Fog," *Daily Mirror* (London), December 11, 1924, 2; "London Fogbound for 36 Hours," *Daily Mail*, December 11, 1924, 9.

4   C. H. Biddlecombe, "London Fogs from Above," *Meteorological Magazine* 59, no. 708 (January 1925): 277.

5   "London Held to Ransom by the Fog Fiend," *Daily Mirror*, December 11, 1924, 1.

6   On fog as a "cover" for crime, see Christine Corton, *London Fog: The Biography* (Cambridge, MA: Belknap Press of Harvard University Press, 2015), 148–53.

7   "Park-lane Raids," *Daily Mail*, December 12, 1924, 9; "Cat Burglar Again," *Daily Mail*, December 11, 1924, 7; "Cat Burglars' £3,000," *Daily Mirror*, December 12, 1924, 2; "Jewel Thieves' Coups in Great Fog," *Daily Mirror*, December 11, 1924, 1.

8   "Girl Stabbed with Stiletto in the Fog," *Daily Mail*, 9 December 1952, 1; Charlotte Brunsdon, *London in Cinema: The Cinematic City Since 1945* (London: British Film Institute, 2007), 46.

9   Bruno Latour, *Reassembling the Social: An Introduction to Actor-Network-Theory* (Oxford: Oxford University Press, 2005), 114–15.

10 Latour, *Reassembling the Social*, 39–40, 108; see also Lynda Nead, *The Tiger in the Smoke: Art and Culture in Post-War Britain* (New Haven, CT: Yale University Press, 2017), 22.

11 Peter Thorsheim, *Inventing Pollution: Coal, Smoke, and Culture in Britain since 1800*, 2nd ed. (Athens: Ohio University Press, 2017), 5.

12 Jesse Oak Taylor, *The Sky of Our Manufacture: The London Fog in British Fiction from Dickens to Woolf* (Charlottesville: University of Virginia Press, 2016), 1; Heidi C. M. Scott, *Chaos and Cosmos: Literary Roots of Modern Ecology in the British Nineteenth Century* (University Park: Pennsylvania State University Press, 2014), 62. This argument follows Benson's claim that concepts of the environment come into being only when "materialized in particular environments": Etienne S. Benson, *Surroundings: A History of Environments and Environmentalisms* (Chicago: University of Chicago Press, 2020), 11.

13 Taylor, *Sky of Our Manufacture*, 28–29.

14 Sascha Auerbach, *Armed with Sword and Scales: Law, Culture, and Local Courtrooms in London, 1860–1913* (Cambridge: Cambridge University Press, 2021), 285. Under the Town Clauses Act, 1847, "importuning" meant approaching people to offer sex for payment. See Charles Edward Vincent, *Vincent's Police Code and General Manual of the Criminal Law*, 16th ed. (London: Butterworth, 1924), 201.

15 Fog here is understood similarly to John Durham Peters's conceptualization of clouds as "media": as the ground for existence, conditioning ways of being and acting, and as the way through which these conditions are also conceptualized. John Durham Peters, *The Marvelous Clouds: Towards a Philosophy of Elemental Media* (Chicago: University of Chicago Press, 2015), 14–15.

16 Drew Leder, *The Absent Body* (Chicago: University of Chicago Press, 1990).

17 Alain Pottage, "Introduction: The Fabrication of Persons and Things," in Pottage and Mundy, *Law, Anthropology, and the Constitution of the Social*, 3.

18 This history is that of a growing awareness of air as the biological and ontological condition of existence, and of its subsequent mobilization as an object and method of thought: Peter Sloterdijk, *Foams: Spheres III*, trans. Wieland Hoban (South Pasadena, CA: Semiotext(e), 2016), 34–38, 61–64. Thanks to Chris Otter for this reference. See also Luce Irigaray, *The Forgetting of Air in Martin Heidegger*, trans. Mary Beth Mader

(London: Athlone, 1999); Steven Connor, *The Matter of Air: Science and the Art of the Ethereal* (London: Reaktion, 2010).

19   TBPC minute book, December 10, 1924.

20   See Latour's distinction between "matters of fact" and "matters of concern," based on Yan Thomas's analysis of the Roman legal concept of *res* (thing): Latour, *Reassembling the Social*, 87–120; Alain Pottage, "Law After Anthropology: Object and Technique in Roman Law," *Law, Culture & Society* 31, no. 2–3 (2014): 150–51.

21   Vincent, *Vincent's Police Code*, 124–25.

22   TBPC minute book, April 21, 1927, LMA, PS/TOW/B/01/167; Report of Sergeant P. Rosie, November 24, 1927, in Criticism of Elderly Judges' Treatment of Homosexual Offences (1922–28), TNA, HO/144/22298. Thanks to Matt Houlbrook for this reference.

23   Walk with Sergeant Saltmarshe, District 31 (Lambeth and St Saviour's Southwark), April 28, 1899, Charles Booth Police Notebook, LSE, B363, 39.

24   J. A. Johnston, *The Metropolitan Police Guide: Being a Compendium of the Law Affecting the Metropolitan Police*, 7th ed. (London: HMSO, 1922), 1246.

25   Criticism of Elderly Judges' Treatment.

26   Johnston, *Metropolitan Police Guide*, 1246. On the ad hoc ways in which the police dealt with this ambiguity, see Houlbrook, *Queer London*, 27–31.

27   Pottage, "Law After Anthropology," 154–55. This resists Latour's conceptualization of law as a discrete "mode of existence." See Pottage, "Materiality of What?" 167, 172–74. My argument here is inspired by recent work on the materiality of law and its constitution of the material world. See also Vismann, *Files*; Latour, *Making of Law*; Tomlins, "Historicism and Materiality"; Tom Johnson, "Medieval Law and Materiality: Shipwrecks, Finders, and Property on the Suffolk Coast, ca. 1380–1410," *American Historical Review* 120, no. 2 (2015): 407–32; T. Johnson, "Legal History and the Material Turn."

28   See Russell Hogg cited in David Delaney, *The Spatial, the Legal and the Pragmatics of World-Making: Nomospheric Investigations* (London: Routledge, 2010), 7; also 22. The notion of law "inscribing" meaning into the material world lingers in legal geography even when critiqued. See, for example, Irus Braverman et al., "Introduction: Expanding the Spaces of Law," in *The Expanding Spaces of Law: A Timely Legal Geography*, ed. Irus Braverman et al. (Stanford, CA: Stanford University Press, 2014), 1, 17. For an example of a study examining the legal "construction" of reality, see Brigham, *Material Law*.

29   Tomlins, "Historicism and Materiality," 67–68, 73.

30   Frederick J. Brodie, "On the Prevalence of Fog in London during the 20 Years 1871 to 1890," *Quarterly Journal of the Royal Meteorological Society* 18, no. 81 (January 1892): 40–45; Frederick J. Brodie, "Some Remarkable Features in the Winter of 1890–91," *Quarterly Journal of the Royal Meteorological Society* 17, no. 79 (July 1891): 160–61; Frederick J. Brodie, "Decrease of Fog in London during Recent Years," *Quarterly Journal of the Royal Meteorological Society* 31, no. 133 (January 1905): 15–28. Robert Scott found no discernible increase in fog prevalence between 1870 and 1890, but the frequency of major episodes over this period as a whole was still markedly greater than in the twentieth century: Robert H. Scott, "Fifteen Years' Fogs in the British Islands, 1876–1890," *Quarterly Journal of the Royal Meteorological Society* 19, no. 88 (October 1893): 229–38; Thorsheim, *Inventing Pollution*, 128.

31 Harper, *Queer Things about London*, 36. See "Occurrences of fog which may be comparable in duration or intensity with that of December 5–9, 1952," n.d. (ca. 1953), TNA, MH 55/2659.

32 "Fog Fables," *Daily Mail*, December 28, 1916, 5.

33 The *Daily Mail* reported a "gradual diminution" in London fogs from forty-one in 1905 to four in 1909. "Fog-Free London," *Daily Mail*, March 14, 1910, 4; E. G. Bitham, "On the Variation in the Incidence of Bright Sunshine and Fog in London during the 45 Years 1881 to 1925," March 1930, Disamenities (Smoke etc), New Survey of London, LSE, NSOL/1/5/3, 3.

34 Meteorologist Rollo Russell made one of the first attempts to determine the causal relation between smoke and fog: Rollo Russell, *Smoke in Relation to Fogs in London: A Lecture* (London: National Smoke Abatement Offices, 1889); Rollo Russell, "Haze, Fog, and Visibility," *Quarterly Journal of the Royal Meteorological Society* 23, no. 101 (January 1897): 10–24. Writer James Bone preferred to maintain their distinction: James Bone, *The London Perambulator* (London: Jonathan Cape, 1925), 53–54.

35 Meteorologists Napier Shaw and John Owens provided a more detailed account of the smoke-fog relation, but theirs outlined only the correlation between smoke buildup and fog formation, not their causal relation. Napier Shaw and John Switzer Owens, *The Smoke Problem of Great Cities* (London: Constable, 1925), 13–16, 117–19. Greater statistical evidence was available by 1953 to strengthen causal claims: C. K. M. Douglas and K. H. Stewart, "London Fog of December 5–8, 1952," *Meteorological Magazine* 82, no. 969 (March 1953): 70. Yet even these claims were subject to cautionary caveats: A. L. Kelley, "Fog and Smog," *Smokeless Air* 24, no. 89 (Spring 1954): 140, WL, SA/EPU/H/1/2/1/6.

36 "The Origin of 'Smog,'" *Smokeless Air* 25, no. 91 (Autumn, 1954): 12, WL, SA/EPU/H/1/2/1/7.

37 *Royal Commission on London Traffic. Volume II: Minutes of Evidence*, Cd. 2751 (London, 1905), 499. The *Builder* was less optimistic, claiming it was "morally certain that London must always be subject to fogs, even if coal fires were entirely abolished." "London Fogs'" *Builder*, 87, no. 3229, (December 24, 1904): 656.

38 *Royal Commission on London Traffic. Volume I: Report*, Cd. 2597 (London, 1905), 69, 73.

39 "Fog-Free London." Despite the *Mail*'s optimism, Harold des Voeux and John Owens calculated that average annual soot deposit for the following year (June 1910–June 1911) totaled 260 tons per square mile in London. "Appendix D: Soot-fall of London," in Julius B. Cohen and Arthur G. Ruston, *Smoke: A Study of Town Air* (London: Edward Arnold, 1912), 84–85.

40 Extracts from minutes of proceedings of the Council, July 3, 1923, LMA, LCC/PC/GEN/01/016, 1–2.

41 Extracts from minutes of proceedings of the Council, July 3, 1923, LMA, LCC/PC/GEN/01/016, 3.

42 Meteorological Council, *London Fogs* (London: Meteorological Office, 1904), 6, 16.

43 The independent Committee for the Investigation of Atmospheric Pollution was established in 1912 and received annual funding from the Department of Scientific and Industrial Research from 1917 until absorbed by the Meteorological Office in 1919. In 1926, the LCC began contributing one hundred pounds to the scheme annu-

ally. Shaw and Owens, *Smoke Problem*, vi–viii; extract from a report of the London County Council Housing and Public Health Committee, May 15, 1934, LMA, LCC/PC/GEN/01/016, 1. The fog-filtering apparatus was designed by John Owens, the committee's honorary secretary. Harold Lake, "The Man Who Weighs Fog," *Daily Mail*, November 6, 1920, 6.

44 Herbert G. Clinch, *The Smoke Inspector's Handbook: Or, Economic Smoke Abatement* (London: H. K. Lewis, 1923), 70–75; report by the Chief Officer of the Public Control Department on Atmospheric Pollution, June 22, 1931, LMA, LCC/PC/GEN/01/016, 1–2.

45 Mort, *Capital Affairs*, 27, 39, 122–23.

46 "Weather of December 1952," *Meteorological Magazine* 82, no. 968 (February 1953): 63; "Burglar Gets £12,000 in Fog," *Daily Mail*, December 8, 1952, 1.

47 Henri Lefebvre, *Rhythmanalysis: Space, Time and Everyday Life*, trans. Stuart Elden and Gerald Moore (London: Continuum, 2004), 17–18.

48 Bone, *London Perambulator*, 56; "Our London Correspondence," *Manchester Guardian*, November 18, 1901, 5.

49 "The New Link Boys," *Times*, October 29, 1919, 13.

50 Nead, *Tiger in the Smoke*, 39.

51 Bone, *London Perambulator*, 55–56; also "The King in the Fog," *Daily Mail*, October 14, 1912, 5.

52 "London's Great Christmas Fog," *Daily Mail*, December 23, 1904, 5.

53 Lefebvre, *Rhythmanalysis*, 20.

54 "London's Great Christmas Fog."

55 "Densest Fog of the Year," *Daily Mail*, December 1, 1899, 3.

56 "Ghostly Throngs of Excited Passengers," *Daily Mail*, December 12, 1905, 7.

57 "A Christmas Fog," *Daily Mail*, December 24, 1900, 5.

58 Nead, *Tiger in the Smoke*, 39.

59 "London Fog-Bound," *Daily Mail*, October 28, 1901, 3.

60 Ruth Mayhew to Henry Head, November 4, 1901, WL, PP/HEA/D.4/10.

61 "Fog-Bound Country," *Daily Mail*, November 6, 1901, 5.

62 "Fogged," *St Dunstan's Review* 2, no. 20 (March 1918): 26.

63 "A Christmas Fog."

64 Leder, *Absent Body*, 1–5.

65 Bone, *London Perambulator*, 53–54.

66 "London Fog-Bound," *Daily Mail*, December 22, 1904, 5.

67 Connor, *Matter of Air*, 30–31; Irigaray, *Forgetting of Air*, 8–9.

68 "London's Great Christmas Fog."

69 "Fog-Bound Land," *Daily Mail*, November 28, 1921, 9.

70 "Fog Brings Burglars," *Daily Mail*, November 5, 1907, 5; "The King in the Fog," *Daily Mail*, January 22, 1908, 5; "Robberies in the Fog," *Daily Mail*, January 28, 1909, 5.

71 "Murder in the Fog," *Daily Mail*, November 8, 1909, 5; "Murder in a Fog," *Daily Mail*, November 9, 1909, 12; "Tragedy in the Fog," *Daily Mail*, November 12, 1909, 10; TBPC register, November 8, 16, 18, and 24, 1909, LMA, PS/TOW/A/01/104, ; Old Bailey Proceedings Online, version 7.2, "December 1909, trial of BRANNAN, Luke" (t19091207–15), accessed 16 July 16, 2015, www.oldbaileyonline.org.

72 "Murder in the Fog."

73 "Come-and-Go Fog Slows up London," *Daily Mail*, December 6, 1952, 1; "Burglar gets £12,000 in Fog," *Daily Mail*, December 8, 1952, 1. A "cosh" was a truncheon or length of metal originally used as a "life-preserver." In 1953, just after the fog of December 1952, the term "cosh-boy" was coined to refer to thugs who attacked people with coshes. See *Oxford English Dictionary*, s.v. "cosh, n.³, sense a," last modified July 2023, https://doi.org/10.1093/OED/1892542725; and *Oxford English Dictionary*, s.v. "cosh-boy, n.," last modified July 2023, https://doi.org/10.1093/OED/1019492703.

74 Margery Allingham, *The Tiger in the Smoke* (London: Chatto & Windus, 1952), 9, 23; also Maurice Lane Richardson, "On the Run," *Times Literary Supplement*, August 1, 1952, 497.

75 See also the film *Footsteps in the Fog*, dir. Arthur Lubin (Frankovich Productions, 1955), based on the play *The Interruption* by W. W. Jacobs (in W. W. Jacobs, *Sea Whispers* [London: Hodder & Stoughton, 1926], 257–84) and the film version of Allingham's novel, *Tiger in the Smoke*, dir. Roy Baker (Rank Organisation, 1956). In fiction, see Christianna Brand, *London Particular* (London: Michael Joseph, 1952), Arthur Conan Doyle, "The Adventure of the Bruce-Partington Plans," in *Complete Sherlock Holmes & Other Detective Stories* (Glasgow: HarperCollins, 1994), 1080–98; Sax Rohmer, "The Si-Fan Mysteries" [1917], in *The Fu-Manchu Omnibus*, vol. 1 (London: A&B, 1995).

76 The concept of "translation" derives from Bruno Latour. See Nead, *Tiger in the Smoke*, 22; Latour, *Reassembling the Social*, 39–40, 108.

77 Carmel Haden Guest, *Children of the Fog: A Novel of Southwark* (London: G. G. Harrap, 1927); F. Klingender, "Southwark," October 1930, in Borough background: Shoreditch to Willesden, New Survey of London, LSE, NSOL/1/8/4, 3–4.

78 Walk with Police Constable Sommersgill, District 32 (Trinity Newington and St Mary Bermondsey), May 25–26, 1899, Charles Booth Police Notebook, LSE, B364, 31.

79 Walk with Sommersgill, 19–21.

80 Thomas Burke, *City of Encounters: A London Divertissement* (London: Constable, 1932), 182. See also Cecil Chapman, *From the Bench* (London: Hodder & Stoughton, 1932), 44.

81 Hugh R. P. Gamon, *The London Police Court: To-day and To-morrow* (London: J. M. Dent, 1907), 104; Chapman, *From the Bench*, 34–35. As Sascha Auerbach argues, however, magistrates' intimate knowledge of their districts could be limited by their rapid turnover, responsibilities in other districts, and reliance on those enforcing the law: Auerbach, *Armed with Sword and Scales*, 336–38.

82 Lambeth Police Court (LPC) minute book, April 11, 1930, LMA, PS/LAM/B/01/092.

83 LPC minute book, April 21, 1930, LMA, PS/LAM/B/01/092; LPC minute book, March 26, 1930, LMA, PS/LAM/B/01/091. The case was heard at Lambeth Police Court on March 17 and 26 and April 3, 11, 15 and 21, 1930, and at Sessions House, Newington (the Court of Appeal under the Summary Jurisdiction Act, 1879) on May 30, 1930: LPC registers, LMA, PS/LAM/A/069–070.

84 Bone, *London Perambulator*, 143–45.

85 Charles Booth Police Notebook, 33. Author Arthur Morrison claimed that York Corner had already lost its status as "the chief hiring market in the 'show' business" by 1901, although this reputation evidently lingered decades after. Arthur Morrison, "Loafing London," in Sims, *Living London*, 1:357.

86 TBPC minute book, January 6, 1921, LMA, PS/TOW/B/01/087.

87 TBPC minute book, January 6, 1921.

88 Charles Booth Police Notebook, 37.

89 Walter Besant, *London: South of the Thames* (London: Black, 1912), 81.

90 TBPC minute book, February 1, 1921, LMA, PS/TOW/B/01/087.

91 TBPC minute book, February 8, 1921, PS/TOW/B/01/087; See also the case of Ellen Perrin and Janny Flack, arrested for harassing a drunk American soldier on York Road in December 1924 and referring to the barman of the Duke of York as an alibi: TBPC minute book, December 10, 1924, LMA, PS/TOW/B/01/139.

92 TBPC minute book, January 17, 1923, LMA, PS/TOW/B/01/115.

93 TBPC minute book, January 4, 1921, LMA, PS/TOW/B/01/087.

94 Besant, *London: South of the Thames*, 81; Walk with Sergeant Waters, May 1–2, 1899, Charles Booth Police Notebook, 55.

95 TBPC minute book, February 9, 1914, LMA, PS/TOW/B/01/001.

96 Besant, *London: South of the Thames*, 81.

97 Charles Booth Police Notebook, 29.

98 Edward D. Ward, "The Union Jack Club: What We Want," in *The Flag: The Book of the Union Jack Club*, ed. H. F. Trippel (London: Daily Mail, n.d., ca. 1908), 108–9; Houlbrook, *Queer London*, 121.

99 T. Burke, *London Spy*, 220–21.

100 TBPC minute book, January 4, 1921. See also cases of Alice Keen and Lottie Haynes on January 20, 1921, TBPC minute book, LMA, PS/TOW/B/01/087; and of Rose Rutter on December 17, 1918, TBPC minute book, LMA, PS/TOW/B/01/059.

101 E. Ward, "Union Jack Club," 108; Houlbrook, *Queer London*, 121.

102 TBPC minute book, January 17, 1927, LMA, PS/TOW/B/01/164.

103 Besant, *London: South of the Thames*, 81.

104 TBPC minute book, December 27 and 29, 1920, LMA, PS/TOW/B/01/088.

105 TBPC minute book, December 29, 1920.

106 TBPC register, December 27 and 29, 1920, LMA, PS/TOW/A/01/146.

107 Gamon, *London Police Court*, 151, 153.

108 Gamon, *London Police Court*, 89.

109 TBPC minute book, December 29, 1920.

110 TBPC minute book, December 29, 1920.

111 J. R. Roberts, ed., *Stone's Justices' Manual*, 52nd ed. (London: Butterworth, 1920).

112 On the complexities involved in the magistrate's "preliminary inquiry" of indictable offenses, see J. A. R. Cairns, *The Sidelights of London* (London: Hutchinson, 1923), 97–98.

113 Cairns, *Sidelights of London*, 110.

114 Henry Waddy Turner, *The Police Court and Its Work* (London: Butterworth, 1925), 60–61.

115 Evidence of previous offenses committed would usually be inadmissible until judgment had been reached and a sentence was to be decided upon. Turner, *Police Court*, 109, 111.

116 TBPC register, January 5, 1921, LMA, PS/TOW/A/01/145; Inner London Sessions Register, January 13, 1921, LMA, ILS/B/04/019.

117 Latour, *Making of Law*, ch. 2; Vismann, *Files*.

118 This argument differs from those that reduce "Law," assumed a priori, to its material

manifestations or "social" causes, as found in critical legal theory or legal realism. See Pottage, "Materiality of What?" 178–81; Ronald Dworkin, *Law's Empire* (Oxford: Hart, 1998), 12–14.

119 Gamon, *London Police Court*, 156–57, 90–91.

120 "The Night Patrol," loose insert in TBPC minute book, January 13, 1930, LMA, PS/TOW/B/01/198.

121 Charles Graves, "Flotsam and Jetsam of London: The Down-and-Outs—and their Rescuers," *Sphere*, January 2, 1932, 17.

122 Clodagh Anson, *Book: Discreet Memoirs* (London: Blackshaw, 1931), 306–16. For an account of the van and the microgeography of down-and-outs, see the memoirs of Dorothy Peto, the Superintendent responsible for Metropolitan policewomen beginning in April 1930: Dorothy Peto, *The Memoirs of Miss Dorothy Olivia Georgiana Peto* (Bramshill, UK: printed by the author, 1993), 64.

123 Minute by H. Martin, "Silver Lady" Coffee Stall: free food and clothing to vagrants, TNA, MEPO 3/2522, August 30, 1929.

124 Minute by A. C. L., TNA, MEPO 3/2522, October 26, 1929.

125 Minute by H. Martin, TNA, MEPO 3/2522, August 30, 1929.

126 Minute by H. Martin, TNA, MEPO 3/2522, November 24, 1931.

127 "Police Threat to Free-Meal Men," *Star*, 27 November 1931, n.p., TNA, MEPO 3/2522.

128 Letter from constituents to Sir Philip Cunliffe-Lister, November 27, 1931; "The Silver Lady (Miss Betty Baxter)," December 21, 1937, TNA, MEPO 3/2522.

129 E. Hanmore, *The Curse of the Embankment and the Cure* (Westminster: P. S. King & Son, 1935), 93.

130 Evidence of Harry Conniham and "The Night Patrol," TBPC minute book, January 13, 1930.

131 TBPC minute book, January 13, 1930.

132 Cairns, *Sidelights of London*, 108.

133 "Night Patrol," TBPC minute book.

134 Latour, *Making of Law*, 85. That is, a particular instance of a general case *in law* (such as indecency) rather than simply a case brought before a court.

135 Latour, *Making of Law*, 211–12.

136 Vismann, *Files*, xiii.

137 Houlbrook, "Songs of Seven Dials," in Houlbrook, email message to author.

138 Report of Cannon Row Police Station, "A" Division, September 12, 1929, TNA, MEPO 3/2522.

139 G. Bernard Shaw, "Mr. Shaw on Film Censorship," *Times*, February 17, 1930, n.p., LSE, 4NVA/4/01/11 Box FL098.

140 Betty Baxter, "Shadows of the Night," in *The Sunday at Home, 1929–30*, ed. George J. H. Northcroft (London: Religious Tract Society, 1930), 342. On the hostel, see Eileen Ascroft, "Stranded," *Daily Mirror*, September 12, 1938, 9.

141 Shaw, "Mr. Shaw on Film Censorship."

142 "Film Censorship," *Times*, February 22, 1930, n.p., 4NVA/4/01/11 Box FL098. See also "Censorship," *Evening Standard*, February 17, 1930, n.p., and "'Film Censorship Must Go,' says G. B. S.," *Evening Standard*, February 17, 1930, n.p., 4NVA/4/01/11 Box FL098. Also "The Banned Film," *Daily News*, February 18, 1930, 6.

143 "Mr G. B. Shaw on Film Censorship," V[igilance] R[ecord], March 1930, n.p., 4NVA/4/01/11 Box FL098.

144 236 Parl. Deb. H.C. (5th ser.) (1930) col. 1469.

145 "Censor Bans a Film the Police Helped to Make," Daily News, February 18, 1930, 9.

146 Latour, Making of Law, 211–12, 221–22.

147 Cairns, Sidelights of London, 100–102; Latour, Making of Law, 211–12.

148 Alfred Chichele Plowden, Grain or Chaff? The Autobiography of a Police Magistrate (London: T. Fisher Unwin, 1903), 283–84. This "judicial temper" contrasts with the tearful theatricality of mid-Victorian courtrooms, indicating a significant shift in emotional regimes. See Thomas Dixon, "The Tears of Mr Justice Willis," Journal of Victorian Culture 17, no. 1 (2012): 1–23.

149 Anson, Book, 326–27.

150 Clodagh Anson to the clerk of Tower Bridge Police Court, loose insert in TBPC minute book, January 13, 1930, LMA, PS/TOW/B/01/198.

151 "Night Patrol," TBPC minute book.

152 Anson, Book, 326–27. This was not the last time that Anson was deceived, whether for good or bad intentions, by the down-and-outs on whose behalf she intervened. "Viper Fable in Real Life: Man Who Defrauded Lady Clodagh Anson," Daily Mirror, October 25, 1932, 5.

153 TBPC register, January 13, 1930, LMA, PS/TOW/A/01/172.

154 Anson, Book, 326–27. This antipathy was likely the result of a recent public bruising Anson had received from Magistrate Oulton, of Marlborough Police Court, who criticized her for employing twenty-year-old Cyril Cronshaw to covertly verify the statements of unemployed patrons of the coffee van. "A Free Coffee Stall," Daily Mail, October 14, 1930, 7; Anson, Book, 324–25.

155 For a longue durée account of the segregation of court space and its relation to changing rules of evidence, legal procedures, and forms of social disciplining, see Linda Mulcahy, Legal Architecture: Justice, Due Process, and the Place of Law (London: Routledge, 2011), 51–56. On police court architecture, see Clare Graham, Ordering Law: The Architectural and Social History of the English Law Court to 1914 (Aldershot, UK: Ashgate, 2003), 177–95.

156 Gamon, London Police Court, 57. Designed by John Dixon Butler (1861–1920), Metropolitan Police architect and surveyor since 1895, Tower Bridge Police Court exemplified the "austere" interpretation of Free Classic architecture for which Butler became known. A. Stuart Gray, Edwardian Architecture: A Biographical Dictionary (London: Duckworth, 1985), 132. On Tower Bridge Police Court as spatializing "social distance" between magistrates and defendants, see Auerbach, Armed with Sword and Scales, 332.

157 Gamon, London Police Court, 57–64, 72–73; Turner, Police Court, 61, 203–4; "The Tower Bridge Police Court," The Builder, 88, no. 3242 (March 25, 1905): 331.

158 Physical distance also maintained the magistrate's authority during a period of the public's growing use of police courts: Auerbach, Armed with Sword and Scales, 332, 285.

159 Gamon, London Police Court, 57–64.

160 Gamon, London Police Court, 102; Plowden, Grain or Chaff? 246.

161 H. L. Cancellor, The Life of a London Beak (London: Hurst & Blackett, 1930), 14.

162 Gamon, London Police Court, 57–64.

163 Gamon, *London Police Court*, 106–7.

164 Gamon, *London Police Court*, 57–64.

165 Gamon, *London Police Court*, 106–7.

166 Gamon, *London Police Court*, 108–9.

167 Clodagh Anson, *Another Book* (privately published, 1937), 211; Cairns, *Sidelights of London*, 152. See reference to a "chitty" (a letter or note) sent as an affidavit for Evan Rowlands, charged, alongside Ernesto Randolfi, with indecency in Dulwich Park lavatories in October 1937. LPC minute book, November 1937, LMA, PS/LAM/B/01/284; LPC register, November 1937, PS/LAM/A/01/097.

168 Gamon, *London Police Court*, 70–71.

169 "Marylebone—Ventilation of the Court," *Daily Telegraph* (London), March 4, 1878, 2.

170 "The Weather," *Times*, February 9, 1878, 11; "The Weather," *Times*, February 11, 1878, 11; "The Weather," *Times*, February 12, 1878, 6.

171 238 Parl. Deb. (3d ser.) (1878) col. 973. This debate in the House of Commons took place on March 8, 1878.

172 238 Parl. Deb. (3d ser.) (1878) [no col.]. This debate in the House of Commons took place on March 11, 1878.

173 "Report of *The Lancet Special Commission* on the Ventilation of the Police-Courts," *Lancet* 111, no. 2846 (March 16, 1878): 399.

174 "Report of *Lancet Special Commission*," 400.

175 Graham, *Ordering Law*, 193–94. The classic statement on this is Corbin, *Foul and Fragrant*.

176 "Report of *Lancet Special Commission*," 400.

177 "Report of *Lancet Special Commission*," 400.

178 Cairns, *Sidelights of London*, 101.

179 "Hygiene and the Metropolitan Police Courts," *Lancet* 165, no. 4250 (February 11, 1905): 378; Graham, *Ordering Law*, 194.

180 "Hygiene and the Metropolitan Police Courts," *Lancet*, 165, no. 4256 (March 25, 1905): 811.

181 "Street Offences and Police Evidence," *Law Journal* 64 (October 1, 1927): 206; "The Police Courts and the Public," *Law Times* 164, no. 4409 (October 1, 1927): 225; "Police Courts and the Public," *Law Times* 165, no. 4444 (June 2, 1928): 469. For more on the effect Champain's acquittal had on police procedure, see Houlbrook, *Queer London*, 28–29, 31–32, 208–9.

182 "Street Offences and Police Evidence," 206.

183 "The Police and the Public," *Spectator* (London), October 8, 1927, 533.

184 Report of the Street Offences Committee, 1928, Cmd. 3231.

185 "Police Courts and the Public" (1927), 225.

186 "Metropolitan Police Courts," *Law Times* 165, no. 4424 (January 14, 1928): 27.

187 "Metropolitan Police Courts," *Law Times* 165, no. 4435 (March 14, 1928): 276; Report of the Committee on Metropolitan Police Courts and Juvenile Courts, 1929, LMA, LCC/CH/D/04/003, 3, 5–6.

188 "'Scullions of the Judiciary,'" *Daily Mail*, June 12, 1928, 7.

189 "Mr J. A. R. Cairns," *Daily Mail*, July 12, 1928, 9.

190 "Mr Clarke Hall," *Daily Mail*, July 25, 1928, 9.

191 J. Hasloch Potter, *Inasmuch: The Story of the Police Court Mission, 1876–1926* (London: Williams & Norgate, 1927), 24–25.

192 Metropolitan Police Courts and Juvenile Courts Committee (MPCJCC), TNA, HO 73/120, 6, 14.

193 Report of the Committee on Metropolitan Police Courts and Juvenile Courts, 4.

194 MPCJCC, TNA, HO 73/120, 8.

195 MPCJCC, TNA, HO 73/120, 1.

196 MPCJCC, TNA, HO 73/120, 20.

197 MPCJCC, TNA, HO 73/120, 5.

198 Extracts from minutes of proceedings of the London County Council on July 3, 1923, LMA, LCC/PC/GEN/01/016, 5–6.

199 These provisions were "consolidated" through the Public Health (London) Act (1936). W. R. Hornby Steer, *The Law of Smoke Nuisances*, 2nd ed. (London: National Smoke Abatement Society, 1948), WL, SA/EPU/H/4/1, 12, 14, 30–32.

200 Robert Sinclair, *Metropolitan Man: The Future of the English* (London: G. Allen & Unwin, 1937), 181.

201 Michael John Law, *The Experience of Suburban Modernity: How Private Transport Changed Interwar London* (Manchester: Manchester University Press, 2014), 23.

202 MPCJCC, TNA, HO 73/120, 12, 30–31.

203 Report of the Departmental Committee on the Treatment of Young Offenders, 1927, Cmd. 2831, 11, 27, 36; L. Jackson, *Women Police*, 140–45; Houlbrook, *Queer London*, 232–36.

204 Report of the Committee on Metropolitan Police Courts and Juvenile Courts, 10–11.

205 Solicitor [pseud.], *English Justice* (London: G. Routledge & Sons, 1932), 239, 248. On the increasing disconnect between police courts and working-class petitioners in the 1930s, see Auerbach, *Armed with Sword and Scales*, 26, 41.

206 Solicitor, *English Justice*, 247.

207 Solicitor, *English Justice*, 246.

208 R. Sinclair, *Metropolitan Man*, 146–47.

209 Report of the Departmental Committee on Courts of Summary Jurisdiction in the Metropolitan Area, 1937, LMA, PS/LAM/H/013, 11.

210 Report of the Departmental Committee, 12.

211 Report of the Departmental Committee, 35; Cecil Chapman, *The Poor Man's Court of Justice: Twenty-Five Years as a Metropolitan Magistrate* (London: Hodder & Stoughton, 1925), 180–81.

212 This argument draws on Lakoff and Johnson's productive claim that "*no metaphor can ever be comprehended or even adequately represented independently of its experiential basis*": George Lakoff and Mark Johnson, *Metaphors We Live By* (Chicago: University of Chicago Press, 2003), 19.

213 Gerald J. Postema, *Legal Philosophy in the Twentieth Century: The Common Law World; A Treatise of Legal Philosophy and General Jurisprudence*, ed. Enrico Pattaro (Dordrecht, Neth.: Springer, 2011), 31–32.

214 Postema, *Legal Philosophy*, 18–19.

215 See Dworkin, *Law's Empire*, 6.

216 Latour, *Making of Law*, 191.

217 Pottage, "Law After Anthropology," 154–55.

218 Report of the Royal Commission on Police Powers and Procedure, 1929, Cmd. 3297, 103.

219 Yan Thomas on the "property of law," cited in Pottage, "Law After Anthropology," 154.

220 My thinking here has been much shaped by the discussion of *dispositifs* in Pottage, "Materiality of What?" 180–82; see also Giorgio Agamben, "What Is an Apparatus?" in *"What Is an Apparatus?" and Other Essays*, trans. David Kishik and Stefan Pedatella (Stanford, CA: Stanford University Press, 2009), 2–12.

EPILOGUE

1 Varela, Thompson, and Rosch, *Embodied Mind*, 135.

2 Gallagher, *Enactivist Interventions*, 6.

3 For a recent example, see Sushma Subramanian, *How to Feel: The Science and Meaning of Touch* (New York: Columbia University Press, 2021), 16–21.

4 Thank you to Santanu Das for pointing me toward Lawrence's thoroughly fleshy poems. See also Santanu Das, "D. H. Lawrence's Sense-Words," *Essays in Criticism* 62, no. 1 (January 2012): 58–82.

5 Lawrence, "Noli Me Tangere," in *Complete Poems*, 468–69.

6 D. H. Lawrence, "Touch," in *Complete Poems*, 468.

7 D. H. Lawrence, "Touch Comes," in *Complete Poems*, 470–71.

8 The distinct depictions of touch and change in these three poems were not absolute: the third continues an idea of linear, if utopian, sensory development in its title's anticipation of a more tactile future—"Touch Comes"—and repeats the division between a waking mind and preconscious touch. But the poems nevertheless offer competing ideas of touch that both set the terms for the opposition between touch and mind in "modernity" and offer a way of thinking outside these terms.

9 Jacques Derrida, *On Touching—Jean-Luc Nancy*, trans. Christine Irizarry (Stanford, CA: Stanford University Press, 2005), 93.

10 Merleau-Ponty understood this existential unity in terms of an underlying "flesh" of the world in which all perceivers and things perceived participate. It is this shared condition of existence that allows things to be perceived, provisionally, as it were, as distinct from one another and from the person perceiving. Merleau-Ponty, "Intertwining," 130–40.

11 Didier Anzieu, *The Skin Ego*, trans. Chris Turner (New Haven, CT: Yale University Press, 1989), 62–63.

12 Luce Irigaray, *Elemental Passions*, trans. Joanne Collie and Judith Still (London: Athlone, 1992), 17.

13 "Yesterday's Law, Police, etc.," *Reynolds's Newspaper*, September 23, 1888, 8.

14 J. A. Charlton Deas, "What the Blind May 'See': Some Museum and Other Experiments in Tactile Sight," unpublished manuscript, June 26, 1929, TWAM, TWCMS: 2006.7988, 1–2.

15 Deas, "What the Blind May 'See,'" 6–7.

16 Deas, "What the Blind May 'See,'" 8–11.

17 Deas, "What the Blind May 'See,'" 22–23.

18 Deas, "What the Blind May 'See,'" 21.

19 Deas, "What the Blind May 'See,'" 20–25.

20 G. I. Walker to J. A. Charlton Deas, cited in J. A. Charlton Deas, "The Showing of Museums and Art Galleries to the Blind," *Museums Journal* 13, no. 3 (September 1913): 94.

21 Deas, "What the Blind May 'See,'" 7.

22 Walker to Deas, in Deas, "Showing of Museums," 93–94.

23 Walker to Deas, in Deas, "Showing of Museums," 94.

24 Walker to Deas, in Deas, "Showing of Museums," 94.

25 Deas, "Showing of Museums," 87.

26 Deas, "What the Blind May 'See,'" 3–4.

27 Deas, "What the Blind May 'See,'" 12.

28 Deas, "What the Blind May 'See,'" 12.

29 "Models on Display," TWAM, TWCMS: K13565.

30 Walker to Deas, in Deas, "What the Blind May 'See,'" 15.

31 Rembis, "Challenging the Impairment/Disability Divide," 377.

32 Tanya Titchkosky and Rod Michalko, "The Body as the Problem of Individuality: A Phenomenological Disability Studies Approach," in *Disability and Social Theory: New Developments and Directions*, ed. Dan Goodley, Bill Hughes, and Lennard Davis (Basingstoke, UK: Palgrave Macmillan, 2012), 128–29.

33 Dan Goodley et al., "Key Concerns for Critical Disability Studies," *International Journal of Disability and Social Justice* 1, no. 1 (November 2021): 40–41; Malafouris, *How Things Shape the Mind*, 9.

34 Gilson, "Vulnerability and Victimization," 74.

35 Danielle Petherbridge, "How Do We Respond? Embodied Vulnerability and Forms of Responsiveness," in *New Feminist Perspectives on Embodiment*, ed. Clara Fischer and Luna Dolezal (Basingstoke, UK: Palgrave Macmillan, 2018), 73.

36 Gilson, "Vulnerability and Victimization," 75–77.

37 Transport for London, "New Campaign Launches to Stamp Out Sexual Harassment on Public Transport," press release, October 27, 2021, https://tfl.gov.uk/info-for/media/press-releases/2021/october/new-campaign-launches-to-stamp-out-sexual-harassment-on-public-transport.

38 "Staring at Tube Passengers Could Earn Conviction for Harassment," *Daily Telegraph*, March 11, 2022, 15.

39 "Great Eastern Railway Company's New Station at Liverpool Street," *Engineer*, June 11, 1875, 403.

40 For a comparable trend at Heathrow Airport's Terminal 3, renovated over the same years as Liverpool Street Station, see James Vernon, "Heathrow and the Making of Neoliberal Britain," *Past and Present* 252 (August 2021): 225–26.

41 Transport for London, "Step-Free Access," accessed September 17, 2023, https://tfl.gov.uk/travel-information/improvements-and-projects/step-free-access.

42 City of London, *Bishopsgate Conservation Area: Character Summary and Management Strategy SPD*, September 2014, 17, https://www.cityoflondon.gov.uk/assets/Services-Environment/bishopsgate-conservation-area-character-summary-management-strategy.pdf.

Select Bibliography

The following is a selection of the archival materials and published sources that have been most important to me; for further details of manuscript and periodical sources, see the notes.

ARCHIVES

BBC Written Archives, Caversham
British Library, London
British Library of Political and Economic Science, London
Cadbury Research Library Special Collections, Birmingham
Education Library, University of Birmingham
Lambeth Palace Library, London
Library of Experimental Psychology, Cambridge
London Metropolitan Archives, London
London Transport Museum Archives and Depot, London
The National Archives, London
New College Worcester, Worcester
Norwich Record Office, Norwich
Royal London Hospital Archives, London
Royal National Institute of Blind People, London
Transport for London Archives, London
Tyne & Wear Archives and Museums, Newcastle-upon-Tyne
Wellcome Library, London
Whipple Museum of the History of Science, Cambridge
Wolfson Centre for Archival Research, Birmingham

NEWSPAPERS AND OTHER PERIODICALS

Advertiser (Adelaide)
Age (London)

Daily Express (London)
Daily Mail (London)
Daily Mirror (London)
Daily News (London)
Daily Telegraph (London)
Era (London)
Evening Mail (London)
Girl's Own Paper (London)
Globe (London)
Hackney and Kingsland Gazette (London)
Hearth and Home (London)
Illustrated London News (London)
John Bull (London)
Leader (Melbourne)
Lloyd's Illustrated Newspaper (London)
Lloyd's Weekly Newspaper (London)
London Evening Standard
London Journal
Manchester Guardian
Morning Post (London)
Pall Mall Gazette (London)
Pick-Me-Up (London)
Portsmouth Evening News
Quiver (London)
Review of Reviews (London)
Reynolds's Newspaper (London)
Spectator (London)
Sphere (London)
Standard (London)
Star (London)
Sunderland Daily Echo and Shipping Gazette
Sydney Morning Herald
Sydney Wool and Stock Journal
The Times (London)
The Times Literary Supplement (London)
Westminster Gazette (London)
The Woman at Home (London)
Woman's Herald (London)
York Herald
Yorkshire Post & Leeds Intelligencer (Leeds)

BOOKS, JOURNALS, AND OTHER PUBLISHED SOURCES

Abernethy, Simon. "Moving Wartime London: Public Transport in the First World War."
   London Journal 41, no. 3 (2016): 233–48.

Adcock, Arthur St. John. *London from the Top of a Bus*. London: Hodder & Stoughton, 1906.

Adrian, E. D. "The Activity of the Nerve Fibres: Nobel Lecture, December 12, 1932." In Nobelstiftelsen, *Nobel Lectures: Physiology or Medicine, 1922–1941*, 293–300. Amsterdam: Elsevier, 1965. First published 1932.

Agamben, Giorgio. *Homo Sacer: Sovereign Power and Bare Life*. Translated by Daniel Heller-Roazen. Stanford, CA: Stanford University Press, 1998.

Agamben, Giorgio. "On Potentiality." In *Potentialities: Collected Essays in Philosophy*. Edited and translated by Daniel Heller-Roazen, 177–84. Stanford, CA: Stanford University Press, 1999.

Agamben, Giorgio. *The Use of Bodies*. Translated by Adam Kotsko. Stanford, CA: Stanford University Press, 2016.

Agamben, Giorgio. "What Is an Apparatus?" In *"What Is an Apparatus?" and Other Essays*, translated by David Kishik and Stefan Pedatella, 1–24. Stanford, CA: Stanford University Press, 2009.

Ahmed, Sara. *Queer Phenomenology: Orientations, Objects, Others*. Durham, NC: Duke University Press, 2006.

Ahmed, Sara, and Jackie Stacey. "Introduction: Dermographies." In *Thinking Through the Skin*, edited by Sara Ahmed and Jackie Stacey, 1–19. London: Routledge, 2001.

Alcoff, Linda Martín. *Visible Identities: Race, Gender, and the Self*. Oxford: Oxford University Press, 2006.

Allen, Mary S. *Lady in Blue*. London: Stanley Paul, 1936.

Anderson, Julie. *War, Disability, and Rehabilitation in Britain: "Soul of a Nation."* Manchester: Manchester University Press, 2011.

Anson, Clodagh. *Another Book*. Privately published, 1937.

Anson, Clodagh. *Book: Discreet Memoirs*. London: Blackshaw, 1931.

Anzieu, Didier. *The Skin Ego*. Translated by Chris Turner. New Haven, CT: Yale University Press, 1989.

Armitage, Thomas. *The Education and Employment of the Blind: What It Has Been, Is, and Ought to Be*. London: Harrison & Sons, 1871.

Ashford, David. *London Underground: A Cultural Geography*. Liverpool: Liverpool University Press, 2013.

Asquith, Anthony, dir. *Underground*. British Instructional Films, 1928. New York: Kino Lorber, 2019. DVD or Blu-Ray, 83 min.

Assael, Brenda. *The London Restaurant, 1840–1914*. Oxford: Oxford University Press, 2018.

Auerbach, Sascha. *Armed with Sword and Scales: Law, Culture, and Local Courtrooms in London, 1860–1913*. Cambridge: Cambridge University Press, 2021.

Baedeker, Karl. *London and Its Environs: Handbook for Travellers*. 14th ed. Leipzig: Baedeker, 1905.

Bailey, Peter. "Adventures in Space: Victorian Railway Erotics, or Taking Alienation for a Ride." *Journal of Victorian Culture* 9, no. 1 (2004): 1–21.

Bailey, Peter. "Parasexuality and Glamour: The Victorian Barmaid as Cultural Prototype." *Gender & History* 2, no. 2 (Summer 1990): 148–72.

Bailey, Peter. *Popular Culture and Performance in the Victorian City*. Cambridge: Cambridge University Press, 1998.

Barad, Karen. *Meeting the Universe Halfway: Quantum Physics and the Entanglement of Matter and Meaning.* Durham, NC: Duke University Press, 2007.

Barad, Karen. "On Touching—The Inhuman That Therefore I Am." *differences* 23, no. 3 (2012): 206–23.

Barclay, J. *In Good Hands: The History of the Chartered Society of Physiotherapy, 1894–1994.* Oxford: Butterworth Heinemann, 1994.

Barker, T. C., and Michael Robbins. *A History of London Transport: Passenger Travel and the Development of the Metropolis.* 2 vols. London: Allen & Unwin, 1974.

Barnes, Colin. "Understanding the Social Model of Disability." In *Routledge Handbook of Disability Studies,* edited by Nick Watson, Alan Roulstone, and Carol Thomas, 12–29. London: Routledge, 2012.

Barrow, Robin J. "Rape on the Railway: Women, Safety, and Moral Panic in Victorian Newspapers." *Journal of Victorian Culture* 20, no. 3 (September 2015): 341–56.

Barthes, Roland. *A Lover's Discourse: Fragments.* Translated by Richard Howard. London: Vintage, 2002.

Baxter, Betty. "Shadows of the Night." In *The Sunday at Home, 1929–30,* edited by George J. H. Northcroft, 341–42. London: Religious Tract Society, 1930.

Beecher, Ruth, and Stephanie Wright. "Historicising the Perpetrators of Sexual Violence: Global Perspectives from the Modern World." *Women's History Review,* April 19, 2023. https://doi.org/10.1080/09612025.2023.2197790.

Behal, Rana Pratap. "Forms of Labour Protest in Assam Valley Tea Plantations, 1900–1930." *Economic and Political Weekly* 20, no. 4 (January 1985): PE19–26.

Behal, Rana Pratap. *One Hundred Years of Servitude: Political Economy of Tea Plantations in Colonial Assam.* New Delhi: Tulika Books, 2014.

Benjamin, Walter. *The Arcades Project.* Edited by Rolf Tiedemann. Translated by Howard Eiland and Kevin McLaughlin. Cambridge, MA: Belknap Press of Harvard University Press, 2002.

Benjamin, Walter. "Paris, the Capital of the Nineteenth Century." In *Walter Benjamin: Selected Writings,* vol. 3, edited by Howard Eiland and Michael W. Jennings, translated by Edmund Jephcott, 32–49. Cambridge, MA: Belknap Press of Harvard University Press, 2002. First published 1935.

Bennett, Tony. "Habit, Instinct, Survivals: Repetition, History, Biopower." In Vernon and Gunn, *Peculiarities of Liberal Modernity in Imperial Britain,* 102–18.

Bergwik, Staffan. "An Assemblage of Science and Home: The Gendered Lifestyle of Svante Arrhenius and Early Twentieth-Century Physical Chemistry." *Isis* 105 (2014): 265–91.

Berlant, Lauren. *Desire/Love.* New York: Punctum Books, 2012.

Besant, Walter. *London City.* London: A. & C. Black, 1910.

Besant, Walter. *London: South of the Thames.* London: Black, 1912.

Biddlecombe, C. H. "London Fogs from Above." *Meteorological Magazine* 59, no. 708 (January 1925): 277–80.

Bird, Peter. *The First Food Empire: A History of J. Lyons & Co.* Chichester, UK: Phillimore, 2000.

Bishop, George Holman. "Neural Mechanisms of Cutaneous Sense." *Physiological Reviews* 26, no. 1 (January 1946): 77–102.

Black, Clementina. *Sweated Industry and the Minimum Wage.* London: Duckworth, 1907.

Bone, James. *The London Perambulator.* London: Jonathan Cape, 1925.

Booth, Charles, ed. *Life and Labour of the People in London*, 1st Series. Vol. 3, *Poverty: Blocks of Buildings, Schools, and Immigration*. London: Macmillan, 1902.

Booth, Charles, ed. *Life and Labour of the People in London*, 2nd Series. Vol. 4, *Industry: Public, Professional and Domestic Service, Unoccupied Classes, Inmates of Institutions*. London: Macmillan, 1903.

Booth, Charles, and Jesse Argyle, "Household Service, &c.," in Booth, *Life and Labour of the People*, vol. 4, *Industry*, 211–51.

Boring, Edwin G. *Sensation and Perception in the History of Experimental Psychology*. New York: D. Appleton-Century, 1942.

Bourdieu, Pierre. *Distinction: A Social Critique of the Judgement of Taste*. Translated by Richard Nice. London: Routledge, 2010. First published 1981.

Bourke, Joanna. *Disgrace: Global Reflections on Sexual Violence*. London: Reaktion, 2022.

Boutin, Aimée. *City of Noise: Sound and Nineteenth-Century Paris*. Urbana: University of Illinois Press, 2015.

Brain, Walter R., and Eric B. Strauss. *Recent Advances in Neurology*. London: J. & A. Churchill, 1929.

Brand, Christianna. *London Particular*. London: Michael Joseph, 1952.

Braverman, Irus, Nicholas Blomley, David Delaney, and Alexandre Kedar. "Introduction: Expanding the Spaces of Law." In *The Expanding Spaces of Law: A Timely Legal Geography*, edited by Irus Braverman, Nicholas Blomley, David Delaney, and Alexandre Kedar, 1–30. Stanford, CA: Stanford University Press, 2014.

Brigham, John. *Material Law: A Jurisprudence of What's Real*. Philadelphia: Temple University Press, 2009.

Broad, W. H. "The Blinded Soldier as a Masseur." *Beacon* 4, no. 37 (January 1920): 10–11.

Brodie, Frederick J. "Decrease of Fog in London during Recent Years." *Quarterly Journal of the Royal Meteorological Society* 31, no. 133 (January 1905): 15–28.

Brodie, Frederick J. "On the Prevalence of Fog in London during the 20 Years 1871 to 1890." *Quarterly Journal of the Royal Meteorological Society* 18, no. 81 (January 1892): 40–45.

Brodie, Frederick J. "Some Remarkable Features in the Winter of 1890–91." *Quarterly Journal of the Royal Meteorological Society* 17, no. 79 (July 1891): 155–67.

Bruce, Graeme J. *The London Underground Tube Stock*. Surrey: Ian Allen, 1988.

Burke, A. "Games as a Regular Part of the Equipment of the Classroom." *Teacher of the Blind* 20, no. 2 (November 1931): 45–51.

Burke, Thomas. *City of Encounters: A London Divertissement*. London: Constable, 1932.

Burke, Thomas. *The London Spy*. London: Thornton Butterworth, 1922.

Burke, Thomas. *Out and About: A Note-book of London in War-time*. London: Allen & Unwin, 1919.

Butler, Judith. *Precarious Life: The Powers of Mourning and Violence*. London: Verso, 2004.

Butler, Judith. *Senses of the Subject*. New York: Fordham University Press, 2015.

Butler, Judith, Zeynep Gambetti, and Leticia Sabsay, eds. *Vulnerability in Resistance*. Durham, NC: Duke University Press, 2016.

Caeton, D. A. "Blindness." In *Keywords for Disability Studies*, edited by Rachel Adams, Benjamin Reiss, and David Serlin, 34–37. New York: NYU Press, 2015.

Cahill, Ann. *Overcoming Objectification: A Carnal Ethics*. New York: Routledge, 2011.

Cairns, J. A. R. *The Sidelights of London*. London: Hutchinson, 1923.

Campbell, G. M. "Physical Training of the Blind." *Teacher of the Blind* 3, no. 1 (January 1915): 20–21.

Cancellor, H. L. *The Life of a London Beak.* London: Hurst & Blackett, 1930.

Cantlie, James. *Physical Efficiency: A Review of the Deleterious Effects of Town Life upon the Population of Britain, with Suggestions for their Arrest.* London: G. P. Putnam's Sons, 1906.

Carr, Harvey. "Head's Theory of Cutaneous Sensibility." *Psychological Review* 23, no. 4 (July 1916): 262–78.

Casper, Stephen T. *The Neurologists: A History of a Medical Speciality in Modern Britain, c. 1789–2000.* Manchester: Manchester University Press, 2014.

Chapman, Cecil. *From the Bench.* London: Hodder & Stoughton, 1932.

Chapman, Cecil. *The Poor Man's Court of Justice: Twenty-Five Years as a Metropolitan Magistrate.* London: Hodder & Stoughton, 1925.

Cherniavsky, Eva. "#MeToo." *differences* 30, no. 1 (2019): 15–23.

Chevigny, Hector. *My Eyes Have a Cold Nose.* London: Michael Joseph, 1947.

Chiang, Yee. *The Silent Traveller in London.* London: Country Life, 1938.

Classen, Constance, ed. *A Cultural History of the Senses in the Age of Empire.* London: Bloomsbury, 2014.

Classen, Constance. *The Deepest Sense: A Cultural History of Touch.* Urbana: University of Illinois Press, 2012.

Clifford, W. G. *The Ex-Soldier: By Himself.* London: A. & C. Black, 1916.

Clinch, Herbert G. *The Smoke Inspector's Handbook: Or, Economic Smoke Abatement.* London: H. K. Lewis, 1923.

Clunn, Harold. *The Face of London: The Record of a Century's Changes and Development.* 7th ed. London: Simpkin Marshall, 1937.

Coen, Deborah R. "The Common World: Histories of Science and Domestic Intimacy." *Modern Intellectual History* 11, no. 2 (2014): 417–38.

Coen, Deborah R. *Vienna in the Age of Uncertainty: Science, Liberalism, and Private Life.* Chicago: University of Chicago Press, 2007.

Cohen, Deborah. *Household Gods: The British and Their Possessions.* New Haven, CT: Yale University Press, 2006.

Cohen, Deborah. *The War Come Home: Disabled Veterans in Britain and Germany, 1914–1939.* Berkeley: University of California Press, 2001.

Cohen, Julius B., and Arthur G. Ruston. *Smoke: A Study of Town Air.* London: Edward Arnold, 1912.

Cohen-Portheim, Paul. *The Spirit of London.* London: B. T. Batsford, 1935.

College of Teachers of the Blind. *The Education of the Blind: A Survey.* London: Edward Arnold, 1936.

College of Teachers of the Blind. *Handbook for School Teachers of the Blind.* Bristol, UK: College of Teachers of the Blind, 1956.

Connor, Steven. *The Matter of Air: Science and the Art of the Ethereal.* London: Reaktion, 2010.

Corbin, Alain. *The Foul and the Fragrant: Odor and the French Social Imagination.* Translated by Miriam L. Kochan, Roy Porter, and Christopher Prendergast. Cambridge, MA: Harvard University Press, 1986.

Corbin, Alain. *Time, Desire, and Horror: Towards a History of the Senses.* Translated by Jean Birrell. Cambridge: Polity, 1995.

Corbin, Alain. "Urban Sensations: The Shifting Sensescape of the City." In Classen, *Cultural History of the Senses*, 47–67.

Corton, Christine. *London Fog: The Biography*. Cambridge, MA: Belknap Press of Harvard University Press, 2015.

Couser, G. Thomas. *Recovering Bodies: Illness, Disability, and Life-Writing*. Madison: University of Wisconsin Press, 1997.

Crook, Tom. *Governing Systems: Modernity and the Making of Public Health in England, 1830–1910*. Oakland: University of California Press, 2016.

Crook, Tom. "Secrecy and Liberal Modernity in Victorian and Edwardian England." In Vernon and Gunn, *Peculiarities of Liberal Modernity*, 72–90.

Danziger, Kurt. *Constructing the Subject: Historical Origins of Psychological Research*. Cambridge: Cambridge University Press, 1990.

Dark, Sidney. *The Life of Sir Arthur Pearson*. London: Hodder & Stoughton, 1922.

Das, Santanu. "D. H. Lawrence's Sense-Words." *Essays in Criticism* 62, no. 1 (January 2012): 58–82.

Das, Santanu. *Touch and Intimacy in First World War Literature*. Cambridge: Cambridge University Press, 2005.

Daston, Lorraine, and Peter Galison. *Objectivity*. 2nd ed. New York: Zone, 2010.

Davidson, M. "Physical Training for the Blind." Letter to the editor. *Teacher of the Blind* 9, no. 1 (May 1921): 15–19.

Davin, Anna. "City Girls: Young Women, New Employment, and the City, London, 1880–1910." In *Secret Gardens, Satanic Mills: Placing Girls in European History, 1750–1960*, edited by Mary Jo Maynes, Birgitte Søland, and Christina Benninghaus, 209–23. Bloomington: Indiana University Press, 2005.

"A Day in the Life of a Nippy." *Picture Post* 2, no. 9 (March 4, 1939): 29–34.

D'Cruze, Shani. *Crimes of Outrage: Sex, Violence, and Victorian Working Women*. London: UCL Press, 1998.

Delaney, David. *The Spatial, the Legal and the Pragmatics of World-Making: Nomospheric Investigations*. London: Routledge, 2010.

Delap, Lucy. *Knowing Their Place: Domestic Service in Twentieth-Century Britain*. Oxford: Oxford University Press, 2011.

Dennis, Richard. "The Architecture of Hurry." In *Cityscapes in History: Creating the Urban Experience*, edited by Katrina Gulliver and Heléna Tóth, 115–35. Farnham, UK: Ashgate, 2014.

Dennis, Richard. *Cities in Modernity: Representations and Productions of Metropolitan Space, 1840–1930*. Cambridge: Cambridge University Press, 2008.

Dennis, Richard. "Making the Underground Underground." *London Journal* 38, no. 3 (November 2013): 203–25.

Dennis, Richard, Phillip Gordon Mackintosh, and Deryck W. Holdsworth, "Architectures of Hurry: An Introductory Essay." In *Architectures of Hurry: Mobilities, Cities, and Modernity*, edited by Richard Dennis, Phillip Gordon Mackintosh, and Deryck W. Holdsworth. London: Routledge, 2018.

Derrida, Jacques. *Copy, Archive, Signature: A Conversation on Photography*. Translated by J. Fort. Stanford, CA: Stanford University Press, 2010.

Derrida, Jacques. *Of Grammatology*. Translated by Gayatri Chakravorty Spivak. Baltimore: Johns Hopkins University Press, 1976.

Derrida, Jacques. *On Touching—Jean-Luc Nancy*. Translated by Christine Irizarry. Stanford, CA: Stanford University Press, 2005.

Dixon, Thomas. "The Tears of Mr Justice Willis." *Journal of Victorian Culture* 17, no.1 (2012): 1–23.

Doan, Laura. *Disturbing Practices: History, Sexuality, and Women's Experience of Modern War*. Chicago: University of Chicago Press, 2013.

Dworkin, Ronald. *Law's Empire*. Oxford: Hart, 1998.

Deas, J. A. Charlton. "The Showing of Museums and Art Galleries to the Blind." *Museums Journal* 13, no. 3 (September 1913): 85–108.

The Descriptive Album of London: A Pictorial Guide Book. London: Descriptive Album Publishing Co., 1896.

Desmond, Shaw. *London Nights of Long Ago*. London: Duckworth, 1927.

Douglas, C. K. M., and K. H. Stewart. "London Fog of December 5–8, 1952." *Meteorological Magazine* 82, no. 969 (March 1953): 67–71.

Douglas, Robin. *Well, Let's Eat*. London: Cassell, 1933.

Drake, Barbara. "The Tea-Shop Girl, being a Report of an Enquiry Undertaken by the Investigation Committee of the Women's Industrial Council." *Women's Industrial News* 17, no. 61 (April 1913): 115–29.

Drake, Barbara. "The Waiter." In *Seasonal Trades: By Various Writers*, edited by Sidney Webb and Arnold Freeman, 92–105. London: Constable, 1912.

Drake, Barbara. *Women in Trade Unions*. London: Labour Research Department, 1920.

Earle, F. M. "Principles Underlying the Teaching of Blind Children." *Teacher of the Blind* 15, no. 4 (June 1927): 105–11.

Earle, F. M. "Principles Underlying the Teaching of Blind Children." *Teacher of the Blind* 16, no. 1 (September 1927): 4–9.

Eckermann, Johann. *Conversations of Goethe with Eckermann*. Translated by John Oxenford. London: J. M. Dent & Sons, 1930.

Edelman, Lee. *No Future: Queer Theory and the Death Drive*. Durham, NC: Duke University Press, 2004.

Edensor, Tim. "The Social Life of the Senses: Ordering and Disordering the Modern Sensorium." In *A Cultural History of the Senses in the Modern Age*, edited by David Howes, 31–54. London: Bloomsbury, 2014.

Elden, Stuart. *Foucault's Last Decade*. Cambridge: Polity, 2016.

Ellis, Havelock. *Studies in the Psychology of Sex*. Vol. 4, *Sexual Selection in Man*. Philadelphia: F. A. Davis, 1905.

"The Enlargement of Liverpool-Street Station, Great Eastern Railway: No. 1." *Engineer*, June 8, 1894, 493–94.

"Eurhythmics for the Blind." *Beacon* 7, no. 77 (May 1923): 11–12.

Evans, E. "Physical Activity Exercises for the Blind." *Teacher of the Blind* 8, no. 4 (February 1921): 81–83.

Evans-Gordon, William E. *The Alien Immigrant*. London: Heinemann, 1903.

F., J. *The Law of Compensation: Blind, but Self-Reliant*. London: printed by the author, 1904.

Flack, Martin, and Leonard Hill. *A Textbook of Physiology*. London: Edward Arnold, 1919.

Flint, Kate. "The Social Life of the Senses: The Assaults and Seductions of Modernity." In Classen, *Cultural History of the Senses*, 25–45.

Flint, Kate. "Sounds of the City: Virginia Woolf and Modern Noise." In *Literature, Science, Psychoanalysis, 1830–1970: Essays in Honour of Gillian Beer*, edited by Helen Small and Trudi Tate, 184–94. Oxford: Oxford University Press, 2003.

Flint, Kate. *The Victorians and the Visual Imagination*. Cambridge: Cambridge University Press, 2000.

"'Fogged.'" *St Dunstan's Review*, 2, no. 20 (March 1918): 26.

Foucault, Michel. *The Courage of Truth: The Government of Self and Others II: Lectures at the Collège de France, 1983–1984*. Edited by Frédéric Gros. Translated by Graham Burchell. New York: Palgrave Macmillan, 2012.

Foucault, Michel. *The Hermeneutics of the Subject: Lectures at the Collège de France, 1981–1982*. Edited by Frédéric Gros. Translated by Graham Burchell. New York: Palgrave Macmillan, 2005.

Freeman, Elizabeth. *Beside You in Time: Sense Methods & Queer Sociabilities in the American 19th Century*. Durham, NC: Duke University Press, 2019.

Freeman, R. Austin. "Afflicted London." In Sims, *Living London*, 3:28–31.

Fretwell, Erica. *Sensory Experiments: Psychophysics, Race, and the Aesthetics of Feeling*. Durham, NC: Duke University Press, 2020.

Galison, Peter. *Image and Logic: A Material Culture of Microphysics*. Chicago: University of Chicago Press, 1997.

Gallagher, Shaun. *Enactivist Interventions: Rethinking the Mind*. Oxford: Oxford University Press, 2017.

Gallagher, Shaun, and Dan Zahavi. *The Phenomenological Mind*. 3rd ed. London: Routledge, 2020.

Galton, Francis. *Inquiries into Human Faculty and Its Development*. 2nd ed. London: Dent, 1907.

Gamon, Hugh R. P. *The London Police Court: To-day and To-morrow*. London: J. M. Dent, 1907.

Garland-Thompson, Rosemarie. "Misfits: A Feminist Materialist Disability Concept." *Hypatia* 26, no. 3 (Summer 2011): 591–609.

Garrington, Abbie. *Haptic Modernism: Touch and the Tactile in Modernist Writing*. Edinburgh: University of Edinburgh Press, 2013.

Gibson, James J. "The Theory of Affordances." In *The Ecological Approach to Visual Perception*, 119–35. Dallas: Houghton Mifflin, 1979.

Gilson, Erinn. "Vulnerability and Victimization: Rethinking Key Concepts in Feminist Discourses on Sexual Violence." *Signs* 42, no. 1 (2016): 71–98.

Goodley, Dan. "The Dis/ability Complex." *DiGeSt: Journal of Diversity and Gender Studies* 5, no. 1 (2018): 5–22.

Goodley, Dan, Rebecca Lawthom, Kirsty Liddiard, and Katherine Runswick-Cole. "Key Concerns for Critical Disability Studies." *International Journal of Disability and Social Justice* 1, no. 1 (November 2021): 27–49.

Goodley, Dan, Rebecca Lawthom, Kirsty Liddiard, and Katherine Runswick-Cole. "Provocations for Critical Disability Studies." *Disability & Society* 34, no. 6 (2019): 972–97.

Gorham, Maurice. *Londoners*. London: Percival Marshall, 1951.

Gowing, Laura. *Common Bodies: Women, Touch, and Power in Seventeenth-Century England*. New Haven, CT: Yale University Press, 2003.

Graham, Clare. *Ordering Law: The Architectural and Social History of the English Law Court to 1914*. Aldershot, UK: Ashgate, 2003.

"Great Eastern Railway Company's New Station at Liverpool Street." *Engineer*, June 11, 1875, 403.

Greenwood, Major Jr. *Physiology of the Special Senses*. London: Edward Arnold, 1910.

Griffiths, Percival. *The History of the Indian Tea Industry*. London: Weidenfeld & Nicholson, 1967.

Guest, Carmel Haden. *Children of the Fog: A Novel of Southwark*. London: G. G. Harrap, 1927.

Hacking, Ian. "Making Up People." In *Historical Ontology*, 99–114. Cambridge, MA: Harvard University Press, 2002.

Haddon, A. C., ed. *Reports of the Cambridge Anthropological Expedition to Torres Straits*. Vol. 2, 2 pts., *Physiology and Psychology*. Cambridge: Cambridge University Press, 1901, 1903.

Hadley, Elaine. *Living Liberalism: Practical Citizenship in Mid-Victorian Britain*. Chicago: University of Chicago Press, 2010.

Hall, G. S., and A. Allin. "The Psychology of Tickling, Laughter, and the Comic." *American Journal of Psychology* 9, no. 1 (October 1897): 1–41.

Hanmore, E. *The Curse of the Embankment and the Cure*. Westminster: P. S. King & Son, 1935.

Harper, Charles G. *More Queer Things about London*. London: Cecil Palmer, 1924.

Harper, Charles G. *Queer Things about London: Strange Nooks and Corners of the Greatest City in the World*. London: Cecil Palmer, 1923.

Harvey, Elizabeth. "The Portal of Touch." *American Historical Review* 116, no. 2 (April 2011): 385–400.

Harvey, Elizabeth, ed. *Sensible Flesh: On Touch in Early Modern Culture*. Philadelphia: University of Pennsylvania Press, 2002.

Hayward, Rhodri. "Neurology and the Resurgence of Demonology in Edwardian Britain." *Bulletin of the History of Medicine* 78, no. 1 (2004): 37–58.

Head, Henry. *Destroyers and Other Verses*. London: Humphrey Milford, 1919.

Head, Henry. *Studies in Neurology*. 2 vols. London: Hodder & Stoughton, 1920.

Head, Henry, and W. H. R. Rivers. "A Human Experiment in Nerve Division." *Brain* 31, no. 3 (November 1908): 323–450.

Head, Henry, and James Sherren. "The Consequences of Injury to the Peripheral Nerves in Man." *Brain* 28, no. 2 (November 1905): 116–338.

Head, Ruth. *A History of Departed Things*. London: Kegan Paul, 1918.

Head, Ruth. *Pictures and Other Passages from Henry James*. London: Chatto & Windus, 1916.

Hindmarch-Watson, Katie. *Serving a Wired World: London's Telecommunications Workers and the Making of an Information Capital*. Oakland: University of California Press, 2020.

Hirst, Alfred. *My Dark World*. London: British & Foreign Blind Association, 1898.

Hirst, Alfred. *Types for the Blind*. London: Elliott and Sons, 1894.

Hitchcock, Alfred, dir. *The Lodger: A Story of the London Fog*. Gainsborough Pictures, 1927. New York: Criterion, 2017. DVD or Blu-Ray, 91 min.

Hitchcock, Alfred, dir. *Rich and Strange*. British International Pictures, 1931. New York: KL Studio Classics, 2021. DVD or Blu-Ray, 83 min.

Hochschild, Arlie Russell. *The Managed Heart: Commercialization of Human Feeling*. 2nd ed. Berkeley: University of California Press, 2012.

Höhne, Stefan. *Riding the New York Subway: The Invention of the Modern Passenger.* Cambridge, MA: MIT Press, 2021.

Holland, Eugene W. *Deleuze and Guattari's "Anti-Oedipus": Introduction to Schizoanalysis.* London: Routledge, 1999.

Hollins, Alfred. *A Blind Musician Looks Back: An Autobiography.* Edinburgh: W. Blackwood & Sons, 1936.

Holmes, Gordon. *Selected Papers of Gordon Holmes.* Edited by Charles G. Phillips. Oxford: Oxford University Press, 1979.

Holmes, Gordon. "Sir Henry Head: 1861–1940." *Obituary Notices of Fellows of the Royal Society* 3, no. 10 (December 1941): 665–89.

Hornsey, Richard. "'He Who Thinks, in Modern Traffic, Is Lost': Automation and the Pedestrian Rhythms of Interwar London." In *Geographies of Rhythm: Nature, Place, Mobilities and Bodies,* edited by Tim Edensor, 99–112. Farnham, UK: Ashgate, 2010.

Houlbrook, Matt. "'A Pin to See the Peepshow': Culture, Fiction, and Selfhood in Edith Thompson's Letters, 1921–1922." *Past and Present* 207, no. 1 (May 2010): 215–49.

Houlbrook, Matt. *Prince of Tricksters: The Incredible True Story of Netley Lucas, Gentleman Crook.* Chicago: University of Chicago Press, 2016.

Houlbrook, Matt. *Queer London: Perils and Pleasures in the Sexual Metropolis, 1918–1957.* Chicago: University of Chicago Press, 2005.

Houlbrook, Matt. "Thinking Queer: The Social and the Sexual in Interwar Britain." In *British Queer History: New Approaches and Perspectives,* edited by Brian Lewis, 135–64. Manchester: Manchester University Press, 2013.

Howes, David. *Sensual Relations: Engaging the Senses in Culture and Social Theory.* Ann Arbor: University of Michigan Press, 2003.

Hulme, Tom. "'A Nation Depends on Its Children': School Buildings and Citizenship in England and Wales, 1900–1939." *Journal of British Studies* 54 (April 2015): 406–32.

Hunt, Paul, ed. *Stigma: The Experience of Disability.* London: Chapman, 1966.

"Hygiene and the Metropolitan Police Courts." *Lancet* 165, no. 4250 (February 11, 1905): 378.

"Hygiene and the Metropolitan Police Courts." *Lancet* 165, no. 4256 (March 25, 1905): 811.

Illingworth, W. H. *History of the Education of the Blind.* London: S. Low, Marston, 1910.

Ingold, Tim. *The Perception of the Environment: Essays on Livelihood, Dwelling, and Skill.* London: Routledge, 2011.

Irigaray, Luce. *Elemental Passions.* Translated by Joanne Collie and Judith Still. London: Athlone, 1992. First published 1982. Page references are to the 1992 edition.

Irigaray, Luce. *The Forgetting of Air in Martin Heidegger.* Translated by Mary Beth Mader. London: Athlone, 1999.

Jackson, Louise. "Making Sexual Harassment History: The UK Context." Gender Equalities at Work. June 24, 2021. https://www.genderequalitiesat50.ed.ac.uk/2021/06/24/making -sexual-harassment-history-the-uk-context/.

Jackson, Louise. "The Unusual Case of 'Mrs Sherlock': Memoir, Identity and the 'Real' Woman Detective in Twentieth-Century Britain." *Gender and History* 15, no. 1 (April 2003): 108–34.

Jackson, Louise. *Women Police: Gender, Welfare and Surveillance in the Twentieth Century.* Manchester: Manchester University Press, 2006.

Jackson, Michael. *The Varieties of Temporal Experience: Travels in Philosophical, Historical, and Ethnographic Time*. New York: Columbia University Press, 2018.

Jacyna, L. S. *Medicine and Modernism: A Biography of Sir Henry Head*. London: Pickering & Chatto, 2008.

Jaques-Dalcroze, Émile. "Eurhythmics and the Education of the Blind." Translated by E.R. Hutchinson. *Teacher of the Blind* 4, no. 2 (March 1918): 26–31.

James, C. L. R. *Letters from London*. Edited by Nicholas Laughlin. Oxford: Signal Books, 2003. First published 1932.

James, Henry. *The Art of the Novel: Critical Prefaces*. New York: Scribner, 1934.

James, Henry. "London." In *Essays in London and Elsewhere*, 1–46. London: James R. Osgood, McIlvaine, 1893.

James, Henry. *The Wings of the Dove*. Westminster: Archibald Constable, 1902.

Jenner, Mark. "Tasting Lichfield, Touching China: Sir John Floyer's Senses." *Historical Journal* 53, no. 3 (September 2010): 647–70.

Johnson, Mark. *Embodied Mind, Meaning, and Reason: How Our Bodies Give Rise to Understanding*. Chicago: University of Chicago Press, 2017.

Johnson, Tom. "Medieval Law and Materiality: Shipwrecks, Finders, and Property on the Suffolk Coast, ca. 1380–1410." *American Historical Review* 120, no. 2 (2015): 407–32.

Johnson, Tom. "Legal History and the Material Turn." In *The Oxford Handbook of Legal History*, edited by Markus D. Dubber and Christopher Tomlins, 497–513. Oxford: Oxford University Press, 2018.

Johnston, J. A. *The Metropolitan Police Guide: Being a Compendium of the Law Affecting the Metropolitan Police*. 7th ed. London: HMSO, 1922.

Josipovici, Gabriel. *Touch*. New Haven, CT: Yale University Press, 1996.

Joyce, Patrick. *The Rule of Freedom: Liberalism and the Modern City*. London: Verso, 2003.

Joyce, Patrick. *The State of Freedom: A Social History of the British State since 1800*. Cambridge: Cambridge University Press, 2013.

Joyce, Patrick, and Tony Bennett. "Material Powers: Introduction." In *Material Powers: Cultural Studies, History, and the Material Turn*, edited by Patrick Joyce and Tony Bennett, 1–21. London: Routledge, 2010.

Kennedy-Cox, Reginald. *Reginald Kennedy-Cox: An Autobiography*. London: Hodder & Stoughton, 1931.

Kenny, Nicholas. *The Feel of the City: Experiences of Urban Transformation*. Toronto: University of Toronto Press, 2014.

Kern, Stephen. *The Culture of Time and Space, 1880–1918*. Rev. ed. Cambridge, MA: Harvard University Press, 2003. Reprint of 1983 first edition, with new preface. Page references are to the 2003 edition.

Kerner, Annette. *Further Adventures of a Woman Detective*. London: Werner Laurie, 1955.

Kerner, Annette. *Woman Detective*. London: Werner Laurie, 1954.

Kimmins, C. W. "Special Features in the Training of the Blind." *Beacon* 7, no. 76 (April 1923): 13–14.

Kleege, Georgina. *More than Meets the Eye: What Blindness Brings to Art*. New York: Oxford University Press, 2018.

Koselleck, Reinhart. "Historia Magistra Vitae: The Dissolution of the Topos into the

Perspective of a Modernized Historical Process." In *Futures Past: On the Semantics of Historical Time*, translated by Keith Tribe, 26–42. New York: Columbia University Press, 2004.

Koselleck, Reinhart. *Sediments of Time: On Possible Histories*. Edited and translated by Sean Franzel and Stefan-Ludwig Hoffmann. Stanford, CA: Stanford University Press, 2018.

Koven, Seth. *The Match Girl and the Heiress*. Princeton, NJ: Princeton University Press, 2014.

Koven, Seth. "Remembering and Dismemberment: Crippled Children, Wounded Soldiers, and the Great War in Britain." *American Historical Review* 99, no. 4 (October 1994): 1167–1202.

Koven, Seth. *Slumming: Sexual and Social Politics in Victorian London*. Princeton, NJ: Princeton University Press, 2006.

Kudlick, Catherine J. "Disability History: Why We Need Another 'Other.'" *American Historical Review* 108, no. 3 (June 2003): 763–93.

Kuklick, Henrika. "Fieldworkers and Physiologists." In *Cambridge and the Torres Strait: Centenary Essays on the 1898 Anthropological Expedition*, edited by Anita Herle and Sandra Rouse, 158–80. Cambridge: Cambridge University Press, 1998.

Kuriyama, Shigehisa. *The Expressiveness of the Body and the Divergence of Greek and Chinese Medicine*. New York: Zone Books, 1999.

Laite, Julia. "Immoral Traffic: Mobility, Health, Labor, and the 'Lorry Girl' in Mid-Twentieth-Century Britain." *Journal of British Studies* 52 (2013): 693–721.

Lakoff, George, and Mark Johnson. *Metaphors We Live By*. Chicago: University of Chicago Press, 2003.

Landes, Donald A. *The Merleau-Ponty Dictionary*. London: Bloomsbury, 2013.

Lang, Hugo. *A German-English Dictionary of Terms Used in Medicine and the Allied Sciences*. Edited by Bertram Abrahams. London: J. & A. Churchill, 1905.

Laqueur, Thomas. *Solitary Sex: A Cultural History of Masturbation*. New York: Zone, 2003.

Latour, Bruno. *The Making of Law: An Ethnography of the Conseil d'Etat*. Translated by Marina Brilman and Alain Pottage. Cambridge: Polity, 2010.

Latour, Bruno. *Reassembling the Social: An Introduction to Actor-Network-Theory*. Oxford: Oxford University Press, 2005.

Latour, Bruno. *We Have Never Been Modern*. Translated by Catherine Porter. New York: Harvester Wheatsheaf, 1993.

Latour, Bruno, and Steve Woolgar. *Laboratory Life: The Construction of Scientific Facts*. 2nd ed. Princeton, NJ: Princeton University Press, 1986.

Law, Michael John. *The Experience of Suburban Modernity: How Private Transport Changed Interwar London*. Manchester: Manchester University Press, 2014.

Lawrence, Christopher, and Steven Shapin, eds. *Science Incarnate: Historical Embodiments of Natural Knowledge*. Chicago: University of Chicago Press, 1998.

Lawrence, D. H. *Complete Poems*. Edited by Vivian de Sola Pinto and Warren Robert. Harmondsworth, UK: Penguin, 1993.

Leder, Drew. *The Absent Body*. Chicago: University of Chicago Press, 1990.

Lefebvre, Henri. *Rhythmanalysis: Space, Time and Everyday Life*. Translated by Stuart Elden and Gerald Moore. London: Continuum, 2004.

Linden, David J. *Touch: The Science of Hand, Heart, and Mind*. London: Viking, 2015.

Linker, Beth. "On the Borderland of Medical and Disability History: A Survey of the Fields." *Bulletin of the History of Medicine* 87, no. 4 (Winter 2013): 499–535.

Linstrum, Erik. *Ruling Minds: Psychology in the British Empire*. Cambridge, MA: Harvard University Press, 2016.

A Little Book of Sunshine: A Collection of Articles, Stories and Poems on Sunshine House, the Blind Babies' Home at Chorley Wood, Herts. N.p., n.d. ca. 1918.

"London Fogs." *Builder* 87, no. 3229 (December 24, 1904): 656.

London Trades Council. *London Trades Council, 1860–1950: A History*. London: Lawrence & Wishart, 1950.

Longmore, Paul K. *Why I Burned My Book and Other Essays on Disability*. Philadelphia: Temple University Press, 2003.

Lynd, Robert. "The Morning and Evening Rush." In *Wonderful London: The World's Greatest City Described by its Best Writers and Pictured by its Finest Photographers*, vol. 2, edited by Arthur St. John Adcock, 580–91. London: Amalgamated Press, 1926.

Maccheroni, A. "The Montessori Method." *Beacon* 4, no. 43 (July 1920): 8.

Mack, Adam. *Sensing Chicago: Noisemakers, Strikebreakers, and Muckrakers*. Urbana: University of Illinois Press, 2015.

Mackenzie, Catriona, Wendy Rogers, and Susan Dodds, eds. *Vulnerability: New Essays in Ethics and Feminist Philosophy*. New York: Oxford University Press, 2014.

Malafouris, Lambros. *How Things Shape the Mind: A Theory of Material Engagement*. Cambridge, MA: MIT Press, 2013.

Malm, Andreas. *Fossil Capital: The Rise of Steam Power and the Roots of Global Warming*. London: Verso, 2016.

Mann, Tom. *Tom Mann's Memoirs*. London: Labour Publishing, 1923.

Manning, Erin. *Politics of Touch: Sense, Movement, Sovereignty*. Minneapolis: University of Minnesota Press, 2006.

Mansell, James G. *The Age of Noise in Britain: Hearing Modernity*. Urbana: University of Illinois Press, 2017.

Marriott, F. R. "How the Blind Travel." *Beacon* 4, no. 38 (February 1920): 7–8.

Marx, Karl. "Economic and Philosophical Manuscripts (1844)." In *Early Writings*, translated by Rodney Livingstone and Gregor Benton, 279–400. London: Penguin, 1992.

"Massage by the Blind." *British Journal of Nursing* 29 (1902): 526.

Matera, Marc. *Black London: The Imperial Metropolis and Decolonization in the Twentieth Century*. Oakland: University of California Press, 2015.

Maurette, Pablo. *The Forgotten Sense: Meditations on Touch*. Chicago: University of Chicago Press, 2018.

Mayhew, Henry. "Metropolitan Railway." In *The Shops and Companies of London and the Trades and Manufactories of Great Britain*, vol. 1, edited by Henry Mayhew, 142–53. London, 1865.

McComas, Alan J. *Galvani's Spark: The Story of the Nerve Impulse*. Oxford: Oxford University Press, 2011.

Meier, William M. "Going on the Hoist: Women, Work, and Shoplifting in London, ca. 1890–1940." *Journal of British Studies* 50, no. 2 (April 2011): 410–33.

Merleau-Ponty, Maurice. "The Intertwining—The Chiasm." In *The Visible and the Invis-*

ible, ed. Claude Lefort, trans. Alphonso Lingis, 130–55. Evanston, IL: Northwestern University Press, 1968.

Merleau-Ponty, Maurice. *Phenomenology of Perception*. Translated by Colin Smith. London: Routledge, 2002. First published 1945.

Merleau-Ponty, Maurice. *Phenomenology of Perception*. Translated by Donald A. Landes. London: Routledge, 2012. First published 1945.

Meredyll, M. "Eurhythmics and the Blind!" *Teacher of the Blind* 5, no. 5 (September 1917): 55–57.

Meteorological Council. *London Fogs*. London: Meteorological Office, 1904.

"Metropolitan Police Courts." *Law Times* 165, no. 4424 (January 14, 1928): 27.

"Metropolitan Police Courts." *Law Times* 165, no. 4435 (March 31, 1928): 276.

Michalko, Rod. *The Difference that Disability Makes*. Philadelphia: Temple University Press, 2002.

Mitchell, Sally. *The New Girl: Girls' Culture in England, 1880–1915*. New York: Columbia University Press, 1995.

Morris, E. W. *A History of the London Hospital*. London: Edward Arnold, 1910.

Morrison, Arthur. "Loafing London." In Sims, *Living London*, 1:357–362.

Mort, Frank. *Capital Affairs: London and the Making of the Permissive Society*. New Haven, CT: Yale University Press, 2010.

Mosely, Sydney. *The Night Haunts of London*. London: Stanley Paul, 1920.

Moshenska, Joe. *Feeling Pleasures: The Sense of Touch in Renaissance England*. Oxford: Oxford University Press, 2014.

Mulcahy, Linda. *Legal Architecture: Justice, Due Process, and the Place of Law*. London: Routledge, 2011.

Müller, Johannes. *Elements of Physiology*. 2 vols. Translated by William Baly. London: Taylor and Walton, 1838–42.

Mullin, Katherine. *Working Girls: Fiction, Sexuality, and Modernity*. Oxford: Oxford University Press, 2016.

Murphy, Ann V. *Violence and the Philosophical Imaginary*. Albany: State University of New York Press, 2012.

Nafe, John Paul. "A Quantitative Theory of Feeling." *Journal of General Psychology* 2 (January 1, 1929): 199–211.

Nash, Jennifer C. "Pedagogies of Desire." *differences* 30, no. 1 (2019): 197–217.

National Council of Public Morals. *The Cinema: Its Present Position and Future Possibilities*. London: printed by the author, 1917.

Nead, Lynda. *The Haunted Gallery: Painting, Photography, Film, c. 1900*. New Haven, CT: Yale University Press, 2007.

Nead, Lynda. *The Tiger in the Smoke: Art and Culture in Post-War Britain*. New Haven, CT: Yale University Press, 2017.

Nead, Lynda. *Victorian Babylon: People, Streets and Images in Nineteenth-Century London*. New Haven, CT: Yale University Press, 2000.

"A New Development in Dalcroze Eurhythmics." *Teacher of the Blind* 11, no. 4 (February 1924): 65–67.

Newen, Albert, Leon De Bruin, and Shaun Gallagher. "4E Cognition: Historical Roots,

Key Concepts, and Central Issues." In *The Oxford Handbook of 4E Cognition*, edited by Albert Newen, Leon De Bruin, and Shaun Gallagher, 3–16. Oxford: Oxford University Press, 2018.

Newman, George. *The Building of a Nation's Health*. London: Macmillan, 1939.

Ngo, Helen. *The Habits of Racism: A Phenomenology of Racism and Racialized Embodiment*. Lanham, MD: Lexington Books, 2017.

Nippy. British Pathé, Film ID 1024.20, February 9, 1931. Video, 6:16. https://www.britishpathe.com/asset/64379/.

Noë, Alva. *Action in Perception*. Cambridge, MA: MIT Press, 2004.

No Longer Alone. British Pathé, Film ID 2717.04, 1961. Video, 17:47. https://www.britishpathe.com/asset/196064/.

Norrsell, Ulf, Stanley Finger, and Clara Lajonchere. "Cutaneous Sensory Spots and the 'Law of Specific Nerve Energies': History and Development of Ideas." *Brain Research Bulletin* 48, no. 5 (1999): 457–65.

Olsén, Jan Eric. "Vicariates of the Eye: Blindness, Sense Substitution, and Writing Devices in the Nineteenth Century." *Mosaic* 46, no. 3 (September 2013): 75–91.

Opitz, Donald L., Staffan Bergwik, and Brigitte Van Tiggelen, eds. *Domesticity in the Making of Modern Science*. Basingstoke, UK: Palgrave Macmillan, 2016.

O'Rourke, Chris. *Acting for the Silent Screen: Film Actors and Aspiration between the Wars*. London: I. B. Tauris, 2017.

Otter, Chris. *The Victorian Eye: A Political History of Light and Vision in Britain, 1800–1910*. Chicago: University of Chicago Press, 2008.

Owens, Emily A. "Consent." *differences* 30, no. 1 (2019): 148–56.

P., S. B. "Childhood's Royal Road to Learning: The Montessori Methods of Education." *Beacon* 4, no. 38 (February 1920): 3–4.

Palmer, Arnold. *Straphangers*. London: Selwyn & Blount, 1927.

Panagia, Davide. *The Political Life of Sensation*. Durham, NC: Duke University Press, 2009.

Parisi, David. *Archaeologies of Touch: Interfacing with Haptics from Electricity to Computing*. Minneapolis: University of Minnesota Press, 2018.

Parkinson, Harry B., and Frank Miller, dirs. *London Old and New*. H. B. Parkinson Productions, 1924. in Harry B. Parkinson and Frank Miller, *Wonderful London*. London: British Film Institute [BFI], 2012. BFI ID 18731.

Pater, Walter. *The Renaissance: Studies in Art and Poetry*. 6th ed. 1901. Reprint, London: Macmillan, 1904.

Paterson, Mark. *How We Became Sensorimotor: Movement, Measurement, Sensation*. Minneapolis: University of Minnesota Press, 2021.

Paterson, Mark. *Seeing with the Hands: Blindness, Vision, and Touch after Descartes*. Edinburgh: Edinburgh University Press, 2016.

Paterson, Mark. *The Senses of Touch: Haptics, Affects and Technologies*. Oxford: Berg, 2007.

Pearson, Arthur. *Victory Over Blindness: How It Was Won by the Men of St Dunstan's and How Others May Win It*. London: Hodder & Stoughton, 1919.

Peel, C. S. *A Hundred Wonderful Years: Social and Domestic Life of a Century, 1820–1920*. London: John Lane, 1926.

Peters, John Durham. *The Marvelous Clouds: Towards a Philosophy of Elemental Media*. Chicago: University of Chicago Press, 2015.

Petherbridge, Danielle. "How Do We Respond? Embodied Vulnerability and Forms of Responsiveness." In *New Feminist Perspectives on Embodiment*, edited by Clara Fischer and Luna Dolezal, 57–79. Basingstoke, UK: Palgrave Macmillan, 2018.

Peto, Dorothy. *The Memoirs of Miss Dorothy Olivia Georgiana Peto*. Bramshill, UK: printed by the author, 1993.

Pettit, Michael. *The Science of Deception: Psychology and Commerce in America*. Chicago: University of Chicago Press, 2013.

Phillips, Adam. *On Kissing, Tickling, and Being Bored*. London: Faber, 2016. First published 1993.

Phillips, Gordon. *The Blind in British Society: Charity, State and Community, c. 1780–1930*. Aldershot, UK: Ashgate, 2004.

Picker, John M. *Victorian Soundscapes*. Oxford: Oxford University Press, 2003.

Pictorial and Descriptive Guide to London and its Environs. 27th ed. London: Ward, Lock, 1906.

Pike, David L. "London on Film and Underground." *London Journal* 38, no. 3 (2013): 226–44.

Pireau, M. *Massage Manual: Intended for the Use of Students for the I.S.T.M. Examination*. London: Scientific Press, 1912.

Plowden, Alfred Chichele. *Grain or Chaff? The Autobiography of a Police Magistrate*. London: T. Fisher Unwin, 1903.

"The Police Courts and the Public." *Law Times* 164, no. 4409 (October 1, 1927): 225.

"Police Courts and the Public." *Law Times* 165, no. 4444 (June 2, 1928): 469–70.

Postema, Gerald J. *Legal Philosophy in the Twentieth Century: The Common Law World; A Treatise of Legal Philosophy and General Jurisprudence*. Edited by Enrico Pattaro. Dordrecht, Neth.: Springer, 2011.

Post Office London Directory: Part III: Commercial and Professional Directory. London: Kelly, 1899.

Pottage, Alain. "Law After Anthropology: Object and Technique in Roman Law." *Law, Culture & Society* 31, no. 2–3 (2014): 147–66.

Pottage, Alain. "The Materiality of What?" *Journal of Law and Society* 39, no. 1 (March 2012): 167–83.

Pottage, Alain, and Martha Mundy, eds. *Law, Anthropology, and the Constitution of the Social: Making Persons and Things*. Cambridge: Cambridge University Press, 2004.

Potter, J. Hasloch. *Inasmuch: The Story of the Police Court Mission, 1876–1926*. London: Williams & Norgate, 1927.

Price, H. H. "Touch and Organic Sensation: The Presidential Address." *Proceedings of the Aristotelian Society*, n.s., 44 (1943–1944): i–xxx.

Priestley, J. B. *Angel Pavement*. London: William Heinemann, 1930.

Priestley, J. B. "Man Underground." In *Self-Selected Essays*, 75–80. London: William Heinemann, 1932.

Priestley, J. B. *Margin Released: A Writer's Reminiscences and Reflections*. London: Heinemann, 1962.

Priestley, J. B. *Midnight on the Desert: A Chapter of Autobiography*. London: William Heinemann, 1937.

Priestley, J. B. *They Walk in the City: The Lovers in the Stone Forest*. London: William Heinemann, 1936.

"The Psychology Course." *Teacher of the Blind* 16, no. 4 (March 1928): 82–83.

Pugh, Edwin. *The City of the World: A Book about London and the Londoner.* London: Thomas Nelson & Sons, 1912.

Purves, Alex, ed. *Touch and the Ancient Senses.* London: Routledge, 2018.

Rancière, Jacques. *The Politics of Aesthetics: The Distribution of the Sensible.* Edited and translated by Gabriel Rockhill. London: Continuum, 2004.

Rappaport, Erika D. "The Senses in the Marketplace: Stimulation and Distraction, Gratification and Control." In *A Cultural History of the Senses in the Age of Empire*, ed. Constance Classen, 69–88. London: Bloomsbury, 2014.

Rappaport, Erika D. *Shopping for Pleasure: Women in the Making of London's West End.* Princeton, NJ: Princeton University Press, 2000.

Rappaport, Erika D. *A Thirst for Empire: How Tea Shaped the Modern World.* Princeton, NJ: Princeton University Press, 2017.

Reinarz, Jonathan. *Past Scents: Historical Perspectives on Smell.* Urbana: University of Illinois Press, 2014.

Rembis, Michael. "Challenging the Impairment/Disability Divide: Disability History and the Social Model of Disability." In *Routledge Handbook of Disability Studies*, edited by Nick Watson and Simo Vehmas, 2nd ed., 377–90. London: Routledge, 2019.

Renn, Jürgen, and Tilman Sauer. "Errors and Insights: Reconstructing the Genesis of General Relativity from Einstein's Zurich Notebook." In *Reworking the Bench: Research Notebooks in the History of Science*, edited by Frederic L. Holmes, Jürgen Renn, and Hans-Jörg Rheinberger, 253–67. Dordrecht, Neth.: Kluwer Academic, 2003.

"Report of *The Lancet Special Commission* on the Ventilation of the Police-Courts." *Lancet* 111, no. 2846 (March 16, 1878): 399–401.

Rheinberger, Hans-Jörg. *An Epistemology of the Concrete: Twentieth-Century Histories of Life.* Durham, NC: Duke University Press, 2010.

Rheinberger, Hans-Jörg. *On Historicizing Epistemology: An Essay.* Translated by David Fernbach. Stanford, CA: Stanford University Press, 2010.

Ricoeur, Paul. "The Hermeneutical Function of Distanciation." In *Hermeneutics and the Human Sciences: Essays on Language, Action, and Interpretation*, translated by John B. Thompson, 131–41. Cambridge: Cambridge University Press, 1981.

Riddle, Christopher A. "The Ontology of Impairment: Rethinking How We Define Disability." In *Emerging Perspectives on Disability Studies*, edited by Matthew Wappett and Katrina Arndt, 23–39. New York: Palgrave Macmillan, 2013.

Ritchie, J. M. *Concerning the Blind: Being a Historical Sketch of Organised Effort on Behalf of the Blind of Great Britain, and Some Thoughts Concerning the Mental Life of a Person Born Blind.* Edinburgh: Oliver & Boyd, 1930.

Ritchie, J. M. "The Mental Life of a Person Born Blind." *Teacher of the Blind* 19, no. 3 (January 1931): 61–65.

Rivers, W. H. R. "Observations on the Senses of the Todas." *Journal of Psychology* 1, no. 1 (December 1905): 321–96.

Roberts, J. R., ed. *Stone's Justices' Manual.* 52nd ed. London: Butterworth, 1920.

Robinson, Louis. "On the Anthropological Significance of Ticklishness." In *Report of the Sixty-Fourth Meeting of the British Association for the Advancement of Science held at Oxford in August 1894*, 778. London: BAAS, 1894.

Robinson, Louis. "The Science of Ticklishness." *North American Review* 185, no. 617 (June 21, 1907): 410–19.

Robinson, Louis. "Ticklishness, and the Phenomena of Tickling." In *A Dictionary of Psychological Medicine* [. . .], vol. 2, edited by D. H. Tuke, 1294–96. London: J. & A. Churchill, 1892.

Roper, Michael. *The Secret Battle: Emotional Survival and the Great War*. Manchester: Manchester University Press, 2009.

Roper, Michael. "Splitting in Unsent Letters: Writing as a Social Practice and a Psychological Activity." *Social History* 26, no. 3 (October 2001): 318–39.

Rose, Jacqueline. *On Violence and On Violence against Women*. London: Faber, 2021.

Rubery, Matthew. "From Shell Shock to Shellac: The Great War, Blindness, and Britain's Talking Book Library." *Twentieth Century British History* 26, no. 1 (2015): 1–25.

Russell, C., and H. S. Lewis. *The Jew in London: A Study of Racial Character and Present-Day Conditions*. London: T. Fisher Unwin, 1900.

Russell, Rollo. "Haze, Fog, and Visibility." *Quarterly Journal of the Royal Meteorological Society* 23, no. 101 (January 1897): 10–24.

Russell, Rollo. *Smoke in Relation to Fogs in London: A Lecture*. London: National Smoke Abatement Offices, 1889.

Salisbury, Laura, and Andrew Shail. Introduction to *Neurology and Modernity: A Cultural History of Nervous Systems, 1800–1950*, edited by Laura Salisbury and Andrew Shail, 1–40. Basingstoke, UK: Palgrave Macmillan, 2010.

Salmi, Hannu. "Cultural History, the Possible, and the Principle of Plenitude." *History and Theory* 50, no. 2 (May 2011): 171–87.

Sanders, Lise Shapiro. *Consuming Fantasies: Labor, Leisure, and the London Shopgirl, 1880–1920*. Columbus: Ohio State University Press, 2006.

Sanders, Lise Shapiro. "'Indecent Incentives to Vice': Regulating Films and Audience Behaviour from the 1890s to the 1910s." In *Young and Innocent? The Cinema in Britain, 1896–1930*, edited by Andrew Higson, 97–110. Exeter: University of Exeter Press, 2002.

Schivelbusch, Wolfgang. *Disenchanted Night: The Industrialization of Light in the Nineteenth Century*. Translated by Angela Davies. Berkeley: University of California Press, 1988.

Schivelbusch, Wolfgang. *The Railway Journey: The Industrialization of Time and Space in the 19th Century*. Berkeley: University of California Press, 1986.

Schmidgen, Henning. *The Helmholtz Curves: Tracing Lost Time*. Translated by Nils F. Schott. New York: Fordham University Press, 2014.

Scott, Heidi C. M. *Chaos and Cosmos: Literary Roots of Modern Ecology in the British Nineteenth Century*. Pennsylvania: Pennsylvania State University Press, 2014.

Scott, Robert H. "Fifteen Years' Fogs in the British Islands, 1876–1890." *Quarterly Journal of the Royal Meteorological Society* 19, no. 88 (October 1893): 229–238.

Sedgwick, Eve Kosofsky. *Tendencies*. London: Routledge, 1994.

Serres, Michel. *The Five Senses: A Philosophy of Mingled Bodies*. Translated by Margaret Sankey and Peter Cowley. London: Bloomsbury Academic, 2016. First published 1985.

Sewell, William H. Jr. "Connecting Capitalism to the French Revolution: The Parisian Promenade and the Origins of Civic Equality in Eighteenth-Century France." *Critical Historical Studies* 1, no. 1 (Spring 2014): 5–46.

Shapin, Steven. "The Philosopher and the Chicken: On the Dietetics of Disembodied

Knowledge." In *Never Pure: Historical Studies of Science as if It Was Produced by People with Bodies, Situated in Time, Space, Culture, and Society, and Struggling for Credibility and Authority*, 237–58. Baltimore: Johns Hopkins University Press, 2010.

Shapira, Michal. "Indecently Exposed: The Male Body and Vagrancy in Metropolitan London before the Fin de Siècle." *Gender & History* 30, no. 1 (March 2018): 52–69.

Sharma, Jayeeta. *Empire's Garden: Assam and the Making of India*. Durham, NC: Duke University Press, 2011.

Shaw, Napier, and John Switzer Owens. *The Smoke Problem of Great Cities*. London: Constable, 1925.

Sherrington, Charles Scott. "Cutaneous Sensations." In *Text-Book of Physiology*, vol. 2, edited by E. A. Schäfer, 920–1001. Edinburgh: Pentland, 1900.

Sherrington, Charles Scott. *The Integrative Action of the Nervous System*. New Haven, CT: Yale University Press, 1906.

Simmel, Georg. "The Metropolis and Mental Life." In *The Blackwell City Reader*, edited by Gary Bridge and Sophie Watson, 11–15. Oxford: Blackwell, 2002. First published 1903.

Simmel, Georg. "Sociology of the Senses." In *Simmel on Culture: Selected Writings*, edited by David Frisby and Mike Featherstone, 109–20. London: Sage, 1997.

Sims, George R. *Glances Back*. London: Jarrolds, 1927.

Sims, George R, ed. *Living London: Its Work and Its Play, Its Humour and Its Pathos, Its Sights and Its Scenes*. 3 vols. London: Cassell, 1901–1903.

Sims, George R. "London Street Corners." In Sims, *Living London*, 2:87–93.

Sinclair, David C. *Cutaneous Sensation*. Oxford: Oxford University Press, 1967.

Sinclair, David C. "Cutaneous Sensation and the Doctrine of Specific Energy." *Brain* 78, no. 4 (December 1, 1955): 584–614.

Sinclair, Robert. *Metropolitan Man: The Future of the English*. London: G. Allen & Unwin, 1937.

Skinner, Quentin. "Meaning and Understanding in the History of Ideas." In *Visions of Politics: Regarding Method*, vol. 1, 59–89. Cambridge: Cambridge University Press, 2002.

Sloterdijk, Peter. *Foams: Spheres III*. Translated by Wieland Hoban. South Pasadena, CA: Semiotext(e), 2016.

Smith, David Woodruff. "Science, Intentionality, and Historical Background." In *Science and the Life-World: Essays on Husserl's "Crisis of European Sciences,"* edited by David Hyder and Hans-Jörg Rheinberger, 1–26. Stanford, CA: Stanford University Press, 2010.

Smith, Hubert Llewellyn. "Influx of Population (East London)" [1888]. In Booth, *Life and Labour of the People in London*, vol. 3, *Poverty*, 58–119.

Smith, Hubert Llewellyn, ed. *The New Survey of London Life and Labour*. Vol. 8, *London Industries III*. London: P. S. King and Son, 1934.

Smith, Mark M. *How Race Is Made: Slavery, Segregation, and the Senses*. Chapel Hill: University of North Carolina Press, 2006.

Smith, Mark M. *Listening to Nineteenth-Century America*. Chapel Hill: University of North Carolina Press, 2001.

Solicitor [pseud.]. *English Justice*. London: G. Routledge & Sons, 1932.

Spencer, Herbert. *The Principles of Psychology*. 2nd ed. Vol. 1. London: Williams and Norgate, 1870.

Stanley, Liz. "The Epistolarium: On Theorizing Letters and Correspondences." *Auto/Biography* 12 (2004): 201–35.

Stanley, Liz. "The Epistolary Gift, the Editorial Third-Party, Counter-Epistolaria: Rethinking the Epistolarium." *Life Writing* 8, no. 2 (June 2011): 135–52.

Steedman, Carolyn. "A Woman Writing a Letter." In *Epistolary Selves: Letters and Letter-writers, 1600–1945*, edited by Rebecca Earle, 111–33. Aldershot, UK: Ashgate, 1999.

Stephens, Winn. "Underground." *Film Weekly*, April 15, 1929, 14–15.

Stoler, Ann Laura. *Along the Archival Grain: Epistemic Anxieties and Colonial Common Sense.* Princeton, NJ: Princeton University Press, 2009.

Stopford, John S. B. *Sensation and the Sensory Pathway.* London: Longmans, 1930.

"Street Offences and Police Evidence." *Law Journal* 64 (October 1, 1927): 206.

Sully, James. *An Essay on Laughter: Its Forms, Its Causes, Its Development and Its Value.* London: Longmans, 1902.

Sully, James. *Sensation and Intuition: Studies in Psychology and Aesthetics.* London, 1874.

Suvilehto, Juulia, Enrico Glerean, Robin I. M. Dunbar, and Lauri Nummenmaa. "Topography of Social Touching Depends on Emotional Bonds Between Humans." *Proceedings of the National Academy of Sciences* 112, no. 45 (October 2015): 13811–16.

Suvilehto, Juulia T., Lauri Nummenmaa, Tokiko Harada, Robin I. M. Dunbar, Riitta Hari, Robert Turner, Norihiro Sadato, and Ryo Kitada. "Cross-Cultural Similarity in Relationship-Specific Social Touching." *Proceedings of the Royal Society B* 286, no. 1901 (April 2019): 1–10.

"The System of Training in Rhythm and Rhythmic Movement." *Beacon*, 4, no. 43 (July 1920): 4.

Taylor, Jesse Oak. *The Sky of Our Manufacture: The London Fog in British Fiction from Dickens to Woolf.* Charlottesville: University of Virginia Press, 2016.

Teashop Strike. British Pathé, Film ID 218.29, August 19, 1920. Video, 0:47. https://www.britishpathe.com/asset/48432/.

Thomas, Kate. *Postal Pleasures: Sex, Scandal, and Victorian Letters.* Oxford: Oxford University Press, 2012.

Thompson, Emily. *The Soundscape of Modernity: Architectural Acoustics and the Culture of Listening in America, 1900–1933.* Cambridge, MA: MIT Press, 2004.

Thompson, Evan. *Mind in Life: Biology, Phenomenology, and the Sciences of Mind.* Cambridge, MA: Belknap Press of Harvard University Press, 2007.

Thornberry, Elizabeth. *Colonizing Consent: Rape and Governance in South Africa's Eastern Cape.* Cambridge: Cambridge University Press, 2018.

Thorsheim, Peter. *Inventing Pollution: Coal, Smoke, and Culture in Britain since 1800.* 2nd ed. Athens: Ohio University Press, 2017.

Tilley, Heather. *Blindness and Writing: From Wordsworth to Gissing.* Cambridge: Cambridge University Press, 2017.

Tilley, Heather, and Jan Eric Olsén. "Touching Blind Bodies: A Critical Inquiry into Pedagogical and Cultural Constructions of Visual Disability in the Nineteenth Century." In *The Edinburgh Companion to the Critical Medical Humanities*, edited by Anne Whitehead and Angela Woods, 260–75. Edinburgh: Edinburgh University Press, 2016.

Titchener, E. B. "On Ethnological Tests of Sensation and Perception with Special Reference to Tests of Color Vision and Tactile Discrimination Described in the Reports of the Cambridge Anthropological Expedition to Torres Straits." *Proceedings of the American Philosophical Society* 55, no. 5 (1916): 204–36.

Titchkosky, Tanya. "The Ends of the Body as Pedagogic Possibility." *Review of Education, Pedagogy, and Cultural Studies* 34, no. 3–4 (2012): 82–93.

Titchkosky, Tanya, and Rod Michalko. "The Body as the Problem of Individuality: A Phenomenological Disability Studies Approach." In *Disability and Social Theory: New Developments and Directions*, edited by Dan Goodley, Bill Hughes, and Lennard Davis, 127–42. Basingstoke, UK: Palgrave Macmillan, 2012.

Tomlins, Christopher. "Historicism and Materiality in Legal Theory." In *Law in Theory and History: New Essays on a Neglected Dialogue*, edited by Maksymilian Del Mar and Michael Lobban, 57–83. Oxford: Hart, 2016.

Topik, Steven C., and Allen Wells. "Commodity Chains in a Global Economy." In *A World Connecting, 1870–1945*, edited by Emily S. Rosenberg, 593–812. Cambridge, MA: Belknap Press of Harvard University Press, 2012.

"The Tower Bridge Police Court." *Builder* 88, no. 3242 (March 25, 1905): 331.

Trotter, Wilfred. "The Insulation of the Nervous System." In *The Collected Papers of Wilfred Trotter, F.R.S.*, 47–70. Oxford: Oxford University Press, 1941. First published in 1926.

Tuke, D. Hack, ed. *A Dictionary of Psychological Medicine: Giving the Definition, Etymology, and Synonyms of the Terms Used in Medical Psychology, With the Symptoms, Treatment, and Pathology of Insanity and the Law of Lunacy in Great Britain and Ireland*. Vol. 1. London: J. & A. Churchill, 1892.

Tullett, William. *Smell in Eighteenth-Century England: A Social Sense*. Oxford: Oxford University Press, 2019.

Turner, Henry Waddy. *The Police Court and Its Work*. London: Butterworth, 1925.

"'Underground.'" *Bioscope*, August 1, 1928, 41.

"'Underground.'" *Kinematograph Weekly*, August 2, 1928, 41–42.

Varela, Francisco J., Evan Thompson, and Eleanor Rosch. *The Embodied Mind: Cognitive Science and Human Experience*. Cambridge, MA: MIT Press, 1991.

Verlaine, Paul. *One Hundred and One Poems by Paul Verlaine: A Bilingual Edition*. Translated by Norman R. Shapiro. Chicago: University of Chicago Press, 1999.

Vernon, James. *Distant Strangers: How Britain Became Modern*. Berkeley: University of California Press, 2014.

Vernon, James. "Heathrow and the Making of Neoliberal Britain." *Past and Present* 252 (August 2021): 213–47.

Vernon, James. *Hunger: A Modern History*. Cambridge, MA: Belknap Press of Harvard University Press, 2007.

Vernon, James, and Simon Gunn, eds. *The Peculiarities of Liberal Modernity in Imperial Britain*. Berkeley: University of California Press, 2011.

Vernon, James, and Simon Gunn. "What Was Liberal Modernity and Why Was It Peculiar in Imperial Britain?" In Vernon and Gunn, *Peculiarities of Liberal Modernity in Imperial Britain*, 1–18.

Vincent, Charles Edward. *Vincent's Police Code and General Manual of the Criminal Law*. 16th ed. London: Butterworth, 1924.

Virilio, Paul. *The Original Accident*. Translated by Julie Rose. Cambridge: Polity, 2007.

Vismann, Cornelia. *Files: Law and Media Technology*. Translated by Geoffrey Winthrop-Young. Stanford, CA: Stanford University Press, 2008.

Villey, Pierre. *The World of the Blind: (A Psychological Study)*. Translated by A. H. Ward. London: Simpkin, Marshall, 1922.

Wagg, H. J. *A Chronological Survey of Work for the Blind: From the Earliest Records up to the Year 1930*. London: Sir Isaac Pitman & Sons, 1932.

Walshe, F. M. R. "The Anatomy and Physiology of Cutaneous Sensibility: A Critical Review." *Brain* 65, no. 1 (1942): 48–112.

Ward, Edward D. "The Union Jack Club: What We Want." In *The Flag: The Book of the Union Jack Club*, edited by H. F. Trippel. London: Daily Mail, n.d., ca. 1908.

Ward, M. "At School with the Blind." *Beacon* 1, no. 5 (May 1917): 6–8.

Walkowitz, Judith R. *City of Dreadful Delight: Narratives of Sexual Danger in Late-Victorian London*. London: Virago, 1992.

Walkowitz, Judith R. "Going Public: Shopping, Street Harassment, and Streetwalking in Late-Victorian London." *Representations* 62 (Spring 1998): 1–30.

Walkowitz, Judith R. *Nights Out: Life in Cosmopolitan London*. New Haven, CT: Yale University Press, 2012.

Warne, Vanessa. "Between the Sheets: Contagion, Touch, and Text." *19: Interdisciplinary Studies in the Long Nineteenth Century* 19 (2014): 1–9.

Warne, Vanessa. "'So That the Sense of Touch May Supply the Want of Sight': Blind Reading and Nineteenth-Century British Print Culture." In *Media, Technology, and Literature in the Nineteenth Century: Image, Sound, Touch*, edited by Colette Colligan and Margaret Linley, 43–64. Farnham, UK: Ashgate, 2011.

Watt Smith, Tiffany. *On Flinching: Theatricality and Scientific Looking from Darwin to Shell Shock*. Oxford: Oxford University Press, 2014.

Way, Percy L. "Choosing a Career: The Future of the Blind Child." *Beacon* 9, no. 102 (June 1925): 12–15.

Wearden, John. *The Psychology of Time Perception*. London: Palgrave Macmillan, 2016.

"The Weather of December, 1924." *Meteorological Magazine* 59, no. 708 (January 1925): 295–97.

"Weather of December 1952." *Meteorological Magazine* 82, no. 968 (February 1953): 62–63.

Weber, Ernst Heinrich. *E. H. Weber on the Tactile Senses*. 2nd ed. Edited and translated by Helen E. Ross and David J. Murray. Hove: Erlbaum UK, 1996.

Weddell, G. "The Anatomy of Cutaneous Sensibility." *British Medical Bulletin* 3, no. 7–8 (1945): 167–72.

Wexler, Abraham. *Experimental Science for the Blind: An Instruction Manual*. Oxford: Pergamon, 1961.

Weiss, Gail. *Body Images: Embodiment as Intercorporeality*. New York: Routledge, 1999.

Weiss, Gail. "The Normal, the Natural and the Normative: A Merleau-Pontian Legacy to Feminist Theory, Critical Race Theory, and Disability Studies." *Continental Philosophy Review* 48 (2015): 77–93.

Whitburn, Ben, and Rod Michalko. "Blindness/Sightedness: Disability Studies and the Defiance of Di-Vision." In *Routledge Handbook of Disability Studies*, edited by Nick Watson and Simo Vehmas, 2nd ed., 219–33. London: Routledge, 2019.

Winch, W. H. "Review: *Reports of the Cambridge Anthropological Expedition to Torres Straits: Volume II*: [. . .], 1901, 1903." *Mind*, n.s., 13, no. 50 (April 1904): 273–77.

Wittgenstein, Ludwig. *Philosophical Investigations*. 4th ed. Translated by G. E. M. Anscombe, P. M. S. Hacker, and Joachim Schulte. Chichester, UK: Wiley-Blackwell, 2009.

Wolmar, Christian. *The Subterranean Railway: How the London Underground Was Built and How It Changed the City Forever*. Rev. ed. London: Atlantic Books, 2012.

Woolf, Virginia. "Oxford Street Tide." [1932.] In *The Essays of Virginia Woolf*, vol. 5, 1929–1932, edited by Stuart N. Clarke, 283–88. London: Vintage, 2009.

Woolf, Virginia. "Street Haunting: A London Adventure." [1927.] In *The Essays of Virginia Woolf*, vol. 4, 1925–1928, edited by Andrew McNeillie, 480–90. London: Hogarth, 1994.

Woolf, Virginia. "Street Music." [1905.] In *The Essays of Virginia Woolf*, vol. 1, 1904–1912, edited by Andrew McNeillie, 27–32. London: Hogarth, 1986.

Woolf, Virginia. "An Unwritten Novel." In *Monday or Tuesday*, 18–25. London: Harcourt, Brace, 1921.

Young, Iris Marion. *On Female Body Experience: "Throwing Like a Girl" and Other Essays*. Oxford: Oxford University Press, 2005.

Zimmeck, Meta. "Jobs for the Girls: the Expansion of Clerical Work for Women, 1850–1914." In *Unequal Opportunities: Women's Employment in England, 1800–1918*, edited by Angela V. John, 153–77. Oxford: Blackwell, 1986.

Zotterman, Yngve. *Touch, Tickle, and Pain*. 2 vols. Oxford: Oxford University Press, 1969–71.

Zweiniger-Bargielowska, Ina. *Managing the Body: Beauty, Health, and Fitness in Britain, 1880–1939*. Oxford: Oxford University Press, 2010.

Index

Page numbers in italics refer to figures.

A.B.C. tea shop(s). *See* Aerated Bread Company (A.B.C.) tea shop(s) (London)
Action in Perception (Noë), 15
Adrian, Edgar D., 64
Aerated Bread Company (A.B.C.) tea shop(s) (London), 3, 137, 143–48, *144*, 151, 154, 156, 168, 172, 225, 281n8
"Afferent Nervous System from a New Aspect, The" (Head, Rivers, Sherren), 64
After Office Hours (film), 174
Agamben, Giorgio, 136, 248–49n63, 304n220
age: and power, 222, 225; and touch, 230–31; and vulnerability, 230–31
Ahmed, Sara, 250n81
Akinyemi, Emanuel, 103
Alder Hey Military Orthopaedic Hospital (Liverpool), 71
alienation: modern urban, 165; and spectacle, 11; and synoptic knowledge, 5
Allen, Mary, 165–66
Allin, A., 35
Allingham, Margery, 194, 298n75
Amongst the Nerves of the World (Nevinson painting), 43–45, *45*
amorality, 52–53. *See also* immorality
anatomy, and physiology, 32, 75

Angel Pavement (Priestley), 165
Anson, Clodagh, Lady, 208–9, 212, 300n122, 301n152, 301n154, 302n167
anthropology, 29, 36, 221
Argyle, Jesse, 147–48, 151
Armitage, Thomas, 77–78, 86
Armstrong, Constable, 199–200
Ashfield, Stanley, Lord, 126–27
Asquith, Anthony, 171–72, *172*, 174
Asquith, Herbert, Home Secretary, 72
assault, and touch, 8–9, 149, 158, 201
Athlete Wrestling with a Python, An (plaster cast), 226
Atkinson, Constable, 185
Auerbach, Sascha, 294n14, 298n81, 301n156, 301n158, 303n205
Austin, John, 219
authenticity, and trust, 246n41
autodidacticism, sensory, 83
autofiction, and love letters, self-experimentation in, 31, 58–63
autonomy: bodily, 8, 23–24, 108, 231; and consent, 230, 283n38; and governmentality, 275n21; of law, 203, 219; personal, 21; and tactile, 24; and touch, 6; violation of, 24; and vulnerability, 21, 24, 108, 129, 142, 230–31; of women, 142

Ayres, Frederick, 129–30
Azoulay, Ariella, 264n7, 264n9

BAAS. *See* British Association for the Advancement of Science (BAAS)
Bachelard, Gaston, 254n28
Bainbridge, General, 72
Bakerloo Line (tube), 115, 118–19, 124
Barad, Karen, 250n81, 252n94, 254n29
Barber, Charles, Constable, 197
Barker, Winifred, 172–74
barmaids, 2, 140–42
Baudelaire, Charles, 245n30
Baxter, Elizabeth (Betty), 204, 207
Baxter's Hostel for Stranded Women and Girls, 207
BBC. *See* British Broadcasting Corporation (BBC)
BBFC. *See* British Board of Film Censors (BBFC)
BD8 (BBC television program), 93–95
Beckwith, William, 199–201
Beecher, Ruth, 141
being-in-the-world, 18–19, 184, 248n63, 249n65, 251n90
being-in-time, and individual, temporal, cultural variability of, 278n81
Belcher, William, 147
Benjamin, Walter, 4–5, 9, 244n18, 246n36
Benson, Etienne S., 294n12
Bentley, Albert, 199–202, 212
Bentley, Thomas, 174
Besant, Walter, 197
Beswick, Alice, 2
BFBA. *See* British and Foreign Blind Association (BFBA)
BFI. *See* British Film Institute (BFI)
Bickley, William, 90
Biddlecombe, C. H., 181
Billingsgate (London), 209
Biron, Chartres, Magistrate, 214–15
Bishopsgate Institute (London), 2
Bishopsgate Station (London), 1–3
Blackness, as difference, 131, 133
Bleak House (Dickens), 186–87, 217–18

"Blinded Soldiers at St Dunstan's" (*St Dunstan's Review*), 75
blindness: and anatomy training for massage, 75, 75; blind, term usage, 264n8; and Braille, 68–69, 74, 80, 90, 93; and canes to aid navigation, 272n176; and compensation, contesting, 68, 93–100, 101; as deficiency, 228; definitions of, medical and legal, 264n8; as disability, 20, 22, 69–72, 95, 97, 100–102, 221, 225, 227; and education/training, 22–23, 70–94, 75, 87, 101–2, 221, 225–29, 227, 268n81, 269n97, 269nn103–4, 270n113, 270n121; and employment, 267n66, 271n150; and equality, 70; and eurhythmics, 80–83; in fog, 191; and hearing, 81, 99–100, 99–101, 264n10; hypothetical blind man and philosophical theories of mind, 249n64; as impairment, 18–19, 20, 22, 100, 264n8; and independence, 68–70, 101; and intelligence, 81–82, 89–90, 96; *longue durée* history of educational provision for, 264–65n15; and massage, 71–90, 75, 266n25, 266n32, 266n37, 266n39; and masturbation, 85; and mental images from memory, 270n131; and Montessori education, 229, 269n103; ontology of, 101–2; and perception, 15; and physical exercise, 79–83, 268n81; and physiology training for massage, 75; and physiotherapy, 72–73, 75–76; psychology of, 80–82, 86–87, 89–90; and public transportation, 269n97; and self-representation, 86–93; and senses/sensations, 68–70, 95–96, 100, 101; shifting conceptualization of, 264n8; of sighted people, 191; as social effect, 20; and social equality, 100; and subordination, 100; and tactile, 29–30, 71–76, 80, 88, 101, 229; and tactual images, 86–93; and talking books, 264n10; and touch,

6–7, 16–23, 67–102, 227–30; under-standing of, 270n131; and violability, 228; and vulnerability, 228. *See also* disability

Blindness (Carroll), 96

Blind Set, The (BBC radio program), 93–102, 272n181, 272n185

Blix, Magnus, 33

BMJ. See British Medical Journal (BMJ)

Bodkin, Archibald, Sir, 216

body: autonomy of, 8, 23–24, 108, 231; biographies, 262n204; and difference (bodily), 22; ethics of, 22; in fog, 191–92; and governmentality, 107; integrity of, 24; knowledge of, 22; and law, 184, 186; and letters, writing and receiving, 260n144; mechanistic models of, 19; and mind, 6–7, 13, 16, 18–20, 29–31, 64–66, 80–84, 88, 221, 223, 229; narratives of, 260n144; ontology of, 22, 248n63; and perfor-mance, 140–41; porosity of, 12; and power inequalities, 129; on public transportation, 191; schema (sense of self), 14–15, 17–19, 83–84; scientific knowledge of, 20; and self, 12, 19, 248n63; and spaces, 7, 13, 15, 191, 193, 228–29; and tactile, 13–18, 22, 24; and touch, 8, 17–20, 22–24, 64, 221–22; understandings of, 22; and vulnera-bility, 24; and world, 13, 16–17, 22, 66, 184, 191–92, 221, 248n63, 252n94. *See also* embodiment

Bone, James, 189, 192, 296n34

Booth, Charles, 147–48, 151, 194–95

Bosanquet, F. A., Sergeant, 152

Bourdieu, Pierre, 246n42

Bourke, Joanna, 141–42

Braille, 68–69, 74, 80, 90, 93

Brain (Jackson), 44, 49, 258n117

Bramble, Albert, 174

Brannan, Luke, 193–95

Britain: cerebral age, 6, 223–24; contem-porary, 233; as global empire, 19–20; and touch, history and importance

in, 19–20, 223, 233; and underground railway, world's first, 20. *See also* London

British and Foreign Blind Association (BFBA), 68, 78

British Association for the Advancement of Science (BAAS), 256n55

British Board of Film Censors (BBFC), 207

British Broadcasting Corporation (BBC), 70, 93–100, 290n180

British Film Institute (BFI), 290n187

British Medical Journal (BMJ), 72

Broad Street Station (London), 1, 232

Broom, J., Mr., 121

Browning, Elizabeth Barrett, 54

Browning, Robert, 54

Bulwer-Lytton, Edward, 170

Burke, Thomas, 130, 198

Burn, Dorothy, 158, 166, 169, 175

Burnett, David, Sir, Magistrate, 155

buses: commandeered for frontline service, 108–9; double-decked, 127; fares, 126, 146; financial integration with tubes, 112; in fog, 181, 188–93, 192, 198; horse-powered forerunners of pirate motor, 278n93; and link-boys, 188–93; motor-, 122, 124, 126–27, 189, 278n93; omni-, 1, 122, 188–93, 198; open-top, 7, 117; and passengers, number of, 127–28; prevalence of increased, 189; and rush hours, 126–28; standing on, 127; and time (schedules), 122–23; and tubes, 112, 125–28, 278n94

Butler, John Dixon, 301n156

Butler, Judith, 251nn89–91, 283n37

Butler, Percival, 159

Cadby Hall (Hammersmith), 161

Cairns, J. A. R., Magistrate, 202, 207, 209, 214–15, 218

Cambridge Scientific Instrument Com-pany, 263n221

Campbell, Francis, Lady, 87

Campbell, Jean, 196

Campbell, R. F. Graham, Magistrate, 216
Cann, Tom, 160–61
Cantlie, James, 79
capillary electrometer, 64
capitalism: abstracting forces of, 291n211;
    and civic equality, 291n211; and
    commodities, 4–5, 20, 161, 169, 180;
    and desire, 138, 140; history of, 140;
    and imperialism, 20; industrial, and
    private property, 9; and inequal-
    ity, 233; and intimacy, 140; and
    labor, 138–40, 168; and liberalism,
    5; local, 225–26; and modernity, 5;
    and private property, 9; and public
    spaces, 225–26; and social relations,
    291n211; and street life, 4–5; and tem-
    poralities, 141–42; and touch, 8–9,
    140, 180, 222, 225–26. See also global
    capitalism; labor
Carroll, Thomas, 96
Central Line (London tube), 119, 128
Central London Railway (CLR), 118–19
Central Telegraph Office (London),
    258n116
cerebral age, touch in, 6, 223–24
Certeau, Michel de, 282n29
Challis, Detective Constable, 153
Champain, Frank, 214–15, 302n181
Charing Cross Line (London tube), 118–19,
    121
Charing Cross (Embankment) Station
    (London), 124, 143
Chick (film), 174
Chorleywood College, 270n121, 271n150
Christian Herald, 204
Church House (Westminster), 138, 178
Church of England Temperance Society,
    216
Circle Line (London tube), 120–21
cities. See urban life
citizenship, and touch, 221
City and South London Line (tube),
    109–10
City and South London Railway (CSLR),
    112–14, 113–14, 119

class: and inequality, 140–41; and personal
    space, 23–24; and power, 24, 222, 225;
    and tea shops, 140–41; and touch,
    23–24; and tube (transport), 119–21;
    and vulnerability, 23–24, 230–31
CLR. See Central London Railway (CLR)
Coal Smoke Abatement Society (CSAS)
    (UK), 187
cognition: and embodiment, 15, 223,
    248n52, 252n93; and perception, 223,
    230
cognitive science, 14, 230
Cohen, Deborah, 260n156, 272n178
Coke, Talbot, 143
cold, and sensations/touch, 32–43, 49, 59–
    61. See also heat
College of Teachers of the Blind, 78, 82–
    83, 86, 90, 269n104
Collyer, Constable, 184–85
colonialism, 19–20, 38, 67, 139–40; anti-,
    162–63. See also imperialism
commuting, 274n12; and tea shops, 21, 139;
    and tube (transport), 104, 109, 126.
    See also public transportation; rush
    hours
Concerning the Blind (Ritchie), 82
Condover Hall (Shropshire), 94
Conniham, Harry, 157, 203–9, 212, 220
Conran Smith, Monica, 152–53
consent: and autonomy, 230, 283n38;
    history of, 251n88, 283n38; legal and
    social understandings of, 251n88;
    and politics, 251n88; and touch, 7, 23,
    129; and vulnerability, 108, 142, 230
consumerism, 140–41, 246n36
Coombes, Barbara, 173
Cooper, H., Constable, 3
Corbin, Alain, 10, 244n19, 245n30, 245n32,
    246n42, 302n175
Corps of Commissionaires (UK), 156–58,
    288n128, 288nn138–39
correspondence: and absence of contact,
    52, 54; and feelings, 50–58, 61–63; as
    figurative and literal touch, 51–52;
    and literature, 261n174; as mutual

representation/self-constitution, 55, 260n144; and relationships, 51, 53–54. *See also* epistolary exchanges; letters and letter writing

cosmopolitanism, 141

crime: cosh-boys and cosh attacks, 183, 194, 298n73; disorderly conduct, 153–56, 214–15; and fog, 21, 181–220; homosexuality, 130–35, 280n121, 295n22; importuning (soliciting), 184, 196, 214–15; importuning, defined, 294n14; indecency, 153, 181, 183–86, 196–97, 207, 300n134, 302n167; larceny, 201; loitering, 201, 205–6, 219–20; phenomenology of, in fog, 193–99; pickpocketing, 2, 109, 175, 184, 199–200; prosecution of, 193–99, 216; prostitution, 21, 138, 142, 153, 185, 194–98; during rush hours, 2; and senses, in fog, 194; shoplifting, 288n134; Teddy boys, and threatening behavior, 121, 277n68; and tube (transport), 2, 109, 195–96; vagrancy, 202. *See also* law; violence and violation

Crisis of European Sciences and Transcendental Phenomenology, The (Husserl), 252n93

Cronshaw, Cyril, 301n154

CSAS. *See* Coal Smoke Abatement Society (CSAS) (UK)

CSLR. *See* City and South London Railway (CSLR)

Cunliffe-Lister, Philip, Sir, 205

Daily Express (London), 173

Daily Mail (London), 160–61, 190–91, 193–94

Daily Mirror (London), 172, 183

Daily Telegraph (London), 213

Darwin, Charles, 36, 256n57

Davidson, Harold, Rev., 22, 137–45, 148–51, 156–59, 166–80, 178, 281n4, 290n195; death of, 180

Davidson, Molly, 168, 176–77

Dean, Henry, 27

Deas, J. A. Charlton, 226–29

Deleuze, Gilles, 283n31, 293n243

Derrida, Jacques, 224–25

desire: and capital, 138, 140; and discipline, in tea shops, 163–71; and empathy, 138; history of, 283n31; and knowledge, 4; and labor, 138–39, 176, 179; and phenomenology, 283n31; in tea shops, 21, 138–41, 148, 152, 163–71, 176, 179–80; and touch, 4, 6, 21, 138–41, 163–71, 179–80, 222; and vulnerability, 140, 180

Desmond, Shaw, 143, 278n93

Destroyers and other Verses (Head), 62

Devan, Vivian Russell, Dr., 103

Devonshire Chambers (London), 233

Devonshire House Hotel (London), 2, 25, 233

Dickens, Charles, 186–87, 217–18

Dickinson, Kate, 104

disability: and ability, 20, 22–23, 69, 100–102, 221, 225, 230, 265n17; activism, 70–71, 100, 225, 227, 250n84; constitution of, 22; as critical tool, 265n20; dual conceptual and activist history of, 250n84; and embodiment, 22–23; history of, 23, 250nn83–84, 265n20; and impairment, 20, 23, 70, 100, 102, 229–30; and misfit, 23; as problem, 230; and rehabilitation and support of returning and disabled servicemen and soldiers, 101, 221, 265n16, 267n52, 272n178, 288n128; social model of, *vs.* medical model of, 102, 229–30, 265n20, 273n208; studies, 22–23, 100, 229–30; and touch, 8, 17, 22–23, 102, 222, 229–30; and vulnerability, 17. *See also* blindness

dispositifs, 304n220

distanciation, hermeneutic, 261n165

Distant Strangers (Vernon), 274n10

Distinction (Bourdieu), 246n42

District and Bakerloo/Northern Line tube platforms, Charing Cross Station (London), 124

District Line (London tube), 109, 190

Doan, Laura, 280n113

domesticity, 254n22

domestic servants, 207, 290n182

Donnellan, Philip, 93–95

Drake, Barbara, 150–51

Drake, Tom, 96

dualism, 184, 193, 275n21

Dudley, H., 97

Ealing Common Station (London), 132, 135

Earl's Court Station (London), 103, 123, 135

Eastwood, Mary, 130

Eckermann, Johann, 56–57, 261n179

Economic and Philosophical Manuscripts (Marx), 9

Education and Employment of the Blind, The (Armitage), 77–78

Eichholz, Alfred, 79, 81

electrophysiology, and sensation experiments, 64–65

Elizabeth Baxter's Hostel for Stranded Women and Girls, 207

Elizabeth Line (London tube), 232

Ellis, George W. F., 192

Ellis, Rose, 138

embodiment: and awareness of place, 191; of being-in-the-world, 18–19; and cognition, 15, 223, 248n52, 252n93; and disability, 22–23; and entanglements, 15; in fog, 184, 186, 189, 191–95, 199; and intercorporeality, 251n90; interdisciplinary debates about, 22; and knowledge, 22; and law, 25, 184, 186, 191–95, 199–212, 203, 205, 215, 217–18, 220; methodological claims within interdisciplinary debates about, 22–25; and mind, 17, 19, 240; ontology of, 283n37; and perception, 17, 19, 223; and precariousness, 283n37; and science, 66; and senses, 13–14, 17, 23, 223; and shared ontological precariousness, 283n37; of social spaces, 18; and subjectivity, 142, 192; in tea shops, 5, 8, 141–42, 170, 179,

225–26, 286n99; and temporalities, 222–23; and touch, 5–6, 8–9, 13–14, 17–19, 22–24, 66, 141, 179, 184, 222, 225; universality and uniqueness of, 23; and vulnerability, 24; and world, 66, 223, 230. *See also* body

empiricism, 29, 32, 81, 87

employment. *See* labor

Englishness, 37, 272n181

entanglements: and cognition, 15, 230; and desire, 4, 138; and embodied cognition, 15; of feelings, 61; and law, in fog, 194; of neurology, 59; and perception, 16, 230; and science, 254n27; sensory, 5, 13, 16–17, 20, 66, 76, 252n94; and spaces, 13; of temporalities, 16; of tenderness, 225; of touch, 1–26, 51, 66, 138, 194, 222–23, 225, 233

environmental adaptation, and evolution, 29

epistemology: of experimental instruments, and epistemic objects, 255n45; of science and scientific knowledge, 252n94; of senses, 16, 18; of ticklishness and touch, 34–39; of uncertainty, 176

epistolary exchanges, 54, 260n146. *See also* correspondence; letters and letter writing

Erlanger, Joseph, 65

erotics: of epistolary exchanges, gendered, 260n146; in tea shops, 152, 155, 165; of touch, 7–8, 20, 22, 25, 152, 155, 165

ethics: of body, 22; and politics, 229; sexual, 108, 230; of touch, 16, 22–23, 229, 233

etiology, and psychiatry, 178

eurhythmics, and blindness, 80–83

Euston Station (London), 275n17

evolution: and environmental adaptation, 29; history of, 46; of nervous system/ neurology, 6, 29, 35, 38, 44, 46; and perception, 15; phylogenetic, 35; Spencerian, 38; and touch, 16, 19–20, 38, 44, 46

Excursion, The (Wordsworth), 63
explanation, and experience, 9
Expressiveness of the Body (Kuriyama), 244n23, 254n21

Fage, Ethel, 163, 165
Fanon, Franz, 133, 280n114, 280n124
Farmer, Lee, 95–96
Farrell, Alice, 3, 137–38, 225, 231
Fawcett, Eveline, 154, 286n108
Febvre, Lucien, 10
Fechner, Gustav, 18–19, 28–29
feelings: and correspondence, 50–58, 61–63; entanglements of, 61; in letters and letter writing, 51; and nervous system, 61; and sensations, 65; and tenderness, 227; and thoughts, 85; and touch, 32, 50–58, 221; and vision/ seeing, 47. *See also specific feeling(s)*
feminism, 19; and caress, 225; and sexual danger, melodrama of, 142; and victimhood, 283n35; and vulnerability, 24, 140, 142, 230. *See also* women
Flaubert, Gustave, 54–55
Fletcher, Richard, Headmaster, 91
fog: and air, as biological and ontological condition of existence, 294–95n18; being-in-the-world in, 184; and Big Smoke, 194; blindness in, 191; body in, 191–92; buses in, 181, 188–93, 192, 198; and clouds as elemental media, 294n15; and coal, 20, 187–88, 296n37; and crime, 21, 181–220; and disorientation, 183, 194; and displacement, 184; duality of, 184, 193; and embodied experience, 184, 186, 189, 191–95, 199; and environment, 183–84, 294n12; episodes and incidents in, 16, 187–88, 295n30, 296n33; in film, 183; filtering apparatus, 297n43; and Great Smog of 1952, 183, 194; and greyness, 189, 192–93; history of, 184; intangible tangibility of, 192–93; and law, 21, 181–220; and linkboys, 188–93; measuring and weighing,

182, 182–83, 186–88, 296n43; as metaphor, 21, 184, 218–19; as metonym for crime, 194; and modernity, 189; origins of, 183–84; perception of, 219; and phenomenological history of air, 184; prevalence and episodes/ incidents, 16, 187–88, 295n30, 296n33; and senses, 20–21, 181, 189–94, 219; and sightlessness in, 22; and smog, 183, 187, 194; and smoke, 183, 187–88, 190, 194, 213–14, 216–17, 296nn34–35; and soot, 296n39; spatial reality of, 183; and steam, 190; tactile in, 206; tea shops as refuge in, 143; and touch, 16, 21–22, 181–220; as uncanny, 189–90, 194; weighing and measuring, 182, 182–83, 186–88, 296n43
Footsteps in the Fog (Lubin film), 298n75
Foucault, Michel, 18, 107–8, 248–49n63, 282n29
Foul and the Fragrant, The: Odor and the French Social Imagination (Corbin), 10, 244n19, 245n32, 246n42
Fowler, Harry, 196
Francis, Albert, 114–15
Freeman, R. Austin, 267n66
Freud, Sigmund, 178, 293n243

Gallagher, Shaun, 16
Galton, Francis, 256n61, 257n77
Gamon, Hugh R. P., 201, 210–11
Garland-Thompson, Rosemarie, 23
Gaskell, Elizabeth, 67
Gasser, Herbert, 65
Gay Lord Quex, The (Pinero play), 52–53
gender: and corporeal responses, 131; and epistolary exchanges, erotics of, 260n146; and inequality, 19, 141; and labor, 139–41, 161, 163, 282n23; and personal space, 23–24; and power, 19, 24, 222, 225; and public spaces, 6; and touch, 6, 8, 23–24, 222, 225; and tube (transport), 119–21, 129; and vulnerability, 23–24, 230–31. *See also* sexuality

George, Saint, 96, 272n181
GER. *See* Great Eastern Railway (GER), London
G. E. R. Hotel (London), 232
Gibson, James J., 15, 248n56
Gibson, Millicent, 155
Gilson, Erinn, 230, 283n35
global capitalism, 225–26, 233; and tea shops, 137–80. *See also* labor
Gloucester Road Station (London), 103, 114–15, 128, 133–34
Gluckstein, Montague, 159–60
Goffman, Erving, 282n29
Goldscheider, Alfred, 33
Gordon, Arthur, 166, 175–76, 290n195
governmentality, 107, 135–36, 275n16, 275n21. *See also* politics
Grant, Kathleen, 166–68, 171
Grassi, Giovanni and Salvatore, 195, 197
Great Eastern Hotel (London), 2
Great Eastern Railway (GER), London, 1–3, 232
Great War (World War I), 30, 59; blinded during, 71–76; and buses, increased usage, 189; and prostitution after, 198; and public transportation, 189, 279n97, 279n100; and rehabilitation and support of disabled servicemen and soldiers, 101, 221, 265n16, 267n52, 272n178, 288n128; and rush hours, 279n97; and shell shock, 72; and tea prices, 160; and tea shops, 149–50, 155, 157; and tube traffic increases and usage, 108–10, 127
Grey, Nippy (fictional character), 169–71
Griffin, Michael, 132, 134
Guattari, Félix, 283n31, 293n243

Haddon, Alfred Cort (A. C.), 36
Haeckel, Ernst, 36
Hale, Binnie, 169–70, 291n217
Hall, G. S., 35
Handbook of Physiological Optics (Helmholtz), 33

harassment, 299n91; and embodied interactions in tea shops, 142; of female travelers, 117; history of, 7, 142; and nonconsensual touch in public, 7; and power, 141; and sexual violence, 7; in tea shops, 22, 139, 142; unreported, 142; as violation of bodily integrity, 24; and vulnerability, 140; and women service workers, 141. *See also* sexual harassment
Hardcastle, Leonard, 88–89
Harris, Barbara, 138
Harrisson, Tom, 293n261
Hawes, Marian, 151–53, 156, 286n100
Hawkes, George, 137–38
Haynes, Susan, 125
Head, Henry, 19, 39–66, 41, 48, 229, 253n7, 257n85, 258n117, 262n193, 262n200; and Holmes, 13–15, 27–28, 223; and human experiment in nerve division, 39–50, 63–64; and Mayhew, 7, 17, 22, 27–28, 30–31, 50–63, 191, 259n138, 260n144; and Rivers, 3, 27–32, 36–51, 58–61, 66, 258n92; and Sherren, 27, 38–39, 46, 257n81
hearing: and blindness, 81, 99–101, 264n10; and talking books, 264n10; and touch, 100
Hearth and Home (London), 143
heat, and sensations/touch, 32–43, 49, 59, 61. *See also* cold
Heathrow Airport's Terminal 3 (London), 305n40
Helmholtz, Hermann von, 33, 43, 253n12
Henshaw's Blind Asylum (Manchester), 73, 266n25
Henson, Commissioner, 152
hermeneutics, and distanciation, 261n165
heterogeneity, 21, 24, 104, 141
Hindmarch-Watson, Katie, 258n116, 286n99
Hirst, Alfred, 67–70, 69, 264n5
History of Departed Things, A (Mayhew), 62–63

History of the Education of the Blind (Illingworth), 73
Hitchcock, Alfred, 116–17, 183
Hochschild, Arlie Russell, 152
Hodgkinson, Lewis, 197
Holmes, Gordon, 259n124; and Head, 13–15, 27–28, 223
Holt, Phyllis, 137–38, 142, 168
homosexuality, 130–35, 280n121, 295n22
Hormaid, Constable, 205
Horsley, Victor, 95
Houlbrook, Matt, 246n35, 246n41, 260n148, 261n174, 280n113, 280n119, 280n121, 292n239, 293n250, 295n22, 295n26, 302n181
household gods, 52–53, 260n156
House of Commons (London), 207, 213
Hugo, Victor, 56, 261n175
"Human Experiment in Nerve Division, A" (Head), 39–50, 63–64
Husserl, Edmund, 252n93
Hutchings, Alice, 3–4

Illingworth, W. H., 73
immanence, 17, 186, 248–49n63
immorality, 52–53, 175–76, 179
impact, meaning of, 99
impatience, 121–26, 127–28
Imperial College London, 90, 271n149
imperialism, 20, 29. *See also* colonialism
importuning, 184, 196, 214–15; defined, 294n14. *See also* prostitution
impressionism, literary, 223
Incorporated Society of Trained Masseuses (ISTM), London, 72–76, 266n39
individuation, 79, 135, 251n91
industrialization, 9, 19–20
inequality: and class, 140–41; crisis of, 233; and gender, 19, 141; and global capitalism, 233; and power, 19, 24, 129, 141; and tenderness, 225; and touch, 233; of vulnerability, 22, 24
Institute of Journalists (UK), 52–53

intelligence: and character, 50; and drive, 237; and sensory acuity, 257n77; and ticklishness, 35–36
interracial sex, 280n124
"Intertwining—The Chiasm, The" (Merleau-Ponty), 251n90, 304n10
intimacy: and anomie, 135; and capitalism, 140; and isolation, 2; of letters and narratives, 260n144; and touch, 7, 104; of tube cars, 117, 130–31
Introduction to the Study of Embryology, An (Haddon), 36
introspection, 31, 37–39, 41–42, 46–47, 49–50, 84
Irigaray, Luce, 225
isolation, and intimacy, 2
ISTM. *See* Incorporated Society of Trained Masseuses (ISTM)

Jackson, John Hughlings, 35, 44, 258n117
Jackson, Michael, 278n81
James, C. L. R., 177
James, Henry, 8, 50–51, 259nn138–39
Jews and Jewish communities, in London, 38, 141, 257n72
Johnson, Detective, 155
Johnson, Mark, 247n46, 303n212
Johnston, Charles, Sir, Lord Mayor, 286n100
Johnston, J. A., 185
Jones, E., 80
Jones, Mary, 181, 183–85, 197
Joseph, Bertie, 164, 290n187
Joyce, Patrick, 107
Joynson-Hicks, William, Sir, 215

Kimmins, C. W., 269n104
King, Ernest, Constable, 196
Kinkaid, Alexander, Constable, 195
Kitchin, June, 106
Kittler, Friedrich, 18
Knight, Henry, Alderman, 187
Knightsbridge Station (London), 109, 129

knowledge: of bodies, 22; and desire, 4; and embodiment, 22; and feel/touch, 221; juridical, 8; and senses, 86; synoptic, and alienation, 5; tactile conditions of, 24–25; and touch, 4, 6, 8–9, 18, 20, 24–25. *See also* legal knowledge; scientific knowledge

Koselleck, Reinhart, 16, 245n27

Koven, Seth, 78, 140, 260n144, 260n150, 262n204, 267n52, 282n18, 284n55, 284n63

Krafft-Ebing, Richard von, 262n199

Krzyzanowski, Kazimerz, 135

Kuriyama, Shigehisa, 244n23, 254n21

labor: bodied, 286n99; and capitalism, 138–40, 168; cinema attendants, 288n134; in commercial leisure spaces, 282n23; and commodity, 169; and consumption, 140; and desire, 138–39, 176, 179; diversification of, 104; domestic servants, work interpreted by, 290n182; emotional, and uncertain limits of, 148–58; female private detectives in department stores, 288n134; gendered, 139–41, 161, 163, 282n23; and imperialism, 20; indentured, 139–40; match girls, 145–46, 282n18, 284n55, 284n63; shopgirls, 116–18, 140, 142, 276–77n53; socially or physically distanced, connections between, 282n18; unions, 8, 138–39, 146–51, 160–61; and unrest, 149; and unrest, in Britain and India, 158–63; West End and East End, 277n53. *See also* capitalism; tea shops, labor

Lady of Lyons, The (romantic melodrama), 170

Laite, Julia, 282n18

Lakoff, George, 303n212

Lancet medical journal, 213–14

Landi, Elissa, 171

Lapping, Anne, 95

Latour, Bruno, 219, 252n94, 295n20, 295n27, 298n76

law: atmosphere of, 212–19; autonomy of, 203, 219; body of, 209; conception of, 219; and consent, 251n88; and courtroom layouts, 211; courts, architecture of, 301nn155–56; courts, judicial *vs.* emotional temper in, 301n148; courts, laughter in, 292n239; as discrete mode of existence, 295n27; and embodiment, 25, 184, 186, 191–95, 199–212, 203, 205, 215, 217–18, 220; and evidence of previous offenses committed as inadmissible, 299n115; and fog, 21, 181–220; history of, 8, 21; and magistrates' authority, 301n158; and magistrates' knowledge, 298n81; and magistrates' physical distance in courts, 301n158; and magistrates' preliminary inquiry of indictable offenses, 299n112; and magistrates' social distance in courts, 301n156; materiality of, 295nn27–28; matters of fact and matters of concern, distinction between, 295n20; objectivity of, 25, 203; and obscured vision, 184; and police courts, 4, 8, 21, 25, 184, 186, 194–95, 199–220, 211, 301nn154–68, 303n205; property of, 304n219; and psychoanalysis, 293n250; and reality, legal construction of, 295nn28; and science, 8, 17, 22, 24–25, 226; and senses, 25, 212; and social causes, 299–300n118; and tactile, 25; and tangibility, 25; and touch, 8, 17, 21, 24–25, 186, 194, 200, 212, 220–22, 226. *See also* crime; legal knowledge

Law Journal, 215

Law of Compensation: Blind but Self-Reliant (pamphlet), 101

Lawrence, D. H., 6, 223–25, 231, 304n4

Lawrie, Allan, Justice, 202

Law Times, 215

LCC. *See* London County Council (LCC)

Lee, Norman, 206

Leeds School for the Blind, 88

legal knowledge, 8, 24–25, 186, 199, 201, 221–22, 226

Leighton, Lord, 226

leisure, and commerce, 11, 225. *See also* travel and leisure

Leonard, Elsie, 197

Leonard, J. A., 94

letters and letter writing, 56; and autofiction, 58–63; counter-epistolaria or unordinary, 263n216; fictional, 63; literature in, 55; love, 7, 54–55, 58–63, 263n216; as performance, openended, 260n148; real message of, 63; as real-time observation of feelings, 51; and relationships, 260n144; and self-experimentation, 58–63; and social difference, mediated, 260n150; spatiality and temporality of, 52; as substitute for absence that simultaneously reestablishes it, 52, 56–58, 260n150; and touch, 51–52. *See also* correspondence; epistolary exchanges

Levy, Richard, 158, 175, 177, 179

LGOC. *See* London General Omnibus Company (LGOC)

Lhermitte, Jean, 19, 249n71

liberalism, 5, 12–13, 107, 136, 244n21

liminality, of tube (transport), 21, 130–33

Linden Lodge School (London), 89

linearity, 13, 16, 223–24

Lineham, D., 97

Ling, Pehr, 84

literature: aesthetic, 221; and correspondence, 261n174; and impressionism, 223; and letter writing, 55; and love, 30; and neurology, 30, 59, 254n23

Little, Fletcher, 79

Liverpool Street Station (London), 1–5, 3, 221–22, 231–33, 305n40

Locke, John, 87, 270n131

Lodger, The: A Story of the London Fog (Hitchcock), 183

London: as most populous city in world (1900), 20; population growth, 104, 109; and routinization of life, 165; tearooms, tea shops, temperance restaurants within, rise of in West End, 281n13; and touch, history of, 20–21. *See also* fog; tube (transport)

London after Dark (travelogues series), 206

London and North Western Railway, 232

London Bridge Station, 209

London County Council (LCC), 187–88, 216–17, 296–97n43

London Figaro, 73

London General Omnibus Company (LGOC), 125–27, 181, 189, 278n94

"London Held to Ransom by the Fog Fiend," 183

London Hospital (Whitechapel), 3, 27, 38–39, 46–48, 71, 257n72

London Institute for Massage by the Blind, 71, 265n21

London Perambulator, The (Bone), 196, 296n34

London Police Court, The (Gamon), 211

London Trades Council (LTC), 161

London Traffic Act, 122

London Traffic Enquiry, 109, 120

London Zoological Gardens, 35

love: and autofiction, 58–63; letters and letter writing, 7, 30, 54–55, 58–63, 263n216; and literature, 30; and neurology, 27–66

LTC. *See* London Trades Council (LTC)

Lubienska, Teresa, murder of, 103, 105–6, 108, 129, 132–33, 135

Lubin, Arthur, 298n75

Lucas, Keith, 64

Lucock, Florence, 197

Lyons Corner House(s) (London tea shops), 125, 133, 139, 141, 146–49, 157–74, 164, 167, 285n77, 290n187, 292n222, 292n228; Lujeri Estate, Nyasaland, 162

Lyons Mail, 164, 166, 171

MacKinnon, Catharine, 19
Magill, Adrian, 90–91
Manchester Guardian, 189
Mann, Tom, 146–47, 160
Mansfield, Magistrate, 213–14
Mansfield, Mr., 213–14
Marshman, Constable, 197
Marston, H. J. R., Rev., 101
Martin, H., 204–5
Marx, Karl, 9
masculinity, and power, 141
Mass Observation (UK), 293n261
masturbation: and blindness, 85; contemporary anxiety over, 270n119
match girls, 145–46, 282n18, 284n55, 284n63. *See also* shopgirls
May, Lily, 197
Mayhew, Ruth, 66, 263n216; and Head, 7, 17, 22, 27–28, 30–31, 50–63, 191, 259n138, 260n144
McCartney, Wilf, 161
McCrae, Helen, 290n180
McDougall, William, 36–37
McEleney, Thomas, 196
McNally, Edward, Corporal, 280n121
Mead, Frederick, Magistrate, 214–15
Merleau-Ponty, Maurice, 14–15, 17, 19, 224–25, 248n52, 248n56, 249n65, 249n71, 251n90, 252n93, 280n114, 304n10
metaphors, 303n212
Meteorological Office (London), and fog measurements, 181–83, *182*, 186–88, 296–97n43, 296n43
#MeToo movement, 19
Metropolitan Asylum Board Night Office (Charing Cross), 204–5
Metropolitan Police Guide (Johnston), 185–86
Metropolitan Railway (London), 1, 109–10, 118–19, 121, 190
Miatt, Patricia, 128–29, 131
Midlands Mobility Centre (UK), 94
Midwives' Institute (London), 72
mind: and blindness, 249n64; and body, 6–7, 13, 16, 18–20, 29–31, 64–66,

80–84, 88, 221, 223, 229; and embodiment, 17, 19, 240; and modernity, 107; and perception, 222; representational model of, 247n46; sciences, 6; and touch, 6, 19–20, 59, 64, 223–24, 229, 304n8
Mitchell, Silas Weir, 71
Model Course in Physical Training, 79–80
modernity: and capitalism, 5; and fog, 189; and governmentality, 107; and liberalism, 5; and linearity, 223–24; and mind, 107; of Nippies in tea shops, 163; and personal space, 135; pluralization of as analytic category, 274n11; and senses, 9, 108, 222–23, 245n30; and social relations, 105; and subjectivity, 107; and touch, 9, 223–25, 304n8; and tube (transport), 107, 274nn10–11
Montessori, Maria, 229
Moorland Mystery, The (film), 173
morality, of women, 148. *See also* immorality
Morley, E., 80
Morrison, Arthur, 298n85
Mosely, Sydney, 287n119
movement, on tube (transport), 107, 134
Müller, Johannes, 32–33, 37
Munro, John, 258n116
Murray, Graham Bell, Major, 214–15
My Dark World (Hirst pamphlet), 68–70, *69*

Nafe, John Paul, 65
Nairn, Mr., 218
National British Women's Temperance Association, 73
National Federation of Women Workers (NFWW), 150–51
National Foundation for Educational Research (NFER), England and Wales, 89–90
National Hospital for the Paralysed and Epileptic (London), 35
National Institute for Massage by the Blind (NIMB), 71–79

National Institute for the Blind (NIB), 74–76, 81–90, 267n53, 271n152. *See also* Royal National Institute for the Blind (RNIB)

National Vigilance Association, 207

Nead, Lynda, 189, 194, 278n88

nervous system: and experiments, 39–50, 64–66; and feelings, 61; functional levels of, 35; "newspaper office" of, analogy, 43–45; and psychology, 35; in spatial and temporal terms, 64–65; telegraph and telephone lines, analogy, 43–44, 258n116; and touch, 20, 22, 33, 43, 263n227

neurology: as branch of medicine, advances in, 27–28; and electrical stimulation experiments, 64; evolution of, 6, 29, 35, 38, 44, 46; experiments, 6–7, 39–50, 64, 253n4, 253n12; and human experiment in nerve division, 39–50; intellectual and institutional context of experiments within, 253n4; and literature/language, 30, 59, 254n23; and love, 27–66; physiology of, 7, 31–34, 65; and psychology, 6, 29–30, 34–36, 63–65, 253n12; and selfhood, 59; and sensations, 34, 40, 64–65; and touch, 6, 8, 18–19, 25, 27–66, 226

neuropsychiatry, 19

neuroscience, and perception, 19

Nevinson, Christopher R. W. (C. R. W.), 43–45

Newman, George, 80–81, 268n81

newsboys, 149, 151

Newsboys' Club (London), 149

News of the World, 44, 205

Newton, Kathleen, 154, 286n108

New York Subway, 274n11

NFWW. *See* National Federation of Women Workers (NFWW)

NIB. *See* National Institute for the Blind (NIB)

NIB School of Massage, 75–76, 81–90, 267n53

NIB Sunshine Homes, 82–83, 269n102

Night Patrol, The (film), 203–8, 204

"Night Patrol, The" (play), 203–9

NIMB. *See* National Institute for Massage by the Blind (NIMB)

Nippy (Wylie musical comedy), 169–71, 173

"Nippy" (*Picture Post*), 164

Noë, Alva, 15

Noel, Gerard, 213–14

No Longer Alone (British Pathé film), 94, 272n169

Noona Be Nippy (film), 164

North, Frederick Keppel, Chancellor, 138, 168, 173, 176, 177–78, 180

Northcote, Constable, 199–201

Northern Line (tube), 124, 159

North London Railway, 1

Nuffield Foundation (London), 91, 94

objectivity: of law, 25, 203; of science, 20, 25, 28. *See also* subjectivity

Oliver, Roland, 138, 158, 175–76

O'Mahony, Mark, 132

O'Malley, Mark, 132

One Bishopsgate Plaza (London), 233

ontogeny, 36

ontology: of body, 22, 248n63; of embodiment, 283n37; of immanence, 248–49n63; of precariousness, 283n37; of touch and vision in blindness, 101–2

Orme, Eliza, Asst. Commissioner, 145–47

Otter, Chris, 244n21, 294n18

Owens, Emily, 283n38

Owens, John Switzer, 296n35, 296n39, 297n43

Oxford Circus Station: buses, 109; tubes, 137

pain, and sensations/touch, 32–43, 49, 225, 255n47

Pall Mall Gazette, 52, 145

Parisi, David, 249n67, 254n20

Parker, Albert, 181, 183–85, 197

Parker, Charles, 93–100, 102

Parker, Harold, Sergeant, 195

Parkinson, Harry B. (H. B.), 206

Pass Down the Car Please (Stingemore poster), 111

Pater, Walter, 31, 55–56, 66, 261n179

paternalism, 142

Paterson, Mark, 264n8, 270n131, 271n142

Pearson, Arthur, 74, 82

pedagogies, of touch, 6, 23, 67–102

Pentecostal revivalism, 59

perception: and being-in-the-world, 19; and blindness, 15; and cognition, 223, 230; and embodiment, 17, 19, 223; as emerging process, 16; and entanglements, 16; and evolution, 15; of fog, 219; and intertwining, 304n10; limits of, 230; and mental pictures/standards, 227–28; and mind, 222; and neuroscience, 19; and phenomenology, 14, 17, 19, 223; and physiology, 83; and politics, 70–71, 100, 221; and psychology, 14; self-reporting of, 256n68; and senses, 16; and thinking, 16; and touch, 6, 15–16, 18, 22, 222–23, 227–28, 230; visual, 15

performance and performativity, 12, 51–52, 140–42, 246n41, 282n29

Perkins Institution for the Blind (Watertown, MA), 87

Perryman, May, 153–56

personal space: and bodily autonomy, 8; and class, 23–24; and gender, 23–24; and modernity, 135; in public spaces, 20–21, 23–24; and subjectivity, 136; in tea shops, 21, 23–24; and touch, 17, 222, 225; and tube (transport), 8, 23–24, 104, 106–18, 121, 128–30, 134–36, 172, 276n47; and vulnerability, 23–24. *See also* public spaces

Peters, John Durham, 294n15

Petley, Mabel, 120

Peto, Dorothy, 300n122

phenomenology: and being-in-the-world, 19, 249n65; of crime, in fog, 193–99; and desire, 283n31; and intra-actions

between phenomena, 254n29; and perception, 14, 17, 19, 223; and racial differences, 280n114; and science/scientific knowledge, 65–66, 254nn28–29; and scientific knowledge, 31

Phenomenology of Perception (Merleau-Ponty), 14–15, 17, 19, 248n52, 249n65, 249n71, 252n93, 280n114

phenomenotechnique, 254n28

Phillips, Joseph, 198

photographs and photography, 9, 264n7, 264n9

phylogenetics and phylogeny, 35–38, 46–47, 65

Physical Efficiency (Cantlie), 79

physiology: and anatomy, 32, 75; electro-, 64–65; experimental, 18, 29–32, 64–65, 253n12; German, 36; mechanistic, 19; of neurology, 7, 31–34, 65; and perception, 83; and psychology, 19, 29–30, 34–36, 63–65; of touch, 31–34, 63–65

physiotherapy, for blind people, 72–73, 75–76

Piccadilly Circus (London), 131, 192, 280n119

Piccadilly Circus Station (London), 125, 132, 280n121

Piccadilly Line (London tube), 118–19, 121, 129–30

Pickles, W. J., 91–93

Picture Post, 164, 292n22

Pilcher, Ann, 128–29, 131

Pinero, Arthur, 52–53

Piper, Ivene, 287n124

Pitt, A., Rev., 145, 281n8

Plowden, Alfred Chichele, Magistrate, 208

police courts. *See* law, police courts

politics: and consent, 251n88; and ethics, 229; and perception, 70–71, 100, 221; and touch, 229–30, 248n58; and tube (transport), 136. *See also* governmentality

Pottage, Alain, 304nn219–20

power: and age, 222, 225; and class, 24, 222, 225; and gender, 19, 24, 222, 225; and harassment, 141; and inequality, 19, 24, 129, 141; and masculinity, 141; and race, 24, 222, 225; and sexuality, 222, 225; and vulnerability, 24

Power, Cyril, 104–5, 115–16

Precarious Life: The Powers of Mourning and Violence (Butler), 251n89, 251n91, 283n37

Priestley, J. B., 107, 165–66, 174–75, 275n17, 290n192, 292n233

Principles of Psychology, The (Spencer), 35

prostitution, 21, 138, 142, 153, 185, 194–98. *See also* importuning

proximity, and tube (transport), 20, 104

psychiatry: and etiological explanations, 178; German, 262n199; neuro-, 19; and psychical twilight, 262n199

psychoanalysis, 178, 225, 293n250

psychology: comparative, 19; experimental, 6, 18, 19–20, 29–30, 36, 65, 221, 253n17; Gestalt, 19; mechanistic, 19; and nervous system/neurology, 6, 29–30, 34–36, 63–65, 253n12; and perception, 14; and physiology, 19, 29–30, 34–36, 63–65; and touch, 34–35, 63–65, 249–50n75

public displays of affection, and touch, 177

Public Health Acts, 217, 303n199

public spaces: changing constituency of, 6; and embodied encounters/habits, 7, 225–26; and gender, 6; and personal boundaries, 20–21; touch in, 6–7, 20–21, 23–24, 106, 108, 140, 142, 221–22, 225–26; tube (transport) as, 106, 108; and violability, 228, 230; and vulnerability, 23–24, 228. *See also* personal space; tea shops; tube (transport); urban life

public transportation, 6, 21, 140, 187, 189, 191, 225, 231, 269n97. *See also* buses; commuting; rush hours; tube (transport); *specific railway(s)*

queans, 280n119

queerness, 279–80n113; as transhistorical analytic category, 134; and tube stations, 130–35

queer spaces, 280n119, 280n121; and tube (transport), 130–35

race: and being out of place, 133; and corporeal responses, 131; and power, 24, 222, 225; and vulnerability, 24, 230–31

racial differences: and Blackness, 131, 133; and evolutionary development, 19–20, 29; and liminality, 133–34; and phenomenology, 280n114; and sensory acuity/discrimination, 29, 253n17, 256n61; and skin, 250n81; and social spaces, 133–34; and touch, 19–20

Radford, C., Mr., 213

railway, underground. *See* tube (transport)

Rake, Walter, Constable, 197–98

Rake's Progress, The (Hogarth painting), 164

RAMC. *See* Royal Army Medical Corps (RAMC)

Rancière, Jacques, 265n18

Randolfi, Ernesto, 302n167

Renaissance, The (Pater), 31, 55–56, 66, 261n179

Rheinberger, Hans-Jörg, 254n28, 255n45

Rich and Strange (Hitchcock film), 116–17

Richardson, B. W., 145

Richardson, Ryder, 148

Ritchie, J. M. (John), 82–83, 86–89, 270n131

Rivers, W. H. R. (William), 41; and Head, 3, 27–32, 36–51, 58–61, 66, 258n92

RNIB. *See* Royal National Institute for the Blind (RNIB)

Road Traffic Act (UK), 217

Robinson, Louis, 35–36, 256n55

Robinson, Mollie, 287n124

Robinson, Peggy, 197

Rogers, Thelma, 137–39

Rowen, Samuel, 199–202, 212

Rowlands, Evan, 302n167
Royal Army Medical Corps (RAMC), London, 73
Royal Commission on Labour (UK), 145–47
Royal Commission on London Traffic (UK), 187
Royal Commission on Police Powers and Procedures (UK), 219–20
Royal Commission on the Blind, the Deaf and Dumb (UK), 77–78
Royal National Institute for the Blind (RNIB), 90, 93–97, 228, 265n21, 269n102, 271n152. See also National Institute for the Blind (NIB)
Royal National Institute of Blind People (RNIB), 265n21
Royal Normal College for the Blind (Upper Norwood), 86–87, 87, 101, 269n97
rush hours, 10, 279n97; crime during, 2; and tube (transport), 126–30. See also commuting
Russell, Edward, Sir, 52–53
Russell, Rollo, 296n34
Rye, Fred, 180

Salmon, Alfred, 161
Salmond, John, 219
Salter, Rose (fictional character), 165, 174–75
Schilder, Paul, 19
science: cognitive, 14, 230; and embodiment, 66; epistemology of, 252n94; history of, phenomenological, 254n28; and law, 8, 17, 22, 24–25, 226; neuro-, 19; objectivity of, 20, 25, 28; and phenomenology, 65–66, 254nn28–29; and senses, 20, 25; and tactile, 25; and technology, 64, 230; and touch, 8, 18, 19–20, 24–25, 64, 91, 222, 226; and world-making, 254n27
scientific knowledge: of body, 20; emotional and embodied constitution of, 254n21; epistemology of, 252n94;

history of, 8, 30; and particular intentionality, 252n93; and phenomenology, 31, 65–66, 254nn28–29; and senses, 20, 25, 64–65; sensory origins of, 221–22; and touch, 8, 20, 24–25, 64–65, 221–22, 226
Scott, Robert, 295n30
Scott, Viola, 170–71
Scottish Blind School, 94
Scott's Hotel (Euston), 4
seeing. See blindness; vision
self and selfhood: and body, 12, 19, 248n63; fragility of, 12; and neurology, 59; and ontology of immanence, 248–49n63; performativity of, 12, 51–52, 246n41; and psychology, 51–52; and touch, 249n63
semiotics: tactile, 88; visual, 47
Sennett, Richard, 244n19
sensations: and electrophysiology experiments, 64–65; epicritic, 43–44, 46, 49, 61–63; and experiments, 64–65; and feelings, 65; history and experience of, 245n27; and modernity, 222; muscular, 255n36; and neurology, 34, 40, 64–65; and pain, 32–43, 49, 225, 255n47; protopathic, 43–44, 46, 49, 61–62; self-reporting of, 256n68; and sensibility, common, 61; and social distinctions/order, 12; and social order, 5, 12; and stimuli, 6, 12, 18, 28–30, 32, 34, 42, 49–50, 64–66, 253n12; and temperatures, 32, 42–43, 49; and thoughts, 86; and ticklishness, 34–36; and time, 245n27; and touch, 6, 18, 32–33, 47, 49, 64–65, 222, 253n12, 263n227; and understanding of distribution of the sensible, 223, 265n18
senses: and autodidacticism, 83; and crime in fog, 194; and desensitization, 10–11; and embodiment, 13–14, 17, 23, 223; and entanglements, 13, 16–17, 66, 252n94; epistemology of, 16, 18; and fog, 20–21, 181, 189–94, 219;

history of, 5, 9–13, 14–15, 17–18, 30, 245n30; and knowledge, 86; and law, 212; and legal knowledge, 25, 221–22; and linearity, 16, 223; as mingled, 16–17; and modernity, 9, 108, 222–23, 245n30; nonvisual, 70; and overstimulation, 10–11; and perception, 16; and science, 20, 25; and tactile, 18, 25; and tactile interactions, 18; and touch, 4, 7, 8, 14, 16–18, 25, 30–31, 33, 60, 194, 222, 304n8; and tube/subway travel, 274n11; and urban environment, 12; and urban spaces, 18. *See also* sensations; sensibility, common; sensory acuity; sensory life; *specific sense(s)*
sensibility, common: defined, 32; epicritic, 62; and sensations, 61; and touch, 32–36, 255n36
sensory acuity, 14, 29–30, 36, 90, 252n94, 253n17, 256n61, 257n77
"Sensory Disturbances from Cerebral Lesions" (Head and Holmes), 13–14
sensory life, 9–10, 20, 29, 222–23
Serres, Michel, 16
Sewell, William H., Jr., 179, 291n211
sexual exploitation, 174
sexual harassment, 19, 21, 142, 230–31, 250n80. *See also* sexual violence
sexuality: and corporeal responses, 131; and power, 222, 225. *See also* gender; homosexuality
sexual violence, 7, 19, 24, 141–42. *See also* sexual harassment
Shaw, George Bernard, 207
Shaw, Napier, 296n35, 297n44
Sherren, James, and Head, 27, 38–39, 46, 257n81
Sherrington, Charles Scott, 33–34, 61
shopgirls, 116–18, 140–42, 276–77n53. *See also* match girls
shoplifting, 288n134
Shops Act (UK), 149
sight. *See* blindness; vision

Silver Lady, The (travelling tea café), 203–8, 204
Simmel, Georg, 4, 9–10, 222, 245n30, 246n42, 274n8
Sinclair, Robert, 218
Slater, Audrey, 92–93
slumming, 138
Smith, Amy, 276n50
Smith, Mark M., 246n42
Smith, Nellie, 197
Smith, Roger, 255n36
Smith, Watt, 258n92, 262n193, 262n200
social bonding, and touch, 19, 249–50n75
social order, and sensations, 5, 12
social relations, 9, 291n211; and modernity, 105; and movement, 134; and touch, 6; and tube (transport), 134–35, 274n8, 274n10
social spaces, 18, 23–24, 130, 134
Society for Promoting Female Welfare (London), 73–74
society of strangers, 12
Society of Trained Masseuses (STM). *See* Incorporated Society of Trained Masseuses (ISTM)
"Sociology of the Senses" (Simmel), 10, 246n42
soliciting. *See* importuning; prostitution
Sommersgill, Constable, 194
South Eastern Railway (London), 196
space and time. *See* time and space
space(s). *See* personal space; public spaces; queer spaces; social spaces; urban spaces
Sparkes, F., 160–61
Spearman, Charles, 82
spectacle: and alienation, 11; and social performance, 141, 282n29
Spencer, Herbert, 34–35, 38
spiritualism, 59
Stacey, Jackie, 250n81
Stanley, Liz, 263n216
Staples, Florence, 193–95
Star, 145, 205

St. Dunstan's Hostel for Blind Soldiers
and Sailors, 73–75, 75, 191
St Dunstan's Review ("Blinded Soldiers at
St Dunstan's"), 75, 191
Stevens, Frederick, 148–49, 158
St. George's Circus (London), 198–99
Stigma: The Experience of Disability (Hunt,
ed.), 100
Stingemore, F. H., 111
St. John's College, Cambridge, 39–41, 41, 59
STM (Society of Trained Masseuses). See
Incorporated Society of Trained
Masseuses (ISTM)
St Mary Abbots Hospital (London), 103
Stoler, Ann Laura, 250n83
strangers, society of, 12
St. Thomas' Hospital (London), 36, 71–72,
128
Studies in Neurology, 47–48, 48, 62, 63–64
subjectivity: of city inhabitants, 247n44;
and embodiment, 142, 192; and
governmentality, 107; history of, 107;
and modernity, 107; and personal
space, 136; and tea shops, 142; and
tube (transport), 107, 136. See also
objectivity
subject-object, in self-experiments,
262n193
subway. See tube (transport)
Sully, James, 34
Sunday at Home, The, 204
Sunday Dispatch, 176–77
Sunday Express, 205
Sunday Magazine, 68
Sunderland Museum and Art Gallery
(Sunderland, England), 226–29, 227
Sunderland School for the Blind (Sunderland, England), 226–29, 227
Sunshine Homes (NIB), 82–83, 269n102
Swiss Cottage for the Blind (London),
86–89

tactile: acuity, and blindness, 71–76; and
autonomy, 24; and body, 13–18, 22,
24; in fog, 206; and knowledge,
24–25; and public transportation,
269n97; and science, 25; and senses,
18, 25; and social spaces, 18; in tea
shops, 18, 138, 152, 176, 179, 286n99;
and touch, 13–18, 20, 24–25, 31, 222;
and tube (transport), 18, 22, 190; and
vulnerability, 24
Tamylon, Josiah, 4
tangibility: and intangible of fog, 192–93;
and law, 25; spectral, 57; and touch,
17, 25, 31
taste: as gustatory as well as aesthetic,
246n42; and senses/touch, 31
Tate Gallery (London), 17, 57
Tatler, 170
Taylor, Henry, 94
tea shops: and capital, 138; and class,
140–41; and commuting, 21, 139; for
daytime and nighttime, 139; and
desire, 21, 138–41, 148, 152, 163–71,
176, 179–80; discipline in, 163–71;
disorderly conduct in, 153–57; and
embodied encounters/interactions
in, 5, 8, 141–42, 170, 179, 225–26,
286n99; and emotional labor, uncertain limits of, 148–58, 168; erotics in,
152, 155, 165; in film, 138–40, 171–79,
172, 178, 292n225; and fog, as refuge
in, 143; and global capitalism, 137–
80; harassment in, 22, 139, 142; and
labor, emotional, 148–58, 168; and
labor relations, 8, 21, 138–39, 145–51,
158–63, 166, 176–77, 179–80; ladies
rooms in, 144; misconduct, 287n119;
new social and spatial opportunities
of, 21; Nippies (waitresses) in, 163–74,
164, 172, 290n187, 292n222; personal
boundaries and space in, 21, 23–24;
and precarious lives, 143–48, 176,
251n89, 251n91, 283n37; prosecuted,
154–55, 287n120, 287n124; as refuges
for women, 139, 143; as social spaces,
18; spatial and social conditions

in, 21, 23–24; and subjectivity, 142; tactile interactions in, 18, 138, 152, 176, 179, 286n99; touch in, 4, 17, 18, 21, 23–24, 137–80, 221, 286n99; and vulnerability, 24, 142; waitresses, and public service, 163; waitresses, and routinization of habitus, 164–66; waitresses, bodily behavior of, 163, 165; waitresses, charged for breakages, 285n92; waitresses, great risks for, 145; waitresses, industrious femininity of, 164; waitresses, wages, 145–46, 151, 281n8, 292n222; in West End, rise of, 281n13

technology, and science, 64, 230

Teddy boys, and threatening behavior, 121, 277n68

telegraph and telephone lines, and nervous system, analogy for, 43–44, 258n116

Temperance Society, Church of England, 216

temporalities, 245n27; and capitalism, 141–42; and embodied encounters, 222–23; entanglements of, 16; linear, 13; and linearity, 13; and nervous system, 65; and queerness, 279–80n113; and spatial, 6, 64–65, 141–42; and touch, 6, 64–65, 222

tenderness: and conflicting feelings, 227; cultivating, 233; entanglements of, 225; history of, 225; inequalities and dangers of, 225; multiple meanings of, 239; shared, 224–25; and touch, 221–33; understanding, 240; utopian, 224–25

TfL (Transport for London) 2021-2024 campaign, 231

They Walk in the City (Priestley), 165–66, 174–75

Thomas, Sibyl, 198

Thomas, Yan, 220, 295n20, 304n219

Thomson, Sidney, 145

ticklishness, 32, 34–39, 256nn55–57

Tiger in the Smoke, The (Allingham), 194, 298n75

time and space, 9–10, 13, 123–24, 131, 189–90, 233, 262n199, 278n75

Times, The (London), 11, 52–53, 76, 207

togetherness, and touch, 224–25

touch: aversions to, 6, 19, 21; and change, 304n8; as differences, 26; as disparaged, 6; as dwindled, 224; everyday vicissitudes of, 25–26; as experience, 66; experiments and investigations, 6, 18, 19–20, 24–25, 39–50, 64–66, 221–22; forms of, 180; as haptic subject, 254n20; history of, 4, 6–9, 17–28, 102, 108, 140, 142, 186, 221–33, 244–45n23, 263n227; illicit, 21, 151, 158, 166, 168–69, 183, 197, 199, 219, 232; immanent history of, 17; inappropriate, 172, 225; longing for, 4, 25, 57; lower and higher levels of, 62; meanings of, 7, 229; measurement of, 30, 47; as object, 65–66; phantasmic importance of, 19; in poetry, 8, 304n8; prohibitions against, 21; routinization of, 107; in spatial and temporal terms, 5–6, 23–24, 64–65; themes, 22–25, 226; and thought, 86–87; transgression of, 21; types and capacities of, 28; understanding of, 19–22, 222; unwanted, 9, 19, 23, 24, 104, 125, 139, 224; uses of, 4–9

Trade Facilities Act (UK), 112

trains. See tube (transport); specific railway(s)

transport. See buses; public transportation; tube (transport); specific railway(s)

Transport for London (TfL) 2021–2024 campaign, 231

travel and leisure, 23, 225

Trenchard, Lord, Police Commissioner, 205

triad valve amplifier, 64

Tribe, Arthur, 106

Truscott, George, Sir, Alderman, 154

trust, and authenticity, 246n41

tube (transport): architecture and technology, 106; and buses, 112, 125–28; and class, 119–21; and coal power stations, 118–21; and commuting, 104, 109, 126; containment of, 21; and crime, 2, 109, 195–96; and de-compartmentalization, 106, 119; electrification of, 16, 106, 118–21, 123, 187, 190, 277n72; elevators, 103, 123–25, 232; and embodied encounters/existence/relations, 5, 104, 135–36, 225–26; encounters, 108, 123–24; escalators, 10, 23–24, 106, 117, 123–25, 124, 131–33, 232; and etiquette of space, 106; everyday encounters on, 107–8; fares, 126; funding of, 110, 112; and gender, 119–21, 129; and governmentality, 107, 135–36; heterogeneity of, 21; history of, 275n14; impatience on, 121–26, 127–28; intimacy of, 117, 130–31; liminality of, 21, 130–33; and mail/post, 275n17; as meeting places of would-be lovers, 280n118; and minding the gap, 106–8, 114–15; and modernity, 107, 274nn10–11; padded cell carriages, 112–13, 113; and passengers, number of, 127–28; and personal space, 8, 23–24, 104, 106–18, 121, 128–30, 134–36, 172, 276n47; as popular, 104; poster, 111; prevalence of, 108; and proximity, 20, 104; and queer spaces, 130–35; and rush hours, 126–30; and social relations, 134–35, 274n8, 274n10; as social spaces, 18, 130, 134; spread outward, 139; standard stock railcar, 114; standing on, and straphangers, 106, 116, 119–20, 126–30, 190; strangers on, 104, 115, 274n10; and subjectivity, 107, 136; tactile interactions in, 18, 116, 118, 130, 190; tactile norms in, 22; and time (schedules), 121–23; and touch, 4–8, 16, 17, 20–24, 103–36,

221; transitory quality of, 131; and tunnels, 112, 118, 121, 126–28, 190, 232; and vulnerability, 21, 24, 104. *See also specific line(s) and station(s)*

Tube Train, The (Power linocut), 104–5, 105, 115–16

Tuke, Marian, 155–56

Turner, Henry Waddy, Magistrate, 202

Types for the Blind (Hirst pamphlet), 68

UERL. *See* Underground Electric Railways Company of London (UERL)

uncertainty, epistemology of, 176

Underground (film), 7, 116–18, 124, 171–74, 172

Underground Electric Railways Company of London (UERL), 118–19, 126–27, 171

underground railway. *See* tube (transport)

urbanization, and industrialization, 19–20

urban life: and alienation, 165; and consumerism, 246n36; desensitizing effects of, 9; individualism, and mutual indifference, 244n19; and material transformations, 247n44; and noise, 247n43; and sensory changes, 9–10, 247n44; and subjectivity of inhabitants, 247n44; and touch, 6, 8, 104, 140, 222; visibility in, 11, 246n36; and vulnerability, 104. *See also* public spaces

urban spaces, 18, 222

Vanbrugh, Irene, 52–53

VanClute., W., 91

Varieties of Temporal Experience, The (Jackson), 278n81

Verlaine, Paul, 60, 262n198, 262n200

Vernon, James, 12, 274nn10–11, 305n40

Vickery, T. G., Asst. City Solicitor, 153–55

victimhood, 142, 283n35

Vierordt, Karl von, 277–78n73

Villey, Pierre, 82, 87–88

Vincent's Police Code, 185

violability, 180, 228, 230

violence and violation: and care, 225; and difference, 225; and fear, 7–8; of touch, 7–8, 23, 180, 222–24; and vigilance, 129; and vulnerability, 180, 228. *See also* sexual violence

vision: and feelings, 47; history of, 9, 244n21; and touch, 16, 19, 32–33, 67–70, 100–102, 184, 200, 202, 221, 225–26; and visibility, in city, 11, 246n36

Voeux, Harold des, 187, 296n39

von Frey, Max, 33–34, 40

vulnerability: and autonomy, 21, 24, 108, 129, 142, 230–31; and being-in-the-world, 251n90; and bodily encounters, 24; of city life, 104; and class, 23–24; and consent, 108, 142, 230; contextual nature of, 21; and desire, 140, 180; and disability, 17; and embodiment, 24; and feminism, 24, 140, 142, 230; and gender, 23–24, 230–31; and harassment, 140; inequality of, 22, 24; of newsboys alone on streets at night, 149; and personal space, 23–24; and power, 24; and precarity, 251n89; and public spaces, 23–24; and race, 24; and tactile, 24; and tea shops, 24, 142; and touch, 8–9, 17, 21, 23–24, 180, 230–31, 251n90; and transgression, 21; and tube (transport), 21, 24, 104; and victimhood, 283n35; and violability, 180, 228

Waechter de Grimston, Evelyn, Lady, 177–79, *178*

Walker, Edith, 169

Walker, G. I., 226–28

Walkowitz, Judith R., 24, 140–41, 164, 250n80, 251n91, 281n13, 283n35

Walshe, Francis (F. M. R.), 49

Walton, Constable, 153

Warnham, Charles, 196–97

Warnham, Eliza, 197

Waterloo Underground Station, 115, 171–72, *172*, 185

Way, Percy, 75–76

Webber, Detective Inspector, 202

Weber, Ernst Heinrich, 18, 28–37

Welcome Free Travelling Café. *See* Silver Lady, The (traveling tea café)

West African Student Union House (London), 280n124

Westminster Bridge Station (London), 174

Wetherell, Marmaduke, 173

Wexler, Abraham, 90–91

"What the Blind May 'See'" (Deas), 229

Wildeblood, Peter, 280n121

Williams, Frederick, 133–34, 138

Williams, Myfanwy, 89–90

Wilson, Ernest, 47–48, 61

Wilson, S., 97

Winch, W. H., 37

Winckelmann, Johann, 55–57, 261n179

Wings of the Dove, The (James), 50–51

Winsor, Violet, 155

Wolfenden Committee (London), 132

Woman's Herald (London), 145

women: autonomy of, 142; and consumerist cosmopolitanism, 141; and film industry, economic and sexual exploitation of, 174; and indentured labor, 139–40; police, 138–39; private detectives in department stores, 288n134; public role, expansion of, 142; in public urban sphere, 140–41; questionable morality of, 148; safety of, 138–42, 145, 231; service workers, 141; and sexual danger/risks, 140–41; and spatial boundaries, 140; tea shops as refuges for, 139, 143; traveling alone, 23, 129, 131, 231; unaccompanied, and cultural implications, 23, 250n80; victimhood of, 142; violability of, 230. *See also* feminism

Women's Auxiliary Service (UK), 165

Women's Trade Union League (UK), 147

Woolf, Constable, 205

Woolf, Virginia, 11–12, 223, 247n43

Woolwich Military Academy (London), 71–72

Worcester College for the Blind, 90–91
Wordsworth, William, 63
working girls, 21, 142, 173
World of the Blind, The (Villey), 82
World War I (Great War). *See* Great War
    (World War I)
Wright, Florence, 169
Wright, Robert, 203–9, 212

Wright, Stephanie, 141
Wylie, Julian, 169

Yeats, W. B., 57, 261n183

Zoological Society of London, 256n55
zoology, 35–36, 256n55
Zotterman, Yngve, 64